Austria

Anthony Haywood

Kerry Walker

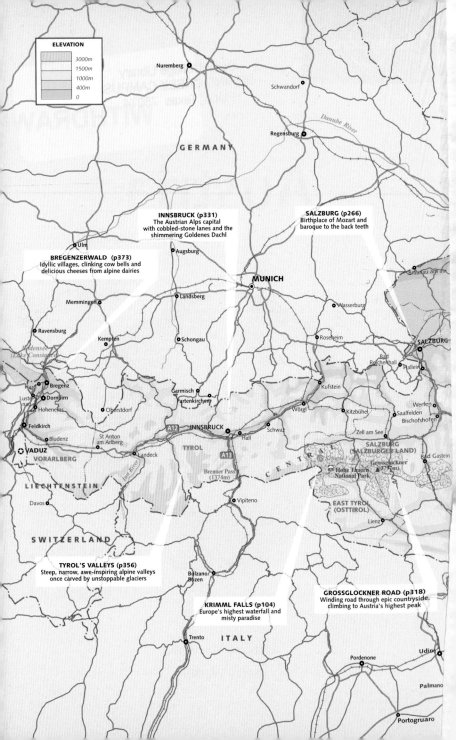

ELEVATION

3000m
1500m
1000m
400m
0

Nuremberg

Schwandorf

Danube River

Regensburg

GERMANY

INNSBRUCK (p331)
The Austrian Alps capital
with cobbled-stone lanes and the
shimmering Goldenes Dachl

SALZBURG (p266)
Birthplace of Mozart and
baroque to the back teeth

Ulm

Augsburg

Braunau am Inn

BREGENZERWALD (p373)
Idyllic villages, clinking cow bells and
delicious cheeses from alpine dairies

Memmingen

MUNICH

Landsberg

Wasserburg

Ravensburg

Kempten

Schongau

Roseheim

SALZBURG

*Bodensee
(Lake Constance)*

Bad
Reichenhall

Hallein

Hard
Bregenz

Garmisch

Kufstein

Werfen

Lustenau
Dornbirn

Partenkirchen

Wörgl

Kitzbühel

Saalfelden
Bischofshofen

Hohenems

Oberstdorf

A12
INNSBRUCK

Schwaz

Hall

Zell am See

**SALZBURG
(SALZBURGER LAND)**

Feldkirch

Bludenz

St Anton
am Arlberg

A13

Bad Gastein

VADUZ

VORARLBERG

Landeck

TYROL

Inn River

CENTRAL

Krimml Falls

**Hohe Tauern
National Park**

Grossglockner
(3772m)

LIECHTENSTEIN

Brenner Pass
(1374m)

Davos

Vipiteno

**EAST TYROL
(OSTTIROL)**

Lienz

SWITZERLAND

TYROL'S VALLEYS (p356)
Steep, narrow, awe-inspiring alpine valleys
once carved by unstoppable glaciers

Bolzano/
Bozen

KRIMML FALLS (p104)
Europe's highest waterfall and
misty paradise

GROSSGLOCKNER ROAD (p318)
Winding road through epic countryside,
climbing to Austria's highest peak

Trento

ITALY

Pordenone

Udine

Palmano

Portogruaro

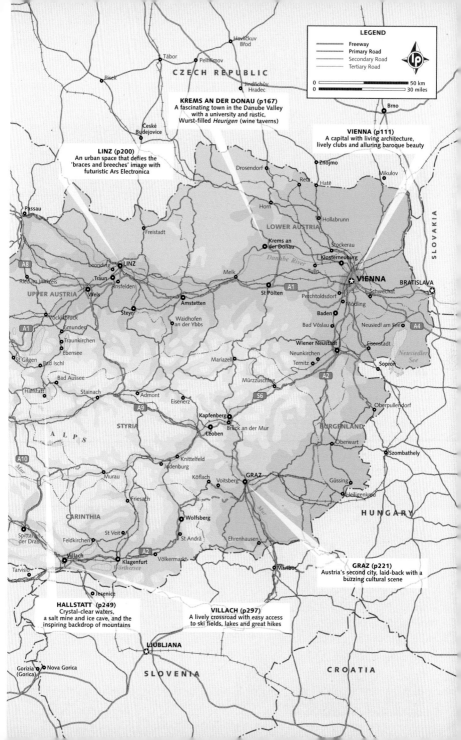

LEGEND
Freeway
Primary Road
Secondary Road
Tertiary Road

0   50 km
0   30 miles

KREMS AN DER DONAU (p167)
A fascinating town in the Danube Valley with a university and rustic, Wurst-filled *Heurigen* (wine taverns)

VIENNA (p111)
A capital with living architecture, lively clubs and alluring baroque beauty

LINZ (p200)
An urban space that defies the 'braces and breeches' image with futuristic Ars Electronica

GRAZ (p221)
Austria's second city, laid-back with a buzzing cultural scene

HALLSTATT (p249)
Crystal-clear waters, a salt mine and ice cave, and the inspiring backdrop of mountains

VILLACH (p297)
A lively crossroad with easy access to ski fields, lakes and great hikes

CZECH REPUBLIC

SLOVAKIA

LOWER AUSTRIA

UPPER AUSTRIA

STYRIA

BURGENLAND

CARINTHIA

HUNGARY

ALPS

SLOVENIA

CROATIA

Havlíčkův Brod
Pelhřimov
Tábor
Písek
Jindřichův Hradec
Brno
České Budějovice
Znojmo
Mikulov
Drosendorf
Retz
Hatě
Horn
Hollabrunn
Freistadt
Krems an der Donau
Stockerau
Klosterneuburg
Passau
Leonding
LINZ
Traun
Ansfelden
Melk
Tulln
VIENNA
BRATISLAVA
Ried im Innkreis
Wels
St Pölten
Schwechat
Vöcklabruck
Steyr
Perchtoldsdorf
Mödling
Neusiedl am See
Gmunden
Amstetten
Baden
Traunkirchen
Waidhofen an der Ybbs
Bad Vöslau
Eisenstadt
Ebensee
Wiener Neustadt
St Gilgen
Bad Ischl
Mariazell
Neunkirchen
Ternitz
Sopron
Neusiedler See
Hallstatt
Bad Aussee
Stainach
Admont
Mürzzuschlag
Oberpullendorf
Eisenerz
Kapfenberg
Bruck an der Mur
Leoben
Murau
Knittelfeld
Judenburg
Köflach
Voitsberg
GRAZ
Oberwart
Szombathely
Friesach
Güssing
Heiligenkreuz
Wolfsberg
St Veit
St Andrä
Ehrenhausen
Spittal an der Drau
Feldkirchen
Villach
Klagenfurt
Wörthersee
Völkermarkt
Maribor
Tarvisio
Jesenice
LJUBLJANA
Gorizia (Gorica)
Nova Gorica
Mur

On the Road

ANTHONY HAYWOOD Coordinating Author

Mariazell (p238) in Styria is an unusual town in that it's Austria's most important place of pilgrimage. Wayfaring pilgrim-hikers clack to its basilica with Nordic walking stocks; stalls outside the basilica peddle devotional objects; and incense hangs in the air. Not to be forgotten though are its couple of good mountain-bike trails, pretty forest hiking and the glistening Erlaufsee (Lake Erlauf; p238). Leaving the tumult around the basilica, I went up to Bürgeralpe, the local peak. I think this photo captures the 'other side' of Mariazell: the backdrop of low mountains, some highly atmospheric clouds and Erlaufsee.

KERRY WALKER There's something special about a place that, for all its beauty, remains untouched. The Tennengebirge (p97) in Salzburger Land is one of those rare places. This karst plateau is a lonely wilderness of otherworldly rock formations, sheer precipices and rounded heights. The ascent was tough going: a dizzying 1000m scramble in the sweltering midday sun. Exhausted yet exhilarated, I sat beside a cool snowfield at the summit and watched shafts of light pick out the contours of the Northern Limestone Alps, rippling across to Germany. It was breathtaking in every sense of the word.

See full author bios page 421

AUSTRIA

Vienna's jewel-box palaces and Mozart melodies, sparkling Alps and problems like Maria naturally still have their place in Austria's heart. But venture further for experiences that defy expectations: from slinging on a backpack to stride through the Tennengebirge's lunar landscape to slurping cider with grizzled farmers in Mühlviertel orchards, from catapulting down the jaw-dropping Harakiri in Mayrhofen to bathing in Salzkammergut's tingly lakes. Cosmic spas and cities with newfound street cred are adding a twist to Austria's tale. So cast aside the well-thumbed picture-book, as the real story is even more enchanting…

Historical Highlights

Austria flaunts its heritage in exuberant fashion. Vienna's bombastic Habsburg palaces and Salzburg's baroque splendour are worthy, but dig deeper and you'll unearth Stone Age settlements, Roman archaeological sites and medieval festivals. In the country where Mozart composed and Strauss taught the world to twirl, you won't need to search hard for culture – it waltzes right up to you.

① Imperial Riches

When it came to palaces, the Habsburgs knew how to pick 'em. Vienna's Hofburg (p125) never fails to impress with its lavish state apartments, majestic Prunksaal (pictured), prancing Lipizzaner stallions and Schatzkammer stuffed with jewels the size of golf balls.

② Medieval Spirit

Feldkirch (p374) whisks you back to the Middle Ages with cobblestone squares and labyrinthine streets lined with half-timbered houses. Celebrate with the locals at summer festivals full of jousting, jesters and medieval feasting.

③ Abbeys & Castles

Make the pilgrimage to the Wachau for abbeys and ruined castles galore. One of the greatest ecclesiastical treasures is Stift Melk (p172), a pristine Benedictine abbey perched high above the Danube Valley.

④ Baroque Symphonies

The city that inspired Mozart to strum and Maria to sing, Salzburg (p266) is a baroque beauty of incredible proportions. Built high by the prince-archbishops, its hilltop fortress, whimsical palace and sumptuous churches beckon.

⑤ Prehistoric Sites

Take a giant leap back to the Stone Age at Ötzi Dorf (p356), recreating the Neolithic world of Ötzi, the 5400-year-old mummy discovered frozen in the Similaun Glacier in 1991.

⑥ Roman Rocks

Under the watchful eye of Emperor Claudius, Aguntum (p325) mushroomed into a centre of trade in Roman times. Explore the reconstructed artisan quarter and villa at this archaeological site in the shadow of the Dolomites.

⑦ Bohemian Rhapsody

Grazing the border to the Czech Republic, the misty woodlands of the little-known Mühlviertel hide some fine Gothic gems. Be sure to glimpse the outstanding Flügelaltar (winged altar) in Kefermarkt (p216).

Natural Icons

Over millennia, raw elemental forces have
sculpted a landscape of sublime natural
beauty, where glacial rivers carve deep gullies and mountains tower above undulating
pastures. Pick a random spot – the theatrical
mountainscape of Hohe Tauern National
Park, the icy underworld of Eisriesenwelt –
and you'll discover that the wilderness on
Austria's doorstep is pure drama.

❶ Eisriesenwelt
A blast of artic air hits you at Eisriesenwelt (p285), the world's largest accessible ice caves. Twisting past frozen sculptures and lakes, this warren of teeth-chattering tunnels is perfect for summertime chilling.

❷ Grossglockner Road
The high-altitude Grossglockner Road (p318) unleashes a rollercoaster of emotions as it corkscrews past dazzling glaciers, spiky peaks and the godfather of Austria's mountain mafia, Grossglockner (3797m).

❸ Dolomites
Rearing up above Lienz and its nearby hamlets, the scaly peaks of the Dolomites (p323) give East Tyrol a sense of wilderness. Rough around the edges, these rocks reveal their soft side when the evening light turns their turrets and towers pink.

❹ Liechtensteinklamm
A jaw-dropping ravine south of Salzburg, the Liechtensteinklamm (p286) is well hidden and worth seeking. Among the deepest and longest gorges in the Alps, its centrepiece is a torrent that glints opal blue in the afternoon sun.

❺ Krimml Falls
Feel the spray of the awesome Krimml Falls (p104), Europe's highest waterfall. Seducing visitors with its thunderous rumble and rainbows, the 380m-high cascade is a water feature not every country has in its backyard.

❻ Hintertux Glacier
Soar above a sea of ice to the Hintertux Glacier (p349). At the summit, skiers and vista vultures kick back to enjoy wide-screen views of the Tuxer Alps, Grossglockner and Zugspitze.

❼ 5Fingers
Get giddy on alpine views at 5Fingers (p250). Spreading out like a hand, the precipitous platform clings to 400m-high cliffs that tumble down to the bright blue waters of Hallstätter See.

❶ Skiing & Snowboarding

Downhill doesn't get much hairier than the Harakiri (p348), Mayrhofen's sultan of swoosh. The almost vertical slope makes even accomplished skiers quiver in their boots with its incredible 78% gradient. It's steep, scary and there ain't no going back.

❷ Rafting

The frothing, milky blue waters of Tyrol's rivers are tailor-made for getting wet beneath the region's brooding summits. Try rollin' on down the Inn River – it's all the rage in Landeck (p359).

❸ Paragliding

If hurling yourself off the edge of a mountain appeals, the snow-dusted pinnacles of the Zillertal are the place to give flight to your fantasy. Grab a parachute in Zell am Ziller (p347) to catch those thermals and glide.

❹ Hiking

Ever dreamed of being an extra in *Cliffhanger*? Scrambling up the jagged cliffs of the Tennengebirge (p97) is your chance to flirt with mountaineering. The vast karst plateau that unfolds at the top makes the sweating and swearing worthwhile.

❺ Bungee Jumping

Dangling from a rubber band is a gravity-defying way to see Austria; the perfect springboard to go take a run and jump is Tyrol's 192m-high Europabrücke (p337).

❻ Kitesurfing

A haven to migrating birds, the wind-buffeted waters of Neusiedler See also reel in flocks of thrillseeking kitesurfers. Slip into a wetsuit at Podersdorf am See (p196) for some big-wave action.

Local Flavours

Austria's cuisine is inextricably linked to the land. The real treat is grazing each region for homegrown flavours, from dairy-hopping through the Bregenzerwald to sipping wine in the Wachau's vineyards. Ingredients are wholesome, portions generous and Austrians don't skimp on calories; here you're encouraged to skip the main course and go straight for pudding!

① Say Cheese
The Käsestrasse (p374) runs through the mountainous Bregenzerwald like a vein through a slab of Stilton. Stop off at alpine dairies to meet the cheese-makers and indulge in pungent Bergkäse and tangy Räskäse.

② Vine Time
If you want to sip Grüner Veltliners and Rieslings, join the merry men in the *Heurigen* dotted around Lower Austria (p162) and Burgenland (p188). These traditional wine taverns exude rustic charm.

③ Sugar & Spice
Ditch the diet and devour the cake: try redcurrant-filled *Linzer Torte* in Linz (p207), flaky apple strudel in Salzburg (p276) and chocolaty *Sacher Torte* in Vienna's whirl of elegant coffee houses (p151).

④ Big Apple
Pick your way through mile upon mile of apple orchards in the rural Mostviertel (p177) and Traunviertel (p210). Pause at local farms for a glass of juice, zingy *Most* (cider) or fiery schnapps.

⑤ Alpine Cure
Silky in texture, wafer-thin and deliciously savoury, the *Schlegeis-Speck* in Mayrhofen (p349) is cured for three months at 1800m above sea level. The crisp air from the Zillertal Alps gives it a distinctive aroma.

⑥ Poppy Power
Monet-like fields of scarlet poppies are the source of the specialities that land on your plate in the Waldviertel (p177). In villages south of Zwettl, poppy-seed favourites include cheese, pasta and an incredibly rich cake.

⑦ Freshwater Fish
There's no sea, but Austria's crystal-clear brooks and lakes are teeming with tasty fish. Savour fresh trout beside the lakes of Salzkammergut (p245) and *Felchen* (whitefish) on the banks of Bodensee (p369).

New Dimensions

So long cuckoo clocks, farewell Heidi-esque kitsch; Austria is slowly abandoning old-style designs in favour of cutting-edge architecture. With a visual flair and desire to innovate, it's pushing aesthetic boundaries to become one of the most progressive countries on the planet, from sci-fi spas to Vorarlberg's glass-and-wood wonder walls and Zaha Hadid's smooth contours shaping Innsbruck.

Museum Moderner Kunst Stiftung Ludwig Wien 4

❸ Kunsthaus Graz
With its acrylic skin and voluptuous curves, the Kunsthaus in Graz (p226) is like some magnificent space-age sea slug. British architects Peter Cook and Colin Fournier dreamed up this contemporary art space.

❹ MUMOK
Behind a dark basalt exterior, MUMOK (p130) showcases a peerless collection of 20th-century art, from nouveaurealism to pop art. Both mesmerising and repellent, the Viennese Actionism works have prime shock value.

❺ Bregenz
Tired of alpine cuteness? Vorarlberg's a hotbed of design, with a growing crop of ecofriendly larch and glass edifices that blend seamlessly with the natural surrounds. Its nerve centre, Bregenz, features cubic wonders like the Kunsthaus (p369) and Festspielhaus (p369).

❶ Zaha Hadid
The queen of daring design, Iraqi-born Zaha Hadid has almost single-handedly revamped Innsbruck's architectural landscape. Her head-turning creations include the glass-and-steel Bergisel ski jump (p336; pictured) and the spacey Hungerburgbahn funicular (p336), soaring spectacularly above the city.

❷ Aqua Dome
Ahhh... Surely the best way to absorb the wonders of modern design and views of the Ötztal Alps is by drifting in the flying saucer-shaped pools at Tyrol's slickest spa, Aqua Dome (p356).

❻ Hangar 7
Close to Salzburg Airport, Hangar-7 (p278) is a stroke of genius. Celebrity chefs cook up a storm at Ikarus, while the sphere-shaped May Day Bar is the place to converse with virtual bar staff and watch Flying Bulls flit past.

❼ Linz
Linz is a beacon for avant-garde art and technological wizardry. Its giant glass rectangle, the Lentos Kunstmuseum (p203) shelters modern masterpieces. Step across the Danube and into a virtual world at the Ars Electronica Center (p203).

Walker near Ölperer Hütte on the Berliner Höhenweg walking route (p88).

Contents

Regional Map Contents

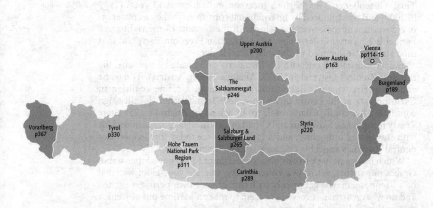

Destination Austria

Let's say you wake one morning in Austria and make your way bleary-eyed to a newspaper stand. What you see in the press will probably be at odds with this country you imagine: nothing about those idyllic mountain lakes or spectacular snow-dusted peaks, or even a picture of sweaty mountain bikers in centrifugal frenzy on a windswept forest trail. You are more likely to be greeted by the news that Austrian farmers are dying out, that state finances have been squandered on 18 Eurofighter jets, the ruling coalition government lacks true leadership, and that Austria's youth is guzzling itself comatose on alcopops. Maybe on another page, you see a picture of a somehow familiar politician holding up what looks like a town signpost.

It's no surprise that beautiful landscapes rarely get a showing in the national press – not unless they're being threatened, at any rate. What may strike you, though, is that these are not issues that break a country's back.

Austria has invested a lot into political and social calm. The result today is that while some countries lack direction, Austria is flying ahead with the continent's highest growth rates and standard of living. It has weird architecture, a buzzing capital with an even weirder dialect, and the tendency small countries sometimes have to occasionally drive themselves into strange mental and cultural landscapes. Part of this quality of life also comes from the wonderful physical landscape and opportunities outdoors. Meanwhile, it has a 50th anniversary of neutrality under its belt, and in that same year (2005) Austria joined the European Community while still officially staying neutral.

The death of former president and UN secretary Kurt Waldheim in 2007 did, however, give cause for retrospection. Waldheim had been at the centre of an international uproar in the 1980s after it was alleged he knew about or participated in war crimes during WWII. He died without ever understanding how he had suddenly become a world issue. For Austria, he symbolised a generation of silence post-WWII.

On the political stage, in 2007 a grand coalition between the Sozial-demokratische Partei Österreichs (SPÖ; Social Democrats) and the conservative Österreichische Volkspartei (ÖVP; Austrian People's Party) was revived, this time under the tutelage of SPÖ's Chancellor Alfred 'Gusi' Gusenbauer. The previous incarnation had lasted 13 years (1987 to 2000) and was followed by international controversy when a conservative government took over the reins with the support of the right-wing Freiheitliche Partei Österreichs (FPÖ; Austrian Freedom Party), at that time strongly influenced by populist Jörg Haider.

Haider himself fell out with his own party and headed a new one, the Bündnis Zukunft Österreich (BZÖ; Alliance Future Austria). Today, he and his party, which is the dominant partner in a ruling coalition in Carinthia, are at the centre of the so-called Ortstafelstreit (locality sign conflict). This conflict dates back to an article in Austria's 1955 State Treaty recognising Slovenian and Croatian as official languages in regions with substantial minorities, and it is the one issue today that jeopardises neutral Austria's amicable relations with its neighbours.

Which brings us back to our bleary-eyed jaunt to the newspaper stand. Grab a newspaper, retire to a coffee house, tolerate your aloof waiter if he's Viennese, maybe get prickly with him at your own peril, get excited and do what Austrians everywhere seem to make a pastime out of – enjoy this quality of life that is Austria.

FAST FACTS

Population: 8,281,950

GDP: €257.9 billion

Inflation rate: 1.8%

Unemployment rate: 6.3%

Growth rate: 2.7%

Median net income per year: €16,626

Number of dogs in Austria: 560,000

Percentage overweight or obese: 43.3% women & 57.7% men

Getting Started

When it comes to planning for your trip, Austria is a breeze. Infrastructure and services are excellent, which means the amount of advance preparation you need to do in order to ensure access to cash, or to special dietary and other personal needs, is minimal. Nor do you need to spend much time planning how to get from A to B, even if you've set a tight schedule. The distances between sights are usually easily manageable by foot or a short ride, and catching a distance train or bus will require just a quick check of timetables. In terms of budgets, almost all towns have a very good range of accommodation options – from the cheapest to four-star hotels or the occasional five-star-spangled option. See p380 for more accommodation information.

WHEN TO GO

Visiting Austria at any time of year is a great experience, but remember that the season will influence what you can do. Summer is the obvious time for hiking, mountain biking and lake swimming, but ski conditions also make Austria a fantastic place for winter breaks. Festivals take place year-round, but the majority of music festivals are held between May and October.

For warm weather, aim for the months between April and October, although these two months can be changeable. Crowds and prices peak in the July and August high season, when temperatures can also climb to uncomfortable levels and many famous institutions close down, including the opera, the Spanish Riding School and the Vienna Boys' Choir. Consequently, June and September are often the best times for city trips.

You'll find cities less crowded in winter and (except in ski resorts and over Christmas and Easter) hotel prices lower, although it can get bitingly cold. Winter sports are in full swing from mid-December to late March, with the high season over Christmas and New Year and in February. Alpine resorts are very quiet or close down from late April to mid-June, and in November and early December.

Austria lies within the Central European climatic zone, though the eastern part of the country has a Continental Pannonian climate, with low rainfall, hot summers and mild winters. The Alps have high precipitation, short summers and long winters, and visitors should be prepared for all temperatures there. Seasons are distinct. Summer falls between June and August and has the highest temperatures, but also the highest levels of rainfall. Winter can bite hard, especially in December, January and February. Spring and autumn bring changeable weather, but quite often the most comfortable temperatures.

COSTS & MONEY

Compared to other European cities, Vienna is cheaper than London, Paris, Zürich or Rome, similar to Munich, and more expensive than Prague or Budapest. With the exception of ski resorts such as Lech and Kitzbühel, the Austrian countryside is noticeably cheaper than Vienna. Overall, Britons and Americans will probably find things very affordable.

Accommodation will be your most expensive item (see p380 for accommodation costs), but it can be significantly reduced if you use hostels or share in twin rooms and doubles. If you are travelling alone on midrange options, expect to pay about €50 to €60 per night (with breakfast) in a hotel. Prices for a lunch special are around €6 to €9. An evening meal with a glass of wine or beer costs about €15 to €20, while a day pass on public transport in cities averages about €4.50. Museum entry is €5 to €7 in most cases (though

The three most popular provincial capitals in terms of overnight stays by visitors are Vienna, Salzburg and Innsbruck.

See Climate Charts (p383) for average temperatures and precipitation in Austria's major cities.

Don't spend it all at once – visitors spend €13 billion each year in Austria, compared to the €7 billion spent by Austrians travelling abroad.

DON'T LEAVE HOME WITHOUT...

■ Double-checking the visa situation and your passport expiry date (p392).

■ Organising a good health-insurance policy (p387).

■ A spattering of the language, or a phrase book – a little goes a long way (p411).

■ Polite servitude; Austrians love their greetings, titles, pleases and thank yous (p413).

■ A good relationship with dogs; in Vienna, owners take them everywhere, including bars and restaurants.

■ Good hiking boots and a swimming suit; this is the land of mountains and lakes.

■ A curling tattoo across your lower back – *Arschgeweih* (ass antlers) are still almost cool.

HOW MUCH?

Deerskin *Lederhose* €600

Achtel (wine) at a *Heurigen/Buschenshank* €1 to €1.50

Wiener schnitzel €8 to €15

Double room in pension from €45

A 24-hour ticket on Vienna's public transport €5.70

many are cheaper and a few €12 or more); everyday toiletries (buy them in a *Drogerie* or supermarket, not a pharmacy) as well as splurges, blow-outs and luxuries, plus transportation will also need to be budgeted. We arrived at almost €350 for The Big Trip itinerary (p26) with side trips by public transport but excluding city transport. Taking these into account, about €125 per day is realistic.

If you're on a tight budget and choose to stay in hostels, eat cheaply, buy your drinks from supermarkets, and walk rather than use public transport in cities, you should be able to manage on about €70 or €80 per day. If you want to go below that budget level, you'll need to pick and choose the sights you visit carefully. Students and children get discounts for some museums and activities, and family deals often apply.

TRAVEL LITERATURE

Austria is still waiting for its definitive travel description because most writers focus on its rich cultural heritage rather than the trials and tribulations of the everyday traveller. There are a few very interesting ones around, though, providing a fine backdrop for your journey.

A superb starting point is *A Time of Gifts,* the first volume of Patrick Leigh Fermor's trilogy detailing his epic and inspiring walk from the Hook of Holland to Constantinople in 1933–34. Written 40 years after his feet took him along the Danube Valley and through Vienna, this rich, evocative tale gives an insight into Austria between the world wars.

In *Danube,* Claudio Magris passes an erudite, Italian eye over the length of the Danube in his travel journal from the mid-1980s, and naturally spends time in Austria. His sharp, individual style tackles topics like the source of the Danube (a leaky tap in a remote mountain farmhouse, according to one sedimentologist) and larger-than-life characters such as Wittgenstein and Kafka.

Edward Crankshaw combines travel literature and historical detail in *Vienna: The Image of a Culture in Decline.* This study of the golden city in the early and mid-1930s is certainly nostalgic but still manages to tell it like it is.

Arguably the best account of Jewish life in Vienna between the world wars is *Last Waltz in Vienna: The Destruction of a Family 1842–1942,* by George Clare. This heartbreaking autobiography details one family's fate at the hands of the Nazis; it's a superb read and an insight into how the ordinary lives of so many were forever changed from one day to the next.

Stefan Zweig's *The World of Yesterday* is an extraordinary account of *fin de siècle* Vienna, a time when intellectual brotherhood tried to stop the destruction of Europe. It's all that more poignant considering Zweig,

Want to stay in a castle? Check out www.schloss hotels.co.at.

who had been forced into exile by the Nazis, committed suicide in 1942 on completion of the book.

TRAVELLING RESPONSIBLY

Since our inception in 1973, Lonely Planet has encouraged our readers to tread lightly, travel responsibly and enjoy the magic independent travel affords. International travel is growing at a jaw-dropping rate, and we still firmly believe in the benefits it can bring – but, as always, we encourage you to consider the impact your visit will have on both the global environment and the local economies, cultures and ecosystems.

On the whole, Austrians are very much aware of ecology issues, including those on the big issues of winter sports in the Alps and the impact of tourism. Along with seven other countries it has signed up to the Alpine Convention to promote sustainable development in the Alps, while also implementing its own sustainability plan. With such a large tourism industry, the contribution of individuals travelling in the country can also make a big difference (see p85).

Getting There & Around

Getting to Austria by train or bus is easy from within Europe. From London, this can reduce your footprint by about 90% or more compared to plane travel. Once inside the country, avoid using cars when it's not necessary. In this guide we've included two driving tours, as sights are otherwise difficult to do in one grab. If you're fit or have the time, you can do exactly the same tours by bicycle. In Vienna, a nifty bicycle rental scheme in summer will help you get home from late-night clubbing on an ecofriendly footing (p159), Tulln has a free city bicycle scheme (p173) and Waidhofen an der Ybbs in the awkward-to-travel Mostviertel solves the problem by offering free use of mountain bikes for up to a week.

Using public transport is another obvious alternative – and easy because it's so good in Austria. Trains run through some beautiful and isolated spots, and any gaps in local networks can be plugged by taking along a bicycle or hiring locally. Although using buses becomes a problem on Sundays, you can get around this by planning a weekday trip.

One of the best sources of information about carbon offsetting in Austria is the German-language website www.myclimate.at. There you can read around the issue locally, such as one proposal to set up donation boxes in Austrian travel agencies so travellers can make a direct donation to a carbon offsetting scheme. Whether this proposal can be implemented, however, remains to be seen. The website also allows you to calculate your carbon emissions from a flight and buy a myclimate ticket online (London to Vienna is €6) to offset your footprint.

For more information on reducing carbon footprints, see p396.

Sleeping & Eating

Austria is on the move in regard to ecofriendly accommodation. Using water wisely (and towels more than once) is where you can make the biggest contribution. Some hotels have low-allergy, ecofriendly fittings, serve organic breakfasts, or have sound waste management principles; you can help by disposing of recyclable materials separate from the rest in your hotel room. Restaurants serving organic foods are plentiful in Austria, even more bountiful are those serving local produce, and markets always have at least one stall selling organic produce. The Greendex (p436) at the back of this book lists many establishments with environmentally friendly practices.

Austria's most popular festival is the Salzburg Festival in summer, when over 200,000 people descend upon the venues.

'Austria is a labyrinth in which everyone knows the way.'
KABARETT ARTIST HELMUT QUALTINGER (1928–86)

TOP 10

Switzerland Vienna • Slovaki

AUSTRIA

BEST READS

There's no better way to get a sense of place than by immersing yourself in a good book – these page-turners have won critical acclaim in Austria and abroad. See p55 for more.

1 *Measuring the World* by Daniel Kehlmann

2 *Lust* by Elfriede Jelinek

3 *Night Games: And Other Stories and Novellas* by Arthur Schnitzler

4 *Play of the Eyes* by Elias Canetti

5 *Cutting Timber* by Thomas Bernhard

6 *Setting Free the Bears* by John Irving

7 *Radetzky March* by Joseph Roth

8 *Man Without Qualities, Vol 1* by Robert Musil

9 *Vienna Coffeehouse Wits, 1890–1938* by Bernhard Harold B Segel (ed)

10 *Burning Secret and Other Stories* by Stefan Zweig

MUST-SEE FILMS

One of the best ways to do a bit of pre-departure planning is to curl up on a sofa with a bowl of popcorn and press play. These flicks range from the best-known films about Austria to the cheesiest. See p56 for more details.

1 *The Edukators* (2004) directed by Hans Weingartner

2 *The Third Man* (1949) directed by Carol Reed

3 *Amadeus* (1984) directed by Milos Forman

4 *Foreigners Out!* (2002) directed by Paul Poet

5 *Funny Games* (1997) directed by Fritz Lang

6 *Siegfried* (1924) directed by Michael Haneke

7 *Dog Days* (2001) directed by Ulrich Seidl

8 *Lovely Rita* (2001) directed by Ernst Marischka

9 *The Sissi Trilogy* (1955–57) directed by Jessica Hausner

10 *Der Bockerer* (1981) directed by Franz Antel and Rainer C Ecke

OUR FAVOURITE FESTIVALS & EVENTS

Austrian is never short of a good festival – you can always count on some kind of celebration going on around the country. These are some favourites, but others appear in the Directory chapter (p385) and throughout this book.

1 *Wiener Festwochen* (Vienna Festival Weeks), May and June (p141)

2 *Musikwochen Millstatt* (Millstatt Music Weeks), May to September (p309)

3 *Styriarte* (Graz), June and July (p229)

4 *Milka Schokoladenfest* (Bludenz; Milka Chocolate Festival), July (p377)

5 *Bregenzer Festspiele* (Bregenz Festival), July and August (p370)

6 *Salzburger Festspiele* (Salzburg Festival), July and August (p274)

7 *Lange Nacht der Museen* (countrywide; Long Night of the Museums), September (p141)

8 *Halleiner Stadtfestwoche* (Hallein City Music Weeks), September (p284)

9 *Viennale* (Vienna International Film Festival), October (p141)

10 *Wörthersee Festspiele* (Klagenfurt; Wöthersee Festival), late June to mid-August (p293)

GET HITCHED IN STYLE

This is probably going to set the father of the bride back €1000. For that he'll cover the local registry costs and the expense of hiring a staggeringly romantic venue. That might be, say, an Art Nouveau cabin on the 65m-high Ferris wheel in Prater, or the west wing of Lower Belvedere palace (with 'a splendid outlook on the Upper Belvedere as the local spin doctors put it). Sure, getting married in Vienna is kitsch, but it's an idea that seems to have taken off.

The city council offers seven palaces; four sights (including the Ferris wheel); seven 'locations' (which include a city tram or the Hotel Sacher); as well as the Danube and four other 'landscape' locations, where couples can tie the knot. For the low down, see the council's website (www .wien.gv.at/english/administration/civilstatus/wedding/dreamwedding.html).

Resources

Websites in English are few and far between, but the government website www.lebensministerium.at does have a large section in English covering sustainability in forestry, water, foodstuffs and the environment.

The internet portal www.nachhaltigkeit.at (in German) is also good place to explore sustainability in Austria. The Austrian Business Council for Sustainable Development (ABCSD; www.abcsd.at, in German) has a small list of companies committed to the concept, or look into the AlpMedia website (www.cipra.org), with lots of information about sustainability and the Alps.

INTERNET RESOURCES

Austrian Federal Government (www.austria.gv.at) Gateway to various ministries of the Austrian government.

Austrian National Tourist Office (www.austria.info) The perfect introduction to Austria in a number of languages, with plenty of information and links.

Austrian Press & Information Service (www.austria.org) US-based site with current affairs and links to a range of topics.

Austro Search (www.austrosearch.at) Exhaustive online directory of Austrian businesses and organisations.

Lonely Planet (www.lonelyplanet.com) General facts on Austria, links to Austrian sites and reports from fellow travellers on the Thorn Tree.

Statistik Austria (www.statistik.at) The government's official number-crunching site, with facts and figures on all aspects of life in Austria.

Tiscover (www.tiscover.com) Useful site for information on the provinces; comes complete with online booking facilities.

An Austrian was the first person to put a propeller on a ship. Other Austrians invented the sewing machine, the typewriter and lithography.

Itineraries
CLASSIC ROUTES

Experience high culture and sharp lifestyles in Vienna and the provincial capitals, bathe in refreshing lakes and hike rugged mountains on a 1500km route that does the whole hog by train (and just a few buses) from the capital to the Austrian heartlands.

THE BIG TRIP
One Month / Vienna to Vienna

Spend several days in **Vienna** (p111) before catching a train to **Neusiedl am See** (p196) and taking a bus to **Nationalpark Neusiedler See-Seewinkel** (p197). Boat over to medieval **Mörbisch am See** (p194) and **Rust** (p193), continuing to Schloss Esterházy in **Eisenstadt** (p190) before getting on a train to **Wiener Neustadt** (p184). Rail across the **Semmering Pass** (p186) towards **Graz** (p221), Styria's relaxed capital, and continue to **Klagenfurt** (p289), capital of Carinthia, which offers great swimming in the **Wörthersee** (p295). Lively **Villach** (p297) beckons, as does a side trip to Hermagor's **Garnitzenklamm** (p105) gorge. Swing northeast to **Spittal an der Drau** (p305) and via **Kitzbühel** (p350) towards **Innsbruck** (p331) for some Tyrolean days. **Bregenz** (p368), on the Bodensee, is another side trip.

From Innsbruck, head to **Salzburg** (p266), cultural highlight and gateway to the lakes region, bussing to **St Gilgen** (p261) on the **Wolfgangsee** (p260) and to **Bad Ischl** (p247), where train lines run to **Hallstätter See** (p249). Wind by train or road via **Gmunden** (p257) to **Linz** (p200) on the Danube and via the **Danube Valley** (p164), **Melk** (p172) and pretty **Krems an der Donau** (p167) back to Vienna.

CITIES & LANDSCAPES
Two Weeks / Vienna to Innsbruck

Wake up bright and early in **Vienna** (p111) and visit the palace and gardens of Schloss Schönbrunn. Kids will enjoy the zoo and Tyrolerhof there too. The route from here leads west along the **Danube Valley** (p164). **Krems an der Donau** (p167) is one highlight in a region that flows with wine and good living, **Dürnstein** (p171) is especially good for splurging in top-notch hotels, and **Spitz** (p172) has a low-key atmosphere and some enjoyable hikes through vineyards and forest to castle ruins. Also try to take in the views and church at **Maria Taferl** (p166), a spectacular hilltop town that brings the faithful to their knees. The road or railway continues west to **Linz** (p200) – an industrial city with exciting museums. The trail to **Steyr** (p211) will restore the rural flavour, from where you make your way to **Eisenerz** (p242), with its larger-than-life mines, and **Graz** (p221), Austria's second-largest city and arguably its most chilled-out. After taking in its restaurants, bars and cultural sights, you might feel ready for the open country again. It's a 200km rail journey from Graz to **Hallstatt** (p250), but along the way spend a few hours in **Leoben** (p241) to visit the MuseumsCenter before rolling into the **Hallstätter See** (p249) region. After that, **Gmunden** (p257) and the **Traunsee** (p257), though less spectacular, will call you gently back into town life, and **Salzburg** (p266), the next stop, will immerse you in the city again. From here zip across to the pistes or trails of **Kitzbühel** (p350), one of Austria's premier ski resorts, to **Innsbruck** (p331), where you can take your choice between culture or hiking trails.

Take in the large cities and spectacular mountain, lake and river landscapes on a 1000km rail and bus/road route that includes a fine taste of culture, food and wine.

ROADS LESS TRAVELLED

Across picturesque farmland, into gouged valleys and over precarious, windswept passes – this 900km rail and bus/road route takes in places ideal for striking out into even more remote parts. It includes a fortress town, national parks, waterfalls and the highest peaks between Vienna and Innsbruck.

MEADOWS, MOUNTAINS & VALLEYS   Three Weeks / Vienna to Innsbruck

From **Vienna** (p111) drive or take the train or bus north to the tiny Czech border town of **Drosendorf** (p178). After walking around its medieval town wall, continue by road to Hardegg and the **Nationalpark Thayatal** (p178). From here, the route runs south through the often neglected Waldviertel (via Retz and Horn if on train or bus) to **Schloss Rosenburg** (p177) and **Krems an der Donau** (p167) for a shot of culture and good living. Explore the Danube on a side trip, especially the lower-key regions on the south bank. Make your way to **Waidhofen an der Ybbs** (p177; via Melk and Amstetten if using rail and bus), the perfect spot to begin exploration of the Mostviertel by bicycle. Continue south on rail or road to the Enns Valley, which will provide a spectacular viaduct for the next section of the route. (A side trip from Hieflau goes to **Eisenerz**, p242, to view the ore mines.) The route closely follows the course of the Enns River to Gstatterboden, gateway to the **Nationalpark Gesäuse** (p243), and continues to **Admont** (p243), where you can peek at the Benedictine Abbey. At Selzthal a side trip to **Graz** (p221) is an option, but this route continues along the Enns Valley before heading west to **Zell am See** (p312). Swing south by road from there to **Grossglockner** (p318), Austria's highest peak, in the Hohe Tauern range, and bus or drive on to **Heiligenblut** (p319) and its pilgrimage church. From here continue south to **Lienz** (p323) before swinging northwest to Mittersill, west via the spectacular **Krimmler Wasserfälle** (p317) to **Zell am Ziller** (p347), near **Mayrhofen** (p348) with great activities, and on to **Innsbruck** (p331). An alternative is to go from Mittersill via **Kitzbühel** (p350) to Innsbruck.

History

Although Austria's territorial heartland has always been modest in size, its monarchy ruled an empire that spanned continents and was once the last word in politics and high culture. How did it happen and how did it all change over time? To really understand this, it's useful to know more about the civilisations and empires that figure in its colourful past. Civilisations & Empires is therefore where this history starts. Afterwards we take a trail through themes of post-WWII neutrality (Neutral, Nice & Not Guilty), uprisings (To the Barricades), Jewry (Jewish History in Austria) and foreign invasion of its territory (The Enemy at the Gate), culminating in one of the world's most enduring family dynasties (Keeping it in the Family – the Habsburgs).

CIVILISATIONS & EMPIRES

It would be an understatement to say that alpine regions of Austria were inhospitable places during the Ice Age some 30,000 years ago. They were virtually impenetrable for human and beast. It's therefore not surprising that while mammoths were lumbering across a frozen landscape, the more-accessible plains and Danube Valley in Lower Austria developed into early showplaces of civilisation. A visit to the Naturhistorisches Museum in Vienna (p129) contains two fascinating stone Venus statuettes that are reminders of this era.

When the Celts settled in the late Iron Age (around 450 BC) they also chose the valley of the Danube River and salt-rich regions around Salzburg, encountering Illyrians who had wandered there from the Balkan region. Gradually an Illyric–Celtic kingdom took shape, known as Noricum, that stretched from eastern Tyrol to the Danube and eastern fringes of the Alps in Carinthia.

The Romans, who crossed the Alps in force in 15 BC and settled south of the Danube River, carved up these regions into administrative areas and built fortresses (Limes) and towns such as Carnuntum (p178), Vindobona (the forerunner of Vienna), Brigantium (Bregenz; p368), Juvavum (Salzburg; p266), Flavia Solva (Leibnitz in Styria), Aguntum (p325) and Virunum (north of Klagenfurt). However, the Western Empire created by the Romans collapsed in the 5th century, leaving a vacuum that was filled by newly arriving tribes: the Germanic Alemanni in Vorarlberg, Slavs who pushed into Carinthia and Styria, and Bavarians who settled south of the Danube in Upper and Lower Austria, Tyrol and around Salzburg. The Bavarians proved to be the most successful, and by the 7th century they had most regions of Austria in their grip, creating a large German-speaking territory.

Discover more about the history of Austria from the Babenbergs through to the country's entry into the EU in *The Austrians: A Thousand Year Odyssey* by Gordon Brook-Shepard.

TIMELINE

30,000–25,000 BC	5300 BC	800–400 BC
The 30,000-year-old Venus of Galgenberg (aka Dancing Fanny) and the 25,000-year-old buxom beauty, the Venus of Willendorf, are crafted – both are now in Vienna's Naturhistorisches Museum.	The Neolithic 'Ötzi' dies and is mummified in a glacier in the Ötztal. He's found in 1991 and several Austrian and Italian women ask to be impregnated with his frozen sperm.	The Iron Age Hallstadtkultur (Hallstadt Culture) develops in the southern Salzkammergut, where settlers work salt mines. Around 450 BC Celts arrive in the region and build on this flourishing culture.

THE CAROLINGIANS STRIKE BACK

But at this time it was still possible to talk only about tribes, not fully fledged empires. This changed in Europe and in Austria itself with the growth of the so-called Carolingian Empire in the 6th century. This was Europe's most powerful empire in its day. It originated in western France and Belgium, grew into a heavyweight under Charlemagne (747–814) and took its inspiration from the Romans. Significantly for future Austria, Charlemagne created a buffer region in the Danube Valley, later dubbed Ostmark (Eastern March), which shored up the eastern edge of his empire, and in 800 he was crowned Kaiser (see boxed text, below) by the pope.

The patron saint of Austria is Saint Leopold III of Babenberg (1096-1135).

Fate took another decisive turn in 976, when the Eastern March landed in the hands of Leopold von Babenberg (940–94), a descendent of a noble Bavarian family. The Babenbergs were a skilful family who in the 11th century expanded their small territory to include most of modern-day Lower Austria (with Vienna), and a century later Styria (1192) and much of Upper Austria. In 1156, under the Babenberg monarch Heinrich II 'Jasmirogott', the Eastern March (still a political fence at that time) was elevated to a duchy (ie with its own duke and special rights) and Vienna became its capital.

THE EMPIRE OF THE HABSBURGS

The Babenberg dynasty, however, ran out of heirs in 1246 when one of its rulers, Duke Friedrich II, died in battle with neighbouring Hungarians over a border dispute. This had enormous ramifications for future Austria because it led to the catapulting of another noble family, the Habsburgs, to power in Europe. In a twist of bad fortune, a Bohemian monarch of the day, Ottokar II, married Friedrich's widow and in 1273 refused to recognise the election to king by prince-electors (see boxed text, opposite) of a another noble whose star was rising in Central Europe – the Habsburg Rudolf I (1218–91).

The distended lower jaw and lip, a family trait of the early Habsburgs, is discreetly downplayed in official portraits.

This caused one of the most celebrated clashes in Austrian history when in 1278 the House of Habsburg and Bohemian arch rival Ottokar II (who also controlled Styria and Carinthia) fought it out on the Marchfeld, situated 30km northeast of Vienna. Ottokar, held up while trying to penetrate Drosendorf's fortress en route to the battle (p178), was killed in battle, allowing the Habsburg family to reign over the Holy Roman Empire.

That was pretty much the way things remained for over 500 years. It's only a modest simplification to say that between the era in which mammoths roamed the frozen wastes and the next important change – the arrival of 164cm, low-rise Napoleon in the early 19th century – Austria had seen early human settlers (the ones who carved those Venus statuettes), two major civilisations (Illyrians and the Celts), one Roman Empire and two families (the Babenbergs and the Habsburgs) control the land.

15 BC–AD 600	800	976 & 996
The Romans establish relations with Celts and Celtic-influenced Noric tribes. From 15 BC Roman occupation begins in the three provinces of Rhaetia, Noricum and Pannonia. Slavic, Germanic and other tribes later overrun the territories.	The Frankish king Charlemagne is crowned Holy Roman Emperor. The troublesome Avars are routed and disappear, creating an Eastern March that passes into the hands of Charlemagne's successors Otto I (912–73) and Otto II (955–83).	The Babenbergs are entrusted with the Eastern March in 976, administer it as margraves, and in 996 this appears for the first time in a document as Ostarrîchi.

AUSTRIA & THE HOLY ROMAN EMPIRE

The Holy Roman Empire was Europe's oddest 'state'. Its foundations were laid when Charlemagne's father, Pippin, rescued a beleaguered pope and became Patricius Romanorum (Protector of Rome), making him Caesar's successor. The title 'Kaiser' is derived from 'Caesar'. Pippin, with Italian spoils on his hands (one being the present-day Vatican), gave these to the pope. Charlemagne continued this tradition as protector, and in 962, with the crowning of Otto I (912–73) as Holy Roman Emperor, the Empire was officially born.

Kings in the Empire were elected in political horse-trading by a handful of prince electors, but to take the next step and become Kaiser (and protector of the pope), the pope had to crown the king. Depending on how feisty the pope happened to be, this brought other troubles. In 1338 enough was enough, and the electors threw the pope overboard, deciding they could elect their own Kaiser.

In 972, just before Otto I died, borders of the Empire included present-day Austria, Slovenia, Czech Republic, Germany, Holland, Belgium and much of the Italian peninsula. These borders ebbed and flowed with the times. When Rudolf I arrived in 1273, it all – or what remained of it – belonged to the Habsburgs.

The Empire was formally buried in 1806 when Napoleon Bonaparte tore through Europe, and by the time the Austro–Hungarian Empire took shape in 1867 (a dual monarchy of Austria and Hungary), it was little more than a dim and distant reminder of medieval times.

The French Revolution of 1789–99 was a political explosion that ushered in a new age of republicanism in Europe, and it challenged surviving feudal-istic anachronisms like the Holy Roman Empire. Thus, although Napoleon was soundly defeated in Leipzig in 1813 and, finally, at Waterloo in 1815, his advance across Europe caused its collapse. The Habsburgs survived, however, and in the post-Napoleon Vormärz (Pre-March) years, they dominated a loose Deutscher Bund (German Alliance) comprising hundreds of small 'states' cobbled together in a period of cultural flourish – called the Biedermeier period.

Given that ordinary citizens at the time were kept on a short leash by their political masters, it's not surprising that they began to seek new freedoms. In 1848, inspired by the February 1848 revolution in France, Austrians demanded their own parliament (p33). One was created and met (without Hungary, a Habsburg possession at the time, and without parts of Italy that had been in Habsburg hands) in July that year. But revolution and a democratic parliament failed to endure in Austria.

In 1867 a dual monarchy was created in Austria and Hungary, arising out of an attempt by the Habsburgs to hold onto support for the monarchy among Hungarians by giving them a large degree of autonomy. This Austro-Hungarian Empire would grow to include core regions of Austria, Hungary, the Czech Republic, Slovakia, Slovenia, Croatia and Bosnia-Herzegovine, as well as regions like the Voivodina in Serbia, and small chunks in northern Italy, Romania, Poland and the Ukraine.

The roots of Austria's Österreichische Volkspartei (ÖVP; Austrian People's Party) go back to 1887; a forerunner of the Sozialdemokratische Partei Österreichs (SPÖ; Social Democratic Party of Austria) was founded a year later.

Vienna's population peaked at more than two million between 1910 and 1914. After WWI, Vienna was one of the world's five largest cities.

1156	1192	1246–78
As consolation for relinquishing Bavaria, which fell into Babenberg hands after a local conflict, Austria becomes a duchy (Privilegium Minus) and the Babenberg ruler Heinrich Jasomirgott (1107–77) becomes Austria's first duke, residing in Vienna.	Styria is given to Babenberg Leopold V (1157–94) on the condition that it stays part of Austria forever. Styria at the time includes chunks of Slovenia and various parts of Lower and Upper Austria.	The last Babenberg dies in 1246 and Habsburg rule begins when Rudolf I is elected king of the Holy Roman Empire in 1273; he defeats Bohemian Ottokar II in the Battle of Marchfeld in 1278.

This was the so-called 'KuK' (König und Kaiser; King and Kaiser) monarchy – the Kaiser of Austria was also King of Hungary. In practice, the two countries increasingly went separate ways, united only by the dual monarch and a couple of high-level ministries like 'war' and 'foreign affairs'.

THE MODERN REPUBLICS

The turmoil caused by defeat in WWI, however, brought this to an end, laying the foundations for modern Austria. Austrians demanded a fully fledged republic, and they got one, ending 640 years of Habsburg rule.

This First Republic was the country's first experiment with truly democratic institutions, but the stigma of WWI defeat weakened it. Austria, now reduced almost to the size of the country we know today, lost access to resources beyond its own borders, which caused economic problems. Polarisation was another hurdle. This had a geographical edge in Austria: 'Rotes Wien' (Red Vienna) was controlled by a socialist city government, while rural regions were firmly in the grip of the conservative federal government of the Christian Socials. Chaos broke out in March 1933 when the Christian Socials chancellor Engelbert Dollfuss (1892–1934) dissolved parliament and, in what was virtually a putsch, prevented it from sitting.

Dollfuss' sympathies lay with the Italian dictator Benito Mussolini (1883–1945) and the Catholic Church. He banned the communist party and the pro-German Austrian Nazi Party (this favoured annexation of Austria by Germany), and when he took up the battle with the Social Democrats, he sparked the Austrian Civil War in 1934.

By 1936, however, Hitler and Mussolini had created a Rome–Berlin axis and Austria found itself between a rock and a hard place. In March 1938, Hitler's troops invaded Austria, and Hitler, an Austrian himself, ruled the country as an appendage of Germany until 1945.

Soviet, not Allied, troops liberated Vienna in March 1945, triggering a twilight period in which the Soviet Union, Britain, the USA and France occupied Austria and carved up the capital into zones – the famous 'four men in a jeep' period. It was the beginning of the Second Republic (below) – today's Republic of Austria.

Carl E Schorske magically interlinks seven essays on the intellectual history of Vienna in his seminal work *Fin-de-Siècle Vienna*.

NEUTRAL, NICE & NOT GUILTY

In 1948 the British author Graham Greene flew to Vienna and roamed the bomb-damaged streets looking for inspiration for a film he had been commissioned to write about the occupation of post-WWII Vienna. As chance would have it, Greene penned the script for one of Europe's finest films about the era – *The Third Man*, starring Orson Wells as the penicillin racketeer Harry Lime. In a moment of improvisation the end of the film, Orson Wells as Lime waxes lyrical about how under the bloody reign of the Borgias' Italy produced some of its finest art. 'In Switzerland they

1335 & 1363	1517	1556
Bavarian Ludwig IV (1314–47) gives Carinthia (minus Tyrol) to the Habsburgs in 1335 and territories include Austria (Ostarrîchi), Styria, Krain (in Slovenia) and Carinthia. In 1363 Margarethe Maultasch (1318–63) dies and Tyrol is added.	Theology professor Martin Luther sparks the Reformation when he makes public his 95 Theses that call into question corrupt practices of the Church, and most of Austria becomes Lutheran (Protestant).	Abandoning the idea of uniting an empire under Catholicism, Karl V abdicates – the Spanish part goes to his son Philipp II and Ferdinand I gets Austria, Bohemia and largely Turkish-occupied Hungary.

had brotherly love, 500 years of democracy and peace, and what did they produce? The cuckoo clock.'

Postwar Austria sought the kind of Swiss stability that makes a cuckoo clock fascinating. One day in April 1945, at the instigation of the Soviet Union, the country was proclaimed a republic for the second time in its history. The constitution from 1920 was revived (in its 1929 form), and pre-Nazi laws from March 1933 came back into force; free elections were held in November 1945.

The Soviet Union insisted on Austria declaring its neutrality as a condition for ending occupation in 1955. At the last minute, though, recognition of Austria's guilt for WWII was struck out of the State Treaty that paved the way for neutral independence. Its neutrality differs from the Swiss 'cuckoo clock' model, however, because Austria joined the UN and has even participated in international peace-keeping forces. The Second Republic became a mostly quiet, peaceful period during which the economy enjoyed solid growth or boom conditions, Austria played a moderating role during the East–West frost, and the world forgot about the past.

This silence was shattered in 1986, however, and not surprisingly it was the guilt question again. When accusations surfaced that presidential candidate Kurt Waldheim had been involved in Nazi war crimes, Austria seriously confronted its Nazi past for the first time. Evidence that he had committed war crimes while a lieutenant serving with the German army in the Balkans could never be proved, but nor was Austria's elected president willing to fully explain himself or express misgivings about his wartime role.

TO THE BARRICADES

While empires waxed and waned, Austria was wracked by revolt and resistance. Apart from frequent squabbles between sycophantic monarchs, the first large-scale uprising took place in the mid- and late-15th century, when peasants in Austria (as elsewhere in Central Europe) rose up against their nobility in the Peasants' Wars. These upheavals were spontaneous and directed at local despots, however, rather than against the empire itself. The roots of discontent could be found in a need for cash to finance defences against the Turks, or in some instances demands by an oppressive monarch during the drawn-out anti-reformation.

In April 1809, during the Napoleonic occupation, Tyrol – which had fallen into the hands of Bavaria – was the scene of another rebellion when innkeeper Andreas Hofer (1767–1810) led a rebellion for independence. For his troubles, Hofer was put on trial and executed at Napoleon's behest. His body is entombed in Innsbruck's Hofkirche (see p334).

The next show of strength from the people was the Revolution of 1848. Austrians suffered badly during the system of atrophy under Klemens von Metternich, a diplomat who rose to power in the splash caused by Napoleon's

Hella Pick's *Guilty Victim: Austria from the Holocaust to Haider* is an excellent analysis of modern-day Austria.

When Governor Schwarzenegger allowed an execution to go ahead in California in 2005, some Austrians wanted to revoke his Austrian citizenship. Austria first abolished capital punishment in 1787.

Austria's greatest military hero, Prince Eugène of Savoy, was in fact French. Refused entry to the French army by Louis XIV, Eugène went on to humiliate him on the battlefield.

1618–48	1683	1740–48
Anti-reformer Ferdinand II (1578–1637) challenges Bohemia's confessional freedom. Habsburg counsels are thrown out of a window (the Prague Defenestration), triggering the Thirty Years' War.	Turkish Siege of Vienna. This siege of 1683 comes after an even closer call in 1529 when Turks were thwarted by winter. Christian Europe is mobilised and the threat persists until 1718, after which the Ottoman Empire gradually wanes.	Maria Theresia (1717–80) inherits Habsburg possessions, Prussia seizes Silesia (in Poland today) and the Austrian War of Succession starts a European power struggle between Prussia and a Habsburg-controlled Austria-Hungary.

fall. Metternich believed in the power of absolute monarchy and his police snapped ferociously at the heels of liberals and Austrian nationalists in the decades before revolution. This Vormärz era (ie pre-March 1848, and also called 'Biedermeier') was culturally rich, but socially the air was heavy with political resignation and Austrians grew insular. This was about to change, not least because atrocious industrial conditions were making the country ripe for change. Nationalism – the best chance of liberalising societies in those days – was also threatening to chip the delicate edges of the Habsburg empire.

The sparks of February revolution in Paris (1848) flared in Vienna in March, but, reflecting the city–country divide, failed to really ignite Austria elsewhere except in Styria. In one ironic twist, a similar revolution in Germany meant some Austrian revolutionaries supported being part of a greater, unified and liberal Germany. This was the tricky *Grossdeutsch-Kleindeutsch* (Greater Germany–Lesser Germany) question, and reflects the difficult affinity between Austrians and Germans.

The rebels demanded a parliament, and briefly they got one in May 1848. Kaiser Ferdinand I packed his bags and his family and fled to Innsbruck. This should have been the end of the Habsburgs. It wasn't. Parliament passed a bill improving the lot of the peasants, and Ferdinand cleverly sanctioned this, overnight winning the support of rural folk in the regions. Meanwhile, the Habsburgs received a popular boost when General Radetzky (1766–1858) won back Lombardy (Italy) in successful military campaigns.

In October 1848 revolution reached fever pitch in Vienna. Although this uprising was ultimately quashed, the Habsburgs decided to dispense with Ferdinand I, replacing him with his nephew Franz-Joseph I, who introduced his own monarchical constitution and dissolved the parliament in early 1849. It would only be revived properly in 1867.

By September 1849 it was time to weigh up the damage, count the dead and, most importantly, look at what had been won. Austria was not a democracy, because the Kaiser could veto the Reichstag's legislation. But revolution had swept away the last vestiges of feudalism and made state citizens out of royal subjects.

Women in Austria gained the right to vote in national elections in 1919.

The Nazi Era

By 1927, these citizens inhabited a very different world. WWI had ended in defeat and armed paramilitary groups roamed the streets of Vienna and elsewhere engaging in bloody clashes. A July revolt broke out in 1927 when left-wing groups stormed the Palace of Justice in Vienna. This was prompted by a court having acquitted members of a right-wing paramilitary Frontkämpfer (Front Fighters) group charged with killing two people during demonstrations. The police moved in and regained control of the building, but about 90 people died in the revolt and over 1000 were injured.

1764	1793	1804–05 & 1809
The reformer Kaiser Joseph II (1741–90) takes the throne and the Age of Enlightenment that began under Maria Theresia is in full swing. The power of the Church is curbed, but Hungary drags its feet.	Following a marriage to French king Louis XVI (1754–93), Maria Theresia's 15th daughter Marie-Antoinette (1755–93) – who the French call 'L'Autrichienne' (the Austrian) – is beheaded during the French Revolution. A new European age begins.	Napoleon (1769–1821) occupies Vienna in 1805. The Holy Roman Empire is abolished, Franz II reinvents himself as Austrian Kaiser Franz I, creating a Danube Monarchy. But in 1809 the Frenchman must return to re-take Vienna.

In the late 1920s and the 1930s, the stakes were raised even higher and, with the annexation of Austria by Hitler in 1938, opposition turned to resistance. As elsewhere, whenever Hitler's troops jackbooted over a border, resistance from within was extremely difficult. Communists and Social Democrats were outlawed in the early 1930s and fought from underground. Members of the Social Democratic Worker's Party fought a four-day battle with police in Linz and Vienna before being banned and their leadership was arrested.

The role of Austria during WWII is one of the most controversial aspects of its modern history. Austria's home-grown brand of Austro-Fascism had favoured independence, but Hitler was popular inside Austria, and Austria itself supplied a disproportionately large number of officers for the SS and the German army. In short, what Hitler and the Nazis couldn't achieve through pressure, large numbers of Austrians themselves helped achieve through their active and passive support for Nazism and Hitler's war.

Interestingly, Tyrolean resistance leaders often rallied opposition to Nazism by recalling the revolt of innkeeper Andreas Hofer in 1809 (see p33). An *Österreichisches Freiheitsbataillon* (Austrian Freedom Battalion) fought alongside the Yugoslav People's Liberation Army, and partisan groups in Styria and Carinthia maintained links with other partisans across the Yugoslavian border. Tellingly, unlike other countries, Austria had no government in exile.

Resistance increased once the war looked lost for Hitler. The Austrian Robert Bernardis (1908–44) was involved in the assassination attempt on Hitler by military brass on July 20, 1944 and was then executed by Nazis. Another involved in that plot, Carl Szokoll (1915–2004), survived undetected. The most famous resistance group, however, was called 05, whose members included Austria's president from 1957 to 1965, Adolf Schärf (1890–1965).

With the Red Army approaching Vienna in 1945, 05 worked closely with Szokoll and other military figures in Operation Radetzky to liberate Vienna in the last days of the war. Although they were able to establish contact with the Red Army as it rolled towards Vienna, they were betrayed at the last moment and several members were strung up from street lanterns. The Red Army, not Austrians, would liberate the capital.

The findings of the Historical Commission's report into Austria during the Nazi era can be found at www.historikerkommission.gv.at.

JEWISH HISTORY IN AUSTRIA

When the Nazis stomped into Vienna in March 1938, ordinary Austrians threw bouquets of flowers and cheered. A few days later, Hitler addressed tens of thousands of cheering Austrians on Vienna's Heldenplatz to declare the integration of his 'homeland' into the Third Reich. For those Jews who had not yet managed to flee the country, this must have been a depressing moment. Vienna's 'father' of modern psychoanalysis, Sigmund Freud (1856–1939), had not wanted to read the signs for a long time, but in June that year he fled to England. The 20th century's most innovative classical

'The Viennese are neither more abstinent nor more nervous than anyone else in big cities.'
SIGMUND FREUD

1848	1866	1867
Revolution topples Chancellor Klemens von Metternich, who flees disguised as a washerwoman. Kaiser Ferdinand I abdicates, but successor Franz-Joseph I (1830–1916) abolishes many reforms. Austria's first parliament is formed.	Austria and its allied principalities in Germany fight the Austro-Prussian War (1866), which leads to victory for Prussia and creates the groundwork for a unified Germany that excludes Austria.	Weakened by loss against Prussia, Austria is now forced by Hungary to create a dual Austro-Hungarian monarchy (the Ausgleich) in 1867. Austria establishes a democratic parliament.

composer, Arnold Schönberg (1874–1951), had already been booted out of his job as a lecturer in Berlin in 1933 and fled to the US. They were just two of many prominent Austrian Jews forced into exile.

Others were not as fortunate. The Holocaust (or 'Schoa'), Hitler's attempt to wipe out European Jewry, was a brutal and systematic act that saw some 65,000 Austrian Jews perish in concentration camps throughout Europe. It ruptured a Jewish history in Austria dating back to the early Middle Ages, and even today it's not really possible to talk about a 'recovery' of Jewish culture in the country.

The first mention of Jews in Vienna was in 1194, when a minter by the name of Schlom was appointed by the crown. The very same man was subsequently murdered along with 16 other Viennese Jews by zealous crusaders on their way to the Holy Land. Gradually, a ghetto grew around today's Judenplatz in Vienna (see p127), where a large synagogue stood in the 13th century.

Historically, Jews could only work in some professions. They were seldom allowed into tradesmen's guilds or to engage in agriculture and therefore earned a living through trading goods and selling, or through money lending, which explains many of the clichés of the past and present. Two 'libels' in the Middle Ages made life difficult for Jews. One of these was the 'host desecration libel', which accused Jews of desecrating Christ by such acts such as sticking pins into communion wafers and making them weep or bleed. The second was the 'blood libel', which accused Jews of drinking the blood of Christians during rituals. In 1420 these libels culminated in one of Vienna's worst pogroms, during which many Jews committed collective suicide. The synagogue on Vienna's Judenplatz was destroyed and the stones of the synagogue were used for the building of the old university.

Out of the Darkness

Jews were officially banned from settling in Vienna until 1624, but this law was regularly relaxed. It did mean, however, that Vienna's Jews had a particularly rough time of it, and in 1670 when Leopold I (1640–1705) drove them out of Unterer Werd, the quarter was re-christened Leopoldstadt, the name it bears today. They returned, however, and this district remained Vienna's largest Jewish quarter prior to WWII.

When money was tight following the 1683 Turkish siege, Jews were encouraged to settle in town as money lenders. Interestingly, once the threat subsided from 1718, Sephardic Jews from Spain arrived and were allowed to establish their own religious community. An edict from Kaiser Joseph II (1741–90) improved conditions for Jews and after Kaiser Franz I reinvented himself as Austria's Kaiser and allowed Jews to establish schools, some of Vienna's Jewry rose into bourgeois and literary circles.

The revolution of 1848 (see p33) brought the biggest changes, however. Vienna's Jews were at the forefront of the uprising, and it brought them

Take a virtual tour through Jewish history in Austria from the Middle Ages to the present in the Jewish Virtual Library at www.jewishvirtual library.org/jsource/vjw/Austria.html.

1878	1908	1914
To prevent the Russians increasing their influence in the Balkans after they win the Russo-Turkish War of 1877–78, Austria-Hungary occupy Bosnia and Herzegovina.	Fatefully, Austria-Hungary is given a mandate to occupy and administer Bosnia and Herzegovina, with the expectation that it would later be annexed completely.	Austrian archduke Franz Ferdinand is assassinated in Sarajevo by a Serbian nationalist, triggering World War I, which sees Austria-Hungary in alliance with Germany and the Ottomon Empire.

freedom of religion, press and schooling. Indirectly, it also led to the founding of the *Israelitische Kultusgemeinde* (Jewish Religious Community), more than a century after the Sephardic Jews had founded their own. Today this is the main body that represents religious Jews in Austria.

Legally unfettered, Vienna's Jews nevertheless found themselves walking a high tightrope. They owed much to the Habsburg monarchy and many therefore identified with it. Many also cherished the freedoms of revolution. And all inhabited an 'Austrian–German' cultural landscape. Somewhere in there, they also lived out their strong Jewish identity.

In 1878 Jewry in Austria was shaken up again by the arrival from Budapest of Theodor Herzl (1860–1904), who founded political Zionism, a concept that brought together the ideas of the workers' movement with support for a Jewish state. His book *Der Judenstaat* (1896; The Jewish State) would later be crucial to the creation of Israel.

Beginning with Adolf Fischhof (1816–93), whose political speech on press freedom in 1848 helped trigger revolution, and continuing with Herzl and with the founding father of Austrian social democracy, Viktor Adler (1852–1918), Jews drove ahead reforms in Austria and played a key role during the Rotes Wien (see p32) period of the 1920s and early 1930s.

This, of course, poured oil on the fires of Hitler's ideology. When Hitler's troops reached Vienna in 1938, Jews were subjected to attack and abuse. The tragedy was that the Jewish community had contributed so much to Viennese cultural and political life, and now many of Vienna's non-Jewish citizens simply looked the other way.

The events that followed, culminating in the Holocaust, are etched in the collective memory of Jews everywhere: the prohibitive Nuremberg Laws, the forced sale and theft of Jewish property, the *die Kristallnacht* ('Night of Broken Glass') on 9–10 November, 1939 when synagogues and Jewish businesses burned and Jews were attacked openly on the streets.

Because of this, today the Jewish community is only a fraction of its former size. About 7000 religiously affiliated Jews live in Austria, and about another 3000 to 5000 who are not affiliated with a community. The number was boosted by the arrival of Jews from the former Soviet Union in the 1990s. For a fascinating glimpse of Jewish life from the 13th century to today, don't miss the Jewish Museum and the Museum Judenplatz, both in Vienna (see p127).

> Hear and read stories of Holocaust victims at the website of the US Holocaust Memorial Museum (www.ushmm.org).

THE ENEMY AT THE GATE

The Celts, the Romans and various tribes have all swept across borders at one time or another to lay claim to Austrian lands. In fact, Austria itself was originally founded as a border *March* to keep out tribes (see p30). The Turkish sieges, though, are the ones that really got the European imagination firing.

1918	**1920s**	**1934**
WWI ends and Karl I abdicates after the humiliating defeat; the First Republic is proclaimed in Vienna. Meanwhile, the Habsburg empire is shaved of border nationalities and Austria keeps most German-speaking regions.	The Social Democratic Party of Austria controls 'Red Vienna', its heart set on Austro-Marxism, while the provinces are controlled by conservative forces.	Austrian politics is chronically polarised, paralysed by paramilitary groups and in 1934 parliament is in gridlock and Austria collapses into civil war – hundreds die in three-day fighting culminating in Social Democrat defeat.

The Ottoman Empire viewed Vienna as 'the city of the golden apple', but it wasn't Apfelstrüdel they were after in their great sieges. The first, in 1529, was undertaken by Süleyman the Magnificent, but the 18-day endeavour was not sufficient to break the resolve of the city. The Turkish sultan subsequently died at the siege of Szigetvár, yet his death was kept secret for several days in an attempt to preserve the morale of his army. The subterfuge worked for a while. Messengers were led into the presence of the embalmed body which was placed in a seated position on the throne. They then unwittingly relayed their news to the corpse.

At the head of the Turkish siege of 1683 was the general and grand vizier Kara Mustapha. Amid the 25,000 tents of the Ottoman army that surrounded Vienna he installed his 1500 concubines, guarded by 700 black eunuchs. Their luxurious quarters contained gushing fountains and regal baths, all set up in haste but with great effect.

Again, it was all to no avail, even though Vienna was only lightly defended by 10,000 men. Mustapha's overconfidence was his downfall; failing to put garrisons on Kahlenberg, he and his army were surprised by a swift attack. Mustapha was pursued from the battlefield and defeated once again, at Gran. At Belgrade he was met by the emissary of the Sultan Mehmed IV. The price of failure was death, and Mustapha meekly accepted his fate. When the Austrian imperial army conquered Belgrade in 1718 the grand vizier's head was dug up and brought back to Vienna in triumph.

KEEPING IT IN THE FAMILY – THE HABSBURGS

Possibly no other family has influenced the European continent – or the world for the matter – as much as the Habsburgs. Although its origins could never be described as humble, the family came a long way from its Habichtsburg (Hawke's Nest) castle near Basle in present-day Switzerland.

Marriage, not muscle, was the historic key to Habsburg land grabbing. The Hungarian king Matthias Corvinus (1443–90) once adapted lines from Ovid when he wrote: 'Let others wage war but you, lucky Austria, marry! For the empires given to others by Mars are given to you by Venus.'

The age of the convenient wedding began in earnest with Maximilian I (1459–1519), whose moniker was The Last Knight because of his late predilection for medieval tournaments. His other loves were Renaissance art, his own grave (which he commissioned during his own lifetime) and Albrecht Dürer (1471–1528), who he commissioned to work on the very same grave before he stepped into it. It is now in Innsbruck's Hofkirche (see p334).

But it was Maximilian's affection for Maria of Burgundy (1457–82) that had the greatest influence on the fortunes of the Habsburgs. The two married, and when Maria fell from a horse and died as a result of a miscarriage in 1482, Burgundy, Lorraine and the Low Countries fell into Habsburg hands. In their

Really mad or really handsome? The Habsburg Johanna the Mad kissed the feet of husband Philipp the Handsome when his coffin was opened five weeks after his death in 1506.

1938

Nazi troops march into Vienna and Hitler visits his birthplace Braunau am Inn, his beloved Linz, and Vienna to address 200,000 ecstatic Viennese on Heldenplatz. After a rigged referendum, Austria becomes part of Hitler's Reich.

1939–45

War and genocide in Austria. Over 100,000 of Vienna's 180,000 Jews escape before the Anschluss but 65,000 Jews die. In 1945 the Red Army liberates Vienna. Austria and Vienna are divided among the powers.

1955

The Austrian Staatsvertrag (State Treaty) is ratified. Austria declares its sovereignty and neutral status and a decade of occupation ends. Neutral status draws post-WWII international bodies to Vienna, and the UN later establishes offices here.

WHATEVER HAPPENED TO THE HABSBURGS?

They're still around. Otto von Habsburg (1912–) is the current family head, but he renounced his claims to the Habsburg lands in 1961, a step that allowed him to re-enter Austria and launch a career in European politics.

Once asked why his name never surfaced in the tabloids, the 90-plus year old 'monarch' replied: 'I've not once attended a ball. I prefer to sleep at night. And if you don't go to nightclubs, you don't run into the gossip columnists.' Somewhat of a sporting man, too, when Otto von Habsburg was quizzed about who he thought would win an Austria versus Hungary football match, he reportedly replied 'Who are we playing?'

Most poignant is perhaps a comment by German President Paul von Hindenburg to Otto von Habsburg in 1933 (the year Hitler seized power in Germany): 'You know, your majesty, there's only one person with hostile feelings towards the Habsburgs, but he's an Austrian.'

---

day, these regions were the last word in culture, economic high-kicking and the arts. The downside was a sticky relationship with France that stuck to the Habsburg shoe for centuries.

The 'Spanish Marriage' in 1496 was another clever piece of royal bedding. When Maximilian's son Philipp der Schöne (Philipp the Handsome) married Juana la Loca (1479–55; Johanna the Mad), Spain and its resource-rich overseas territories in Central and South America became Habsburg. When their son, Ferdinand I (1503–64) married Anna of Hungary and Bohemia (1503–47), fulfilling a deal his grandfather Maximilian I had negotiated with King Vladislav II (1456–1516), Bohemia was also in the Habsburg fold. In the same deal, Maria von Habsburg (1505–58) married into this Polish–Lithuanian Jagiellonen dynasty, which traditionally purveyed kings to Poland, Bohemia and Hungary at that time. By 1526, when her husband Ludwig II (1506–26) drowned in a tributary of the Danube during the Battle of Mohács against Turks, Silesia (in Poland), Bohemia (in the Czech Republic) and Hungary were all thoroughly Habsburg.

Under Karl V (1500–58), the era of the universal monarch arrived, and the Habsburgs had added the Kingdom of Naples (southern Italy, including Sicily). That, unfortunately, was about as good as it got.

The rot set in with the Treaty of Augsburg (1555), which regulated religious bickering surrounding the Reformation. This treaty stipulated that each ruler could decide the religion of his or her own region. Not only does this explain the patchwork of Protestant and Catholic religions today in many regions that used to be part of the Holy Roman Empire, but it also made a mess of the Habsburgs because Karl V had dedicated his life to creating his so-called 'universal Catholic monarchy'. Seeing the writing clearly on the wall, he abdicated in 1556 and withdrew to a monastery in Spain to lick his wounds and die.

1955–66	1986	1995
'Grand coalitions' of major parties govern Austria based on a system of Proporz (proportion), whereby ministerial posts are divided among the major parties. This becomes a hallmark of Austrian politics.	Austria confronts its past when Austrian presidential candidate Kurt Waldheim (1918–2007) is accused of war crimes. Waldheim wins a tough election but is stained. An Historian's Commission finds Waldheim unhelpful but no proof of crimes.	Austria joins the European Union (EU) in 1995 but because of guarantees in 1955 to Moscow to remain neutral, it foregoes NATO membership.

The spoils were divided up among Habsburgs. The brother of Karl V – Ferdinand I (the same one who had married Anna of Hungary and Bohemia) – inherited Austria and (yes, you guessed it) Hungary and Bohemia, and Karl V's only legitimate son, Philipp II (1527–98) got Spain, Naples and Sicily, the Low Countries, and the overseas colonies.

Maria Theresia

For a succinct biography of every Habsburg ever born (including the current family), see www.antiquesatoz.com/habsburg.

If Maximilian I was the Last Knight, Maria Theresia (1717–80) was the mother of the nation. Thrust into the limelight when her father died with no male heirs, she held onto power for 40 years, while also managing to give birth to 16 children – among them Marie Antoinette, future wife of Louis XVI. Maria Theresia's fourth child, Joseph II, weighed a daunting 7kg at birth.

Although Maria Theresia pushed through many enlightened reforms, she was remarkably prudish for a family that had married and copulated its way to power. One of her less popular measures was the introduction of the short-lived Commission against Immoral Conduct in 1752, which raided private homes, trying to catch men entertaining loose women – the commission even tried to snare Casanova during his visit to Vienna.

Maria Theresia's low take on fornication was no doubt coloured by the conduct of her husband, Francis I, who was apparently very adept in just that field. Yet despite his philandering, Maria Theresia felt she should remain loyal to her spouse, and when he died suddenly in 1765 she stayed in mourning for the rest of her life. She retreated to Schloss Schönbrunn (p135) in Vienna, left the running of the state in the hands of Joseph II (of 7kg fame), and adopted a low-profile and chaste existence.

Although the last Habsburg ruler abdicated in 1918, the family is still going strong in public life (see boxed text, p39).

1999	2007	2008
Austria introduces the euro and abolishes the Austrian shilling as its currency, having easily satisfied the criteria for the level of debt and the inflation rate.	A grand coalition government of Social Democrats and Austrian People's Party is formed under Alfred Gusenbauer.	Austria co-hosts with Switzerland football's European Cup.

The Culture

THE NATIONAL PSYCHE

Trying to put a finger on the psyche of a country that gave us the likes of psychoanalyst Sigmund Freud is surely fraught with dangers. As Freud himself said, 'I know only one thing for sure. The value judgements of human beings are…an attempt to prop up illusion with argument'. So what was he trying to tell us? Maybe that whatever we decide about Austrians on a visit, some of it will be our own narrative.

Even Freud, though, couldn't deny a few things about the Austrians' mental topography. One is the self-styled conservatism you find in the deeper rifts and valleys of its regions. On top of this come a few historical grains that irritate the Austrian psyche. Once upon a time half the world was its oyster. Now it isn't. But what Austria now lacks in land it makes up for with a grandiose bureaucracy honed with vigour since the 19th century. Inside this bureaucracy you are likely to find (apart from the odd grump) a system of dividing up posts not on merit but consensus. Austrians see themselves – probably quite rightly – as more harmony-seeking than the neighbouring Germans, but they can also be greater sticklers for convention and public opinion is less fragmented, which has much to do with the country's size.

Austrians are self-made rather than born; strikingly 'New World' at times and also fiercely regional. Along with the national symbols, each state has its own anthem, which is sung by schoolchildren on important occasions, and each even has its own patron saint.

The Viennese are different because they see themselves first and foremost as Austrians. The capital lives and thrives from its Wiener Schmäh (Vienna humour), a concoction of morbid, wry, misanthropic wit, personified by dead rock singer Falco (p49). Some of the local Vienna Actionism art did too. Maybe it's also why one of Freud's most important works is his *Jokes*

'In Austria, everyone becomes what they are not.'
COMPOSER GUSTAV MAHLER

The Austrian Federal Government's official website www.austria.gv.at has plenty of information on the country's political situation in English.

DOS & DON'TS

Austria is a society of politeness; to ignore the rules is the height of rudeness. Stick to the following dos and don'ts and you'll do just fine:

- Do greet people with *Grüss Gott* or *Guten Tag*, whether it be in a social setting, shop, café, restaurant or information office. *Servus* is reserved for greetings only between friends or the younger generation. When departing, *Auf Wiedersehen* or *Auf Wiederschauen* is appropriate.
- Do shake hands when introduced to someone, even in younger, informal company. Likewise, shake hands when you leave.
- Do introduce yourself at the start of a phone call by giving your name.
- Do dress up if going to the opera, theatre or a top restaurant. A jacket and tie for men is the norm.
- Do use full titles at the beginning of formal meetings; *Herr* for men and *Frau* for women is the minimum required. If you speak German, always use the *Sie* form with the older generation and on the telephone; it's not so common with the younger generation.
- Don't cross at the traffic lights when the figure is red, even when there is no traffic in sight. Austrians rarely do it, and the cops can instantly fine you for jaywalking.
- Don't strip off or go topless at every beach in Austria. Nude bathing is limited to areas with FKK signs and if no-one else is going topless at other beaches, you shouldn't either.

and their Relation to the Unconscious. All very serious stuff, of course. But it also happens to be a fine collection of Schmäh.

LIFESTYLE

With their high material standard of living, a spectacular landscape on the doorstep lending itself to skiing, hiking and extreme sports, and its exciting cultural metropolises, Austrians enjoy a quality of life that is the envy of other Europeans. The Viennese lifestyle brings the excitement and perks of a big city at a pace that is more relaxed than in most other European capitals. This shows in the favoured Viennese pastime of enjoying a beer, wine or coffee with friends in one of the capital's many bars, restaurants or coffee houses. Vienna is also a magnet for artists, students and professionals from all over Austria, who go there to live and work, but return to their 'homes' in the provinces regularly for a shot of country life.

The roots of tradition still reach down deep into Austrian soil outside the cities, so sometimes Austrians live up admirably to bizarre images the world has of them. Women can still be seen in the *Dirndl* (a full, pleated skirt) with tight bodice, worn with traditional apron, bonnet, and blouse with short, puffed sleeves. Men, meanwhile, can be founding drinking a beer or wine in collarless loden jackets, green hats, wide braces and shorts or knee breeches. In early summer, hardy herders plod to alpine pastures with their cattle and live in summer huts while tending their beasts. Austria also has lots of traditional festivals.

All this is packed into in a small country with the fifth-highest standard of living in the EU and the 10th in the world in terms of earnings and purchasing power. It's coupled with a generous system of social security and healthcare funded by a percentage on the pay packet, and Austrians are also among the best educated in the world; 98% of the population (aged 15 and above) is literate.

ECONOMY

When Soviet tanks rolled into Austria in 1945, the government nationalised many of its industries to prevent them from takeover or wholesale dismantling and transportation to Siberia as war reparations. Since the 1990s, Austrians have watched the pendulum swing back and privatisation is bringing the country into line with current trends. Since joining the EU in 1995, it has also liberalised sectors such as telecommunications, steel and energy.

Women earn about 26% less than men on average (the biggest gap in the EU's 15 countries), and almost half of a person's gross wage goes in tax and social security contributions.

Although its farms still tend to be of the 'two cows, three fences type', it has strong export industries, particularly in chemicals, machine goods, electronics and steel. Most companies are small or medium-sized, however; less than 200 employ more than 1000 people. Tourism accounts for about 10% of GDP, and with 20 million foreign visitors each year, more people per capita visit Austria than any other country. Interestingly, for all this industrial flurry, the landscape has largely been spared the worst and it is not a big polluter – CO_2 emissions are below the Organisation for Economic Co-operation and Development (OECD) average, and less than half the level per person than in the USA.

POPULATION

Given the country's population distribution, Austria might be expected to tilt towards neighbouring Slovakia. Its two largest provinces are Vienna and

A 2007 survey showed Austrians ranked health, a good marriage and good friends as most important for happiness. Hairdressers were the happiest employees.

National service is still compulsory for males in Austria, who can either serve their time in the military or perform civil service duties.

'If you want to abolish Austrian capitalism, first you have to create it.'
HANNES ANDROSCH, BUSINESSMAN AND POLITICIAN

Lower Austria in the east, and it is here, too, that most of Austria's immigrants have settled (see p44).

Austria has a population of 8.3 million. On average, there are 96 inhabitants per sq km, but this figure doesn't really tell us much. Vienna's density is well above this figure, while the rest of Austria's provinces (aside from Vorarlberg) are well below it; Tyrol, with only 53 inhabitants per sq km, is the least populated.

More females than males reside in Austria; at last count, the population was divided: 51.5% females to 48.5% males. Women die about six years later than men: at the ripe old age of 82 compared to the male average of 76. Based on current projections, however, Austria will have almost 9 million people in 2050.

SPORT

Peer into the pantheon of Austrian Olympic Games medallists and one thing becomes clear: Austrians are killer-bee at winter sports. Football, however, draws the largest crowds, and will no doubt be boosted by the European Championship in 2008. Ice hockey, handball, tennis and motor racing also enjoy a strong following. Except for motor racing, Austrians participate in these in large numbers too.

Summer is pretty much a time for niche sports like golf (except for snow golf), paragliding, and anything to do with running, swimming and windsurfing. With the arrival of autumn and winter, things get going on the pistes.

Football

The Austrian humorist and actor Alfred Dorfer (b 1961) reckons that staging a football European Championship in Austria is like putting on ski jumping in Namibia; but co-hosting the championship with Switzerland in 2008 hooks into a proud local history of the 'beautiful game'.

The halcyon days of Austrian football were in 1931–32 when local legend Hugo Meisl (1891–1937) coached the national team through 14 consecutive international matches undefeated. In 1932 the team lost narrowly to the England team at old Wembley and in the 1934 World Cup to Italy in the semifinal.

The national football league, the Austrian *Bundesliga* (www.bundesliga .at, in German), kicks off at the end of autumn and runs until the beginning of spring with a break during the severe winter months. Games are hardly ever sold out, so getting hold of a ticket is usually no problem.

Skiing

As much a national hobby as a sport, nothing gets an Austrian snorting more than the whiff of powder snow. It's hardly surprising, because some of the best conditions worldwide are here. Innsbruck has hosted the Winter Olympics twice (in 1964 and 1976), and World Cup ski races are annually held in Kitzbühel (p350), St Anton am Arlberg (p362) and Schladming.

Stars of the Austrian skiing scene abound, and one person who does this literally is the ski jumper Thomas Morgenstern (b 1986), winner of team and individual gold medals in large hill ski jumping events in the 2006 Winter Olympics in Torino. Another, Salzburg-born Hermann 'The Herminator' Maier (see p44), has achieved superhero status in an alpine career spanning more than a decade and bristling with medals and cups.

Austria's first true superstar, Toni Sailer, is arguably the greatest skier the country has ever produced. At 17 he claimed the Tyrolean championships at downhill, slalom and giant slalom, and four years later won gold medals in all three disciplines at the 1956 Winter Olympics in Cortina d'Ampezzo.

In 2006 Lukas was the most popular boy's name. Leonie topped the list of newborn girls and other popular names were Tobias, David, Lena and Anna.

About 600,000 people play, organise or watch football each weekend during the season in Austria. The Austria Sports Organisation website www.bso.or.at, in German, showcases all sports.

SPORTING LEGENDS – TO HELL & BACK

In a twist of fate, three of Austria's great sportsmen stand out for one feature: they were badly injured at the height of their careers and made sensational comebacks.

The Formula One legend Niki Lauda is possibly most famous of all. He suffered horrific burns in a high speed crash during the 1976 season, yet he was back in his car after missing only two races. That year he narrowly failed to retain the world championship, losing out to James Hunt by a single point on the last race of the season. Undeterred, he regained the title the following year, and proceeded to net his third championship win in 1984.

The somewhat bumbling side of skier Hermann Maier has led to him being likened to Superman's human alter ego, Clark Kent. However, in the 1998 Nagano Olympics, Maier showed the amazing toughness that characterises his all-or-nothing skiing style. During the men's downhill competition, he misjudged a difficult curve, got too close to a gate, somersaulted 30m through the air, bounced over a fence and crashed through two safety nets before finally coming to rest. Austria held its breath as the man known as 'The Herminator' got to his feet, dusted himself down and waved at the crowd. He went on to win two gold medals in the next six days.

But worse was to come. In August 2001 Maier was involved in an horrific motorcycle crash that almost cost him his life. Doctors faced an agonising decision – amputate the hopelessly damaged leg or not. They tried to save it. Maier underwent some painful operations to insert a titanium rod into the leg to hold it together. His recovery was miraculous; in January 2003, only 18 months after the accident, he went on to win the Super G (super giant slalom) at Kitzbühel – his 42nd World Cup victory.

Thomas Muster, Austria's top tennis player during the 1990s, had his kneecap crushed by a drunk driver, just hours after a win at the 1989 Lipton Championship semifinal in Florida. It was doubtful he would ever play tennis again. Images of Muster hitting balls while strapped to an osteopathic bench evoked admiration and bewilderment among tennis fans. He went on to become world number one and in the process earned the nickname 'The Iron Man'.

Other Sports

Motor racing is enormously popular as an armchair sport, and only speed limitations prevent this from spreading to the highways. No Austrian has roared around the Formula One circuit more successfully than Vienna-born star of the 1970s and '80s, Niki Lauda (b 1949; see boxed text, above). Off the circuit, Lauda morphed into a local aviation mogul, and more recently founded the low-cost Niki airline and a car rental firm.

Gone are the days when Austria could claim a tennis ace of the likes of the Styrian *Laufstier* (running bull) Thomas Muster (b 1967; see boxed text, above), although tennis is still popular, and Association of Tennis Professionals (ATP) tennis events are held in Vienna, Pörtschach am Wörthersee and Kitzbühel.

Ice hockey is also popular, and Austria's one and only superstar, Thomas Vanek (b 1984), currently plays in the National Hockey League (NHL) in the USA for the Buffalo Sabres.

MULTICULTURALISM

With just under 10% of her population on foreign passports, Austria has a lower percentage of foreigners than Switzerland and the Benelux countries, and is on par with Germany. In numbers, that means about 815,000 foreigners. The trend is upward: foreigners have a higher birth rate, and more people are arriving than leaving. The other important trend over recent years has been an increase in people taking the plunge to become 'neo-Austrians' (as the local statistical office quaintly puts it). A good indication of the situation on the ground is that almost 17% – or one in six people living in Austria – have a migrant background.

According to the Austrian State Treaty, Croatian and Slovenian minorities have a right to place name signs in both German and the minority language.

A tiny 1.5% of the population is made up of indigenous minorities, mainly from Eastern Europe. Most settled in Austria's eastern parts between the 16th and 19th centuries and include Croatians, Slovenes, Hungarians, Czechs, Slovaks and Sinti or Roma. A number of traditional languages have also crossed the border with them; Slovene is an official language in Carinthia and some town signs – much to the chagrin of the populist governor of Carinthia, Jörg Haider – are bilingual. Croatian and Hungarian are spoken in Burgenland.

The largest immigrant groups are Serbians, Bosnians and Croatians who arrived in the early 1990s, and Turks or descendents of Turks who arrived as guest workers in earlier decades, mainly in the 1950s and '60s.

As a result, Vienna has some fascinating quarters – such as the 16th district – that are colourful places for a plunge into multicultural life, but immigration has also produced a backlash. Anti-foreigner campaigns have been a feature of Austrian politics since the 1990s, particularly by the right-wing nationalist Freedom Party, (FPÖ), which played the anti-Turkish card with a slogan 'Home, not Islam' during the 2006 national elections, and by Haider, whose Alliance Future Austria (BZÖ), a break-away party from the FPÖ, campaigned on the platform of a one-third reduction of the number of foreigners in Austria.

> For a good numbers crunch, visit the English and German language pages of the government statistic internet site at www.statistik.at.

MEDIA

Although mass media and press freedom has a long history in Austria, so too is a tradition of media being concentrated in just a few hands. Austria was the last country in Europe to abolish its state monopoly on TV and radio.

The state-owned *Wiener Zeitung* (www.wienerzeitung.at, in German), first published in 1703, is the oldest newspaper in the world. It is also one of the dullest and least-read, selling only 22,000 copies of a weekday, and is a strong candidate for revamping. *Der Standard* (http://derstandard.at, in German) and *Die Presse* (www.diepresse.com, in German) are at the serious end of a spectrum of about 20 daily national or regional newspapers, but together account for less than 10% of readership. *Kurier* has a readership of about 10%, while the mass-circulation *Kronen Zeitung* (www.krone.at, in German) at the low-brow end of the rack has a massive 43% and wields enormous clout in politics and public opinion.

The TV staples of most Austrians are dished up by ORF1 and ORF2, the two channels of the public broadcaster. There's also a good culture channel, 3Sat, also broadcast in Germany and Switzerland. Local private channels of quality are still thin in the ether, and many Austrians actually watch German private stations. The radio landscape has more depth in the field, although here ORF holds the reins on a swathe of national and local stations. Hitradio Ö3 is the most popular mainstream music station, FM4 serves up an entertaining dish of interviews, some English language programmes and news reports, plus music beyond the chart staples, and Ö1 strokes a classic number.

> For online information on Austria's cultural life, people and movements, see the Austrian Encyclopaedia website www.aeiou.at.

RELIGION

On the surface of things, religion would seem to play an important part in the lives of Austrians, and the country has certainly been a stronghold of Catholicism for centuries. Inquiring whether there's a church in town is bit like asking whether the pope is Catholic. In the latest census, 73.6% of the population said they were Roman Catholic, 4.7% Protestant and 4.2% Muslim. Freedom of religion is guaranteed under the constitution.

All is well for the Catholic Church then, right? It could be worse. Religion for most Austrians means observing the major rituals such as baptism, confirmation and weddings and funerals; about one-third make it regularly to church.

ARTS

Music

What other country can match Austria's musical heritage or the creative tones of its great composers? At the low-brow end of the shelf, Vienna was known as early as the 12th century for its *Minnesänger* (troubadours), and in *Heurigen* (wine taverns) today performers scratch out a uniquely Viennese folk music, known as *Schrammelmusik,* in combos with violin, accordion, guitar and clarinet. In the Alpine regions, *Volksmusik* (folk music), based on traditional tunes but often sawn or pumped out with modern instruments, echoes in hills and valleys.

The Habsburgs were prolific patrons of the arts, and in the 18th and 19th centuries Europe's finest flocked to Vienna in search of their generosity. In fact, some of the Habsburgs themselves were gifted musicians: Leopold I (1640–1705) composed, Karl VI (1685–1740) stroked a violin, his daughter Maria Theresia plucked a decent double bass, and her son Joseph II was a deft hand at harpsichord and cello.

Austria has almost 2000 wind instrument orchestras in which about 100,000 musicians blow horns of one variety or another. Lower Austria has almost 500, Vienna just 19.

Today, Austrian orchestras like the Vienna Philharmonic enjoy a reputation others would die for, and organisations such as the Vienna Boys' Choir, the Staatsoper (p152), the Musikverein (p152) and the Konzerthaus (p152) are unrivalled. Salzburg and Graz complement Vienna as major music centres and, like Vienna, host important annual music festivals. Linz has the international Brucknerfest (p205), Schwarzenberg in Vorarlberg hosts Schubertiade (Schubert Festival; p373), and Innsbruck has its own Festival of Early Music (p338). The Bregenz Festival (p370) is famous for productions performed on a floating stage on the Bodensee.

PAST MASTERS

Austria overflows with past masters and pretty much has been a weather vane registering the current direction of classical music in Europe. Most of the figures will need no introduction. Christoph Willibald von Gluck (1714–87) is important because he brought operatic music and drama together, setting the stage for opera as we know it today. Later in the century, Josef Haydn (1732–1809) ushered in classicism and influenced music like no other in his epoch with opera and operetta, symphonies, string quartets, piano sonatas and piano trios. His greatest works included the oratorios *The Creation* (1798) and *The Seasons* (1801) and Symphony No 102 (1794) in B-flat Major. Haydn thought Wolfgang Amadeus Mozart (1756–91) to be the 'greatest composer' and Schubert effused that the 'magic of Mozart's music lights the darkness of our lives'. Mozart was born in Salzburg, where today his house of birth and his residence give

---

TOP FIVE CDS

- Mozart: *The Magic Flute*
- Schubert: *The Trout Quintet*
- Falco: *Falco 3* (try to get the original LP with the full version of 'Rock Me, Amadeus', rather than the CD)
- Kruder & Dorfmeister: *The K&D Sessions*
- Arnold Schönberg: *Pierrot Lunaire*

wonderful insights into his creative genius; a Mozartwoche (Mozart Week) is celebrated in late January.

Ludwig van Beethoven (1770–1827) was born in Bonn, Germany, but his musical genius blossomed in Vienna under Mozart and Haydn. He was totally deaf by 32, but that didn't stop him composing what many consider to be his best works, including Symphony No 9 in D Minor (1824) and Symphony No 5 (1808). Franz Schubert (1797–1828), a native of Vienna, was the last in the great line of composers from the Viennese School's Classical period (1740–1825). Although syphilis (or typhoid) took him to an early grave at 31, he composed a startling number of symphonies, overtures, masses, choral and piano works, chamber music and *Lieder* (songs).

The waltz originated in Vienna in the early 19th century and early masters of this genre were Johann Strauss the Elder (1804–49), who also composed the *Radetzky March* (1848), and Josef Lanner (1801–43). Johann Strauss the Younger (1825–99) followed up with Austria's unofficial anthem, the *Blue Danube* (1867), *Tales from the Vienna Woods* (1868) and his eternally popular operettas *Die Fledermaus* (1874) and *The Gypsy Baron* (1885).

The 19th century brought forth great composers such as Anton Bruckner (1824–96), who was long associated with the abbey in St Florian (p209); the Hamburg-born Johannes Brahms (1833–97), who worked in Vienna and died there; the director of the Vienna Court Opera from 1897 to 1907, Gustav Mahler (1860–1911); and Hungarian born Franz Lehár (1870–1948), who composed *Die lustige Witwe* (The Merry Widow; 1905).

Vienna also gave us the 20th century's most innovative composer Arnold Schönberg (1874–1951), who stretched tonal conventions to snapping point with his 12-tone style of composition. The most influential of his pupils in this Second Vienna School were Alban Berg (1885–1935) and Anton von Webern (1883–1945); both were born in the capital and both explored and continued the development of Schönberg's technique. Tellingly, at the first public performance of Berg's composition *Altenberg-Lieder*, the concert was cut short because the audience fell over itself in rage.

CONTEMPORARY CLASSIC

Given such a pedigree in classic, the high quality of Austria's contemporary classic scene should come as no surprise. The post-WWII years were finally lifted out of darkness by Friedrich Cerha (b 1926), whose famous compositions include *Spiegel I-VII* (1960–72) and the Brecht opera *Baal* (1974). In the 1960s and '70s Cerha was joined by a wave of brash and exciting young composers. Influenced by Schönberg, MOB art & tone ART was one group of composers and musicians that shook up the scene, formed around Otto M Zykan (1935–2006), Kurt Schwertsik (b 1935) and Heinz Karl Gruber (b 1943). Today Gruber is the most successful of the three. The 1980s brought the next generation. The Swiss-born Beat Furrer (b 1954) founded the Klangforum (Sound Forum), which has developed into the foremost group featuring new music soloists today – not least because it has a long-running residency at the prestigious Paris Opera (Palais Garnier). Others paddling innovative waters are Bernhard Lang (b 1957), who integrates electronic forms into his new music, and Olga Neuwirth (b 1968), who collaborates closely with Nobel Prize-winning author Elfriede Jelinek (see p55) on exciting dramatic works. On a more traditional note, the Tyrolean composer Johannes Maria Staud (b 1974) is very highly regarded. A premiere of his orchestral work *Apeiron* (2005) was performed by the Berlin Philharmonic under the expert baton of Sir Simon Rattle.

'After the call for a republic, the gentry in Austria was abolished. In its place is possession of a season ticket for the Vienna Philharmonic.'
AUSTRIAN WRITER HANS WEIGEL

Before burial, Haydn's head was purloined by phrenologists. The skull was preserved, passed around over the years, and finally reunited with the rest of Haydn in the 1950s.

Beethoven must have been picky with his dwelling; he lived in as many as 60 addresses during his time in Vienna.

JAZZ

Among the figures from the 1980s, Max Nagl (b 1960; www.maxnagl.at, in German) is possibly the most influential, but jazz aficionados abroad will probably be more familiar with Wolfgang Puschnig (b 1956; www.puschnig.com, in German) and the big band Vienna Art Orchestra (www.vao.at), founded with Zürich-born Mathias Rüegg (b 1952) and others.

Since then a new guard has unpacked its instruments in the clubs and bars. The young trumpeter Lorenz Raab (b 1975; www.lorenzraab.at, in German) currently enjoys a very strong following in club culture. Other club performers to watch out for are HDV Trio from Vorarlberg (www.hdvtrio.com, in German), and Vienna's best-known acoustic act, Drechsler, a saxophone trio with its own DJ (www.ulrichdrechsler.com). The guitarist Wolfgang Muthspiel (b 1965; www.materialrecords.com, in German) is also quite well-known internationally, but if the soul sounds of the Hammond organ are your secret vice, Raphael Wressnig (b 1979; www.raphaelwressnig.com, in German) is the man in Austria to watch out for.

A group of ultra contemporary artists are associated with Vienna's Jazzwerkstatt (www.jazzwerkstatt.at), a collective that promotes jazz in Austria and organises an annual three-week jazz festival (free admission) in Vienna each March. Following is a whirlwind tour of the scene; check the websites for current dates and venues.

Austria currently has some great saxophone artists, including Christoph Auer (b 1981; www.christophauer.at), the saxophone quartet Phoen, (http://phoen.at) and the sax and clarinet player Clemens Salesny (b 1980; www.clemens-salesny.at, in German). Christoph Dienz (b 1968; www.dienz.at, in German) plays the bassoon and brings the zither, a stringed folk instrument, to jazz and improvisation, whereas Kelomat (www.kelom.at), which plays traditional and improvised jazz, is the most successful among a new generation on the scene.

Moving on to grooves styles, Peter Rom (b 1972; http://peterrom.com) heads an exciting trio, and Bernd Satziger (b 1977; www.wurschtsemmerl.at, in German) leads a wonderful three-piece outfit that uses a Wurlitzer organ. If your style is more rock, fusion, punk, improvisation or strange noises, Jazzwerkstatt figures to keep an ear open for are the unutterable Brpobr (http://brpobr.klingt.org, in German), some of whose work is reminiscent of early Pink Floyd; the more melody-based Fuzz Noir (www.fuzznoir.com), and Tumido (http://tumido.klingt.org, in German); the latter is a techno-punk-jazz outfit.

Jazz women figure prominently on the scene, and one group to watch out for is Falb Fiction, led by the saxophonist Viola Falb (b 1980; www.falbfiction.com, in German). Her style ranges from 'strictly harmonic to free, melodic ballads to pulsing grooves' and goes into rock. Mosaik, an outfit headed by Angela Tröndle (b 1983) creates vocal and purely instrumental jazz sounds based on clean rhythms and melodies infused with lots of piano, which Tröndle herself plays. Agnes Heginger (b 1973) has an education in classic as well as jazz, and doesn't shy away from throwing in improvisation or pop or anything else for that matter. In the past she's worked with Georg Breinschmidt (b 1973), Austria's virtuoso of contrabass jazz. The Graz-born Elisabeth Harnik (b 1970) composes and improvises on piano, and appears regularly at home-grown jazz events and across Europe, either solo, on piano or improvising with groups. Austria also attracts some talented Balkan and Eastern European jazz artists. The Slovenian Maja Osojnik (b 1976; www.majaosojnik.com), a long-time resident of Vienna, is a hot tip among jazz punters.

'Actually, you don't go to the disco in Linz. You don't really go to Linz. Linz is the ass of the world: chemicals, boredom, drugs. Which means, come to think of it, of course you have to go to Linz if you're in the rap business – the ghetto city of Austria and the toughest Austria's got to offer.'

GERMAN JOURNALIST WOLFGANG HÖBEL

As well as the Jazzwerkstatt events, the three week Jazzfest Wien is held in June-July each year (www.vienna jazz.org).

ROCK, POP & UNDERGROUND

Dig into the rock scene and the depth and variety of Austria's talent will lead to a lot of wild and sleepless nights in dark places. Some of the acts we mention here are well-known, others spend more time underground than above it. The websites will usually give you a taste of the music, and with a bit of surfing and good old-fashioned pencil and paper you can cobble together a 'Sound of Music' tour of a different kind (and more interesting than the Von Trapp variety).

Naked Lunch (www.nakedlunch.de) is currently the best-known Austrian band and have been working sounds for ages, yet it's only been in the last couple of years that they've risen to popularity at home and abroad. Going a bit deeper into the underground, the duo Attwenger (www.attwenger.at) has a large following for its music with flavours of folk, hip-hop and trance. Completing the triumvirate of relative old hands, Graz-based Rainer Binder-Krieglstein (b 1966; performing as binder & krieglstein, www.mikaella.org/bk, in German) does an eclectic blend of headz, hip-hop, groove and nujazz.

For hip-hop pure, Linz-based Texta (www.texta.at, in German) is the most established in the art. Young blood comes in the form of art-house hoppers Mieze Medusa & Tenderboy (www.miezemedusa.com, in German), who are regulars on the Vienna circuit and organise poetry slams in town. Two other bands calling the hip-hop shots are Waxolutionists (www.waxos.com) and the bizarre Bauchklang (www.bauchklang.com), remarkable for

---

FALCO – LIVING HARD, LEAVING BEHIND A WRECK

It may come as a surprise to some, but the music scene in Austria is one of Europe's most exciting at the moment. The roots of a distinctly Austrian sound go back to the 1970s, when 'Austropop' was born. It was influenced by US artists like Bruce Springsteen and Bob Dylan, and this small and still quite close-knit scene often sprinkled its lyrics with local dialect.

One of the most eccentric bands from the very beginning was the rock-punk group Drahdiwaberl, who combined Vienna Actionism with rock and a damned good show. One of its members, a certain Hans Hölzel, played bass in the group and stood out from this chaotic, totally hotwired ensemble, with his tough style and light touch of arrogance. Decked out in a suit, gelled to the brink and performing with idiosyncratic gestures – that was the beginning of the phenomena Falco. In 1982 he went solo, and turned rock music upside down.

According to Helge Hinteregger from the Music Information Center Austria (MICA; www.mica.at, in German), an organisation that promotes Austrian artists, Falco's influence on the development of the scene has been enormous.

Falco brought together the chill of New Wave with a blend of English and German phrased lyrics delivered in spoken chants, which is one reason why he's also known as the inventor of German-language hip-hop. Fatalism was always in there somewhere; drugs and alcohol were almost part of his style. Legendary songs like 'Ganz Wien' (Total Vienna) about heroine abuse, 'Jeanny' and 'Junge Römer' (Young Romans) played with the chill of human life on the edge of a precipice. His innovation and power, his success, and not to forget the musician Falco himself, were a stroke of luck for the Austrian music scene. You can still feel his influence today. Out of the local style of New Wave later came Vienna Electronic.

With a number one hit in the US charts, Falco reached the peak of his career. But Falco himself knew it was also breaking point and the only way now was down. Rock me Amadeus wasn't Falco's last hit, but nor could he recreate its phenomenal success. Right up until his death in a car accident in 1998, he remained a key figure in Austrian music, and Falco events are held every year on his birthday and on the anniversary of the crash.

using only voices – no instruments – for its reggae- and ethnic-influenced hip-hop and trance.

This, of course, is absolutely normal compared to the equally remarkable Fuckhead (www.fuckhead.at), who, alone for a tendency to perform in plastic robes or gear that looks suspiciously like underwear, will obviously not be everyone's cup of tea. This is high-voltage turbo industrial grunge and it's akin to listening hard while a surgeon removes your eardrum; afterwards you might be ready to tune into the saccharine flavours of teeny rocker Christina Stürmer (b 1982; www.christinastuermer.de, in German), or indeed to the very soft lounge rhythms of Saint Privat (www.saintp rivat.com).

Stage diving into the DJ scene, Electric Indigo (Susanne Kirchmayr, b 1965; www.indigo-inc.at) is the most influential of the female DJs, she organises a platform (female: pressure) for gals who DJ and an online sound base (Open Sounds), and performs with a Club Crazy residency in Vienna's Flex venue (see p153). Tanja Bednar (aka tibcurl; www.tibcurl.com), is possibly Vienna's best-known DJ act; she regularly puts on the Icke Micke Club (www.ickemicke.at), whose wintering ground in the past has included Vienna's Camera Club (p153). Among the guys, DJ Patrick Pulsinger (b 1970; www.feedback-studio.com) spins a variety of genres, including jazz, new music and experimental. Peter Kruder (b 1967) and Richard Dorfmeister (b 1968) together form the production and DJ and production team Kruder & Dorfmeister, who are Austria's most successful act, which ranges from downtempo to trip-hop and electronic rhythms.

Architecture

The earliest 'architecture' you'll find in Austria is a funereal form – the 700 grave mounds located outside Grossklein (p236), illustrating how the Iron Age Hallstatt Culture buried its dead. Also surviving from the early days of settlement are numerous Roman ruins dating from 15 BC to AD 500, including those excavated in Carnuntum (p178), and on Michaelerplatz (p137) in Vienna.

ROMANESQUE

Learn more about Austrian architecture at the Architekturtage (Architectural Days) in June. For more information go to www.architekturtage.at, in German.

The Romanesque period in Austria dates from about AD 1000 to 1250 and features heavy walls, closely spaced harmonising columns and heavy, rounded arches, along with the use of statues and reliefs on the portals and apses. Dig below any Gothic church and you'll often find Romanesque foundations. This style was almost entirely religious in nature and flourished under the Babenberg dynasty, which threw plenty of cash at craftsmen to build cathedrals and abbeys. Some of the best surviving Romanesque buildings today are the cathedral in Gurk (p302) and the Benedictine abbey in Millstatt (p308), both in Carinthia, and the funerary chapel of the Pfarrkirche St Stephan in Tulln (p173). You can also find some Romanesque features today in the main entrance and towers of Vienna's breathtaking Stephansdom (see p124).

GOTHIC

Around 1250 the Romanesque style gave way to Gothic, which petered out in the 16th century. Its hallmarks are high stained-glass windows, pointed arches and ribbed ceiling vaults, external flying buttresses to support the walls, and elaborately carved doorway columns. Stephansdom is the heart and soul of the Gothic style, but Austria also has lots of secular Gothic buildings, including the Goldenes Dachl (p337) in Innsbruck, the Kornmesserhaus (p240) in Bruck an der Mur and the Bummerlhaus (p211) in Steyr.

RENAISSANCE

By the 16th century, Gothic flavours began to pall and Austrians discovered a new enthusiasm for classical forms. This obsession with grace, grandeur and symmetry coincided with the rising fortunes of the Habsburgs. Italian architects set to work on designing palaces, mansions and houses that blended Italian and Austrian influences. One of the hallmarks of the era was the arcade courtyard; fine examples are Schloss Schallaburg (p166) and Landhaushof (p224) in Graz. Another feature of Renaissance was the sgraffito façade, which is created by applying two layers of different colours and scratching a design into the top layer to reveal the layer beneath. This effect has been put to good use on houses in St Veit an der Glan in Carinthia (p303).

BAROQUE & ROCOCO

With the end of the Thirty Years' War and a receding Turkish threat, Austria's monarchy discovered urban development. This happened at a time baroque was making huge ground in architecture. Features of the resplendent, triumphal style were marble columns, elaborate sculpture and painting, and rich, gilded ornamentation; it added up to extravagant interiors designed to inspire and impress. Not to be outdone, the Church chipped in with a profusion of decorated interiors rich enough to make worshippers giddy.

Having learnt from the Italian school, Graz-born architect Johann Bernhard Fischer von Erlach (1656–1723) developed an Austrian baroque style, which grew to prominence from 1690 and expired around 1730. This reflected the gushing decorative style of Italian baroque but gave it a specifically Austrian twist, with dynamic colours and irregular or undulating lines. Austria has so many outstanding baroque buildings that it's difficult to know where to start. Some of the best are Fischer von Erlach's Kollegienkirche (p273) in Salzburg and his Karlskirche (p133) in Vienna, Johann Lukas von Hildebrandt's Schloss Belvedere (p132), also in Vienna, and Stift Melk (p172) and Augustiner Chorherrenstift (p209), both by Jakob Prandtauer (1660–1726).

Rococo, the decorative climax of baroque, was the favoured style of the empress Maria Theresia, who chose it for the rooms of Schloss Schönbrunn (p135) when she commissioned Nicolas Pacassi to renovate the palace in 1744.

NEOCLASSICISM

From the 18th century, rococo's extravagance bowed down to a revival of old architectural styles. Known as neoclassicism (because many works had a classical bent) or revivalism, the trend culminated in cold lines and strict forms in the 19th century. The Ancient Greece-inspired historicism of the parliament building (p128) in Vienna from 1883 is a good illustration, symbolising democracy with its impressively soaring columns.

When Emperor Franz Josef I took the Austro-Hungarian throne in 1848, the building boom reached new heights of grandiosity. Vienna's Ringstrasse (p128) is Austria's showcase from this time, and was developed on the site of the old city walls from 1857 onwards. Ringstrasse also demonstrates just how flagrantly builders plundered previous styles, including French Gothic (Votivkirche), Flemish Gothic (Rathaus; p128), Grecian (Parliament; p128), French Renaissance (Staatsoper; p152) and Florentine Renaissance (Museum für angewandte Kunst; p128). If neoclassicism is your thing, this is the best Europe has to offer.

'The obsession with grace, grandeur and symmetry coincided with the rising fortunes of the Habsburgs'

GUSTAV KLIMT & SECESSIONISM

Now usually associated with Art Nouveau, the Viennese Secession movement was formed by 19 artists in the 1890s in order to break away from the historical or revivalist styles that dominated Europe at the time. The painter Gustav Klimt (1862–1918) was its first president, and other Secession artists included architect Otto Wagner (1841–1918), interior designer and painter Carl Moll (1861–1945) and painter Kolo Moser (1868–1918).

Secession artists worked in a highly decorative style. Klimt's famous painting *The Kiss* (1908) is typical of the rich ornamentation, vivid colour and floral motifs favoured by the movement. His later pictures (such as the two portraits of Adele Bloch-Bauer from 1907) employ a harmonious but ostentatious use of background colour, with much metallic gold and silver to evoke or symbolise the emotion.

Otto Wagner, by contrast, began working in historicist styles (some neo-Renaissance buildings on Vienna's Ringstrasse are by his hand), joined the Secessionists, and with Klimt and others split from them and adopted his own more-functional style. His greatest works include the Postsparkasse (Post Office Savings Bank; p131), the Kirche am Steinhof (p136) and the Majolikahaus (p135), but his work can be seen everywhere in the capital; he designed some 35 stations of the current U-Bahn system.

MODERN

In an age of change, something had to give. Late-19th-century Jugendstil (Art Nouveau) was sensuous, decorative and, unlike rococo, neoclassicism or neoclassical revivalism, not intent on bowling over with exaggerated displays of beauty or strict lines. In Vienna the style blossomed with the founding of the Secession movement in 1897, led by painter Gustav Klimt (1862–1918). One of the foremost architects in the movement was Otto Wagner (1841–1918; see above). Another, Adolf Loos (1870–1933) was influenced by Wagner, broke with his style, and became a bitter critic of the Ringstrasse buildings. His Loos Haus (p137) and American Bar (p149) in Vienna offer a good insight into his style.

The influence of the Social Democrats in the Vienna city government of the new republic (from 1918) gave rise to a number of municipal building projects, not least the massive Karl-Marx-Hof apartment complex. This stands in contrast to the multicoloured, haphazard-looking work of Austria's maverick 20th-century architect, Friedensreich Hundertwasser (see boxed text, opposite).

Austria's leading postmodern architect is Hans Hollein (b 1934), designer of the angular glass and stone Haas Haus (1990) in Vienna, near Stephansdom. Impressive but very different in its form, the monumental Hangar-7 (2003; p278) at Salzburg's airport is a spectacular glass and steel hanger housing vintage aircraft, art exhibitions and visitor facilities, designed by Volkmar Burgstaller (b 1944). Meanwhile in Linz, the Zürich architects Weber & Hofer are the force behind the cube-shaped Lentos art museum (2003; p203). One of Austria's most bizarre recent constructions, however, is the 'Friendly Alien' Kunsthaus (2003; p226) in Graz by British architects Peter Cook (b 1936) and Colin Fournier (b 1944), a creation with nozzles and an acrylic skin with electronic morphing capabilities.

Painting

Austria has some of the world's most impressive collections of paintings. Oberes Belvedere (p132) and the Prunkstall (p132) have a wealth of Gothic religious art from the Middle Ages. Come the Renaissance, the focus of the Viennese shifted from biblical motifs to landscapes. The Danube School (unusual because it combined both) included greats such as Rueland Frueauf the Younger (1470–1545), Wolf Huber (1485–1553) and German-born Lukas Cranach the Elder (1472–1553).

Baroque artists were relatively thin on the ground in Austria, but the ceiling frescoes of Johann Michael Rottmayr (1654–1730) in Salzburg's Residenz (p268) and in the Stift Klosterneuburg (p160) are remarkable legacies. The other great baroque master is Daniel Gran (1694–1757), whose major work is in Vienna's Nationalbibliothek (p126). Taking the brush to canvas as well as roofs, Franz Anton Maulbertsch (1724–96) left legacies in the Riesensaal of the Hofburg in Innsbruck (p334) and in the Österreichische Galerie of Schloss Belvedere in Vienna (p132). The other great baroque painter, Paul Troger (1698–1762), created stunning spatial effects in Stift Melk (p172).

The Biedermeier period of the mid-19th century produced leading artists Ferdinand Waldmüller (1793–1865) and Friedrich Gauermann (1807–62), who captured the age in portraits, landscapes and period scenes. Some of Waldmüller's evocative (if idealised) peasant scenes can be viewed in the Oberes Belvedere (p132) in Vienna.

While the neoclassical period certainly produced its local greats, including August von Pettenkofen (1822–89) and Hans Makart (1840–84), Austria's golden age was still just around the corner. The turn of the century brought the Jugendstil period, featuring organic motifs such as plant tendrils, flowing hair, flames and waves. No-one embraced this sensuousness more than Gustav Klimt (1862–1918; opposite).

His contemporary, Egon Schiele (1890–1918), created grittier and more confronting works. Schiele worked largely with the human figure, and many of his works are brilliantly executed minimalist line drawings splashed with patches of bright colour and usually featuring women in pornographic poses. He also produced many self-portraits and a few large, breathtaking painted canvases, most of which can be seen in the Leopold Museum (p130). Vienna's Oberes Belvedere (p132) has a wonderful collection from the era,

> Museum after museum is listed on www .austrianmuseums.net; it's in German but it's pretty easy to navigate.

THE STRAIGHT LINE IS GODLESS

One of Austria's most celebrated architects-artists is Friedensreich Hundertwasser. Thanks to his eccentricity, he is also one of the most entertaining – visually and literally. When you look at his creations, including his last work – a public toilet in his beloved second home, New Zealand – you can understand what lies behind his claim that the 'straight line is godless and immoral'.

Some say his work is a nervous response to Bauhaus or Jackson Pollock. Perhaps. In his famous *Verschimmelungsmanifest* (Mould Manifesto, 1964), he claimed to have once counted 546 straight lines on a razor blade. And while not everyone who has battled with mould in their homes will agree with his (positive) view that 'with the microbes and sponge, life comes into the house'. His claim that his uneven floors 'become a symphony, a melody for the feet, and bring back natural vibrations to man' has won followers.

Hundertwasser lost a good deal of his family in the Nazi death camps and began a career in art at the Akademie der bildenden Künste (Academy of Fine Arts) in 1948, soon afterwards treading his own creative path. He would later move towards spiritual ecology, believing that cities should be harmonious with their (natural) environment. He envisaged buildings semi-submerged beneath undulating meadows, and homes with 'tree tenants', who pay rent in environmental currency. With the air and ozone layer getting thinner, perhaps he was onto something.

Hundertwasser locked horns with the Viennese establishment on many occasions, and he complained that his more radical building projects were quashed by the authorities. Nevertheless, he was commissioned to re-create the façade of the Spittelau incinerator in Vienna. This project opened in 1992 and is probably the most unindustrial-looking heating plant you'll find. Other Hundertwasser creations include the KunsthausWien and Hundertwasserhaus in Vienna (p131), St Barbara Kirche in Bärnbach (p235) and Bad Blumau's spa resort (p237).

VIENNESE ACTIONISM *Dr Ed Baxter*

Viennese Actionism spanned the years 1957–68 and was one of the most extreme of all the modern art movements. It was linked to the Wiener Gruppe (Vienna Group) and had its roots in abstract expressionism. Actionism sought access to the unconscious through the frenzy of an extreme and very direct art: the Actionists quickly moved from pouring paint over the canvas, which was then slashed with knives, to using bodies (live people, dead animals) as 'brushes', and using blood, excrement, eggs, mud and whatever else came to hand as 'paint'. The traditional canvas was soon dispensed with altogether. The artist's body became the canvas, and the site of art became a deliberated event (the scripted action, staged both privately and publicly).

It was a short step from self-painting to inflicting wounds upon the body, and engaging in physical and psychological endurance tests. For 10 years the Actionists scandalised the press and public and incited violence and panic – and got plenty of publicity in the process. Often poetic, humorous and aggressive, the Actions became increasingly politicised, addressing the sexual and social repression that pervaded the Austrian state. Art in Revolution (1968), the last Action to be realised in Vienna, resulted in six months hard labour all-round.

---

and a museum in Tulln (p173) is dedicated entirely to Schiele. The other major exponent of Viennese Expressionism was playwright, poet and painter Oskar Kokoschka (1886–1980), whose sometimes-turbulent works reveal an interest in psychoanalytic imagery and baroque-era religious symbolism. Kokoschka's work is also showcased in the Leopold.

Painting took a backseat between the two world wars, but returned with a vengeance after WWII. In the 1950s HC Artmann (1921–2000) founded the Wiener Gruppe (Vienna Group); its members integrated surrealism and Dadaism into their sound compositions, textual montages, and Actionist happenings. Public outrage and police intervention were regular accompaniments to their meetings. The group's activities came to an end in 1964 when Konrad Bayer (1932–64), its most influential member, committed suicide; much of the legacy of the movement is on show in the MUMOK (p130).

Some of the important names in today's Austria's art scene include Gunter Brus (b 1938) and Hermann Nitsch (b 1938), both former members of the Actionism group, Arnulf Rainer (b 1929), also associated with Actionism but more recently involved in photographing and reworking classic pieces by Schiele, van Gogh and Rembrandt, and Eva Schlegel (b 1960), who works with a wide range of media. Sammlung Essl in Klosterneuburg has many of these artists and should be high on the list of places to visit for contemporary art.

Hermann Nitsch still practices Viennese Actionism; decide for yourself whether it's your cup of tea at www.nitsch .org, in German.

Sculpture

Austria is blessed with two very early pieces of erotic pre-Christian sculpture. At over 30,000 years old, *Venus of Galgenberg* (aka Dancing Fanny) is the oldest-known stone figurine in the world, while the more rapturous *Venus of Willendorf*, discovered in the Danube Valley, has fended off suitors for some 25,000 years. Both are now in Vienna's Naturhistorisches Museum (p129).

The enamel *Verdun Altar* (1181) in Klosterneuburg abbey (p160) is Austria's finest surviving work from the Romanesque period. Some of the most beautiful altars were carved of lime wood during the Gothic era. The best known are today in St Wolfgang (p260) and are the work of Michael Pacher (1440–98), who is one of the most skilful religious artists working in the 15th century. The tomb (1502) of Maximilian I in Innsbruck's Hofkirche (p334) is a highlight of the Renaissance, and the same church has impressive statues in bronze, including several by the German master of all trades, Albrecht Dürer (1471–1528).

Take a peak at the sublime works of the Wiener Werkstätte and learn something of the organisation's history at www.wiener-werk staette.at.

The baroque period is captured in the fountain by George Raphael Donner in Vienna's Neuer Markt (p137), and Balthasar Permoser's statue of Prince Eugène in the Schloss Belvedere (p132). Those with a special interest in baroque funeral caskets should look no further than the giant double sarcophagus created by Balthasar Moll (1717–85) for Maria Theresia and Franz I, located on Vienna's Neuer Markt (p127).

Neoclassicism was the age of the equestrian statue, and nothing typifies this better than the one from 1804 of Emperor Joseph II in Josefsplatz in Vienna's Hofburg (p125). Salzburg also has some distinctive equine marvels in its old town centre.

The Biedermeier period achieved much in furniture and some of this can be seen in Vienna's Museum für angewandte Kunst (Museum of Applied Art; p131). It also gave rise to the technique of 'bending' wood in furniture, particularly in the backs of chairs, and since that time the bentwood chair has also been known as the Viennese chair.

The Secessionist movement not only had a hand in painting and architecture, but also some interesting sculpture. This offshoot was known as the Wiener Werkstätte (Vienna Workshop), which changed the face of domestic design. Wallpaper, curtains, furniture, tiles, vases, trays, cutlery, bowls and jewellery were all targets for design; aesthetics came before practicality, which means that some of it is brilliant but utterly useless. Josef Hoffmann was a prominent figure in the Werkstätte, as was Kolo Moser (1868–1918); many of their works, along with other members, can be seen at the Museum für angewandte Kunst (p131) and Leopold Museum (p130).

Literature

The outstanding Austrian work produced in the Middle Ages was the *Nibelungenlied* (Song of the Nibelungs), written around 1200 by an unknown hand. This epic poem told a tale of passion, faithfulness and revenge in the Burgundian court at Worms. Its themes were adapted by Richard Wagner in his *The Ring of the Nibelungen* operatic series.

Aside from Franz Grillparzer (1791–1872; see p57), Austria's literary tradition didn't really take off until around the turn of the 20th century, when the Vienna Secessionists and Sigmund Freud were creating waves. Influential writers who emerged at this time included Arthur Schnitzler (1862–1931), Hugo von Hofmannsthal (1874–1929), Karl Kraus (1874–1936) and the young poet Georg Trakl (1887–1914). Kraus' apocalyptic drama *Die letzten Tage der Menschheit* (The Last Days of Mankind, 1922) employed a combination of reports, interviews and press extracts to portray the absurdity of war.

Peter Altenberg (1859–1919) was a drug addict and alcoholic whose doctor wrote him off as unfit for work due to an overly sensitive nervous system. Quite sensibly, he dedicated his life to poetry after that and portrayed bohemian Vienna. You'll find an amusing figure of him as you enter his favourite coffee house, Café Central (p151) in Vienna. Hermann Broch (1886–1951) was also very much part of Viennese café society. Broch was a scientist at heart who believed literature could provide the metaphysical explanations for scientific discovery. His masterwork was *Der Tod des Vergil* (The Death of Virgil, 1945) written in a Nazi concentration camp and after his emigration to the USA.

Robert Musil (1880–1942) was one of the most important 20th-century writers, but he only achieved international recognition after his death with his major literary achievement, *Der Mann ohne Eigenschaften* (The Man without Qualities, 1932). This seven-volume unfinished work is a fascinating portrait of the collapsing Austro-Hungarian monarchy. Heimito von

A slice of Viennese life in the late '60s from popular US author John Irving, *Setting Free the Bears* tells a charming, sad and amusing story about a plan to release the animals from the zoo at Schönbrunn.

Set in 1932, *The Radetzky March* by Joseph Roth is the study of one family affected by the end of empire. The themes of *The Radetzky March* are applicable to any society emerging from a long-hated, but at least understood, regime.

Not just a novel, but a complete overhaul of what a novel can be, *The Death of Virgil* by Hermann Broch is as stylistically groundbreaking as Joyce's *Ulysses*. Covering the last day of the poet's life, this book is hard, hard work.

Doderer (1896–1966) grew up in Vienna, which is why his two great works, *Die Strudlhofstiege* (1951) and *Die Dämonen* (The Demons; 1956) depict Vienna society in the first decades of the 20th century.

A friend of Freud, a librettist for Strauss and a victim of Nazi book burnings, Stefan Zweig (1881–1942) certainly had a rich social pedigree. A poet, playwright, translator, paranoiac and pacifist to boot, Zweig believed Nazism had been conceived specifically with him in mind and as a result he when he became convinced in 1942 that Hitler would take over the world, he took an overdose of barbiturates in his chosen exile, outside Rio de Janeiro. Joseph Roth (1894–1939), primarily a journalist, wrote about the concerns of Jews in exile and of Austrians uncertain of their identity at the end of empire. His re-released *What I Saw: Reports from Berlin, 1920–33* (2002) is part of a resurgence of interest in this fascinating writer.

Perhaps it's something in that murky Danube water, but the majority of contemporary Viennese authors (at least, those translated into English) are grim, guilt-ridden, angry and sometimes incomprehensibly avant-garde. Thomas Bernhard (1931–89) was born in Holland but grew up and lived in Austria. Like seemingly many Viennese, he was obsessed with disintegration and death, and in later works such as *Holzfällen* (Cutting Timber, 1984) turned to controversial attacks against social conventions and institutions. His novels are seamless (no chapters or paragraphs, few full stops) and seemingly repetitive, but surprisingly readable once you get into them.

The best-known contemporary writer is Peter Handke (b 1942). His postmodern, abstract output encompasses innovative and introspective prose works such as *Die linkshändige Frau* (The Left-Handed Woman, 1976) and stylistic plays like *Die Stunde, da wir nichts voneinander wussten* (The Hour When We Knew Nothing of Each Other, 1992). The provocative novelist and 2004 Nobel Laureate Elfriede Jelinek (b 1946) dispenses with direct speech, indulges in long flights of fancy and takes a very dim view of humanity, but she is worth persevering with. *Die Klavierspielerin* (The Piano Teacher, 1983), *Lust* (1989), *Die Liebhaberinnen* (Women as Lovers, 1975), *Die Ausgesperrten* (Wonderful, Wonderful Times, 1980) and *Einar* (2006) are all available in English; *The Piano Teacher* has also been made into a film.

Elisabeth Reichart (b 1953) stands out for her novels and essays, and especially for criticism of patriarchy and investigations of Nazi-related Austrian guilt, both during WWII and more recently. Her *Das Haus der sterbenden Männer* (House of the Dying Men, 2005) is a richly textured novel based on the relationship between two very different women, one of whom runs a home for terminally ill men. Novelist and lyricist Wilhelm Aigner (b 1954) was awarded the prestigious *Grosser Österreichischer Staatspreis für Literatur* (Grand Austrian State Prize for Literature) in 2006 and his *Die schönen bitteren Wochen des Johann Nepomuk* (The Beautiful, Bitter Weeks of Johann Nepomuk, 2006) about first love, football and adolescence also appears in English. Contemporary young authors who are shaping the literary scene today include Thomas Glavinic (b 1972), Berlin-based Kathrin Röggla (b 1971), and Vienna-based (Munich-born) Daniel Kehlmann (b 1975), whose historical novel *Vermessung der Welt* (Measuring the World, 2005) about early scientists Alexander von Humboldt and Carl Friedrich Gauss is highly acclaimed and in translation.

Cinema & TV

Austria may have a long history in film (1908 marked the country's first feature film, *Von Stufe zu Stufe*; From Stage to Stage), but its endeavours have generally gone unnoticed outside the German-speaking world. As a cinematic backdrop for film, the story is quite different; two of the most famous films

---

Thomas Bernhard's one-sentence prose poem *On the Mountain* is the story of a man about to die of lung disease. The first book Bernhard wrote and the last he published, it is bleak and bitter. Also try *Cutting Timber* and *Wittgenstein's Nephew*.

Witty and clever, Elfriede Jelinek hates all her characters. Her novel *Lust* is the story of a rural woman preyed on by her husband and lover, told without a gram of sympathy for the filthy habits of humans.

So it's kitsch, tacky and full of cheesy songs, but there's no denying the popularity of *The Sound of Music* (1965) by Robert Wise, the story of the multitalented Von Trapp family and their too-good-to-be-true nanny.

in cinematic history, *The Third Man* (1949) and *The Sound of Music* (1965), are set in Vienna and Salzburg respectively. Both flopped on release in the country, and while most Austrians still haven't a clue about 'Doe, a deer, a female deer', opinions on Harry Lime and his penicillin racket have turned 180 degrees since then (p32). There are literally hundreds of other films and TV programmes filmed in Austria; *Before Sunrise* (1994), *The Living Daylights* (1987) and *Where Eagles Dare* (1968; staring Clint Eastwood and Richard Burton) are three of the more famous examples.

Many of Austria's early big names were successful after they travelled to Berlin or Hollywood. Vienna-born director Fritz Lang (1890–1976) pretty much captures it all: he almost ruined his Berlin film studio with the astronomical budget of *Metropolis* (1926), the story of a society enslaved by technology. This and his *The Last Will of Dr Mabuse* (1932), during which an incarcerated madman spouts Nazi doctrine, were banned under the Nazis; after knocking back a work offer from Hitler, who was besotted Lang's silent classic *Die Nibelungen* (1924), the director went to Hollywood.

Writer and director Billy Wilder (1906–2002), who moved to Vienna in 1916, also worked in Berlin before striking out for Hollywood. Others who are famous internationally are glamour girl Hedy Lamarr (1913–2000), and director Fred Zinnemann (1907–1997; *From Here to Eternity* and *High Noon* in 1952). For many, Klaus Maria Brandauer (b 1944), star of *Out of Africa* (1985) and *Mephisto* (1981) will need no introduction, and Arnold Schwarzenegger (b 1947), has left visiting cards in Hollywood and as Governor of California.

One filmmaker today attracting attention at home and abroad is Michael Haneke (b 1942), whose work often features violence and a theme of self-destruction. His first film, *Funny Games* (1997), played at the Cannes Film Festival, and his *The Piano Teacher* (2001), based on the novel by Viennese writer Elfriede Jelinek went one step further by winning three awards there. Director Hans Weingartner (b 1970) achieved acclaim with *Die fetten Jahre sind vorbei* (The Edukators, 2004), an insightful film that shows the generation problems you take on if you kidnap an ex-student revolutionary-turned-businessman (it's not worth the trouble, it seems). Ground was also broken in *In 3 Tagen bist du tot* (In 3 Days You're Dead, 2006), when director Andreas Prochaska (b 1964) filmed amateur actors speaking local dialect in a teenage thriller set in the bucolic landscape of the Salzkammergut. In the documentary genre, Hubert Sauper (b 1966) received an Oscar nomination for *Darwin's Nightmare* (2004).

Although news coverage is excellent, locally dubbed foreign fare dominates a bland TV landscape. Testing the brain's sleep centre are noble but interminable broadcasts of parliament, Austrian talk shows, local variants on reality TV or specials on folk music. Against this backdrop, the old favourite, *Komissar Rex*, a bizarrely genre-fluid crime series with a dash of slapstick featuring a ham-roll-stealing German Shepherd dog and plenty of local scenery, reaches giddying and thoroughly enjoyable heights.

Theatre & Dance

Vienna's tradition in the theatre was – and still is – bolstered by the quality of the operas and operettas produced in the golden age of music. In addition to these forms, Greek drama, avant-garde, mime, comedy, cabaret, farce and other theatrical genres are regularly part of the vibrant scene. Vienna is home to the four national theatres and opera houses – the Staatsoper (p152), Volksoper (p153), Akademietheater (the Burgtheater's second stage) and the Burgtheater itself (p153), which is one of the premier theatre and opera venues in the German-speaking world. Theater in der

'All my six husbands married me for different reasons.'
AUSTRIAN HOLLYWOOD FILM ACTRESS HEDY LAMARR

For a complete rundown of Austrian films in English, consult the archives of www.afc.at, the Austrian Film Commission's website.

Viennese *enfant terrible* Haneke's first world-renowned work, *Funny Games* (1997) is a disturbing study of sadism and destruction. A family on holiday is taken hostage by two well-educated young men who want to push some boundaries.

Josefstadt (p153) is known for the modern style of acting evolved by Max Reinhardt, while the Theater an der Wien (p152) puts on opera, dance and concerts. All provincial capital cities are blessed with major theatres.

The first great figure in the modern era was the playwright Franz Grillparzer (1791–1872). Other influential playwrights who still get a regular airing are Johann Nestroy (1801–62), known for his satirical farces, and Ferdinand Raimaund, the 19th-century author of *Der Alpenkönig und der Menschenfeind* (The King of the Alps and the Misanthrope, 1828). Adalbert Stifter (1805–68) is credited as being the seminal influence in the development of an Austrian narrative style.

Many Viennese authors are also playwrights – perhaps the Viennese fondness for the avant-garde encourages crossing artistic boundaries. Arthur Schnitzler, Thomas Bernhard, Elfriede Jelinek and Peter Handke (p55) have all had their plays performed at the Burgtheater.

Dance is by no means as popular as the other arts, but it does have a world-class venue in the TanzQuartier Wien (p153) as well as in those venues already mentioned.

Find out what the Austrian Oak's saying these days by visiting the Terminator-cum-governor's slightly wacky personal website at www.schwarzenegger.com.

Food & Drink

Tradition with new, non-regional edges best describes what you can increasingly expect from Austrian restaurants today. Wiener schnitzel (from
veal), *Tafelspitz* (boiled beef with apple and horseradish sauce) and delicious
hams and cheeses from Tyrol are often balanced by dishes with flavoursome
infusions from outside a region or abroad. For many, the best is left for last:
deliciously divine cakes and pastries, with an international reputation hard
to beat, round off a meal perfectly.

STAPLES & SPECIALITIES

Traditionally, the largest meal of the day is at *Mittag* (midday), known as
Mittagessen (midday meal), whereas *Abendessen* (dinner) consists of bread,
cheese, ham and a beer or wine. Snacking between meals is common, and is
often referred to as *Jause*. If they have time, Austrians will still sit down to
a *Tagesteller* (set dish) or *Mittagsmenü* (set lunch, including soup; around
€6 to €9) in a restaurant, which is invariably a cheap way to fill the belly.
Frühstück (breakfast) is less important, and usually consists of coffee or tea
with a *Semmel* (bread roll) and jam, ham or cheese (or all three). On weekends, particularly in Vienna, breakfast is a completely different creature;
people lazily while away the hours over coffee, rolls, and occasionally a full
English breakfast.

www.pumpkinseedoil
.cc – more information
than you will ever need
to know about southern
Styria's liquid gold.

Three courses are usual for traditional meals. Clear soups are a particular
favourite as a *Vorspeise* (starter), such as *Frittatensuppe*, a clear soup with
shreds of crepe-like pancake. *Markknödelsuppe* is a clear bone-marrow soup
with dumplings, while *Leberknödelsuppe* is yet another clear soup with liver
dumplings. *Gulaschsuppe* (goulash soup), a rich beef-vegetable soup with
plenty of paprika, can be taken as a starter or a main. If you're not a soup
fan, then try *Bauernschmaus*, a platter of cold meats and bread.

Wiener schnitzel, a breaded escalope of veal, is Vienna's best-known
culinary concoction, but it is ubiquitous throughout Austria. Variations on
the schnitzel theme include the more common pork schnitzel, *Cordon Bleu*,
with ham and cheese, and the *Natur*, a schnitzel fried on its own.

Other than schnitzel, *Speisekarten* (menus) normally feature classic
Austrian dishes, such as *Backhuhn* (fried chicken; also known as *Backhendl*),
Tafelspitz, *Schweinsbraten* (slices of roast pork) and *Zweibelrostbraten* (slices
of roast beef smothered in gravy and fried onions). A great variety of *Wurst*
(sausage) is available, and not only at the takeaway stands. Common fish
include *Forelle* (trout), *Hecht* (pike), *Fogosch/Zander* (pike-perch), *Karpfen*
(carp), and *Saibling*, a local freshwater fish, similar to trout.

It's estimated that each
year about 73 million
servings of schnitzel,
42 million portions of
goulash and almost 40
million pasta dishes are
spooned into Austrian
digestive systems.

Main dishes commonly appear with *Beilagen* (side dishes) and extras,
which come in a variety of shapes and forms. *Knödel* (dumplings) are an
element of many meals, and can appear in soups and desserts as well as main
courses. *Nockerln* (sometimes called *Spätzle*, especially in the west) is small
homemade pasta with a similar taste to *Knödel*. *Nudeln* is normally flat egg
noodles, except when it's the tiny noodles in a soup. Austrians love potatoes,
and are not satisfied with just boiling them. They appear as *Pommes* (French
fries), *Quellmänner* (boiled in their skins), *Bratkartoffel* (roasted), *Geröstete*
(sliced small and sautéed) and *Erdapfelsalat Erdäpfe* (boiled potatoes with
chopped chives in a watery dressing).

Regional traditional cuisine is where things get really interesting.
Burgenland has strong ties to Hungarian cooking, with lashings of paprika,
beans, potatoes and cabbage, while in Styria it's hard to go anywhere

OUR TOP EATING EXPERIENCES

Vienna

- **Österreicher im MAK** (p147) Classics like tongue of veal find a new edge in this sharp restaurant.
- **Naschmarkt** (p149) Not just the capital's most famous farmers market – nosh houses stand cheek by jowl, tantalising with exotic and local flavours.
- **Halle** (p147) Penne with artichoke hearts meets Styrian chicken on a changing menu in the pulsating Museums Quartier.

Lower Austria

- **Mörwald Kloster Und** (p170) All the hallmarks of the Wachau are here: a lovely setting, good wine and a chef to watch out for (all while enjoying breast of pigeon).
- **Filmbar im Kesselhaus** (p169) A hungry film-lover's dream come true, with delicious salads and meats, an art-house cinema, plus cinema exhibition space.
- **MOKA** (p178) Miss the last bus out, treat yourself to poppy seed cake and – damn it! – stay overnight.

Burgenland

- **Weingut Gabriel** (p194) Wash down smoked sausage with great wine while watching storks mate above the yard of this picturesque Heuriger.
- **Weingut & Weingasthof Kloster am Spitz** (p195) Organically produced wines, game flavoured with ginger and other fusion elements are all at home here.
- **Zur Dankbarkeit** (p196) A regional kitchen in a leafy yard off the pink, shimmering Neusiedler See, plus the best drops from local winegrowers.

Upper Austria

- **k.u.k. Hofbäckerei** (p207) Fritz Rath tempts the sweet-toothed with his famous *Linzer Torte* in the city's oldest café.
- **Knapp am Eck** (p213) Down a cobbled lane, this gorgeous tavern serves sage-stuffed pork in a lantern-lit, ivy-clad garden.
- **Schlossbrauerei Weinberg** (p216) Devour beer-drenched goulash and beer-battered schnitzel in this cavernous brewpub, hidden in the forest above Kefermarkt.

Styria

- **Lendplatz farmers markets** (p231) The finest out of the *Selchkammer* (smoke house), *Hartkäse* (matured cheese), vegetables, breads and flowers from Graz vendors – with views.
- **Aiola Upstairs** (p230) Chilled music, lemongrass risotto and beef, plus a strong wine and cocktail list and views of Graz from Schlossberg.
- **Iohan** (p231) Gothic vaulting, great wines and food, with *Leberpate* (liver pâté) served at the bar.

Salzkammergut

- **Restaurant-Pizzeria Simmer** (p253) Pizza and a bowling alley out back, and views across the swampy meadows to Hallstätter See.

without encountering *Kürbiskernöl*, a rich, dark pumpkin-seed oil. It is also home to Austria's *Almochsen* (shortened to Almo) bulls, delivering the best beef. In Carinthia, look for *Käsnudeln*, pasta made into balls and combined with cheese. *Käsnocken, Kässpätzle* and *Käsnödel* are variations on a the theme. Tyrol specialities include *Tiroler Gröstl*, pan-fried onions, meat and potatoes, and *Tiroler Knödel*, dumplings hiding small pieces of ham.

■ **Im Weissen Rössl** (p261) Braised cheek of veal, colonial sauces, and fine views in two restaurants overlooking the Wolfgangsee.

■ **Rudolfsturm** (p102) Rustic, filling fare while perched some 800m above Hallstätter See – a perfect end to hiking around the lake.

Salzburg & Salzburger Land

■ **Scio's Specereyen** (p278) Few can resist the blinis with caviar and chocolate-coated *Venusbrüstchen* (Venus breasts) at Scio's.

■ **Afro Café** (p277) Hot-pink walls, wacky artwork and African flavours (such as sticky ostrich kebabs) make this Salzburg's coolest café.

■ **Obauer** (p286) Karl and Rudi Obauer reach for the Michelin stars, with local fare like Werfen lamb and trout strudel.

Carinthia

■ **Restaurant Maria Loretto** (p294) Stupendous Wörthersee views, plus classic fare – from local trout and schnitzel with cranberries to Carinthian Almo steak.

■ **Zauberhutt'n** (p294) Mediterranean influenced food, a kitchen full of magicians, and the best squid conjured up this side of the Alps.

■ **Millstätter See** (p308) A romantic dinner for two on a raft on a lake: enjoy a seven course meal ferried out by to you by waiters on a watery mission.

Hohe Tauern National Park Region

■ **Hölzlahneralm** (p317) The *Kaspressknödel* (dumpling in Pinzgauer cheese) is a meal in itself at this farmhouse high above Krimml Falls.

■ **Our's Lounge** (p316) Glass walls, throne-like red velvet chairs and a menu packed with fusion flavours draw trendies to the lounge.

■ **Hotel Haidenhof** (p326) Locals pile into the South Tyrolean tavern for fresh trout, homemade strudel and appetising Dolomite views.

Tyrol

■ **Metzgerei Kröll** (p349) Nip into this family-run butchers for delicious *Schlegeis-Speck* ham, cured at 1800m to achieve its aroma.

■ **Stanz** (p359) High on a plateau, Stanz's 65 distilleries pack a punch with fiery plum schnapps.

■ **Auracher Löchl** (p355) Expect walls festooned with forest animals, low beams and humungous *Schweinshaxe* (pork knuckles) at this medieval haunt.

Vorarlberg

■ **Käsestrasse** (p374) The dairies lining this road through the Bregenzerwald roll out tasty cheeses, from creamy Bergkäse to walnutty Nussknacker.

■ **Cafesito** (p371) Squeeze into this hip café for chilli hot chocolate and Bregenz's freshest bagels and smoothies.

■ **Wirtschaft zum Schützenhaus** (p376) '*Schiessen und Geniessen*' (shoot and enjoy) is the motto at this half-timbered tavern, with lederhosen-clad staff and enormous schnitzels.

No meal in Austria would be complete without *Nachspeise* (dessert). Beating all-comers in the popularity race is the *Apfelstrüdel*, although *Palatschinken* (crepes) comes a close second. A speciality for Salzburg is the *Salzburger Nockerl*, a fluffy baked pudding made from eggs, flour and sugar. *Germknödel* are sourdough dumplings, but more appetising are *Marillenknödel* (apricot dumplings). Look for *Mohr im Hemd*, a chocolate pudding with whipped cream and chocolate sauce, *Guglhupf*, a cake shaped like a volcano, the *Sacher Torte* in Vienna and the *Linzer Torte* in Linz. The ever-present *Mozartkugeln* (Mozart Balls) are another favourite.

DRINKS
Nonalcoholic Drinks

Although herbal and black teas are popular, coffee is the preferred hot beverage, which is drunk mainly in a *Kaffeehaus* (coffee house) or café, or sometimes in a Café-Konditorei. Strong Turkish coffee is a popular variation in coffee houses. Mineral or soda water is widely available and cheap, though tap water is fine and for the asking. *Almdudler,* a cross between ginger ale and lemonade, is one local soft drink found the country over. Come September, *Traubenmost,* a fresh, unfermented grape juice, is available in wine regions.

Alcoholic Drinks

Although *Bier* (beer) is by far the most popular drink in Austria, internationally, *Wein* (wine) outshines the amber fluid. White wine is traditionally Austria's mainstay, but one-third of the country's viniculture is now planted in reds. Austria has four winegrowing regions: Weinland (Lower Austria and Burgenland; see p195), Steierland (Styria; see p236), Wien (Vienna) and Bergland (Upper Austria, Salzburg, Carinthia, Tyrol and Vorarlberg). These bring together 19 different winegrowing areas. Grüner Veltliner is the most common variety, while *Sekt* is the local bubbly.

Come autumn the whole country goes mad for *Sturm* – new wine in its semi-fermented state. It's yeasty, highly drinkable, has a kick like a mule, and hangovers resemble a porcupine waltzing inside your head, but it's an absolute must. *Staubiger* is new wine fully fermented and is more sour and cloudy than *Sturm.* Some of the young wines can be a little sharp, so it is common to mix them with 50% mineral water, called a *Gespritzer* or *G'spritzer.*

The perfect place to sample wine and *Sturm* is a *Heurigen* or *Buschenschank,* Austria's wine taverns. Rustic and rural, these wonderful establishments have plenty of character and traditionally sell only their own wine, but quite often you'll find stock from outside. They're easy to spot; just look for the *Busch'n* (green wreath or branch) hanging over the front door.

Acidic but pleasant, *Most* is an alcoholic beverage made from apples or wild and cultivated pears and similar to cider. It's found almost all over Austria, but especially in Upper Austria, and in Lower Austria, from where the fruit-growing Mostviertel region (between the Ybbs and the Enns Rivers) gets its name.

Austria loves its home-grown beer, which is no surprise considering the quality. It's usually a light, golden-coloured lager or pilsner (there are dark versions too), and is produced by breweries across the country. Common brands include Ottakringer from Vienna, Gösser and Puntigmer from Graz and Stiegl from Salzburg. *Weizenbier* (wheat beer), also known as *Weissbier* (white beer) has a full-bodied, slightly sweet taste and can be light or dark, clear or cloudy, and is sometimes served with a slice of lemon straddling the glass rim. *Vom Fass* (draught beer) comes in a either a 0.5L or a 0.3L glass. In Vienna and some other parts of eastern Austria these are called respectively a *Krügerl* (sometimes spelled *Krügel*) and a *Seidel.* Elsewhere these will simply be *Grosse* (big) or *Kleine* (small). A small beer may also be called a *Glas* (glass). A *Pfiff* is just 0.125L, which will probably satisfy you for all of two seconds. *Radler* is a mix of beer and lemonade.

Austrians have a soft spot for *Schnapps,* made from a variety of fruits and sometimes called *Obstler.* Some of the country's better drops can be bought at *Bauernmärkte* (farmers markets) across the country.

Check out what's happening in the Austrian vineyards and even practice your Austrian wine terms with mp3 at www.winesfromaustria.com.

Vienna is the largest wine-growing city in the world, although it produces only 1.4% of Austrian wine; 91.7% is produced in the Weinland region.

The Ultimate Austrian Wine Guide, by Peter Moser and published by Falstaff, is the wine lover's bible to Austrian wine. It features a rundown on wines from Austria, 200 leading wineries and is in English.

MORE THAN JUST COFFEE

Legend has it that coffee beans were left behind by the fleeing Turks in 1683, however the tradition of the Viennese *Kaffeehaus* developed in the 19th century, when their numbers reached a reputed 600 cafés.

When ordering a cup of the brown stuff, a 'coffee, please' doesn't suffice. Make your choice from the many types, and this will generally be served on a silver platter accompanied by a glass of water, and if you're lucky, a small sweet.

Here's what you'll generally find on offer:

- *Brauner* – black but served with a tiny splash of milk; comes in *Gross* (large) or *Klein* (small)
- *Einspänner* – with whipped cream, served in a glass
- *Fiaker* – Verlängerter with rum and whipped cream
- *Kapuziner* – with a little milk and perhaps a sprinkling of grated chocolate
- *Maria Theresia* – with orange liqueur and whipped cream
- *Masagran* (or *Mazagran*) – cold coffee with ice and Maraschino liqueur
- *Melange* – the Viennese classic; served with milk, and maybe whipped cream too, similar to the cappuccino
- *Mocca* (sometimes spelled *Mokka*) or *Schwarzer* – black coffee
- *Pharisäer* – strong *Mocca* topped with whipped cream, served with a glass of rum
- *Türkische* – comes in a copper pot with coffee grounds and sugar
- *Verlängerter* – *Brauner* weakened with hot water
- *Wiener Eiskaffee* – cold coffee with vanilla ice cream and whipped cream

CELEBRATIONS

Austrian cuisine very much follows the seasons. Game, an integral part of most menus throughout the year, really comes into its own in autumn, when most of the hunting takes place. Expect to find *Hirsch* (venison), *Wildschwein* (wild boar), *Gems* (chamois) and *Reh* (roe deer) on menus around this time. Come early autumn, the hills and forests are crawling with Austrians, with their bums up and their heads down, searching for *Schwammerl/Pilze* (mushrooms). In May, it's hard to avoid *Spargel* (asparagus), but why would you want to miss this crisp, freshly picked stick of goodness? It's often served with a rich, creamy sauce.

St Martin's Day (November 11) is traditionally marked with the serving of *Gans* (goose), St Martin's symbol. The tasty dish is available the entire month of November. Just before *Weihnachten* (Christmas), you might like to check what's splashing in the bathtub before you dip a toe – the Central European tradition of keeping a live *Karpfen* (carp) in store for Christmas festivities is not unknown in Austria. Seasonal celebrations are complemented with *Vanillekipferl*, crescent cookies which have a special place in the hearts of all Austrians.

WHERE TO EAT & DRINK

Restaurants are by far the most common place to eat. Quite often a rural inn will call itself a *Gasthof* or *Gasthaus* to denote a more traditional setting and décor. Restaurants usually open from 11am or 11.30am to midnight (kitchen till 10.30pm); some close the kitchen, or even the premises, during downtime from 2.30pm to 5pm or 6pm.

Heurigen are fairly inexpensive places to eat in wine areas and the capital. Food is usually buffet style and consists of hearty, Austrian cuisine, and is

Ewald Plachutta and Christoph Wagner put together their favourite Austrian dishes in The 100 Classic Dishes of Austria, published by Deuticke.

Legend has it that the origin of the humble bagel dates back to 1683, when a Viennese baker created a *Beugal* (stirrup) for Polish King Jan III Sobieski in celebration of his victory over the Turks.

available from around 11am to 11pm. Take note that a *Kaffeehaus* (coffee house) or *Café* is very different from a *Café-Konditorei*. A coffee house/café serves coffee, tea and other beverages, as well as light warm and cold meals and sometimes a few pastries and cakes. By contrast, a *Café-Konditorei* specialises in cakes, often baked on the premises, and will usually serve coffee too. While it is customary to linger for hours, read the newspapers from the racks, drink a wine or beer and play chess or cards in a coffee house/café, this would be out of line in a *Café-Konditorei*. Hours tend to be different too. A *Café-Konditorei* keeps close to standard shop hours, whereas coffee houses and cafés open their doors early, often between 7am and 8am, and close from anything between 7pm and 1am, depending on the market they're catering to, or even morph into very late-night drinking dens.

In mountainous areas, *Hütte* or *Almhütte* (alpine huts) are atmospheric places for basic Austrian cuisine in stunning surroundings.

Quick Eats
If you need something in a hurry, a *Würstel Stand* (sausage stand) is never too far away. Deli shops sometimes offer hot food, such as spit-roasted chicken (an Austrian favourite). Supermarket delis will always have sandwiches for those on the run.

VEGETARIANS & VEGANS
Vegetarians will do just fine in Vienna, and in Austria's other large cities there are at least a couple of vegetarian restaurants to choose from. In the countryside however, things can get extremely meaty. Many places now offer at least one vegetarian dish, but don't count on it every time; you may have to rely on a combination of salads and side dishes to create a full meal. Note that most soups are made with meat stock.

EATING WITH KIDS
Feeding the little 'uns will prove no problem in Austria; in general, only the very upmarket restaurants have a problem with children. Some restaurants have children's menus but most will be willing to serve smaller portions if you ask nicely.

See p383 for more on travelling with children.

HABITS & CUSTOMS
In general, Austrians are a polite and respectable bunch at the table, and tend to take their time over meals. More often than not, the next course will not be served until everyone at the table has finished, so don't ramble on to your neighbour while the rest of the diners are waiting. Nonsmokers (and some smokers) may be annoyed with smoking habits in restaurants; many smokers won't bat an eyelid lighting up while you're still only half way through your Wiener schnitzel.

Austrians certainly like a drink, and the country has its fair share of teenage binge drinkers and alcoholics, but your average Austrian tends to take his or her time getting sozzled. Every drink bought deserves a *Prost* (cheers) and eye contact with your fellow drinkers; not following this custom is thought of as rude. Even worse, it's believed to result in bad sex for the next seven years.

COOKING COURSES
Places offering cooking courses are rather thin on the ground, but if you're keen to learn how to bread a schnitzel the Austrian way, or roll the perfect *Knödel,* there are a few places in Vienna to check out:

The Wiener schnitzel is not in fact from Vienna; it was brought back to the capital from Milan in 1848 by Field Marshal Radetzky's chief cook.

Food history, wine glossary and menu guide; it's all here under one website: www .globalgourmet.com /destinations/austria.

Get Elisabeth Mayer-Browne's take on the Austrian kitchen in the *Best of Austrian Cuisine,* published by Hippocrene.

Babettes (Map pp116-17; ☎ 01-585 51 65; www.babettes.at, in German; 04, Schleifmühlgasse 17; ◷ 10am-7pm Mon-Fri, 10am-5pm Sat) A food-lover's dream, with a zillion cookbooks and spices, plus cooking courses to boot.

Hollerei (Map pp116-17; ☎ 01-892 33 56; www.hollerei.at, in German; 15, Hollergasse 9; ◷ Mon-Sat) Conducts regular courses on veg cooking with style.

Restaurant zur Traube (☎ 02738-229 80; kochschule@moerwald.at; Kleine Zeile 13-17, 3483 Feuersbrunn) In rural Feuersbrunn (a short hop from Vienna). Offers seminars and courses almost weekly on Austrian and international cuisine.

Wrenkh Kochsalon & Restaurant (Map pp120-1; ☎ 01-533 15 26; www.wrenkh.at, in German; 01, Bauernmarkt 10; ◷ lunch & dinner) Runs some unusual courses: its *Zurufküche* (cooking calling) consists of lining up an array of ingredients and experimenting in style and dish, while *Kochsalon* courses are group cooking events whose multicourse outcome you enjoy together.

Classic dishes and their recipes can be found on the English website www.austrianfoodandwine.com.

In Styria, try the **Erste Steirische Kochschule** (☎ 03135-522 47; www.kochschule.at, in German; Hauptstrasse 168) in Kalsdorf, or **Gasthof Vitalpension Hubinger** (☎ 03861-81 14; www.hubinger.com; 8633 Etmissl 25) in Etmissl for traditional Austrian cooking courses.

EAT YOUR WORDS

Want to know your *Germknödel* from your *Grammelknödel*? Your *Wiener Bachhendl* from your Wiener schnitzel? Get behind the cuisine scene, by getting to know the language.

Useful Phrases

Can you recommend ...?

Können Sie ... empfehlen?	ker-nen zee ... emp-*fay*-len
a restaurant	
ein Restaurant	ain res-to-*rang*
a bar/pub	
eine Kneipe	ai-ne *knai*-pe

A table for ..., please.

Einen Tisch für ..., bitte.	ai-nen tish für ... *bi*-te

I'd like to reserve a table for ...

Ich möchte einen Tisch für ... reservieren.	ikh *merkh*-te ai-nen tish für ... re-zer-*vee*-ren
(two) people	
(zwei) Personen	(tsvai) per-*zaw*-nen
(eight) o'clock	
(acht) Uhr	(akt) oor

Do you have ...?

Haben Sie ...?	hah-ben zee ...?
a menu in English	
eine englische Speisekarte	ai-ne *eng*-li-she shpai-ze-kar-te
vegetarian food	
vegetarisches Essen	ve-ge-*tah*-ri-shes e-sen

What would you recommend?

Was empfehlen Sie?	vas emp-*fay*-len zee

I'd like a local speciality.

Ich möchte etwas Typisches aus der Region.	ikh *merkh*-te et-vas ti-pi-shes ows dair re-*gyawn*

I'd like the set menu, please.

Ich hätte gerne das Tagesmenü, bitte.	ikh ha-te *ger*-ne das ta-ges- me-noo *bi*-te

What are the daily specials?

Was sind die Tagesspezialitäten?	vas zind dee ta-gez-spe-tsya-lee-te-ten

I'm a vegetarian.
Ich bin Vegetarier(in). (m/f)   ikh bin ve-ge-*tah*-ri-e-r/ve-ge-*tah*-ri-e-rin
Is it cooked in meat stock?
Ist es in Fleischbrühe?   ist es in flaish-*brü*-e
What's in that dish?
Was ist in diesem Gericht?   vas ist in *dee*-zem ge-*rikht*
I'd like ..., please.
Ich möchte ..., bitte.   ikh *merkh*-te ... *bi*-te
Can I have some more ... please.
Bitte noch ein ...   *bi*-te nokh ain ...
That was delicious!
Das war sehr lecker!   das vahr zair le-ker
The bill, please.
Die Rechnung, bitte.   dee *rekh*-nung, *bi*-te
Bon appétit.
Güten Appetit.   *goo*-ten a-pe-*teet*
Cheers!
Prost! prawst!

Menu Decoder
SOUPS & STARTERS
Frittattensuppe (free-*ta*-ten-*zu*-pe) – clear soup with chives and strips of pancake
Leberknödelsuppe (*lay*-ber-kner-del-*zu*-pe) – liver dumpling soup
Rindsuppe (*rind*-zu-pe) – clear beef soup

MAINS
Backhendl (*bakh*-hen-del) – fried breaded chicken
Bauernschmaus (*bow*-ern-shmows) – platter of cold meats
Grammelknödel (*gra*-mel-*kner*-del) – pork dumplings
Gulasch/Gulas (*goo*-lash/*goo*-las) – thick beef soup
Schinkenfleckerl (*shin*-ken-flek-erl) – oven-baked ham and noodle casserole
Schweinsbraten (*shvains*-bra-ten) – roast pork
Semmelknödel (*ze*-mel-kner-del) – bread dumplings
Stelze (*shtel*-tse) – roast hock
Tafelspitz (*ta*-fel-spits) – boiled beef, potatoes and horseradish sauce
Tiroler Gröstl (tee-*ro*-ler grer-stel) – potatoes, onions and flecks of meat fried in a pan
Wiener schnitzel (*vee*-ner *shni*-tsel) – breaded veal cutlets (sometimes with pork or turkey)
Zwiebelrostbraten (*tswee*-bel-*rost*-bra-ten) – roast beef slices with gravy and fried onions

DESSERTS
Apfelstrüdel (*ap*-fel-stroo-del) – apple strudel
Germknödel (jairm-*kner*-del) – yeast dumplings with poppy seeds
Kaiserschmarrn (*kai*-zer-shmar-ren) – sweet pancake with raisins
Marillenknödel (ma-*ree*-len-*kner*-del) – apricot dumplings
Mohr im Hemd (*morr* im hemd) – chocolate pudding with whipped cream and chocolate sauce
Palatschinken (*pa*-lat-shing-ken) – crepes
Topfenknödel (*top*-fen-kner-del) – cheese dumplings

Food Glossary
MEAT & FISH

bacon	*Speck*	shpek
beef	*Rindfleisch*	rint-flaish
brains	*Hirn*	heern
carp	*Karpfen*	karp-fen
chicken	*Huhn/Hendl*	hoon/hen-dl

duck	*Ente*	*en*-te
eel	*Aal*	ahl
fish	*Fisch*	fish
goose	*Gans*	gans
ham	*Schinken*	*shing*-ken
hare	*Hase*	*hah*-ze
lamb	*Lamm*	lam
liver	*Leber*	*lay*-ber
minced meat	*Hackfleisch*	*hak*-flaish
plaice	*Scholle*	*sho*-le
pork	*Schweinsfleisch*	*shvai*-ne-flaish
salmon	*Lachs*	laks
tongue	*Zunge*	*tsung*-e
trout	*Forelle*	fo-*re*-le
tuna	*Thunfisch*	*toon*-fish
turkey	*Puter*	*poo*-ter
veal	*Kalbfleisch*	*kalp*-flaish
venison	*Hirsch*	hirsh

VEGETABLES & FRUIT

apple	*Apfel*	*ap*-fel
apricot	*Marille/Aprikose*	ma-*ree*-le/a-pri-*ko*-ze
asparagus	*Spargel*	*shpar*-gel
banana	*Banane*	ba-*nah*-ne
beans	*Bohnen*	*baw*-nen
beetroot	*Rote Rübe*	*raw*-te- *rü*-be
cabbage	*Kohl*	hawl
carrots	*Karotten*	ka-*ro*-ten
cherries	*Kirschen*	*kir*-shen
corn	*Mais*	mais
cucumber, gherkin	*Gurke*	*gur*-ke
garlic	*Knoblauch*	*knawp*-lowkh
grapes	*Trauben*	*trow*-ben
green beans	*Fisolen*	fee-*zo*-len
mushrooms	*Champignons/* *Schwammerl/Pilze*	sham-pee-*nyon/* *shva*-mer/*pil*-tse
onions	*Zwiebeln*	*tsvee*-beln
pear	*Birne*	*bir*-ne
peas	*Erbsen*	*erp*-sen
peppers	*Paprika*	*pap*-ri-kah
pineapple	*Ananas*	a-na-*nas*
plums	*Zwetschgen*	*tsvetsh*-gen
potatoes	*Erdäpfel/Kartoffeln*	*ert*-ep-fel/kar-*to*-feln
raspberries	*Himbeeren*	*him*-bee-ren
spinach	*Spinat*	shpi-*naht*
strawberries	*Erdbeeren*	*ert*-bee-ren
tomatoes	*Paradeiser/Tomaten*	pa-ra-dai-ser/to-*mah*-ten

OTHER ITEMS

bread	*Brot*	brawt
bread roll	*Semmel*	*ze*-mel
butter	*Butter*	*bu*-ter
cheese	*Käse*	*kay*-ze

chocolate	Schokolade	sho-ko-*lah*-de
coffee	Kaffee	ka-fay
cream	Schlagobers/	shlag-o-berz/
	Rahm/Sahne	rahm/zah-ne
dumplings	Knödel	kner-del
eggs	Eier	ai-er
honey	Honig	haw-nikh
jam	Marmelade	mar-me-*lah*-de
mustard	Senf	zenf
nut	Nuss	nus
oil	Öl	erl
pepper	Pfeffer	pfe-fer
rice	Reis	rais
salad	Salat	za-*laht*
salt	Salz	zalts
sugar	Zucker	tsu-ker

COOKING TERMS

baked	gebacken	ge-*ba*-ken
boiled	gekocht	ge-kokht
crispy	knusprig	k-*noo*-sprik
fresh	frisch	frish
fried	gebraten	ge-*brah*-ten
grilled	gegrillte	ge-grilt
homemade	selbst gemacht	selbst ge-*makht*
roasted	braten	bra-ten
steamed	gedämpft	ge-dempft
smoked	geräuchert	ge-roy-khert
sour	sauer	zow-er
sweet	süss	züs

UTENSILS

ashtray	Aschenbecher	a-shen-be-kher
cup	Tasse	ta-se
fork	Gabel	gah-bel
glass	Glas	glahs
knife	Messer	me-ser
plate	Teller	te-ler
spoon	Löffel	ler-fel
toothpick	Zahnstocher	tsahn-shto-kher

Environment

Landlocked in the heart of Europe, Austria may be small but she's a country magnet, surrounded by Germany, the Czech Republic, Slovakia, Hungary, Slovenia, Italy, Switzerland and Liechtenstein. Despite her diminutive size, she's an astounding natural beauty who revels in diversity: from the green vines of Burgenland to Lower Austria's castle-speckled hills, Tyrol's voluptuous mountains to the pure lakes of Salzkammergut. In topographic terms, it's as though someone chalked a line straight down the middle and asked all the Alps to shuffle to the west and all the flats to slide to the east, so stark is the contrast in this land of highs and lows.

THE LAND

Think of Austria and invariably the first thing to pop into your head are mountains. Of the 83,858 sq km of land squeezed within Austria's borders almost two-thirds are mountainous. The glaciers that began carving up the landscape some 2½ million years ago played a big hand in softly sculpting the country's distinctive shape of mountains, valleys and lakes.

Austria's Alps can be split into three mountain ranges running in a west–east direction. The Northern Limestone Alps, bordering Germany, reach nearly 3000m and extend almost as far east as the Wienerwald (Vienna Woods). The valley of the Inn River separates them from the High or Central Alps, the highest peaks in Austria dwarfed by the majestic summit of Grossglockner (3797m). The Southern Limestone Alps, which include the Karawanken Range, form a natural barrier with Italy and Slovenia.

The rest of the country is a mixed bag of alpine foothills, lowlands and granite highlands. By far the most fertile stretch is the Danube Valley, growing 90% of Austria's food. In the northeast the landscape switches to rolling hills and dense forest, thinning out to the east in the pancake-flat Pannonian plains. What these regions lack in mind-blowing scenery they make up for with mile upon mile of vineyards and farmland.

Austria's greatest feature outside the Alps is the thoroughly un-blue Danube (Donau), flowing west–east from Germany through the Danube Valley and Vienna, and eventually exiting in Slovakia. Joining the Danube as it enters Austria is the turquoise Inn River. To the southeast, the main waterways are the Mur and the Drau.

Aside from rivers, Austria is riddled with lakes and it's hard to move without toppling into one in the Salzkammergut region and Carinthia. The country's most unusual lake is Neusiedler See in Burgenland, Austria's lowest point (115m) and one of Europe's few steppe lakes. It's an outdoorsy haven for ornithologists, water-sport fanatics and cyclists.

WILDLIFE

Austria has abundant wildlife and while you'd be lucky to glimpse an elusive lynx or golden eagle in the Alps, there's a good chance you might spy marmots, chamois and ibex. Bird-watchers flock to the banks of Neusiedler See to spot the 150 different species of birds that breed in the area. During the Europe-Africa migration period, the same number of species drop in on the lake during their flight south.

Animals

The critters of Austria's alpine regions are the most intriguing for visitors. There you'll find the ibex, a mountain goat with curved horns, which was

www.naturschutz.at is a one-stop shop for info on Austria's landscape, flora and fauna. It's in German, but there are a few links to English sites too.

Get your skates on at Neusiedler See. When the salt lake freezes it becomes Central Europe's biggest natural ice rink, beckoning anyone that fancies a teeth-chattering twirl.

Cameras and binoculars at the ready…Kaiser-Franz-Josefs-Höhe in the Hohe Tauern National Park is a prime place to spot ibex, chamois and marmots in the late afternoon.

at one stage under threat but fortunately is now breeding again. It's the master of mountain climbing and migrates to 3000m or more come July. The chamois, a small antelope more common than the ibex, is equally at home scampering around on mountain sides. It can leap an astounding 4m vertically and its hooves have rubber-like soles and rigid outer rims – ideal for maintaining a good grip on loose rocks.

A right pair of love birds, golden eagles stay together for life. See www.birdlife.at, in German, to find out more about these elusive raptors and other Austrian birdlife.

The marmot, a fluffy rodent related to the squirrel, is also indigenous to the Alps. It's a sociable animal that lives in colonies of about two dozen members. Like meerkats, marmots regularly post sentries, which stand around on their hind legs looking alert. They whistle once when a predator from the air (like an eagle) and twice when a predator from the ground (such as a fox) is approaching and the whole tribe scurries to safety down a network of burrows. Winged fauna in the Alps include golden eagles, vultures – both bearded and griffin – and a multitude of colourful butterflies.

In the east the picture is completely different. The Neusiedler See, a large steppe lake, is a unique sanctuary for numerous species of bird. Commonly spotted are avocets, Eurasian curlews, yellow wagtails, short-eared owls, great bustards and white storks.

ENDANGERED SPECIES

Like most European countries, Austria has its fair share of endangered species, including the country's 'flagship' species below – those that stand out in a list that's far too long. For more information, consult the Rote Liste (red list; www.umweltbundesamt.at), a comprehensive list of endangered species collated by the Umweltbundesamt (Federal Environment Agency).

Austria's most endangered species is the Bayerische Kurzohrmaus (Bavarian pine vole), which is endemic to Tyrol and found only in six localities. Following close behind is the Kaiseradler (imperial eagle), at one time extinct in Austria but fortunately staging a comeback through re-immigration. The Triel (stone curlew), a rare bird found only in eastern Austria, is also under threat, as is the Europäische Sumpfschildkröte (European pond terrapin), which inhabits the Danube floodplains. The Europäische Hornotter (long-nosed viper) may be a venomous snake at home in Carinthia, but humans are a far greater threat to its survival than its bite will ever be to our survival.

Although still teetering on the brink of extinction, the country's population of brown bears now reaches double figures (estimated at around 15 to 20). This is due to the efforts of organisations like Austria's Brown Bear Life Project and the WWF who have invested millions of euros into bringing the bear back to the Alps. While rarely sighted, brown bears are said to roam in central and southern mountainous regions such as Carinthia and Styria.

Plants

An incredible 47% of Austria is forested, making it one of the most wooded countries in Europe. At low altitudes expect to find shady oak and beech forests; at higher elevations conifers, such as pine, spruce and larch, take over. At around 2200m trees yield to alpine meadows and beyond 3000m, only mosses and lichens cling to the stark crags.

A highlight of the Alps is its flowers, which add a palette of colour to the high pastures from June to September. The flowers here are built to cope with harsh conditions: long roots counter strong winds, bright colours attract few insects and specially developed leaves protect against frost and dehydration. By far the most popular is the edelweiss, which is a white, star-shaped flower found on rocky crags and crevices. Although most alpine flowers are protected and should not be picked, many young, love-struck men have risked life and limb to bring such a flower to the lady of their choice. Delicate orchids, arnica, alpine roses and purple gentian also carpet the slopes in summer.

Of particular note again is the Unesco biosphere reserve of Neusiedler See, whose western shores are lined with a vast, almost impenetrable belt of reeds.

NATIONAL PARKS

For a country of such extraordinary natural beauty, it may come as a surprise to learn that only 2.9% of Austria falls within the boundaries of national parks. Within this 2.9%, commercial operations such as traditional farming and hunting, are still ongoing. However, the national park authorities have managed to strike a good balance between preserving the natural wildlife and keeping local economic endeavours alive. The website www .nationalparksaustria.at has links to all six national parks and a brochure in English to download.

Of Austria's national parks, Hohe Tauern National Park is the most spectacular and frequented hands-down. Neusiedler See-Seewinkel takes second place, due to its closeness to Vienna and the plethora of water sports activities available there.

Aside from the country's national parks, protected areas and reserves are dotted all over Austria and land protected by nature conservation law totals a more impressive 35.5%, which covers landscapes from forest to the Alps and Pannonian steppe.

ENVIRONMENTAL ISSUES

On the whole, Austrians are an ecofriendly bunch who treat their backyard better than most nations. They're well informed about environmental issues and the government, which spends 3% of its Gross Domestic Product (GDP)

> The Dreiländereck in Villach, Carinthia, is the point where Austria, Slovenia and Italy meet. It's quite an experience to hike to the summit and kick back in three countries at the same time.

AUSTRIA'S NATIONAL PARKS

Park (area)	Features	Activities	Best Time to Visit	Page
Donau-Auen (93 sq km)	floodplains, meadows, still rivers; beavers, turtles, catfish	walking, cycling, boating	summer	p180
Gesäuse (110 sq km)	mountains, gorges, meadows, forests; owls, eagles, falcons, woodpeckers	rock climbing, hiking, rafting, caving, mountain biking	spring, summer, autumn	p243
Hohe Tauern (1787 sq km)	mountains; ibex, marmots, bearded vultures, golden eagles	hiking, rock & mountain climbing, skiing, canyoning, kayaking, paragliding	year-round	p310
Kalkalpen (210 sq km)	forests, gorges, mountains; lynx, golden eagles, owls, woodpeckers	cycling, hiking, rock climbing, cross-country skiing	year-round	p213
Neusiedler See-Seewinkel (97 sq km)	saline steppe lake, salt marshes; storks, great bustards, avocets, owls	sailing, swimming, cycling, walking, bird-watching	summer	p193
Thayatal (13 sq km)	rocky outcrops, virgin forest; otters, eagles, storks, bats	walking	spring, summer, autumn	p178

on environmental measures, has happily signed international agreements to reduce pollution and preserve natural resources. See the Getting Started chapter (p21) for practical tips on limiting environmental impact.

Recycling is big in this country; Austrians are diligent about separating recycling material from other waste, and the practice is very much ingrained in society. You'll see recycling bins for metal, paper, plastics and glass on many street corners, and most neighbourhoods have stations for hazardous materials. Some glass containers, in particular beer bottles, have a return value that can be claimed at supermarkets; look for *Flaschen Rücknahme* (bottle return) machines.

Measures have been in place for years to protect the fragile ecosystem of alpine regions, yet some forest degradation has taken place due to air and soil pollution caused by emissions from industrial plants, exhaust fumes and the use of agricultural chemicals. The government has moved to minimise such pollutants by banning leaded petrol, assisting businesses in waste avoidance and promoting natural forms of energy, such as wind and solar power. Wind farms are prevalent in the flat plains in the east of the country and home owners are encouraged through tax breaks to install solar panels. Some buses are gas powered and environmentally friendly trams are a feature of many cities.

One of Austria's biggest environmental concerns is not within the country's sphere of control. In 1978, Austrians voted against developing a nuclear power industry, prompting the federal Nuclear Prohibition Law. The Czech Republic thought otherwise, and in 2000 its Temelín nuclear reactor was brought online just 60km from the Austrian border. Many environmentalists were appalled and their concerns were not unfounded; 2002 saw shutdowns, due to faulty valves and a pipe being welded on incorrectly. While no radiation leaks have yet been reported, environmental agencies believe it is only a matter of time. Border blockades and protests flared again in 2007 when the Czech government announced intentions to withdraw from the bilateral Melk Agreement, which monitors the power station's safety and environmental impact. The dispute is ongoing.

> Melting ice is a hot topic in the Hohe Tauern National Park. The Pasterze Glacier has shrunk to half its size over the past 150 years and is predicted to disappear entirely within 100 years.

> Want to know more about Austrian ski resorts stepping up efforts to save the environment? Check out www.saveoursnow.com.

GREENER SHADE OF WHITE

In a bid to offset the impact of skiing, plenty of Austrian resorts are now taking the green run by implementing ecofriendly policies. The following are green giants that aim to tread lightly:

- **Lech** (p379) in Vorarlberg scores top points for its biomass communal heating plant, the photovoltaic panels that operate its chairlifts and its strict recycling policies.
- **Zell am See** (p313) launched Austria's first ISO-certified cable car at the Kitzsteinhorn glacier. It operates a free ski bus in winter and runs an ecological tree and grass planting scheme.
- **Kitzbühel** (p351) operates green building and climate policies and is taking measures to reduce traffic and the use of non-renewable energy sources.
- **St Anton am Arlberg** (p362) shows its green streak by creating protected areas to reduce erosion and pumping out artificial snow without chemicals. Its excellent train connections mean fewer cars.
- **Ischgl** (p360) uses renewable energy, recycles in all hotels, lifts and restaurants and has a night-time driving ban from 11pm to 6am.
- **Mayrhofen** (p348) operates its lifts on hydroelectricity, separates all waste and has free ski buses to reduce traffic in the village.

SEPP HOLZER: THE REBEL FARMER

With its steep inclines and average temperature of 4.2°C, Ramingstein in Salzburger Land has been dubbed Austria's Siberia – cold and inhospitable. Yet precisely the reverse is true at Krameterhof, where kiwis, figs and lemons hang heavy on the trees at an elevation of 1500m. The green-fingered brainchild of this alpine Garden of Eden is Sepp Holzer, alias 'the rebel farmer'. His concept is permaculture using self-sustaining agricultural systems. Once planted, Holzer does not weed, water, prune or use pesticides. 'There's no need – nature is perfect', he says. 'It's humans that make the mistakes'.

An inquisitive child, Holzer observed and experimented with nature to discover that: 'every leaf, every stone, every plant, every insect has an important role to play'. Together with his wife, he runs the 50-hectare farm according to self-sufficient ecosystems; there are terraces to reduce erosion and catch rain, rocks to trap and emit heat, and foraging pigs to till the wheat fields. Carrots and lettuces grow wildly here not in ruler-straight lines and the cherries are plump despite 25cm of new snow a few days ago. 'I work with nature, not against it', Holzer shrugs. And the results are clear: 18 times the average yield using 10% of the energy.

Holzer has scattered the seeds of permaculture far and wide, with international projects including a self-sufficient orphanage in Thailand and a recultivation programme in Scotland. But it's not all been a bed of roses back home. 'People have branded me a liar, a mad farmer that says *Guten Morgen* to the rain worms. I don't talk to worms, but I do try to put myself in the place of animals and plants to consider what they like and need.' He has been fined and threatened for planting cereal crops in the forest, but sticks to his guns against monoculture. 'Deer eat bark from randomly chosen trees because they feel trapped and instinctively know that if trees fall, light will allow other species to grow. Others mock me, but my forest is still standing when a storm comes. Anyone that thinks they are above nature or can control it is a fool.'

In his summer seminars (see www.krameterhof.at, in German), Holzer encourages people to abandon textbook theories and open their eyes to what nature is telling them; the philosophy is careful thought, minimal action. 'Children should grow up understanding that earth is not dirt but the foundations of life', Holzer stresses. 'It's time to stop the social brainwashing and show some civil courage. Those that don't are slaves in their own farms', he adds. There's no doubting the wisdom in Holzer's words or the method in his madness. He may be a rebel, but he does have a cause.

With global warming on the increase, Austria's ski pistes are on the decrease. A UNEP report on climate change published in 2007 warned that rising temperatures could mean that 75% of alpine glaciers will disappear within the next 45 years, and that dozens of low-lying ski resorts such as Kitzbühel (760m) will be completely cut off from their slopes by 2030. Forecasts suggest that the snowline will shift from 1200m to 1800m by 2100, a prediction that is supported by recent mild winters in the Alps. As well as the impact on Austria's tourist industry, the melting snow is sure to have other knock-on effects, including erosion, floods and an increased risk of avalanches.

Austria's lucrative ski industry is a double-edged sword; on the one hand resorts face mounting pressure to develop and build higher up on the peaks to survive, while on the other their very survival is threatened by global warming. For many years, ski resorts have not done the planet many favours: mechanically grading pistes disturbs wildlife and causes erosion, artificial snow affects native flora and fauna, and trucking in snow increases emissions. However, many Austrian resorts (see opposite) now realise that they are walking a thin tightrope and are mitigating their environmental impact with renewable hydroelectric power, biological wastewater treatment and ecological buildings.

Take the plunge at Montafon's Mountain Beach (www.mountain beach.at, in German). The award-winning complex is the last word in eco-bathing, sheltering two enormous pools filled with spring water and cleaned by micro-organisms.

Outdoor Activities

Austria is a great place to get into the outdoors, with a gigantic backyard full of spiky peaks, clear lakes and raging rivers custom-made for vigorous activities. Skiing and walking (p82) are perennial favourites and share the limelight with gravity-defying sports designed to make you scream. Feeling daring? Catch thermals with a parachute or abseil down a waterfall, bounce down the Alps in a snow tube or on the back of a bone-shaking mountain bike.

If that sounds too hair-raising, there's drama to be had in silent moves – swishing through frozen woodlands on cross-country trails and finding your (very big) feet in a pair of snowshoes. Snow or shine, this country is hyperactive.

A great introduction to the never-ending list of outdoor activities on offer in Austria is the national tourist board's website www.austria.info, in German.

WINTER

SKIING & SNOWBOARDING

Go to Austria in winter and you'll find that skiing and snowboarding still top the list of ways to amuse yourself with an enormous pile of snow. The Austrian Alps are fine specimens of mountains: high enough for one to hurl down black runs in big resorts like Mayrhofen (p348), low enough to give beginners the skitterbug on the nursery slopes in chocolate-box villages such as Filzmoos (p286). Almost every Austrian you meet has skied since they were knee-high and the average four-year-old will ski circles around you on the slopes. The best skiing is in the western reaches of the country, though most resorts in the Alps have T-bars, lifts and cable cars.

While this book features plenty of skiing information, it's not a dedicated skiing guide. Austria has hundreds of excellent ski resorts and no attempt has been made to cover them exhaustively. Many are now taking steps to improve their green credentials and minimise their impact on the environment (p72). For a detailed rundown of resorts based primarily on skiing criteria, consult a specialist book or magazine, such as the UK's *The Good Skiing & Snowboarding Guide*. More information on ski resorts can be provided by Österreich Werbung (p391) and the resort tourist offices.

Get your skates on in Vienna for the Friday night skate sessions from May to September. Like-minded bladers meet up at 10pm on Heldenplatz. For route details, see www .fridaynightskating.at, in German.

Information

The skiing season kicks off in December and lasts till late April in the high-altitude resorts. The biggest crowds descend on the slopes at Christmas–New Year and in February half-term holidays. May to June and late October to mid-December fall between the summer and winter seasons. Some cable cars will be closed for maintenance and many hotels and restaurants will be shut, but you'll avoid the crowds and find prices at their lowest.

Austria offers some of the finest year-round skiing in the Alps at eight glaciers: Dachstein, Mölltaler, Hintertuxer (p349), Pitztaler, Kaunertaler, Sölden (p357), Kitzsteinhorn-Kaprun (p313) and Stubaier (p345). However, most alpine glaciers are now receding in the face of global warming, and snow coverage is less secure at lower elevations in early and late season.

Vorarlberg, Salzburger Land and Tyrol are the most popular destinations, but there is also skiing in Upper Austria, Carinthia and even Lower Austria. Ski passes cover the cost of mountain transport, including ski buses between the ski areas. Pass prices for little-known places may be as little as half that charged in the jet-set resorts. You're usually better off buying half-/full-/multiple-day passes. Count on around €25 to €40 for a one-day ski pass, with substantial reductions for longer-term passes.

Rental prices for carving skis, stocks and shoes are around €20 to €35 for one day for downhill skiing, with reduced rates offered over longer periods; snowboards are roughly the same as carving skis. Most ski resorts have one or more ski schools. Individual tuition and group lessons are available and will normally set you back around €250/60 per day respectively. The more days you take, the cheaper it gets.

Ski Regions & Resorts
The following are the pick of Austria's ski regions and resorts, but they're just a taste of what's up there. Weekly ski passes are quoted here at high-season rates; check with local tourist offices or turn to the regional chapters for details on possible discounts.

SPORTWELT AMADÉ (SALZBURGER LAND)
Salzburg's Sportwelt Amadé (www.sportwelt-amade.com) lures skiers with a whopping 865km of snow-sure slopes in 25 resorts. Among them are Radstadt (p287) and Filzmoos (p286). Filzmoos lies at the foot of the Dachstein massif and is a low-key, family-oriented resort with gentle skiing and village charm. The ski schools are in the heart of the resort, lift queues are short and the pistes uncrowded. Off-slope activities include 50km of winter walking trails and romantic horse-drawn sleigh rides. A weekly pass is €196.

EUROPA SPORTREGION (HOHE TAUERN NATIONAL PARK)
The vibrant resorts of Zell am See and Kaprun (p312) form the Europa Sportregion (www.europasportregion.info) and share 132km of pistes. The Schmittenhöhe challenges experts on nine black runs, while the gentle slopes of the Maiskogel are suited to families and novices. Out-of-season skiing is possible at Kitzsteinhorn glacier and snowboarders should check out the rails, kickers and boxes at the plateau. With its *belle époque* hotels and attractive lakefront, Zell am See retains an authentic feel unlike many purpose-built resorts. The entire region affords gorgeous views of the glacier-capped Hohe Tauern mountain range. A six-day pass costs €179.

SILVRETTA ARENA-ISCHGL (TYROL)
Located in the Paznauntal, Ischgl (p360) forms part of the Silvretta Arena and is swiftly carving its name as Ibiza in the Alps, thanks to its vibrant après-ski and clubbing. The powder is good, the lifts are ultramodern and the skiing mostly intermediate, with 230km of pistes for powder junkies to play on. Those seeking big air should check out the half-pipe and snow-boarding park. The Silvretta Ski Pass costs €247 for seven days; it covers not only Ischgl, but also the neighbouring resorts of Galtür, Kappl and Samnaun (in Switzerland).

KITZBÜHEL-KIRCHBERG (TYROL)
The twin ski resorts of Kitzbühel (p350) and Kirchberg are among the best-known in Austria. Kitzbühel attracts the champagne crowd to the swanky hotels and restaurants in its medieval heart, while Kirchberg is more relaxed. They share 150km of prepared pistes and are linked by the 3S cable car at Pengelstein. A fine mix of intermediate and advanced, the slopes include the nerve-splintering Streif run. Snowboarders are well catered for at Kitzbühler Horn's fun park with a half-pipe, kickers and self-timer course. The only downside is Kitzbühel's comparatively low altitude, which means snow is

Tee time! Austria's golfing pros give a whole new meaning to the word 'snowball' when they hit the powder for the World Golf Championships in Abtenau near Salzburg in February.

Get clicking on www .bergfex.com for piste maps and details of every ski resort in Austria, plus info on summer activities such as hiking and mountain biking.

no longer guaranteed. A weekly pass covering this and nearby ski areas (including Wilde Kaiser-Brixental) costs €202.

ZILLERTAL-MAYRHOFEN (TYROL)

Mayrhofen (p348) in the Zillertal combines steep slopes with broad pistes perfect for carving and cruising. Its varied terrain for skiers and boarders includes enough black runs to keep daredevils on their toes. Austria's undisputed king of scary skiing reigns here – the mogul-free and kamikaze-like Harakiri, with a 78-degree gradient that catapults skiers into the unknown (many take one look and judiciously turn back). Even when snow lies thin on the ground in Mayrhofen, the resort's easy access to the Hintertux Glacier means plenty of skiing is always available. The weekly Zillertal Super Ski Pass (€197.50) covers 157km of piste and 49 lifts in the Zillertal area.

ÖTZTAL-SÖLDEN (TYROL)

Austrian Matthias Zdarsky penned the first skiing manual in 1897, invented the first practical ski binding and organised the first slalom competition in skiing history in 1905.

Sölden (p357) in the Ötztal is one of the country's highest resorts and snow coverage is superb. Most skiers that make it this far have the Big 3 in mind: a trio of 'three-thousanders' that are the ultimate in high-altitude, long-distance skiing. Experienced skiers seeking a leg-burner can attempt the Big 3 Rally, which conquers all three peaks in a marathon 50km, four-hour race. If that seems a little ambitious, the lively resort's 150km of slopes include many red and blue runs. The nearby Rettenbach and Tiefenbach glaciers are great for pre- or late-season cruising. The season here is one of the longest in Austria running from November to May and a weekly ski pass costs €228.50.

ARLBERG (TYROL/VORARLBERG)

Comprising the swish resorts of Lech (p379) and Zürs (p379) in Vorarlberg and devilish St Anton am Arlberg (p362) in Tyrol, the Arlberg (www.skiarlberg.at) features 276km of groomed slopes. Lech and Zürs mainly offer red and blue runs, although there is some trickier off-piste terrain. Thrill seekers head for St Anton to ride the brand-new Galzigbahn gondola, speed down off-piste runs below Valluga and test out Rendl's half-pipe and jumps. The après-ski scene here is unrivalled in Austria. A weekly pass costs €224.

SILVRETTA NOVA-MONTAFON (VORARLBERG)

Weather and avalanche reports in Austria's ski regions are updated daily on www.lawine.at.

Silhouetted by Piz Buin (3312m), the Montafon ski area (p378) stretches along a valley in the southeast corner of Vorarlberg. This peaceful region has a clutch of small, laid-back resorts ideal for finding your ski legs on gentle pistes or getting off the well-bashed slopes with ski touring. Serviced by 62 lifts, the 222km of pistes mostly appeal to beginners and intermediates. Alongside downhill skiing, abundant sledding tracks and winter hiking trails make Silvretta Nova–Montafon a family favourite. A weekly pass (€198.50) covers seven resorts, including Schruns/Tschagguns, Gargellen and Gaschurn.

CROSS-COUNTRY SKIING

Locally known as *Langlauf,* cross-country skiing in Austria is considerably greener and cheaper than skiing. Skis give you the traction to walk uphill at your own pace and live the beauty of the forest and mountains in slow motion. The two main techniques are the classic lift-and-glide method on prepared *Loipen* (cross-country tracks) and the more energetic 'skating' technique. The basics are easy to master and tracks are graded from blue to black according to difficulty. It costs around €15 to €20 to rent a pair of cross-country skis for the day.

Seefeld (p345) features among Austria's top cross-country skiing destinations, with 262km of tracks crisscrossing the region and a 3km floodlit

BEST SLOPES FOR...

■ **Families** Heiligenblut (p319) for its relaxed vibe and Bobo's Kids' Club; Filzmoos (p286) for its central slopes and off-slope activities such as horse-drawn sleigh rides.

■ **Snowboarding** For big air it has got to be Sölden (p357), with a half-pipe, two terrain parks and the Big 3 (three mountains above 3000m).

■ **Cruising** Kitzbühel (p350) for its perfect blend of blues, reds and blacks.

■ **Boozing** Après ski heavyweight? St Anton am Arlberg (p362) wins hands down. Hot contender? Ischgl (p360), dubbed 'Ibiza on skis' for its penchant for Europop and wild inebriation.

■ **Snow-sure slopes** Topping 3000m, the Hintertux Glacier (p349) and the Kitzsteinhorn Glacier (p313) offer deep powder for pre- and post-season skiing.

■ **Celebrity spotting** Lech (p379) and Zürs (p379) in Vorarlberg have earned their exclusive image with five-star pads welcoming royals, the filthy rich and supermodels on skis.

■ **Ultimate scream** Mayrhofen (p348) for the breathtakingly sheer Harakiri run. It's *very* steep, pitch-black, and there's no turning baaaaaack...

■ **Postcard scenery** Eschew the Jägermeister parties in favour of Montafon (p378), a pristine valley with diverse terrain, snug chalets and awesome Piz Buin views.

■ **Vista vultures** The views of the glaciated peaks of the Hohe Tauern National Park from the slopes above Zell am See (p312) will blow you away.

■ **Cross-country** Seefeld (p345) and Bad Gastein (p320) are perfect for living life in the slow lane with glorious mountain scenery and mile upon mile of cross-country trails.

■ **Night skiing** Hermagor (p301) is a great base for skiing Nassfeld's slopes, where one of Europe's longest floodlit runs at 2.2km lures after-dark skiers every Wednesday night.

stretch from Seefeld to Mösern. Zell am See (p312) is hot on its heels with 200km of groomed trails providing panoramic views of the Hohe Tauern mountains. Other great resorts to test your stamina and stride include the Bad Gastein region (p320), combed with 90km of well-marked cross-country trails.

SNOWSHOEING
It's immensely satisfying to make tracks through deep, virgin snow without sinking. Originally little more than strap-on tennis rackets, snowshoes have evolved into lightweight contraptions that allow you to shuffle through twinkling woodlands in quiet exhilaration. Many resorts in the Austrian Alps have marked trails where big-footed snowshoers can head up to the hills. It costs roughly €15 to €20 to hire a set of shoes and sticks for the day.

Prime spots to explore the snowy backcountry include Mayrhofen (p348), with around 45km of prepared trails, and Kitzbühel, (p350) where routes around the Kitzbühel Horn and Reith reveal the resort's tranquil side. During the winter season, guided snowshoe hikes depart from the tourist office at 9.45am from Monday to Friday (register in advance). The treks are €5 or free to visitors with a guest card.

SUMMER

CYCLING & MOUNTAIN BIKING
For many, Austria is best explored with your bum on a seat, freewheeling through the pristine countryside. The country is blessed with miles of well-marked cycle paths that pass through lowlands to the east and

mountains to the south and west. Whether you want to tear down the Alps, pedal through river valleys or ride rings around crystalline lakes, this two-wheel-friendly land has all the right ingredients. Warmer temperatures from May to October beckon cyclists, while downhill mountain bikers head to the Alps from late June to mid-September.

The local tourist offices usually stock brochures and maps on cycling and mountain biking. Cycle clubs are another good source of information; **Argus** (Map pp120-1; ☎ 01-505 09 07; www.argus.or.at, in German; Frankenberggasse 11, Vienna) has offices throughout the country and books (also in English) on the subject. Esterbauer's (www.esterbauer.com, in German) Bikeline books cover Austria's major trails in detail; they are in German but are reasonably easy to navigate. Freytag & Berndt and Kompass hiking maps are reliable sources for cycling, as they invariably have cycle trails marked.

City and mountain bikes are available for hire in most Austrian towns and resorts. Intersport has a near monopoly on rental equipment, offering a selection of quality bikes in 140 stores throughout Austria. Day rates range from €15 to €25 and the seventh day is often free on week rentals. All prices include bicycle helmets and there's a 50% reduction on children's bikes. Those that want to plan their route ahead can search by region and book a bike online (www.intersportrent.at).

Bikes can be taken on Austrian trains ÖBB (see p400). Many of the country's leading resorts have cottoned onto the popularity of downhill mountain biking and now allow cyclists to take their bikes on the cable cars for free or for a nominal charge in the summer season – maximising enjoyment and avoiding the sweat and strain of the uphill slog!

Cycling

The Alps offer a bumpy ride, but Austria has numerous flat trails that are less gruelling and sacrifice none of the splendour. Most of the routes circle lakes or follow the course of rivers and include those outlined following.

BODENSEE TRAIL

Plan your two-wheel adventure online at www.radtouren.at, with excellent info in English on cycling routes and bike-friendly hotels in Austria, plus maps, tips and brochures.

Touching base with Vorarlberg, the vast Lake Constance (p369) is easily explored by bike on a 270km cycleway that circumnavigates the lake through Austria, Germany and Switzerland. The route offers wonderful scenery – from forests to apple orchards and vineyards – fleeting views of the Alps and picnic pitstops at pebbly bays. Marked with red-and-white signs, the trail can be split into shorter chunks (see www.bodensee-radweg .com) making it a great option for families.

DANUBE TRAIL

Shadowing the Danube (p164) for 380km from Passau to Bratislava, this route's smooth trails make it popular with easy riders. The trail cuts a path through woodlands, deep valleys and orchards. A highlight is freewheeling past terraced vineyards, lofty cliffs and baroque abbeys in the Wachau. Green-and-white signs indicate the way on both sides of the river. For more details pick up Esterbauer's *Danube Bike Trail* (containing maps and instructions and practical information) or a free copy of the bilingual Donauradweg – Von Passau bis Bratislava.

INN TRAIL

Starting in Innsbruck (p331) and travelling 302km to Schärding, this trail sticks close to the turquoise Inn River. It's basically downhill all the way, passing through Tyrol, Bavaria and Upper Austria. You'll pedal through fertile farmland on Innsbruck's fringes, then alpine valleys dominated by castles in Kufstein and Bavaria. The final flat stretch zips through quaint villages and rolling countryside to Schärding. The route is well marked, but signage varies between regions.

SALZKAMMERGUT TRAIL

This 345km circular trail explores the lake-studded Salzkammergut, including Hallstätter See (p249), Attersee and Wolfgangsee. It's not exactly flat, but the trail is well marked and only a moderate condition is required. The scenic route contours around lakes set against an alpine backdrop – there's nothing like pausing for a refreshing dip in their waters to relieve saddle sore! To explore the area in greater depth, pick up Esterbauer's *Radatlas Salzkammergut*. The trail is signposted (R2) in both directions.

TAUERN TRAIL

Taking in some of Austria's most spectacular scenery, the 325km Tauern tour is not technically difficult, but cycling at high altitude requires stamina. It begins at the thundering Krimml Falls (p317), then snakes along the Salzach River with vistas of glaciated Hohe Tauern peaks. Veering north, the trail passes the hilltop fortress of Hohenwerfen and the salt mines of Hallein. The final leg leads you through Salzburg and the Saalach Valley onto gentle pastures around Braunau am Inn and Schärding. The trail is marked with green-and-white signs in both directions.

Mountain Biking

The Austrian Alps are a Mecca to mountain bikers, with its hairpin bends, backbreaking inclines and steep descents. The country offers 17,000km of mountain bike routes, with the most challenging terrain in Vorarlberg, Tyrol, Salzburg and Carinthia. Below is a sample of the tours that lure the super-fit and speedy.

SALZBURGER ALMENTOUR

On this 146km trail, bikers pedal through 30 Almen (mountain pastures) in three days. While the name conjures up visions of gentle meadows, the route involves some strenuous climbs up to tremendous viewpoints like Zwölferhorn peak. Green-and-white signs indicate the trail from Annaberg to Edtalm via Wolfgangsee (p260). Route details and highlights are given online (www.almentour.com, in German).

Surf www.bike-gps.com for downloadable GPS tours in Austria where you can get dirty on your mountain bike and www.bike-holidays.com for the best places to clean up afterwards.

DACHSTEIN TOUR

Hailed as one of the country's top mountain bike routes; this three-day tour circles the rugged limestone pinnacles of the Dachstein massif and blazes through three provinces: Salzburger Land, Upper Austria and Styria. You'll need a good level of fitness to tackle the 182km trail that starts and finishes in Bad Goisern, pausing en route near Filzmoos (p286). For details, see the website www.dachste inrunde.at.

SILVRETTA MOUNTAIN BIKE ARENA

Grazing the Swiss border, the Silvretta Mountain Bike Arena in the Patznauntal is among the biggest in the Alps, with 1000km of trails; some climbing to almost 3000m. Ischgl (p360) makes an excellent base with a technique park and plenty of trail information at the tourist office. The 15 freeride trails for speed freaks include the Velill Trail, involving 1300m of descent. Tour details are available at www.ischgl-bikeacademy.at, in German.

KITZBÜHEL

Covering 750km of mountain bike trails, the Kitzbühel (p350) region rates as one of Austria's top freewheeling destinations. Routes range from 700m to 2300m in elevation and encompass trial circuits, downhill runs and bike parks. The must-experience rides include the Hahnenkamm Bike Safari from Kitzbühel to Pass Thurn, affording far-reaching views of Grossglockner and Wilder Kaiser, plus the Ehrenbach trail with jumps, drops and natural obstacles.

STUBAITAL & ZILLERTAL

These two broad valleys (p345 and p346) running south from the Inn River in Tyrol are flanked by high peaks crisscrossed with 800km of mountain bike trails. The terrain is varied and the landscape splendid, with gorges, waterfalls and glaciers constantly drifting into view. Highlights feature the alpine route from Mayrhofen to Hintertux Glacier and the dizzying roads that twist up from Ginzling to the Schlegeisspeicher.

PARAGLIDING

Wherever there's a high mountain accessible by cable car and a constant wind, you'll find paragliding and hang-gliding in Austria. It's particularly exhilarating on bright, sunny days in the Alps, when the sky is dotted with people soaring above the pinnacles and floating effortlessly on thermal drafts.

Of the two, paragliding wins the popularity race, simply because the equipment is more portable. Many resorts have places where you can hire the gear, get a lesson, or go as a passenger on a tandem flight. Tyrol is traditionally a centre for paragliding, with narrow valleys and plenty of cable cars. A good place to head is Fly Zillertal (p347) in Zell am Ziller.

Find the best place to spread your wings in Austria at www.flugschulen.at; it gives a regional rundown of flight schools offering paragliding and hang-gliding.

CANYONING

If the thought of hurling yourself down crevices and abseiling down frothing waterfalls appeals, you'll love canyoning. This adrenaline-fuelled sport has established itself as one of the most popular activities in the Austrian Alps. Sliding through a gorge requires nerve and effort, but the ice-cold pools at the bottom provide welcome respite. Among the hundreds of crag-riddled destinations calling budding Indiana Joneses are Mayrhofen (p349), the Ötztal (p356) and St Anton am Arlberg (p362). Inquire at local tourist offices about canyoning specialists in the region. Canyoning is graded according to difficulty and length, with prices fluctuating between €45 and €90.

ROCK CLIMBING

It's impossible to have mountains without *Klettern* (rock climbing) and Austria is covered with rock-climbing opportunities. A good introduction for would-be Spidermen or women is the **Österreichischer Alpenverein** (p83), which advises on places to go and runs rock-climbing courses. Peilstein, in the Vienna Woods, is often used for such weekend courses. Other rock-climbing centres include Dachstein in Salzkammergut, Hochkönig near Salzburg, the Hohe Tauern National Park and Wilde Kaiser near Kufstein in Tyrol. Austrian mountaineer Peter Habeler (p89) runs a first-rate climbing school in Mayrhofen (p349), taking groups high up into the Zillertal Alps.

And they call it puppy love... If you thought only Brits were soppy about their pooches, check out the dedicated doggy paddle areas on the beaches at Millstätter See, Klagenfurt and Neusiedler See.

WATER SPORTS

Austria is dotted with more than 6000 lakes and a mammoth number of rivers coursing through its valleys that offer more than enough places to enjoy water sports.

GOING TO EXTREMES

■ **Go ahead, jump** Austria's mountains aren't the only high points. To discover Vienna's topsy-turvy side, take a deep breath and leap into oblivion from the needle-thin Donauturm (Danube Tower), the world's highest bungee jump from a tower. Daredevils can also plunge 192m from the Europabrücke bridge spanning the Sill River for a thrilling upside-down bounce.

■ **Gone with the wind** Kite-surfing is all the rage on Austria's lakes and it's about as much fun as you can have wearing a wetsuit. For a taste of the extreme water action, make a beeline for Neusiedler See in Burgenland, one of the few steppe lakes in Central Europe. Podersdorf am See is a great base to grab a board and catch the waves.

■ **An ice climb** If you thought regular climbing was slippery, try getting a grip on ice climbing! Scaling frozen walls and waterfalls is pure adventure, but you'll need a decent pair of crampons and a good instructor. Slide over to the Stubai Glacier (p345) in Tyrol to give it a go.

■ **Mind the gap** This is a tube with a difference – one that glides over hard-packed snow at jaw-dropping speeds. For a change, abandon your skis or sledge for the day and get your hands on one of these robust rings for heaps of fun spinning down the slopes in ski resorts like Sölden (p357) and Mayrhofen (p348).

■ **Going down…** If you think paragliding is for wimps, skydiving may be just the ticket. Rolling out of a plane at 4000m and freefalling for 60 seconds before your parachute opens is the ultimate adrenaline rush. Tandem jumps are available all over Austria – from Vienna to Graz and Salzburg (see www.skydive.at for details).

Got some fantastic tips about Austria that you'd love to share with Lonely Planet readers? Create your own Bluelist and upload it onto our website – www.lonelyplanet.com.

Zipping across lakes by wind power is the most popular water sport in the country, and the locals aren't bad at, if Olympic medals are anything to go by. Sailing, windsurfing and kite-surfing are all here to be had; the **Österreichischer Segel-Verband** (Austrian Sailing Federation; ☎ 02167-40 243-0; www.segel verband.at, in German; Seestrasse 17b, A-7100 Neusiedl am See) can provide a list of clubs and locations in the country. The Neusiedler See (p193) is the number-one lake for such activities (probably because Vienna is so close), followed by the lakes of Carinthia and Salzkammergut. Tyrol has the Achensee (p350) and Vorarlberg the Bodensee (p369).

Rafting, canoeing or kayaking the white waters of Austria's alpine rivers are other favourite pastimes. Big rivers which support such adrenaline sports include the Enns and Salza in Styria, the Inns, Sanna and Ötztaler Ache in Tyrol and the Isel in East Tyrol. Imst (p358) is a well-known centre for rafting. **Absolute Outdoors** (☎ 03612-253 43; www.rafting.at; Ausseerstrasse 2-4, Liezen) is a reputable company offering trips on all the above rivers.

When the sun's out, there's little that's more invigorating than a dip in one of Austria's lakes. Carinthia is famed for its pure waters, which can heat up to a deliciously warm 26°C in summer; Milstätter See (p307) and Wörthersee (p295) offer open-water swimming and scuba diving with great visibility. Salzkammergut is another prime spot for a summertime splash, in lakes such as Hallstätter See (p249) and Attersee (p259).

Austrians prudish? Nah. Ubiquitous nudist beaches reveal there's nothing they love better than stripping off. Hallstättersee, Millstätter See and even the Danube Island in Vienna are set up for skinny-dippers.

The closest thing to bathing in mineral water is taking a dip in one of Austria's pure lakes; these include Thiersee, Urisee and Plansee in Tyrol.

Walking in Austria

With its rugged peaks, crinkly valleys and sparkling rivers, Austria serves up some of Europe's finest landscapes – and the only way to truly discover them is by schlepping a backpack and hitting the trail. To the west the Alps flick out like a dragon's tail, luring hikers to its pointy pinnacles, while to the east the soft tapestry of vineyards and hillocks are tailor-made for lazy ambles. Seeing the morning clouds blanket the mountains, curling up by an open fire after an uphill trudge and witnessing the springtime eruption of violet and pink on alpine pastures are experiences that put hikers' senses on high alert.

Giving a walker the pick of the Alps is like giving a child the run of a sweet shop. Despite its accessibility, this country's high-altitude terrain is still laced with adventure: from flirting with mountaineering on fixed-rope routes in the Tennengebirge to scaling the limestone crags of the Dachstein massif to gazing up at the Hohe Tauern National Park's mantle of glaciers. For families and ramblers seeking something gentler, there are deep gullies, thundering waterfalls and meadows riddled with marmot holes to explore.

But it's the locals that give trekking in Austria its unique flavour. Lithe 70-year-olds nordic walking (walking with ski poles) in the hills and rock climbers limbering up on the north face before breakfast are proof that this land embraces all forms of walking with a passion. Further evidence is the mountain huts perched on every hillside, welcoming walkers with farm-fresh cheese, cool beer and cushy beds. Spending a night in one of these snug refuges is a highlight on any trek – a chance to natter with the locals, savour simple home cooking and delight in tumbling out of your bunk at 6am, just in time to see dawn tint the peaks gold.

UPPER AUSTRIA

★ Spitz-Schwallenbach Circuit

LOWER AUSTRIA

VIENNA

THE SALZKAMMERGUT

BURGENLAND

Gosaukamm Circuit

★ Puchberg to Schneeberg

Kaisergebirge ★ Circuit

Tennengebirge ★ Circuit

★ Obertrauen to Hallstatt

Rosengartenschlucht Circuit ★

Pinzgauer Spaziergang ★

STYRIA

VORARLBERG

TYROL

SALZBURG & SALZBURGER LAND

Krimml Falls Loop ★

HOHE TAUERN NATIONAL PARK

Radsattel ★ Circuit

Zillertal Circuit

CARINTHIA

★ Garnitzenklamm Circuit

GETTING STARTED

Because Austrians are such a well-organised bunch, and many spend their weekends walking in the mountains, an ever-increasing number of walking paths are indicated by red-white-red stripes on a handy tree trunk or rock, and regular signs point out the way ahead. The practice of marking mountain trails according to their difficulty started in Tyrol and is becoming more widespread. Paths are coded with the same colours that are used for ski runs: blue for easy, red for moderate (trails are fairly narrow and steep), and black for difficult (these trails are only for the physically fit; some climbing may be required).

Alpine huts make it easy to tackle many long-distance trails with little more than a day pack, but if you're keen to get out and stride during the summer rush hour (July and August) it's advisable to book ahead as the popular places fill up in a flash.

INFORMATION
Information Sources

The **Österreich Werbung** (Austria National Tourist Office, ANTO; ☎ 0810-10 18 18; www.austria.info) has offices throughout the world and should be your first port of call. A full list of contact details can be found on its website, along with walking information on everything from themed family jaunts to multi-day treks for serious hikers. It produces the free and up-to-date *Walk Austria Guide*, which you can order online and use to plan your route before setting off. Check out the regional tourist offices for details on province-specific hikes and free walking brochures.

Österreichischer Alpenverein (ÖAV, Austrian Alpine Club; ☎ 0512-595 47; www.alpenverein.at, in German; Wilhelm-Greil-Strasse 15, Innsbruck) is an excellent source for more specific and detailed information. Adult membership costs €48.50 per year, with substantial discounts for students and people aged under 25 or over 60; members pay half-price at alpine huts and receive other benefits including insurance. The club also organises walks but you have to either join the club or be a member of an alpine club in your home country; there is an arm of the club in England, the **Austrian Alpine Club** (☎ 01929-556 870; www.aacuk.org.uk; 12A North St, Wareham BH20 4AG). Of the 1000-odd huts in the Austrian Alps, 241 are maintained by the ÖAV; see p380 for further details.

Two other clubs worth contacting for information are the **Naturfreunde Österreich** (NFÖ, Friends of Nature Austria; ☎ 01-892 35 34-0; www.naturfreunde.at, in German; Viktoriagasse 6, Vienna) and the **Österreichischer Touristenklub** (ÖTK, Austrian Tourist Club; ☎ 01-512 38 44; www.touristenklub.at, in German; Bäckerstrasse 16, Vienna). The first concentrates on Austria's lowlands, while the second has an excellent **library** (🕑 4-7pm Thu). The majority of books on the Alps are in German, but there is an extensive collection of maps, which can be photocopied, and staff are supremely knowledgeable.

Maps

A great overview map of Austria is Michelin's 1:400,000 national map No 730 *Austria*. Alternatively, the **Österreich Werbung** (Austria National Tourist Office, ANTO; ☎ 0810-10 18 18; www.austria.info) can send you a free copy of its 1:800,000 country map.

There are plenty of high-quality walking maps to choose from, and paths are clearly indicated on all of them. The standard references at a 1:50,000 scale are produced by Freytag & Berndt (F&B) and Kompass. Both include small booklets, that list contact details for mountains huts and offering background information on trails. If you prefer larger-scale maps for walking, use the clear yet detailed Alpenvereinskarte 1:25,000 series. Many local tourist offices hand out basic maps that may be sufficient for short, easy walks. See the individual walks for specific map requirements.

The best place to stock up on maps in Austria is at a *Tabak* (tobacconist), newsagent or bookshop. Usually only local maps are available in these outlets, although bookshops in the major cities offer a wider selection. Outdoor-activities shops usually sell a limited variety of walking maps.

Books

The standard English-language walking guidebook to Austria has long been Cecil Davies' *Mountain Walking in Austria*. The book concentrates on the alpine areas of the country, but some route descriptions can be up to 20 years old. For a more contemporary treatment of multi-day routes, try *Walking Austria's Alps Hut to Hut* by Johnathan Hurdle. If you're keen to identify the local flora, Kompass publish *Alpine Flowers*, a pocket-sized guide complete with colour illustrations.

WHEN TO WALK

While the wildflowers and tinkling cowbells make summer (June to September) a top choice for *wandern* (walking), the sprightly Austrians don't let the dust gather under their boots the rest of the year – they accessorise. Deep powder? Snowshoes. Ice? Crampons. Slippery autumn leaves? A snazzy pair of walking sticks. Of course, if you're planning multi-day hikes in the Alps, summer is probably your only option, as Alpine huts only open from mid-June to late September.

The busiest months are July and August, when snowfields above 2000m melt and the weather is mostly fine. Spring offers fewer crowds and everything begins to bloom at lower altitudes. Autumn, too, is quieter and is a fantastic season to glimpse the mountains wrapped in a cloak of gold and crimson. Even winter walking isn't out of the question in the Alps; many resorts now cater to nonskiers with prepared *Winterwanderwege* (winter trails), and making tracks through squeaky snow with a crisp blue sky overhead is quite something.

If there's one rule of thumb in the Alps, it's to never take the weather for granted. It may *look* sunny but conditions can change at the drop of a hat – hail, lightning, fog, torrential rain, you name it – so the trick is to pack layers and check the forecast before embarking on long hikes at high altitudes. Taped regional Alpine weather reports can be heard on ☎ 0990-911566 81. Tourist offices also display and/or provide mountain-weather forecasts, while web forecasts also available on website of the ÖAV (www.alpenverein.at, in German).

WHAT TO TAKE

A light pack full of little necessities is the secret to happy hiking. It's tough walking on an empty stomach, so make sure you have enough carbohydrate-rich food for the day (including emergency rations) and at least 1L of water per person to avoid dehydration. High-energy foods such as nuts, dried fruits, bread, cheese and cured meats are ideal.

HUT-TO-HUT HIKING

One of the joys of hiking in Austria is spending the night in a mountain hut. These trailside refuges make great bases for exploring the wilderness without sacrificing creature comforts. The highly evolved system means you're hardly ever further than a five- to six-hour walk from the next hut, which removes the need to lug a tent, camping stove and other gear that weighs hikers down. Most huts have a *Gaststube* (living room), a convivial spot that hums with the chatter of ruddy-cheeked walkers, comparing notes and clinking glasses. With a belly full of dumplings and schnapps, you retreat to your comfy bunk and hope you haven't picked the one next to a champion snorer!

Austria has more than 1000 huts, over 500 of which belong to the **Österreichischer Alpenverein** (ÖAV, Austrian Alpine Club; ☎ 0512-59547; www.alpenverein.at, in German; Wilhelm-Greil-Strasse 15) or **Deutscher Alpenverein** (DAV, German Alpine Club; www.apenverein.de, in German). Huts in popular areas are more like mountain inns, with restaurant facilities, drying rooms and even hot showers (normally at an extra charge). Accommodation is in communal dorms called *Matratzenlager*, two- or four-bed rooms, or in the *Notlager* (emergency shelter – wherever there's space) if all beds have been taken. Blankets and pillows are provided but you might need to bring your own sleeping sheet. The lunchtime and evening menu is usually hearty and good value. Members of the ÖAV can order the *Bergsteigeressen* – literally 'mountaineer's meal' – which is low in price but high in calories, though not necessarily a gastronomic treat! On average, hikers should budget €8 to €10 for a basic meal with a drink. It's also sensible to carry tea or coffee, as *Teewasser* (boiled water) can be purchased from the hut warden.

Most huts open from mid-June to mid-September when the trails are free of snow; the busiest months are July and August, when advance bookings are recommended. Members of the ÖAV are entitled to a discount of up to 50% on the cost of overnight accommodation at ÖAV and DAV huts, so if you plan to undertake a hut-to-hut tour in Austria it's worth joining the UK section (p83); however, allow two months for your application to be processed. The ÖAV publishes the *ÖAV Hut Book for Austria* (in German, with key words in English), a comprehensive book on huts, with contact details and opening times. Consult p380 for further accommodation information.

Take lightweight layers that you can put on or take off to warm up or cool down. The basics include a breathable T-shirt, fleece, loose-fitting trousers, sturdy walking boots and waterproofs. For high-altitude hikes, it may also be worth packing a hat, gaiters, thermals, gloves and walking sticks. The sun can be extraordinarily deceptive in the mountains; while the air temperature may be subzero, the rays are still powerful and sunscreen is essential to avoid the lobster-skin and panda-eye look. Also consider taking a torch, first-aid kit, compass, mobile phone and a whistle for emergencies.

WALK DESCRIPTIONS

The times and distances in this chapter are provided only as a guide. Times are based on the actual walking time and do not include stops for snacks, taking photos, rests or side trips. Be sure to factor these in when planning your walk. Distances should be read in conjunction with altitudes – significant elevation can make a greater difference to your walking time than lateral distance. Grading systems are always arbitrary; however, having an indication may help you choose between walks. Easy refers to a short walk on gentle terrain, medium denotes challenging terrain and longer distances, while difficult indicates walks with long distances, significant elevation change and high-altitude or glacier travel.

RESPONSIBLE WALKING

The popularity of walking puts great pressure on Austria's natural environment, particularly the fragile ecosystem of the Alps. To minimise impact and help preserve Austria's ecology, consider the following tips when walking.

Trail Etiquette

Greeting your fellow walkers with a cheery *Servus* (Hello) and observing a few etiquette basics will stand you in good stead.

- On narrow paths, ascending walkers have right of way over those descending.
- Always leave farm gates as you find them. In summer low-voltage electric fences are set up to control livestock on the open alpine pastures; where an electric fence crosses a path, it usually has a hook that can be easily unfastened to allow walkers to pass through without getting zapped.
- The days of plucking edelweiss to woo your sweetheart are long gone. Alpine wildflowers look lovelier on the mountainsides and many of them are protected species.
- Moving too close will unnerve wild animals, distracting them from their vital summer activity of fattening up for the long winter.

Rubbish

- The idea is to carry out what you have carried in, including easily forgotten items such as tinfoil, orange peel, cigarette butts and plastic wrappers. Empty packaging weighs very little.
- Burying rubbish is not recommended as digging disturbs soil and ground cover, and encourages erosion. Buried rubbish will more than likely be dug up by animals, who may be injured or poisoned by it. It also takes years to decompose, especially at high altitudes.
- Minimise the waste you carry out by taking minimal packaging or unpacking small-portion packages and combining their contents in one container before your trip. Take reusable containers or stuff sacks.
- Condoms, tampons and sanitary pads should also be carried out, despite the inconvenience, as they burn and decompose poorly.

Human Waste Disposal

- Make an effort to use toilets in huts and refuges where provided.
- Where there is no toilet, bury your waste. Dig a small, 15cm-deep hole at least 100m from any watercourse; consider carrying a lightweight trowel for this purpose. Cover the waste with soil and a rock. Use toilet paper sparingly and bury that too. In snow, dig down beneath the soil; otherwise your waste will be exposed when the snow melts.
- Contamination of the local water sources by human faeces can lead to the transmission of giardiasis, a human bacterial parasite. It can cause severe health risks to other walkers, local residents and wildlife.

Erosion

- Mountain slopes and hillsides, especially at high altitudes, are prone to erosion. It's important to stick to existing

LONG-DISTANCE TRAILS

Austria's extensive hut network is ideal for those keen to do some serious trekking in the Alps. The website of the **Österreichischer Alpenverein** (ÖAV, Austrian Alpine Club; ☎ 0512-595 47; www.alpen verein.at, in German; Wilhelm-Greil-Strasse 15) has a dedicated section on the country's 10 *Weitwanderwege* (long-distance trails), which stretch from 160km to 1200km and showcase different areas of Austria's stunning landscape. Accessible from mid-June to late September, the following trails are a taste of what's on offer.

■ **Adlerweg** – Exploring Tyrol's finest scenery, the 280km Adlerweg (Eagle Trail) starts in St Johann near Kitzbühel (p350) and scales the Karwendel massif, before traversing the limestone crags of Wilder Kaiser and eventually landing in St Anton am Arlberg (p362). You'll need to be in good condition to attempt this challenging three- to four-week hike, with highlights including rugged peaks, waterfalls, ice caves and hilltop castles. See www.adlerweg.tirol.at for trail information and maps.

■ **Berliner Höhenweg** – This 42km trail begins in Ginzling (p350) and quickly gains altitude (the highest point is 3133m). There are bewitching views of the Zillertal Alps towering over the trail and the turquoise Schlegeisspeicher below. Some mountaineering experience is required as snow patches are not uncommon and there are several passes to tackle. The hike takes three to four days to complete. Use Kompass 1:25,000 map No 37 *Mayrhofen – Tuxer Tal Zillergrund*.

■ **Arnoweg** – The 1200km Arnoweg rates among Austria's best long-distance walks, making a circuit around Salzburger Land that takes roughly two months to complete. The official start and finish point is Salzburg (p266), but many walkers follow only the southerly stretch of the walk, which leads through the glacial landscape of the Hohe Tauern National Park (p310). The route ascends to 3106m, so a decent level of fitness is required. Rother Wanderführer map *Arnoweg Der Salzburger Rundwanderweg* covers the trail. See www.arnoweg.com for more details.

■ **Stubai Höhenweg** – Austria's showpiece hut-to-hut route, the Stubaier Höhenweg starts at Neustift in Stubaital. You'll need a good level of fitness to tread the well-marked 120km circuit, which affords tremendous vistas of hanging glaciers, rocky ridges and wild alpine lakes. Every section of the seven- to nine-day route involves battling at least one pass, and many sections have fixed wire ropes to assist with difficult steps. Buses run from Innsbruck to the Stubaital (p345). Pick up Kompass 1:50,000 map No 83 *Stubaier Alpen – Serleskamm*.

tracks and avoid short cuts that bypass a switchback. If you blaze a new trail straight down a slope, it will turn into a watercourse with the next heavy rainfall and eventually cause soil loss and deep scarring.

■ If a well-used track passes through a mud patch, walk through the mud; walking around the edge will increase the size of the patch.

■ Avoid removing the plant life that keeps topsoils in place.

SAFETY & EMERGENCIES

Most walker deaths are directly attributable to fatigue, heat exhaustion, and inadequate clothing or footwear. A fall resulting from sliding on grass, scree or iced-over paths is a common hazard; watch out for black ice.

In high-Alpine routes, avalanches and rock falls can be a problem.

As long as you stick to the marked route, it's hard to get lost in Austria, where most trails are signposted and well mapped. Study the weather forecast before you go and remember that weather patterns change dramatically in the mountains. Increase the length and altitude of your walks gradually, until you are acclimatised to the vast Alpine scale.

That said, where possible don't walk in the mountains alone. Two is considered the minimum number for safe walking, and having at least one additional person in the party will mean someone can stay with an injured walker while the other seeks help. Inform a responsible person, such as a family member, hut warden or hotel receptionist, of your plans, and let them know when you return. Under no circumstances should you leave marked trails in foggy conditions. With some care, most walking routes can be followed in fog, but otherwise wait by the path until visibility is clear enough to proceed.

The standard Alpine distress signal is six whistles, six calls, six smoke puffs – that is, six of whatever sign you can make – followed by a pause equalling the length of time taken by the calls before repeating the signal again. If you have a mobile phone, take it with you. **Mountain rescue** (☎ 140) in the Alps is very efficient but extremely expensive, so make sure you have insurance.

TYROL & VORARLBERG

ZILLERTAL CIRCUIT (TYROL)
Duration Five to six hours
Distance 11km
Difficulty Medium
Nearest Town Mayrhofen (p348)
Summary A high-level circuit that leaves a big impression, with relatively easy hiking providing tremendous views over the azure Schlegeisspeicher (Schlegeis Reservoir) to the Zillertal Alps.

The Zillertal Alps reward walkers with mesmerising views of flower-strewn meadows, gin-clear streams and frosted peaks. This scenic loop begins by climbing above the turquoise Schlegeisspeicher to join the high-altitude Berliner Höhenweg trail (opposite) at its westernmost point. It's a great mix of everything this mountainscape has to offer: babbling brooks, 3000m pinnacles, high meadows and pine woodlands. The highlight is the precipitous balcony trail that links two alpine huts. Although the route involves 850m of ascent and descent, the path is well graded and mostly gentle; however, you should use care and judgement in bad weather. Kompass 1:25,000 map No 37 *Zillertaler Alpen – Tuxer Alpen* covers the walk in detail.

Getting to/from the Walk
The Schlegeisspeicher is 25km southwest of Mayrhofen and is accessed by the twisting Schlegeis Alpenstrasse toll road, which is open from May to the end of October and costs €10 for a car. Alternatively, buses run between Mayrhofen and the reservoir (one

way €5.20, one hour, seven daily). The walk starts and finishes at the car park beside the reservoir. For details on transport to/from Mayrhofen, see p350.

The Walk
The circuit starts at the Schlegeisspeicher, which impresses with its sheer scale and colour – it seems like a glittering turquoise gemstone dropped into a sea of ice white pinnacles. From the northeast end of the car park, take the well-worn trail signed to the **Dominikus Hütte** (☎ 05286-52 16; mattresses/beds €19/25; ☽ mid-May–late Oct). The turn-off for this hut comes just 100m along the path, but you should stick to the right and head towards the Friesenberghaus. The trail is shown by red-and-white markings on the rocks, and it soon begins its gradual ascent through shady mixed forest. If you peer back, there are views of the mountains, which rise like the bows of a ship above the glacially cold reservoir.

Weaving through pine trees, the trail soon reaches two streams that flow swiftly over water-worn rocks; both are crossed via wooden footbridges. Pause to dangle your toes in the tingling water before continuing through the forest and past slopes that are speckled with wildflowers such as delicate alpine roses and purple gentian in summer. As the rocky trail snakes upwards, the scenery shifts to fields of dwarf pines, moss-clad slabs, and waterfalls that streak the rugged mountain faces silver. The clang of cowbells and the high-pitched whistle of marmots interrupt quiet contemplation on these upper reaches.

After roughly 45 minutes, you approach the tree line near the wooden cabin at **Friesenbergalm** (2036m). The trail flattens out here to traverse high meadows punctuated by tarns, which are rimmed by tufts of silky cottongrass and reflect the towering pinnacles above. Continue around a shoulder and enter a broad valley overshadowed by the immense bulk of the Hoher Riffler (3231m). Affording superlative views of the peaks crowning the horizon, the snaking path is well graded and largely constructed from rock slabs.

It is a further one- to 1½-hour ascent from the Friesenbergalm to Friesenberghaus, passing through boulder-strewn meadows that give way to patches of scree and the gurgling Lapenkarbach (Lapenkar Stream), which meanders through the valley. If you're lucky, you might spot chamois here, though you're

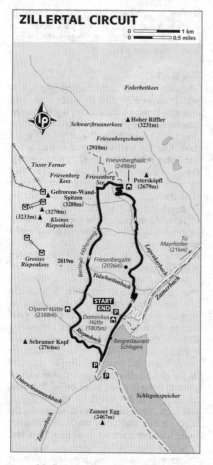

ZILLERTAL CIRCUIT

the valley to magnificent peaks including the Grosser Grainer (3201m) – Zillertal locals nickname it the Grauer (Grey) because of its steely colour – and its smaller sidekick, the Kleiner Grainer (2952m).

Retrace your steps for 50m and turn right along the path signposted to the Olperer Hütte and the Berliner Höhenweg. This begins by descending slightly to cross the outlet stream of the lake, then makes a steep but mercifully short ascent up the rocky slope on the other side. You may need to cross a few patches of snow near the start, which are generally easy to negotiate. Use your hands here for a short section of very easy scrambling. The ascent ends at a path junction; turn left and begin to contour across the mountainside ahead.

The next 1½ hours are spent following a wonderful balcony trail that leads under the 3000m-high glaciers of the Gefrorene-Wand-Spitzen. You'll definitely want to have your camera handy here, as there are fantastic vistas of the azure Schlegeisspeicher and the spiky peaks of the Zillertal Alps. The high-Alpine trail is part of the three- to four-day **Berliner Höhenweg** route, which starts in Ginzling and makes a circuit around the head of the valley. This section makes for interesting and easy-going walking, descending gently as it traverses rock-studded slopes and providing uninterrupted views of the reservoir.

Around two hours from the Friesenberghaus, the 2388m **Olperer Hütte** (☎ 05285-626 71; mattresses/beds €18/24; ✹ early Jun–early Sep) is suddenly revealed, though another stream crossing on wooden planks is necessary before you reach it. The hut is currently being rebuilt from scratch and is scheduled to reopen to walkers in 2008. From here, there are sterling views of the glacier-capped peaks of the Olperer and Zillertal Alps. As well as resident chickens, the hut is home to several Haflinger horses – a beautiful breed of mountain horse unique to this region.

After reaching this point, it's downhill all the way – pass in front of the hut and continue your steady descent to the reservoir. The path begins with more lovely scenery as it winds gently over grassy hummocks and crosses several ice-cold streams. The trail then steepens slightly and zigzags down beside a stream to the road (1½ hours from the Olperer Hütte). Turn left and follow the road for 1km to return to the damside parking area where you started.

more likely to bump into sheep and cows grazing on the pastures. The trail continues to wind uphill in a series of long bends until the Friesenberghaus slides into view. A series of tight switchbacks completes the climb to the hut, which is scenically perched above the valley.

Situated under the glowering face of Hohe Riffler and above a lake that remains ice-bound well into the summer months, the stone-built Deutscher Alpenverein (DAV; German Alpine Club) **Friesenberghaus** (☎ 0676-749 7550; mattresses/beds €16/22; ✹ mid-Jun–late Sep) is a popular base for long-distance hikers. It's a fine spot for a cool beer or a bowl of goulash before tackling the rest of the walk. After a little refreshment, take time out to appreciate the views across

ROCKET MAN: PETER HABELER

Celebrated Austrian mountaineer and ski instructor Peter Habeler was born in Mayrhofen in 1942 and has been scrambling up the glaciated peaks of the Zillertal Alps since the tender age of six. His one-time climbing partner Reinhold Messner said famously of Habeler: 'He's like a sky rocket – really impressive once the fuse is lit.'

By the age of 21, Habeler was a qualified mountain guide and rapidly gaining a reputation as a bold and talented climber. He began a partnership with Messner in the 1960s and together they pushed the boundaries of mountaineering. They soon applied their remarkable Alpine skills to race up the eight-thousanders of the Himalaya and pioneer the first ascent of Everest without supplementary oxygen in 1978. 'We climbed quickly and travelled light, taking only the bare essentials,' Habeler enthuses. 'Other climbers said it was suicide, but we knew that if Sherpas could reach 8500m, Everest was only a couple of hundred metres higher.'

'Extreme Alpinism has always been my goal and I was lucky enough to have fantastic teachers – the best there is,' he says emphatically. He believes, though, that respect for the mountains is declining. 'Alpinism is not about having the latest equipment or proving a point; it's about technique, condition and the ability to predict. There is freedom in the mountains but also restriction.' His secret? 'Taking the time to acclimatise is vital. We spent a couple of months at Everest base camp before making the ascent. Climbers should adapt to the mountains, befriend them. They are not enemies that need to be conquered. It's all about understanding your boundaries and those of the environment. Knowing when to call it a day.'

Today Habeler still stands out as a mountaineer: lean, chiselled and incredibly fit for his age. His passion for climbing is deeply rooted in what he affectionately calls his playground, the Austrian Alps, where he grew up and now runs a guiding company, Ski School Mount Everest (p349). He spends a lot of his time leading tours of the Zillertal Alps and speaks of his love for the Olperer (3476m) and his 'little Everest', the Ahornspitze (2976m). When he's not at home in Mayrhofen, Habeler occasionally pops over to Nepal to guide an expedition or dashes across to Hohe Tauern to climb Grossglockner. It seems there is no keeping this man of the mountains still.

KAISERGEBIRGE CIRCUIT (TYROL)

Duration Six to seven hours
Distance 18km
Difficulty Medium
Nearest Town Kufstein (p354)
Summary Deep ravines, meadows full of wildflowers and the perpendicular turrets of the Kaisergebirge leave walkers awestruck on this high-altitude hike.

The soaring limestone spires of the Kaisergebirge may not count among Austria's highest peaks, but they are undoubtedly some of its most spectacular. Rising abruptly from the valley floor, these distinctive peaks make perfect walking territory. This six- to seven-hour hike passes through beautiful deciduous forest and flower-dotted Alpine pastures before traversing the dizzying Bettlersteig, and affords vistas of both the Wilder Kaiser (Wild Emperor) and the gentler Zahmer Kaiser (Tame Emperor), divided by the fertile Kaisertal (Kaiser Valley). Sturdy footwear and waterproofs are recommended. You can pick up a basic map at the Kufstein tourist office or invest in the more detailed Kompass 1:

25,000 map No 9 *Kufstein-Walchsee-St Johann in Tirol.*

Getting to/from the Walk

The trailhead is Brentenjoch, at the top station of the Sesselbahn Wilder Kaiser in Kufstein (p355). There is a car park at the bottom of the lift (per day €2), or buses 1 and 2 run every 20 minutes from Kufstein to Kaisertal (one way €0.80), five minutes' walk from the bottom station of the chairlift. For full details on getting to/from Kufstein, see p355.

The Walk

The route begins on a high with a giddy ride on a creaking 1970s chairlift, which saves walkers plenty of legwork and certainly gets the adrenaline flowing. The lift glides over slopes wooded with beech and larch trees that are particularly spectacular in autumn when they turn shades of gold, amber and russet. As you approach the top station, the limestone pinnacles of the frost-polished Wilder Kaiser massif come into view.

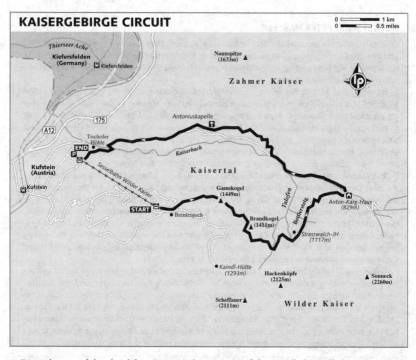

KAISERGEBIRGE CIRCUIT

From the top of the chairlift at **Brentenjoch**, take the narrow trail that veers left and leads downhill through Alpine meadows that are filled with purple thistles and gentian in summer. The zigzagging descent is easy and there are fine views of limestone columns dusted with snow ahead. Bear left onto the well-made path signed for Gamskogel, which initially winds through cool pine and beech forest. A glance left reveals the Kaisertal and pointy Naunspitze (1633m). After roughly 25 minutes, you reach a glade where you can spy Scheffauer (2111m) and Hackenköpfe (2125m).

Continue your gradual ascent on a rocky path, clambering over knobbly roots that form a natural staircase through the forest. The trail steepens on the final climb up to **Gamskogel** (1449m), approximately 50 minutes from the start of the trek. This is chamois territory and close encounters are quite common. At the summit, you are rewarded with stupendous 360-degree views of the rolling Zahmer Kaiser to the north and jagged Wilder Kaiser to the south. Take time out from your hike to relax and enjoy the wonderful pano-

rama of the Nördliche Kalkalpen (Northern Limestone Alps).

The woodland trail begins its descent to the Bettlersteig via a path bordered by dwarf pines and blueberry bushes that cling to crags. To the left is a sheer cliff that drops abruptly to the valley floor; to the right the Kaindl-Hütte drifts into view. The track now runs like a vein through the undulating *Alm* (Alpine meadow) studded with heather and bracken. A slight incline gives way to shady beech and maple forest, and brings the Wilder Kaiser ever nearer; its chiselled north face and rock formations now appear incredibly close.

Around 1½ hours from Brentenjoch is the infamous **Bettlersteig**, the route's toughest and most exhilarating stretch, which traverses a narrow wind-buffeted ridge. While sure-footedness and a head for heights are the only real prerequisites for attempting this stretch, caution should be exercised in bad weather, when the rock becomes slippery and danger-ous. Otherwise, it's easily negotiated via the cables and metal rungs hammered into the rock face that create a real-life high-altitude game of snakes and ladders. The scenery to the north is awesome: a ravine carpeted in luxurious shades of green and the imposing rocky summits of Zahmer Kaiser.

With the arduous bit behind you, the Bettlersteig heads on through beech and fir forest, and crosses the clear Talofen stream. This is about the closest you'll get to the north face of Wilder Kaiser, with its solid wall of limestone thrusting skywards and turrets crowding the horizon. Keep an eye out for chamois and deer in the forest on your way down to Strasswalch youth hostel, where an enormous fir tree provides respite from the midday heat. Further along the Bettlersteig, a trail heads right to **Sonneck** (2260m), a challenging and rewarding ascent for those with suitable experience and climbing equipment.

After another hour of traversing streams and negotiating switchbacks, walkers are generally glad to reach **Anton-Karg-Haus** (☎ 05372-625 78; mattresses/beds €17/22; ☺ May–mid-Oct) for a well-earned rest. The terrace is a pleasant spot for lunch when the sun's out, while a mug of *Milchkaffee* (milky coffee) with homemade shortbread is bound to boost hikers' spirits when the weather is drab.

It's a gentle and scenic 2½ hour descent to Kufstein from here. Tracing the meandering Kaiserbach (Kaiser River), the track leads steadily through the narrow Kaisertal and provides new perspectives of Gamskogel and the surrounding precipices – from this side you can appreciate how steep they really are! There is little change in elevation on the trail, which passes through beech forest and a tunnel hewn out of the rock face. Around an hour from Anton-Karg-Haus, look out for a path on the right that detours to **Antoniuskapelle**, a photogenic 16th-century chapel that is prized for its baroque sculptures.

An hour further on, an easily missed sign points the way to the **Tischofer Höhle**. This 40m-deep karst cave has a long and fascinating history; bones and fossils of *Ursus spelaeus* (cave bear) have been unearthed here, which are believed to date back around 26,000 years to the Pleistocene epoch. When Tyrol went to war in 1809, the cave was also used as a secret hideaway for the freedom fighters.

From the cave, the route continues downhill past overhanging crags and trees forming arches. As you descend, there are great views over Kufstein, and the clang of cowbells in the dairy farms below brings you gently back to civilisation. Finally, the path veers left along a road and crosses a field to the car park at the chairlift.

ROSENGARTENSCHLUCHT CIRCUIT (TYROL)

Duration Three hours
Distance 5km
Difficulty Easy
Nearest Town Imst (p358)
Summary This family-oriented walk has plenty of highs: from climbing a dramatic gorge to racing in a roller coaster to plunging into an Alpine lake.

This three-hour walk is one of Imst's hidden gems and is ideal for families seeking to stretch their legs in summer. The circuit begins by scaling the 200m-high Rosengartenschlucht (Rose Garden Ravine), where boarded walkways make for an easy ascent and the vertiginous views of a cascading river are memorable. The trail then weaves through shady pine forest, providing fine views of the Lechtaler Alps, and reaches a grotto with a glittering blue pool. Before descending to Imst, there is a chance to cool off in the pure waters of a tree-fringed lake and to pick up speed on one of the world's longest Alpine roller coasters. The walking is gentle, but sturdy footwear is recommended as some sections can get slippery.

For more details on this walk, pick up the 1:25,000 *Imst–Gurgltal* map from the tourist office (see p358) opposite the Johanneskirche in central Imst.

Getting to/from the Walk

The walk starts and finishes at the Johanneskirche (St John's Church), just across from the tourist office in central Imst. From here, there are signs to the Rosengartenschlucht, and the trail is well marked and easy to follow. For details on public transport services operating to/from Imst, see p358.

The Walk

The circuit begins on the path behind the frescoed Johanneskirche in Imst and shadows the crystal-clear Schinderbach (Schinder River) upstream to the entrance of the Rosengartenschlucht. On the right-hand side of the trail, take note of the unusual **Berghäusl**, cavelike dwellings that have been hewn out of the sheer rock face. Soon you'll catch your first glimpse of the river, which gushes through a narrow ravine gouged out during the last ice age. The cool, damp environment here supports a tremendous array of flora and fauna; as well as maple, ash, alder and larch trees are rarer species such as the red-winged wallcreeper bird and the wayfaring tree.

The wooden footbridge traversing the river is the first in a series of many that zigzag to the top of the gorge. From this low-level perspective, the scale of the cataract is impressive – vertical dolomite and limestone cliffs tower above, and a torrent of water cascades into pools that glint turquoise in the sun. The climb is gradual and easy, though care should be taken on some sections where rocks are loose underfoot and wooden planks are slippery; cables are occasionally provided to ensure a good grip. After roughly 20 minutes, the chasm narrows and the walk becomes more dramatic – you'll be ducking under overhanging rock faces, contouring around the cliffs and ascending steps carved into the rock. From the bench at **Schöne Aussicht** there are jaw-dropping views of the ravine above and below.

As you pass the fast-flowing river and charcoal grey cliffs speckled with moss, ferns and lichen, the trail twists through two tunnels hollowed out of the rock face that act as resonating chambers for the vibrations from the rumbling water. The fissure narrows further still to barely a slit, and it's almost possible to reach out and touch the other side. Light begins to flood the scene as you emerge at the **Holzbrücke** bridge after around 45 minutes; it's an excellent vantage point above the gorge and rapids, so have your camera handy.

After leaving the gorge, continue straight ahead on the well-prepared trail signed to **Hoch-Imst**. Still following the course of the Schinderbach, the sandy track cuts a path through fragrant pine forest and low scrub, providing panoramic vistas of the surrounding Lechtaler Alps, including the jagged peak of Muttekopf (2774m) and the wooded slopes of Hahntennjoch (1884m). With a bit of luck, you'll hear the cuckoos and woodpeckers that inhabit these woodlands.

A steady and gentle climb leads up through the forest and affords snapshot views of the verdant meadows and snowy summits ahead. Around an hour from the start of the walk, you'll emerge at the **Blaue Grotte**, a cave pool that turns a striking shade of blue when the sun hits it. The history of the grotto dates back 2000 years to when Romans searched these cliffs for semiprecious metals. Shortly after, the path veers right towards Hoch-Imst and

passes a stream flanked by a pebbly beach. Pause on the narrow forest trail to take a refreshing dip in the Badesee, an aquamarine lake ringed by fir trees; it's a peaceful and beautiful spot to while away the hours on a lazy summer afternoon.

Arriving in Hoch-Imst, approximately 1½ hours from the start of the walk, the real fun begins for kids. The **Alpine Coaster** (☎ 05412-663 22; Hoch-Imst 19; adult/child €9.70/7.80; ☺ 10am-5pm May-Sep, 10am-5pm Thu-Sun Oct) is billed as the world's longest Alpine roller coaster and offers a thrilling ride down the mountains. A gondola shuttles passengers uphill to the starting point, where they board self-controlled bobs to catapult 3.5km downhill, negotiating tricky bumps and hairpin bends. If ever there was an incentive to get the little 'uns to walk, surely this must be it!

From here, take the path next to the Sonneck apartments that skirts around the edge of houses and runs parallel to the Fit 2000 track (a fitness trail through the forest that is popular with joggers and nordic walkers). The trail soon begins its gradual and steady descent through fir and pine forest, where blueberries ripen on the bushes in summer. About halfway down, the **Wetterkreuz** comes into view; this cross atop a craggy hillock affords sweeping views across the rooftops of Imst, the broad Gurgltal and the snow-capped mountains that rise beyond.

Aside from occasional slippery roots and rocks, the forest trail is easy walking and winds down to **Am Bergl**, home to the tiny but beautiful Lourdeskapelle (Lourdes Chapel). On the way back down to Imst, culture vultures should also take a peek at the Pestkapelle, a chapel commemorating victims of the 17th-century plague epidemic, and the whitewashed Laurentiuskirche, one of Tyrol's oldest churches, which has a wood-shingle roof and relics dating from the 5th century. This path leads to the Kreuzweg, a centuries-old pilgrim route that eventually brings you back to the Johanneskirche.

RADSATTEL CIRCUIT (VORARLBERG)

Duration Five to six hours
Distance 15km
Difficulty Medium
Nearest Town Bielerhöhe (p378)
Summary A scenic mountain circuit exploring two valleys linked by a pass. Highlights include fabulous glacier scenery and rushing meltwater streams.

This scenic route makes a circuit of two of the valleys near the turquoise Silvretta Stausee reservoir, climbing over the Radsattel at 2652m to cross from one valley to the other. The 700m of ascent and descent means that it's not exactly a walk in the park, but it is relatively straightforward and there are great scenic rewards. The approach route brings you face-to-face with the mighty Piz Buin (3312m), the highest peak in the Silvretta range. Higher up, there are views of shimmering glaciers and long sections of path routed alongside tumbling alpine streams. An alternative finish offers experienced walkers the option of scrambling to the rocky summit of Hohes Rad (2934m). Kompass 1:50,000 map No 41 *Silvretta Verwall-gruppe* and F&B 1:50,000 map No 373 *Silvretta Hochalpenstrasse – Piz Buin* both cover the route, but Alpenvereinskarte 1:25,000 map No 26 *Silvrettagruppe* is more detailed.

Getting to/from the Walk

The circuit starts at the Silvretta Stausee. Situated at the top of the Silvretta Hochalpenstrasse toll road (car €11.50), the reservoir straddles the border of Vorarlberg and Tyrol at an altitude of 2034m. Bielerhöhe is the name given to the pass at the top of the Hochalpenstrasse, adjacent to the Silvretta Stausee. Frequent buses run between Partenen and Bielerhöhe in summer (p378).

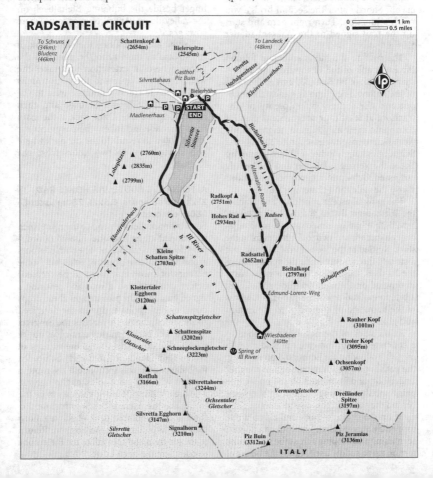

RADSATTEL CIRCUIT

0 — 1 km
0 — 0.5 miles

To Schruns (34km); Bludenz (46km)
To Landeck (48km)

Schattenkopf ▲ (2654m)
Bielerspitze ▲ (2545m)

Silvretta Hochalpenstrasse
Kleinvermuntbach

Gasthof Piz Buin
Silvrettahaus
Bielerhöhe

P P **START END** P
Madlenerhaus

Silvretta Stausee

Bielalbach

Lobspitzen
▲ (2760m)
▲ (2835m)
▲ (2799m)

Klosteralerbach

Ochsental

Bieltal / Alternative Route

Radkopf ▲ (2751m)

Hohes Rad ▲ (2934m) Radsee

Kleine Schatten Spitze (2703m)

Ill River

Radsattel (2652m)

Bieltalkopf ▲ (2797m)

Bieltalferner

Edmund-Lorenz-Weg

Klostertaler Egghorn (3120m)

Schattenspitzgletscher

Wiesbadener Hütte

▲ Rauher Kopf (3101m)

Klosteraler Gletscher

Schattenspitze (3202m)
Schneeglockengletscher (3223m)

Spring of Ill River

▲ Tiroler Kopf (3095m)

▲ Ochsenkopf (3057m)

Rotfluh (3166m)
Silvrettahorn (3244m)

Vermuntgletscher

Dreiländer Spitze (3197m)

Ochsentaler Gletscher

Silvretta Egghorn (3147m)
Signalhorn (3210m)

Silvretta Gletscher

Piz Buin (3312m)

Piz Jeramias (3136m)

ITALY

The Walk

From the Silvretta Stausee car park, walk over the dam and join the well-worn path that skirts around the reservoir's western shore, pausing to admire the views of the milky green lake framed by brooding peaks. Here you'll catch your first glimpse of the cone-shaped Hohes Rad (2934m), which you will be walking around later. A sign warns that stiletto-heeled shoes are not appropriate footwear! The path rounds the southern end of the lake, first crossing a bridge over the fast-flowing Klostertaler Bach; keep to the shoreline as you follow the route. Soon you'll traverse the glacially cold **Ill River**, which cuts a path through the Ochsental Valley at the southeastern corner of the reservoir. Shortly after the second bridge you reach a junction. Turn right here and start up the trail signed to the Wiesenbadener Hütte.

The path to the hut is wide and follows the east bank of the Ill towards the arrow-shaped peak of **Piz Buin** (3312m) at the head of the valley. The climb is steady throughout and the scenery offers plenty of distraction; at least four magnificent glaciers come into view as you gain height: to the west Schattenspitzgletscher (3202m) and Schneeglockengletscher (3223m), and up ahead the Vermuntgletscher and the heavily crevassed Ochsentaler Gletscher suspended above the valley and glistening ice blue.

The gradual ascent continues and reaches the **Wiesbadener Hütte** (☎ 05558-42 33; mattresses/beds €15/20; ☷ mid-Jun–early Oct) and its small adjacent chapel around two to 2½ hours from the start. Nestled at the foot of Piz Buin and just a stone's throw away from the spring where the Ill rises, this alpine hut is a great place to unwind on the sunny terrace, refuel with a bite to eat and enjoy the panoramic vistas of the surrounding snow-dusted mountains and glaciers.

At the back of the hut, signs attached to a concrete shelter indicate the Radsattel to the left. Following the Edmund-Lorenz-Weg, the path is now much narrower and rougher underfoot, and is marked by red-and-white paint splashes. Zigzag steeply up the slope behind the hut and cross a small stream. Keep right on the opposite bank and climb a rise topped by a large cairn. The path can now be seen rising and dipping across the undulating terrain up to saddle itself. Cross the outlet of a shallow pool before making the final steep climb to the narrow **Radsattel**, where a sign marks the Vorarlberg-Tyrol border (one to 1½ hours from the hut).

Drop steeply down the rocky, boulder-strewn eastern side of the pass, possibly crossing a couple of small snowfields near the top. There are great chances of spotting ibex up here (some of them are quite tame), so keep an eye out for their distinctive backward-curving horns. You will pass several small lakes and then the **Radsee**, a sparkling jewel-like lake fringed by greenery, on your way down to the Bieltal (Biel Valley). While this valley is less dramatic than the previous one, the smaller path and lack of hut makes it feel more remote, and it's certainly tempting to linger beside the bubbling Bieltalbach on the valley floor, flanked by meadows where cows graze.

Follow the path along the west bank of the stream all the way to the mouth of the valley, where an extraction unit takes the water from the river and the path widens into a vehicle track. Continue west to the banks of the Silvretta Stausee and turn right along the lake. Once back at the main road turn left and follow the pavement for about 300m to return to the car park where you started (1½ to two hours from the Radsattel).

ALTERNATIVE ROUTE: VIA HOHES RAD
2½ to three hours, 6.5km, 280m ascent, 980m descent

For a more challenging end to the route, turn left (north) at the Radsattel instead of dropping down into the Bieltal. The path contours around the eastern slopes of **Hohes Rad** (some patches of snow may need to be crossed) before climbing over a spur and reaching a signed junction. The path straight ahead drops down to Bielerhöhe and joins the described route shortly before it reaches the Silvretta Stausee. The path to the left scrambles up the rock to the cross that marks the summit of Hohes Rad. Hands will definitely be needed for balance over this section, but the route is marked with red paint splashes throughout. The breathtaking 360-degree views from the top make the extra effort worthwhile: Piz Buin and the pointed peak of Silvrettahorn (3244m) loom large on the horizon. Return to the junction and turn left to the Bielerhöhe to complete the circuit.

SALZBURGER LAND & SALZKAMMERGUT

GOSAUKAMM CIRCUIT (SALZBURGER LAND)

Duration Two days
Distance 22km
Difficulty Medium
Nearest Town Filzmoos (p286)
Summary A satisfying circuit that circumnavigates a limestone massive. It features towering rock pinnacles, a 200m pass and high forest trails.

Gosaukamm is the name given to the most westerly massif in the Dachstein range, a compact group of serrated limestone peaks containing seven summits over 2000m high. The scenery is reminiscent of the Italian Dolomites to the south: pinnacles and spires tower above sheets of scree and there is one section of magnificent limestone pavement. The lower slopes of the massif have vegetation, however, and this circuit undulates around the tree line. As the path circumnavigates the massif, the scenery alternates between pine forest and stark, rocky terrain.

The itinerary given here is for a two-day walk, and much of the climbing comes on the first day of the walk. The most challenging terrain comes around the Steiglpass (2016m), the highest point of the circuit. The ascent to the pass involves a series of ledges and gullies with moderate exposure. Cables are in place for security and most fit walkers should be able to negotiate the section, with a little care.

The porous limestone rock of the Dachstein range means that natural water sources are few and far between. On this route, the huts provide the only reliable sources of water. Make sure to fill up with enough water at each hut to last you until you arrive at the next one. F&B 1:50,000 map No 281 *Dachstein – Ausseer Land – Filzmoos – Ramsau* covers the route. Alternatively, for more detail, use the Alpenvereinskarte 1:25,000 map No 14 *Dachsteingebirge*.

Getting to/from the Walk

The Filzmooser Wanderbus runs regular shuttles between Filzmoos and Hofalm (€3.50, 15 minutes, five daily Sunday to Friday) from the end of May to the end of October. Regular bus services are provided by Postbus between Filzmoos and Eben (adult/child €2.70/1.40, 20 minutes, six daily Monday to Friday, three daily Saturday), where there are connections to Salzburg.

This route can also be accessed from the north, starting and finishing at the Gosausee, 7km south of Gosau village. The advantage of starting here is that you can use the **Gosaukammbahn** (☎ 06134-84 00; one way/return €7.30/10.70; ☽ 8.15am-4.50pm mid-May–Oct) to gain 550m in height and arrive directly at the Gablonzer Hütte.

The Walk

DAY 1: HOFALM TO GABLONZER HÜTTE
Five to six hours, 10km, 1120m ascent, 880m descent

From the Hofalm car park, take the path that leads north past two restaurants. Follow signs for the Hofpürglhütte, veering right after the second restaurant to begin climbing up to the left of a white limestone gully. The path is steep for most of the way, though the gradient eases somewhat towards the end. After climbing for about an hour you reach a junction at the top; turn left and continue for 200m if you want to take a break on the scenic terrace of the large **Hofpürglhütte** (☎ 06453-83 04; mattresses/beds €16/22; ☽ Jun-early Oct). Perched high on a grassy hillock, the hut commands tremendous views of the jagged turrets that frame the horizon.

To continue the route retrace your steps and continue straight ahead at the junction where you joined the path to the hut, following signs to the Steiglpass. The path to the pass can be seen zigzagging up the rock wall ahead, though you must descend across a shallow cirque before you start the climb. Photographers will want to capture the distinctive profile of the **Grosse Bischofsmütze** (2458m) on the left-hand side; shaped like a bishop's mitre, this is the highest peak in the Gosaukamm range. The ascent begins over loose stones but crosses the crags themselves in the upper reaches, negotiating the most challenging terrain of the entire circuit. You are likely to need your hands for balance as you cross rock ledges and mount stony steps, and a moderate amount of exposure keeps your attention on the task at hand. Fortunately cables are in place for security where required.

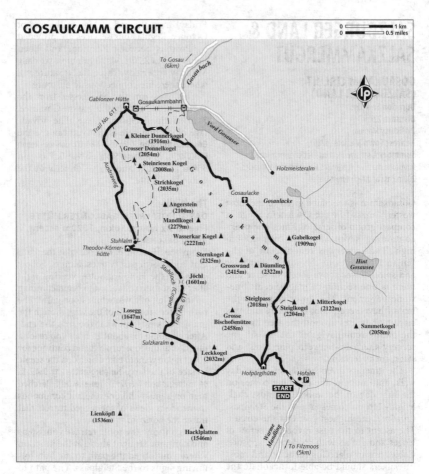

GOSAUKAMM CIRCUIT

Around one hour from the Hofpürglhütte, you arrive at the **Steiglpass** (2018m), where you may have to traverse the occasional snow-field, even in summer. You are now right up amongst the pinnacles and spires on the main ridge of the Gosaukamm massif, and the views are impressive in both directions: Grosse Bischofsmütze, Däumling (2322m), Gabelkogel (1909m) and the formidable glaci-ated peaks of the Dachstein massif are all vis-ible. It's little wonder that for many walkers, the pass is the highlight of the circuit.

The trail continues to cross the pass and be-gins to descend gradually though a wonderful lunar landscape of limestone pavement and escarpments. You descend several rock steps and one small gully, but the obstacles serve

as entertaining distractions rather than real challenges. The path eventually weaves out of the rock, and continues to descend gently through pine and larch woodlands, which are a riot of colour in autumn. Around one hour from the pass you reach a small, triangular-roofed memorial chapel, the **Gedenkkapelle**, in a clearing to the left of the path. The memorial commemorates all those who have perished in the mountains of the area, and in particular the 18-year-old first female ascendant of the nearby Däumling pinnacle, who died during the descent.

Continue to weave through the wood, passing several cabins. The deep green waters of the Gosausee soon come into view to the right and the switchbacks steepen into a steady descent. Keep an eye open for the junction signed to the Gablonzer Hütte. Turn left onto a much fainter trail (a sure sign that most walkers descend to the Gosausee here) and traverse the slopes to join the main Gosausee–Gablonzer path.

This well-trodden path begins by climbing steeply but eases as it passes through a grove of beech trees. Join a gravel track at the top of the climb, turn left and continue for 200m to the **Gablonzer Hütte** (☎ 06136-84 65; mattresses/beds €18/24; ✆ Jun–mid-Oct), around 1½ to two hours from the memorial chapel. The sunny terrace of the hut has a great view southeast to the ice-capped summit of Hoher Dachstein (2995m), which is the highest peak in the Dachstein range.

DAY 2: GABLONZER HÜTTE TO HOFALM
4½ to 5½ hours, 12km, 360m ascent, 600m descent

Begin by climbing the hillock directly opposite the entrance to the hut, following the signs to Austriaweg and Theodor-Körner-Hütte (trail No 611). At the top of the hill, veer right, pass through a metal turnstile, and begin to descend gently through shady fir, pine and larch forest. The path picks a way through the vegetation and re-emerges at the open pasture around the Stuhlalm. Here you join a broad track, turn left and pass a cluster of wooden huts, where refreshments, food and accommodation are available. Continue along the track for a further 500m to reach the picturesque **Theodor-Körner-Hütte** (☎ 0664-916 6303; mattresses/beds €10/14; ✆ Jun–mid-Oct), 1½ to two hours from the start.

From the Theodor-Körner-Hütte, return along the access track for 100m and veer right onto a footpath signed to the Hofpürglhütte. A descent brings you into a cirque bordered by dwarf pines, Stuhlloch, where jagged limestone pinnacles begin to dominate the skyline once more. Contour around the base of the cirque and you will be presented with the most exciting part of the day's route: a steep, zigzagging climb between the sheer rock walls of a narrow gully. Your passage through this dramatic ravine is eased by a long flight of steps and occasional sections of cable. The **Jöchl** (1601m), at the top of the gully, is reached around 40 minutes after leaving the Theodor-Körner-Hütte.

The path now makes an undulating traverse across a series of meadows, passing over several spurs and keeping left at four trail junctions. Alpine roses and gentian bloom on this high grassland in early summer, and there's a chance you'll glimpse chamois and marmots. A final shoulder is rounded and the Hofpürglhütte comes into sight on a ridge ahead. Contour across to the hut, arriving 1¼ to 1¾ hours after leaving the Jöchl.

To return to the Hofalm, retrace your original ascent route from day one (45 minutes). If you plan to return to Filzmoos by foot, however, you may prefer to take the path that leaves from the front terrace of the Hofpürglhütte and descend gently through woodland before joining the Hofalm road for the final few kilometres to the village; if you chose this option, add one to two hours to the day's duration.

TENNENGEBIRGE CIRCUIT (SALZBURGER LAND)

Duration Eight to nine hours
Difficulty Medium to difficult
Distance 15km
Nearest Town Werfen (p285)
Summary A high-altitude trail around a vast limestone plateau. Highlights include enthralling climbs, steep descents and memorable views of the Hochkönig massif.

Slung high above Werfen, the Tennengebirge is a karst plateau that is wild, isolated and beautiful in its austerity. Trekking through this surreal landscape of rounded heights, snow-filled cirques and sheer cliffs is a one-off experience. If you're keen to get off the well-trodden track, this day hike offers challenging walking involving almost 1000m of ascent and some scrambling. Walkers should have a good head for heights and be sure-footed for the initial climb and steep descent; undertaking this trek alone is not recommended.

Snowfields mean that this hike is best attempted from July to early September, and an early start is essential. Aside from emergency shelters, there is very little up here, so you should pack enough food and water for the day. Paths are waymarked, but you'll need a proper map, such as Kompass 1: 50,000 map No 15 *Tennengebirge Hochkönig*, and possibly a compass.

Getting to/from the Walk

Take the cable car (one way €4.50) to Achsenkogel and walk roughly 15 minutes uphill to the trailhead. The trek starts on the right-hand side of the path winding up to Eisriesenwelt. For further details on getting there and away, see p285.

The Walk

Heading up on the path between the cable-car top station and Eisriesenwelt, take the narrow trail on the right, signed Steig (trail No 212), towards Leopold-Happisch-Haus, indicated by a red-and-white stripe on the rocks. The hardest climbing of the day's trek starts here with loose rocks underfoot, a steep incline, and a breathtakingly sheer 1000m drop to your right. While the going isn't easy, the awesome views more than compensate: below, the Salzach River snakes through pastures that form a rich patchwork of greenery, while ahead the towering limestone cliffs are scored with crevices and riddled with caves. The sign *Steinschlag Möglich* reminds hikers to keep their distance from the cliffs because of falling rocks.

The precipitous track contours around the cliff face, passing slopes covered in dwarf pines, and affording head-spinning views of the valley below and the summits above, including **Hühnerkrall** (2289m). Sporadic cables ensure safety, but sure-footedness and a sturdy grip are needed as you clamber up and over the rocks. This exposed section of the trek is undoubtedly exciting, but it can be torturous under a blazing sun, so it's advisable to tackle it early. The zigzagging ascent quickly gains elevation and involves some easy scrambling. The icing on the cake, however, is climbing two (slightly wobbly!) ladders that scale the vertical rocks and get the adrenaline pumping. The trail crosses piles of scree and passes a memorial on the left-hand side, which commemorates two mountaineers who lost their lives here in 1994.

Around two hours from the trailhead, there's a sense of achievement upon reaching the magnificent karst plateau, a vast, grey desert of undulating limestone where snowfields often linger till summer. The Jagdhütte emergency shelter lies to the left, but you should sidle right and follow the signs for Leopold-Happisch-Haus. Bordered by dwarf pines and tussock grass, the path traverses the plateau and leads gently up natural steps hewn into the rock. When clouds cast

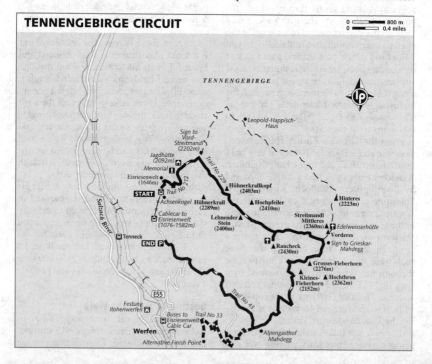

TENNENGEBIRGE CIRCUIT

shadows across the contours of this rugged and starkly beautiful landscape, the effect is otherworldly.

The trail climbs further and, glancing back, the jagged pinnacles of the Hochkönig range are visible. Roughly three hours into the hike, keep an eye out for the sign to Vord-Streitmandl (trail No 229). This track continues to scale the ridges of the plateau, but is now waymarked with a red dot in a white circle (similar to the Japanese flag). It can be tricky to stay on the path if there are snowfields, as the markings are sometimes obscured, so particular care is needed when traversing the bowl-shaped depressions and cirques. Though challenging, the walking here is extremely satisfying and the far-reaching views reveal the Alps tumbling down to the flats, including the twin peaks of Hühnerkrallkopf (2403m) and Hochpfeiler (2410m) to your left.

The trail soon emerges in front of the dramatic **Lehnender Stein** (2400m) precipice, which provides heart-stopping views of the valley below. These cliffs are home to nesting eagles and, while you may spot one if you're lucky, you're far more likely to hear their high-pitched screech. Another pleasant half-hour is spent wandering past steely turrets before weaving up a rocky path to the exposed and wind-buffeted peak of **Raucheck** (2430m), the highest mountain in the Tennengebirge range. The amazing views from the summit, marked by a silver cross, make all the puffing and panting worthwhile: the 360-degree panorama of the Northern Limestone Alps is difficult to drag yourself away from.

Around six hours from the start of the hike, it's all downhill on the trail veering right signed to **Grieskar-Mahdegg**. While the prospect of skipping down the hillside may seem like a breeze after all that climbing, the tough descent is designed to test tired legs and is easily underestimated. The track zigzags down a deep ravine, where care is needed climbing over weatherworn limestone dotted with fissures and sinkholes. Look back to admire the spectacular trio of horned peaks: Grosses Fieberhorn (2276m), Kleines Fieberhorn (2152m) and Hochthron (2362m).

The trail descends relentlessly for roughly another hour, traversing rocks and a ladder before culminating in a series of tight switchbacks down extremely steep slopes of scree and boulders. The fabulous vistas of the **Hochkönig** massif's pinnacles crowding the horizon bolster waning spirits and there are good chances of sighting the nimble-footed chamois that inhabit these upper reaches. It's quite a relief to catch sight of the first dwarf pines speckling the slopes, as these signal your gradual approach to the tree line.

The relief at reaching the tree line is overwhelming – finally earth that does not slip or slide! The narrow trail now weaves through pine forest and becomes much flatter and easier, though the gnarled roots and leaning trees can be a bit of an obstacle course. After a steady hour-long march, the **Alpengasthof Mahdegg** sails into view. Keep your eyes peeled for the small sign indicating the trail (trail No 43) that will take you back to the starting point, which winds through shady beech and fir forest, and provides snapshot views of Werfen. Eventually the path brings you out onto the road to Eisriesenwelt; turn right, and the car park is about 10 minutes' stroll. The alternative is to take the zigzagging route (trail No 33) from Alpengasthof Mahdegg down to central Werfen, which takes just under an hour.

OBERTRAUN TO HALLSTATT (SALZKAMMERGUT)

Duration Six to seven hours
Distance 18km
Difficulty Easy to medium
Nearest Town Obertraun (p252)/Hallstatt (p250)
Summary A picturesque and spectacular walk around the shores of the pristine Hallstätter See (Lake Hallstatt) against a backdrop of towering mountains, with opportunities for swimming.

The Hallstätter See is a magnificently pristine lake in the Salzkammergut region, surrounded by soaring peaks and providing excellent opportunities for summer swimming. Few trails in Austria match this circuit for lakeside beauty. The walk initially follows the shore of the lake along the easy and mostly level Ostuferwanderweg (Eastern Shore Hiking Trail) from Obertraun, joins the historic Soleweg (Brine Pipeline Trail) at the northern end of the lake, then continues along this winding and spectacular trail past a waterfall to Rudolfsturm, a scenic lookout-restaurant above Hallstatt. The section along the eastern shore can be done any time of year and in any conditions, while the Soleweg requires a good level of fitness, good shoes and a reasonable head for heights. Children will need careful supervision in this section. The Soleweg section should be attempted in winter only in good conditions and with appropriate clothing.

Getting to/from the Walk

This walk begins in Obertraun and heads anticlockwise around the lake. It is also possible to start at Rudolfsturm in Hallstatt. From Obertraun train station, follow the line northwest along Bahnhofstrasse for 200m, cross the line and veer right. The trail begins just after the ferry terminal, 10 minutes' walk from the tourist office.

The Walk

After leaving Obertraun, follow the trail above the lake shore around the forested **Sechserkogel**, with its rocky outcrops. If you are combining a hike with a swim, the bluff is one of the more attractive places for swimming off rocks, although it's best approached from the water itself. However, there are plenty of other opportunities to paddle or swim along the eastern shore.

After 1.5km the trail leads across the Hallstatt train station and, shortly after, continues along a walkway attached to the rock face above the water. This is the deepest section of the Hallstätter See (125m). This part of the walk affords some splendid views up the lake between the wonderfully carved rock faces flanking the valley, petering out at the northern tip of the lake at the settlement of Steeg and the mouth of the Traun River.

From the walkway, the trail continues along a gravel path among riverbank acacias, pines, larch, fir and beech. This is also a botanical theme path, so the vegetation is often marked along the way. Keep left at the fork in the trail (and at all forks on this section). From here it is about another 15 minutes' walk along the water's edge to **Seeraunzn** (☎ 0676-433 12 63; Obersee 41; mains €5.50-12; ☼ 10am-8pm Easter Sun-Oct), a lakeside restaurant that is a great place to recover strength for the tougher Soleweg leg of the walk.

About 1½ hours into the Ostuferweg section the trail approaches Steeg and joins a small access road leading under the railway line. Follow the trail left and around. At the T-junction, Strandbadstrasse runs left under the railway line again to the **Steeg public beach**.

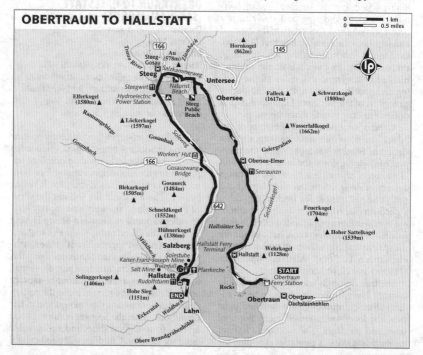

OBERTRAUN TO HALLSTATT

IN THE FOOTSTEPS OF PILGRIMS

A historic path, the Pilgrim's Way (Pilgerweg), connects St Gilgen and St Wolfgang via the western shore of the Hallstätter Sea (Lake Hallstatt). In the past pilgrims followed this path to honour St Wolfgang, the bishop who was said to have founded the church in St Wolfgang village by throwing his axe from the Falkenstein hill into the valley below and building the church on the spot where it fell.

The walk takes half a day and maps are available from the tourist offices in St Wolfgang and St Gilgen. The path starts from Furberg, near St Gilgen, and climbs the Falkenstein (795m) before continuing through the village of Reid to St Wolfgang. Apart from the fairly steep climb to the top of the Falkenstein, the walk isn't too strenuous (remind yourself that many pilgrims did it with lentils in their shoes or naked with iron rings around their necks as a sign of penance!). There are various things to see along the way, including a stone that still apparently bears the marks of the St Wolfgang's buttocks. It became as soft as wax in a miracle sent by God to allow the saint to rest his weary bones.

This (clothed) beach area has sunbathing platforms, a diving board and a children's slide. Beyond this (across the creek) is the rather swampy but lovely **FKK naturist beach**. Experienced swimmers can shorten the walk by tackling the 500m across the mouth of the Traun River (don't forget to bring your watertight bag and check out the water temperature first). If you do this, aim for the small clearing at the camping ground. You will need to walk back towards the power station from there to resume the walk.

Walkers should backtrack from the beach to the T-junction and keep going straight before turning left at the fork with the traffic mirror and crossing the small bridge. Here the Salzkammerweg (trail No A17) ascends into a grove of trees above the cliffs, or alternatively you can take the road (Arikoglstrasse) at the foot of the cliffs. After about 750m, those taking the cliff path will reach the road; head left and about 100m later turn right into the trail at the orchard. Walkers following Arikoglstrasse should turn left into this trail at this orchard; follow it around to the B166 main road.

This section is the least attractive part of the walk, but the lovely beer garden at riverside **Steegwirt** (☎ 06135-8302; Au 12; mains €8-12; 🕑 10am-9pm, closed Tue Nov-Mar) offers relief.

From Steegwirt, cross the Traun River, follow the road south for about 150m past the hydroelectric power station and turn right onto Salzstubenweg. This ascends for another 150m to join the **Soleweg** to Hallstatt.

Forget all about low lakeside trails now. The Soleweg (also called in parts Soleleitungsweg) follows the precarious path hacked into the Ramsau mountains between 1597 and 1607 for a pipeline, which transports brine from the nearby salt mines. It is reputed to be the oldest in the world and was originally made from hollowed-out tree trunks fitted together.

Approximately 1.5km from the point where you join the Soleweg, the trail leads past a small **workers' hut** (admission free; 🕑 summer), which contains a small exhibition (in German) on the pipeline and salt in the region. Just after this is one of the walk highlights: the 43m-high **Gosauzwang** bridge spanning a gorge carved out by the **Gosaubach** (Gosau Brook).

Sections of the walk after the bridge require care in parts, especially the stretch from a 2.5km marker to the turn-off to Hallstatt. In several places you will need to duck beneath rocks and avoid dripping water while making sure you keep your distance from the steep edges of the path. But the rewards here are many, with some great views to the lake.

The trail divides at the 1km marker the trail divides. The path to the left leads 500m down into Hallstatt, emerging behind the 15th-century **Pfarrkirche** (p251). If you're approaching the trail from the opposite direction, this is an easy entry point, but you will miss the sensational views from the Rudolfsturm.

The trail to the right becomes steep and narrower, passing a **Solestube**, where the volume and pressure of brine in the pipes is controlled. As you ascend, Hallstatt can be glimpsed below through the trees. About 300m after a steep climb, you reach a **lookout** and the **Kaiser-Franz-Joseph mine**. Steps from here lead past a **waterfall**, where the Mühlbach tumbles down a rock face towards Hallstatt. Finally, after crossing an iron bridge and negotiating more steps, this dramatic trail reaches a grand climax at **Rudolfsturm** (☎ 06134-206 77; Am Salzberg; dishes €4.50-16; ☽ 9am-6pm May-Oct). The fort, built in the 13th century to protect the salt mines, today offers fine food and views from its hilltop location, 800m above the lake. The historic **salt mine** and archaeological area are just a short walk west of here. To end your walk, the **funicular** (one-way adult/child/family €5.10/3.10/10.80) – or alternatively a switchback trail – take you down to Hallstatt.

HOHE TAUERN NATIONAL PARK REGION

PINZGAUER SPAZIERGANG

Duration Five to six hours
Distance 19km
Difficulty Easy to medium
Nearest Town Zell am See (p312)
Summary Easy walking on grassy ridges allows you to enjoy the fantastic views into the Hohe Tauern National Park without serious effort.

This perennially popular day hike in the Kitzbühel Alps combines gentle walking with wonderful Alpine scenery. Sun-dappled woodlands soon thin out and give way to high pastures that are a delight to walk through. To the south is a host of snow white peaks to ogle, including the glaciated summits of Grossglockner and the pyramid-shaped Kitzsteinhorn, while to the north the limestone turrets of the Kaisergebirge and Watzmann slide into view.

In its entirety, the Pinzgauer Spaziergang stretches 32km from the summertime boating playground of Zell am See in the east right across the crest of the range to Mittersill in the west. Covering the second stretch from Schmittenhöhe to Saalbach, this five- to six-hour amble takes in the highlights of the trek without the hard slog. It's generally easy to stick to the trail, but Kompass 1:30,000 map No 30 *Zell am See – Kaprun* might come in handy.

Getting to/from the Walk

The walk starts from the top station of the **Schmittenhöhebahn** (☎ 06542-789-0; one way €16; ☽ 9am-5pm mid-May–mid-Jun, 8.30am-5pm mid-Jun–Oct) in Zell am See. Gondolas depart roughly every half hour. For details on public transport connections to/from Zell am See, go to p316.

The walk finishes at the bottom station of the **Schattberg X-press** (☎ 06541-62 71 10; one way €6.90; ☽ 9-11.45am & 1-4.15pm mid-Jun–Sep), located right on the main road in Saalbach. Bus 680 runs every hour from Saalbach to Zell am See (€3.70, 30 minutes); the last bus departs at 7.15pm.

The Walk

From the top station of the Schmittenhöhebahn (1965m), follow the signs to Saalbach and the Pinzgauer Spaziergang. The views are immediately spectacular: to the east the glistening Zeller See is a blotch of inky blue on the Salzach Valley more than 1000m below, while to the south the 3000m summits and pearly-white glaciers of the **Hohe Tauern National Park** spread out before you. The well-prepared trail gently descends a ski slope flanked by fir trees, passes a chairlift and emerges at Kettingtörl. A slight incline brings you to a flat ridge bordered by heather and bilberry bushes, commanding views across undulating alpine pastures.

Waymarked by a red-and-white stripe, the path soon narrows. Following the ridge trail through fir forest studded with deep blue tarns, your gaze is often drawn left to a stunning line-up of snowy peaks including Austria's highest, Grossglockner (3798m), and the glistening Kitzsteinhorn glacier (3203m) in the foreground. This view, subtly changing all the time, remains with you for the most of the walk. You soon emerge out of the forest onto a stony trail, where the panorama opens up to the south and the landscape is a patchwork of heather, dwarf pines and ponds that reflect the scenery above. From here, you'll catch your first glimpse of the rounded summit of **Maurerkogel** (2074m), which is still dusted with snow in early summer.

It's now an easy amble along a snaking track through pastures where cows graze peacefully and colourful wildflowers such as gentian and alpine roses bloom. After nearly an hour of walking, the track contours around the southern slopes of the Maurerkogel and you'll see the knobbly summit of Oberer-Gernkogel (2175m) ahead. Continue along the path, crossing the occasional meltwater stream, and you'll spy the wooden hut at Sonnenbergalm on the left-hand side. It's now a short and painless ascent to the saddle of **Rohrertörl** (1918m), where you can contrast the snow-free rocky limestone ranges to the

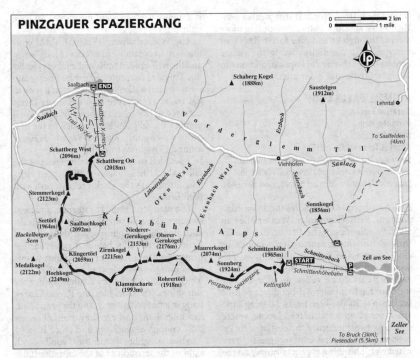

north, such as the chiselled Kaisergebirge range, with the more distinctly alpine, glaciated Hohe Tauern peaks to the south.

Passing two junctions, continue along a fine balcony trail that begins by contouring around the base of Oberer-Gernkogel and gently mounting the slightly lower **Niederer-Gernkogel** (2153m), before making its way down the other side to Klammscharte (1993m). If you're attempting this walk in early season, there is a high possibility that you will have to traverse a few snowdrifts. You're now at the foot of Zirmkogel (2215m) which, if you have the will and expertise, can be climbed in little more than an hour. The rocky trail cuts a path through high meadows carpeted with gold-tinged tussock grass and punctuated by boggy tarns. The sharp peak of Hochkogel (2249m) draws ever nearer.

The narrow trail now runs like a vein through mountains whose mottled greenery resembles a tortoise shell. Shortly you'll reach a small hut near a cool stream that is a great spot to take a break. Around four hours from the start of the trek, the path veers right and ascends a fairly steep incline to **Klingertörl**

saddle (2059m), where a sign next to a stile indicates the way to Saalbach. Temporarily leaving behind the mesmerising views of the Hohe Tauern peaks, traverse the base of cliffs that sweep down from the summit of the Hochkogel and descend for a short while to the wide grassy col of Seetörl (1964m), a nice place to linger and survey the petrol blue lakes of Hackelberger Seen.

Walk north from here, either climbing directly over the summit of the Saalbachkogel (2092m) or contouring around its western slopes. The same option is repeated for the slightly higher **Stemmerkogel** (2123m) where, looking back, there is a final chance to bid farewell to the frosty pinnacles of the Hohe Tauern National Park. Head down the ridge of the mountain and continue towards Schattberg – look right and you'll be able to trace the entire day's trek, including the starting point at Schmittenhöhe. The trail now skirts around the base of Schattberg West before making a final ascent to the top station of the Schattberg X-press gondola down to Saalbach.

If you'd prefer to return to **Saalbach** on foot, however, follow the signs at Schattberg-Ost onto a path (trail No 764) that weaves gently down a ski slope before descending more steeply through fir and pine forest. This trail emerges onto the main road to the village centre; if you choose this option, add one to 1½ hours to the day's duration.

KRIMML FALLS LOOP

Duration Four hours
Distance 15km
Difficulty Easy
Nearest Town Krimml (p317)
Summary This half-day walk takes in Europe's highest waterfall, open meadows and a little-known Celtic trail. Expect mostly gentle walking and dramatic views all the way.

This four-hour walk explores the 380m-high Krimml Falls (Krimmler Wasserfälle) in all their splendour. The first stretch passes through lush forest, pausing at viewpoints for close-up views of the three-tiered falls. The scenic trail then twists up to the Krimmler Achental, an alpine valley sliced in two by the burbling Krimmler Ache and set against a backdrop of 3000m-high peaks. Looping back, you'll travel on a Celtic trade route, where sturdy footwear is needed to negotiate a rocky, root-strewn trail that can become slippery when wet. The going is generally easy on the well-marked trail, which makes it a favourite with families and vista vultures.

Getting to/from the Walk

The walk begins and ends at the ticket office, approximately 10 minutes' stroll from the car park, which costs €4 per day. For further details on transport to/from Krimml, see p318. Should you get tired, a taxi will set you back €6.50 per person from the upper falls or €8 per person from Hölzlahneralm; bookings must be made by telephone (☎ 06564-83 27).

The Walk

From the ticket office (p317), the trail ascends gently through mixed forest of fir, larch and birch. The raging falls nurture a special microclimate here – take note of ostrich ferns, spongy moss and lichen in myriad shades of green, which thrive in this damp atmosphere. Before you actually see the falls, you'll hear their rumble. Soon your attention will be drawn to the lower level of the falls, the **Unterer Achenfall**, which plummet 140m through a steep-sided gorge and are enshrouded in mist. The bronze ibex statue

is a superb vantage point for photos, so have your camera ready.

The Wasserfallweg (Waterfall Path) continues to weave uphill in a series of long loops, and the well-graded trails make for easy walking. This area is a protected nature reserve and signs remind walkers that they should stick to the track. Wandering through shady forest carpeted in clover and bilberry bushes, you'll glimpse the falls on the approach to the first proper viewpoint, **Riemann Kanzel** (1110m), around 15 minutes from the start. Here you'll be rewarded with awe-inspiring views of the falls, which thrash against the jagged cliffs and illuminate the dark green forest with their brilliance.

The path soon begins to steepen, and tight switchbacks lead up through woodlands, affording fleeting glimpses of the village of Krimml in the valley below. A steady incline brings you to a number of lookout points that grant close-up views of the glinting falls, which are often arched by a rainbow when the sun shines. These include the Regen Kanzel, hung in a fine misty spray, and the precipitous Sendtner Kanzl, where the waterfall seems close enough to reach out and touch it.

After roughly 30 minutes you'll catch sight of the second tier of the falls, the 100m **Mittlerer Achenfall**; while they are not as high as the lower and upper falls, this detracts nothing from their drama. Between Jaga Sprung (1220m) and Staubige Reib (1330m), the zig-zagging trail becomes steeper at each bend, contouring around slopes dotted with craggy boulders that shimmer with minerals. By the time you reach Schönangerl, you might need a quick break and this is the perfect spot to kick back with a drink on the terrace, rest your legs and soak up the fabulous views.

At Bergerblick (1390m), you begin your approach to the third tier of the falls, **Oberer Achenfall**, which tumble 140m through a vertical wall of granite. The sheer force of the frothing water is impressive, and the ascent to the final lookout point, Schettkanzel (1460m), is also likely to leave you breathless on a hot summer's day. Approximately an hour from the starting point, you emerge at the top of the falls at Schettbrücke, where the cool forest gives way to open pastures and the Krimmler Ache River runs swiftly over smooth rocks.

Above the falls, the trail flattens and continues to shadow the wild glacial river, making its way through the U-shaped **Krimmler**

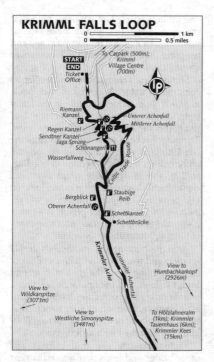

KRIMML FALLS LOOP

Hölzlahneralm (see p317) is like a beacon for weary walkers. Filled with local characters, this rustic hut is a charming place for lunch and a deserved rest; tuck into the homemade *Kaspressknödel* (cheese fritters) with a glass of creamy buttermilk. It's worth taking time here to appreciate the glaciated landscape that unfolds ahead, including the Humbachkarkopf (2926m), the Westliche Simonyspitze (3481m) and the Krimmler Kees glacier, whose meltwaters feed the Krimml Falls. In the early morning and evening, this is prime terrain for animal spotters, as it has a healthy population of marmots, Haflinger horses and chamois.

Retrace your steps along the valley and back to the falls, following the way you came until you reach a fork in the path before Schönangerl. Turn right to reach one of the day's highlights, a little-known **Celtic trade route**, built in about 2000 BC and restored in 1985. Mind your step on the rocky, root-strewn path that twists down through lichen-clad fir trees. This silent area affords an entirely different perspective of the falls and deer can often be seen or heard rustling through the trees. At the bottom, you'll have the final chance to feel the spray of the waterfall from riverbanks daubed with golden marsh marigolds. Make your way across the wooden footbridge and back to the starting point.

CARINTHIA

GARNITZENKLAMM CIRCUIT

Duration Three hours
Distance 6km
Difficulty Medium
Nearest Town Hermagor (p301)
Summary This hike leads through the first two sections of Garnitzenklamm (Garnitzen Gorge) past spectacular waterfalls and pools, returning through mountain forest.

Situated in a province famous for its rugged mountain landscapes, the 6km-long Garnitzenklamm is considered to be the prettiest gorge in Carinthia. The trail follows the course of the Garnitzenbach (Garnitzen Brook) and is officially open between the months of June and September. Although this walk is often possible at other times of year, the path is even more slippery than usual – very good shoes are needed for this walk at

Achental, a highland valley that seems a million miles away from the tourist hordes far below. In June and July, the meadows here are ablaze with wildflowers and you'll spend as much time staring at the ground as you do up ahead; keep an eye out for yellow cowslips, bell-shaped gentian and swaths of bright pink alpine roses. Although the track is reasonably crowd-free, you'll probably bump into a few hikers en route who'll cheerfully bid you *Grüss Gott* (Good day).

About 15 minutes from the falls, 3000m-high peaks begin to slide into view, including the snow-capped Wildkarspitze (3073m) to the west. But the mountains dominating the horizon aren't the only big rocks here – the sea of dwarf pines edging the left-hand side of the path is strewn with huge boulders and bizarre rock formations. Looking right, however, your attention is drawn to the mooing Pinzgauer cows that graze the pastures and the fast-flowing Krimmler Ache. The feeling of peace in this valley is sublime and it's little wonder that it has been dubbed a mini Alaska.

Around two hours from the start of the walk, the fluttering Austrian flag at the best of times – and local authorities warn it is at your own risk. The first two sections are also suitable for children, but kids should be carefully supervised and anyone who suffers from vertigo may encounter problems. Difficult stretches have chains or iron bars to hold onto. After strong rainfall, it is inadvisable to attempt sections 3 and 4. At the end of section 2 is a *Notunterstand* (emergency shelter). All bridges should be crossed one person at a time. Admission to the gorge is €2.50/1 per adult/child.

Getting to/from the Walk

The trailhead is 2.5km southwest of Hermagor, above the small settlement of Möderndorf. From the tourist office in Hermagor take the B111 southwest (left at the fork) and turn left again at the ÖAMTC office. From here continue another 2km through Möderndorf, and across the railway line and bridge to the information stand at the start of the gorge.

The Walk

The walk begins at the lower section of the gorge at an altitude of 612m, where there is an information stand and the Klammwirt restaurant, which has outdoor seating summer that is the perfect spot to gather your strength for strenuous climb ahead. The early section of the walk, which ascends the gorge left of the stream on pebbly ground, is also geologically the oldest (you will see boards along the way explaining the geology), dating back about

460 million years. The youngest stone (at the top of the gorge at an altitude of 1125m) was formed about 200 million years ago and the gorge itself is the product of erosion over about 10,000 years.

Section 1 leads around a **weir** and artificially constructed **waterfall**, as well as rock pools in which it's possible to paddle in the chilly waters. About 30 minutes into section 1 of the gorge, the first **bridge** comes into view. The gorge has been attracting hikers since the late 19th century, but maintaining the trail and crossings is difficult because of flooding. In 2003 five bridges were swept away and replacements had to be flown in and lowered into place by helicopter. This bridge was rebuilt in 2004 (cross it one person at a time); it's worth pausing in the middle for a first view of the gorge from above the water.

After this crossing, the trail ascends steeply on rocks and you pass a tree with an odd root system swelling above the ground. A second bridge follows, and the final leg of section 1 and the early stages of section 2, which begins after **Idawarte**, have some pretty rock formations, spectacular cascades and narrow, bubbling pools flanked with lush vegetation.

From Idawarte the trail crosses another bridge and leads past waterfalls near **Franzenswarte** and along the northern side of the gorge. As the trail ascends, the gorge narrows and the level of difficulty increases. Sections of the trail running along the north side to the next bridge crossing some 500m upstream can get extremely slippery and re-

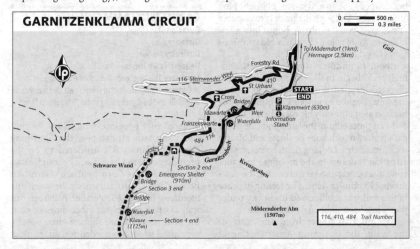

quire care. Parts of the trail have been cut into the cliffs to provide access and have a chain you can hold onto, while other parts run along natural ledges.

Shortly before the end of section 2 of the gorge, the last bridge of this walk is reached. This marks the end of the gorge section of this circuit walk. If you are not walking the entire gorge, cross the bridge just before the end of section 2 and follow Steinernder Weg (trail No 116) for about 1km through some pretty deciduous forest until it joins trail No 410 at the **cross**, where you turn right towards **St Urbani**, some 500m from the junction; this small chapel is set picturesquely in the woods, and has some simple frescoes. The chapel is also a vantage point for more good views over the gorge. From St Urbani, follow the trail through the lush deciduous forest until it rejoins the forestry road. This ends at the road from Möderndorf, just north of the information booth.

ALTERNATIVE ROUTE: SECTIONS 3 & 4 OF GARNITZENKLAMM

If you decide to continue along the gorge, sections 3 and 4 require another 1½ hours in all and involve several steep climbs before you reach the end – at **Klause** – at an altitude of 1125m. It's a spectacular walk at a higher level of difficulty. If you want to hike these sections, instead of turning right and crossing the bridge, continue past the emergency shelter. About 1km further on, the trail crosses a forestry track at the end of section 3, where you have another opportunity to leave the gorge trail; to do this, follow the forestry road north for about 3km and exit back onto the circuit trail (trail No 410).

LOWER AUSTRIA

PUCHBERG TO SCHNEEBERG

Duration 7½ hours
Distance 17km
Difficulty Easy to medium
Nearest Town Puchberg am Schneeberg (p187)
Summary This scenic hike follows the route of a railway line through changing forest landscapes, while the plateau section of the hike also offers tremendous views.

Schneeberg is Lower Austria's highest mountain and is the most popular among the Viennese, who come here to hike its lush forests and spectacular grassy plateau. Rising to 2076m, it is also easily reached by a narrow-gauge cog railway in the summer months. The first section of this trail follows yellow and green markers alongside the railway line for approximately 7km to Baumgarten station (1398m), leaves the railway line for most of the remaining 3km, and finishes at the mountain station (Bergstation). From here the 7km Plateauwanderung (Plateau Hike) begins to the summit of Schneeberg. The entire hike should only be attempted between April/ May and October/November, when the ascent is free of snow; sections of the trail can get a bit slippery in the wet and weather can be changeable. Check the railway timetable for departure times if you are completing one section by rail, and be prepared for all weather conditions.

Getting to/from the Walk

The trailhead is a 10-minute walk north of the railway station in Puchberg. From the train station, follow Bahnstrasse southwest for about 200m until the end, turn right at the T-junction and follow this road until you arrive at the railway line. The trail begins here.

The Walk

From the trailhead, take the path running along the left-hand side of the railway line. After a few hundred metres it crosses the track (watch out for trains!) and follows the course of the line on the right-hand side for most of the hike to Baumgarten station. You will find the trail sublime and picturesque in these early stages, consisting mostly of a forestry track that clings to the side of the Niederer Hengst range. The vegetation in this section is predominantly mixed evergreen and deciduous forest of spruce, beech and some oak. As you climb and wind through the forest you notice views starting to open up into the Hengsttal (Stallion Valley) on the east. After about one hour and a climb of 435m you reach **Hengsthütte** (☎ 02636-21 03; www.hengsthuette .at; Hochschneeberg 1; beds €25; ☺ Tue-Sun May-Oct, Sat & Sun Nov-Apr), where there are spectacular views into the valley and mountains.

The vegetation shows signs of the higher altitude here, with larch and pine trees becoming more frequent. The trail continues along the right of the railway line for another 30

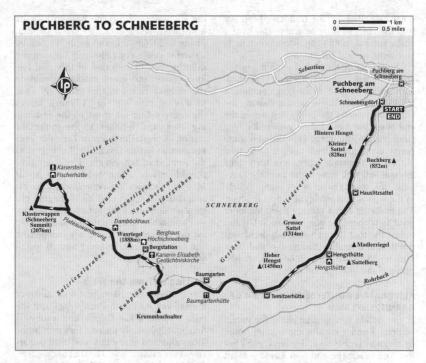

PUCHBERG TO SCHNEEBERG

or 40 minutes before crossing the track and leading to the café at Baumgarten station, **Baumgartenhütte** (☎ 02636-2107; Hochschneeberg 5; light mains €6-8; ☿ daily when train runs). With an evocative game-hunting interior, it's a good spot for a first rest. Few places in the world look like this, and it fills with forestry workers (and train passengers), who step inside to indulge in Baumgarten's famous *Buchtl*, a sweet leavened pastry.

With a *Buchtl* in your belly, follow the yellow trail along the stone embankment of the railway line before crossing the track. From now on you need to keep to the trail marked yellow. A red trail leading to Herminensteig goes off to the right just after the railway crossing; do not take this.

The yellow trail sticks closely to the line for about 200m, then leaves it and ascends through forest that was burned out in bushfires in the 1980s. Gradually you leave the tree line altogether, and the path becomes steep, rocky and uneven. If you are not an experienced hiker, you might find this section difficult in the wet. There are no steep drops, however, and the trail is well marked.

This section is also one of the most panoramic, with magnificent views to Hoher Hengst (1450m) and the valley around Puchberg in the northeast. Finally, about one hour after leaving Baumgarten and about three hours into the walk, you arrive at the stone **Kaiserin Elisabeth Gedächtniskirche**, built in honour of Empress Elisabeth and consecrated in 1901. Across from this is the Bergstation. The first section of the walk ends here.

The **Plateauwanderung**, marked in green and later yellow, starts from the station (1795m) and climbs gently along the side of Waxriegel mountain. A few minutes into the walk you have a wonderful view of what lies ahead: the **Klosterwappen** (Schneeberg summit), whose summit is marked with a cross, and the Fischerhütte perched delicately in the distance. After 20 minutes you reach **Damböckhaus** (☎ 02636-2259; www.damboeckhaus .at; Hochschneeberg 8; mattresses/beds €17/23; ☿ May-Oct), situated at an altitude on 1810m. This is a good place to nip in for sustenance and the host's speciality – game goulash – before you tackle the summit; dishes cost €7 to €9.

About 15 minutes from Damböckhaus the path forks and you follow the trail (marked yellow) to the left to the peak. Not surprisingly, this section is the steepest climb on the trail, rising 225m over 1.5km. About 45 minutes after leaving the fork, you reach the summit. Enjoy the splendid panorama if the weather is good and gather your strength.

The Plateauwandering has one final section, which takes you along the ridge north for 15 minutes towards **Fischerhütte** (☎ 02636-2313; Hochschneeberg 9; mattresses/beds €10/16; ☺ Apr–Oct), on the cusp of the plateau. Near the hut is the **Kaiserstein**, commemorating royal hikes by Kaiser Franz I in 1805 and 1807. From Fischerhütte, complete the circuit on the plateau by taking the direct trail (green) for 40 minutes back past Damböckhaus, and from there walk another 20 minutes to the Bergstation. You can now return to Puchberg by train or, if you would like to stay overnight on the mountain in a pension, the comfortable **Berghaus Hochschneeberg** (☎ 02636-2257; berghaus.hochschneeberg@aon.at; Hochschneeberg 7; s/d €24/40) is situated conveniently close to the Bergstation.

SPITZ–SCHWALLENBACH CIRCUIT

Duration 4½ hours
Distance 11km (round circuit back to Spitz)
Difficulty Easy to medium
Nearest Town Spitz (p172)
Summary This is an easy hike in the Danube Valley through vineyards and forest to hilltop castle ruins. It continues through a nature park and returns via the Danube Cycle Path.

The Wachau region in the Danube Valley is one of the most spectacular river landscapes in Europe. Lush forests and picturesque vineyards cling to high valley walls and crags, while rustic *Heurigen* (wine taverns; ask at the tourist office in Spitz which ones are open) offer the chance to sample local wines direct from the cellar door. Although most towns in the Wachau have hiking trails, this circuit offers the advantage of hiking in almost any weather conditions, and brings together the best qualities of the Wachau: pretty vineyards, deciduous forest, great views of the Danube and a historic castle ruin. Even young children will find the section to the foot of the castle manageable. The climb to the castle and the trail through the nature park to Schwallenbach

are more difficult; here leaves on the path can make it slippery in the wet. Don't stray too far off this path as cliffs are located beyond the trees.

For more details on this walk, pick up the 1:35000 Naturerlebnis Wachau Wandern & Radfahren map (€1) from the tourist office (see p172).

Getting to/from the Walk

The trailhead is on the northern outskirts of Spitz at Rotes Tor, a medieval city gate. From Marktplatz in the centre of Spitz, follow Rote-Tor-Gasse to the right, then go right again at the school gate. Signs point the way.

The Walk

Even as you approach the trailhead from Marktplatz, you pass through small vineyards and an orchard. The Wachau region is famous for its *Marillen* (apricots), which are worked into jams, liqueurs and heady schnapps. Once you arrive at the trailhead you will also see why **Rotes Tor** is considered one of the best spots to take in the view.

Follow the path through the stone portal and into the forest. It's important to keep left at the first fork and follow the blue trail (trail No 10) leading towards Huthof. The path takes you through forest of birch, pine and occasional oak trees; after about 600m a new view over the valley opens up, and you reach a bench and **small cross**.

From here the trail changes direction significantly for the first time by leaving the blue trail and making a switchback southwest up the hill. As the path straightens out, some wooden boxes appear in the forest. These are used for feeding game, and after a while you come across a *Hochsitz* (hunting stool) used by the local forest hunters to wait for their unsuspecting game. More importantly, though, watch out for snakes in this section of forest as they tend to loiter around the woodpiles.

After a fairly moderate climb for another 600m you reach the crest of a ridge that extends up to the 700m-high Buchberg to the north; between the trees there are lovely views of the serpentine **Danube** (Donau).

The trail follows the swath cut into the lower reaches of Buchberg and gradually descends again, offering spectacular views over to the terraced **Michaeler Berg** in the east. At the next fork keep to the right, going in the direction of Erholungswald Jagdriedl; just after this

---

TREKKING WITH LLAMAS

One of the more interesting hikes with llamas in Lower Austria is along a section of the Jakobsweg (Jacob's Path). A two-day trek along this pilgrim's trail begins in Stift Göttweig (near Krems An Der Donau; p167) and goes via the monastery Maria Langegg – where you stay overnight – to Melk. This two-day trek involves about six hours walking each day along pretty forest trails and costs a very reasonable €65 in a group of 15 people. **Donau Niederösterreich Tourismus** (☎ 02713-300 60 60; www.donau.com) handles bookings and can tell you more about the hike.

---

another view opens up, this time over the rooftops of Spitz to the Danube.

From here keep following the trail marked yellow, which leads down towards Radlbach, once a separate town but today a part of Spitz. As the trail heads in a more northerly direction, views shift from the Danube and Spitz to the side valley, the Spitzer Graben (Spitz Basin); from a bluff you get an interesting view of this river valley closed off on three sides by densely wooded mountains. This is a good place to unpack a lunch, and a bottle of local wine or juice.

Continue along the yellow trail (trail No 5) into the gully and across Radlbach (Radl Brook) then stay on the forestry track (yellow; trail No 6) alongside the brook all the way into Radlbach settlement, where there are more vineyards and **Heurigen**. As you walk around Rauch Emma (one of the vineyards), **Burgruine Hinterhaus** (Castle Ruin Hinterhaus) appears in the distance on the bluff.

From Radlbach, go left along the main road and right across the bridge. At the road marked Auf der Wehr, go left again. A sign warns that the climb ahead is steep – and it's serious. The degree of difficulty increases in this section, and for good reason: the approach to the fortress, which was first mentioned in official documents in 1243, was planned in

such a way that attackers stormed it with the right side of the body exposed to the castle defenders. This is typically the side of the body unprotected by a shield in battle. Despite this crafty piece of fortress building and landscape design, the castle gradually fell into disuse from the 1460s. To get to the castle, follow the signs along Weitwanderweg 05.

Views from the castle are superb, and this is a good place to rest up before tackling the second section of the walk. This section takes you through the lush **Jauerling Naturpark** (Jauerling Nature Park) towards Schwallenbach; a small town about 3km from the castle. To walk it, backtrack from the castle and take trail No 6/605 (marked in red) up into the forest. It's another steep climb and will require good shoes in the wet. Walk along the trail through the forest for about 500m, following red-and-yellow markers (trail No 7) until you see the fence; the trail divides here. Take the yellow trail (trail No 7), which winds along the top of **Teufelsmauer** (Devil's Wall) through dense forest, with occasional glimpses over the Danube Valley. After walking for about an hour, you descend gradually through vineyards towards Schwallenbach, from where you have the choice of taking a train or bus back to Spitz or completing the circuit by following the bicycle path alongside the Danube to Spitz.

Vienna

Few cities in the world glide so effortlessly between the present and the past like Vienna. Its splendid historical face is easily recognised: grand imperial palaces and bombastic baroque interiors, museums flanking magnificent squares and, above all, the Hofburg – where the Habsburg rulers lived, loved and married into empires.

But this historical aspect often makes us forget that Vienna is also one of Europe's most dynamic urban spaces. Just a stone's throw from Hofburg, the MuseumsQuartier houses some of the world's most provocative contemporary art behind a striking basalt façade. Outside, a courtyard buzzes on summer evenings with throngs of Viennese drinking and chatting. Nearby, restaurants brim with imbibers enjoying the pleasures of wine and food, while across the yard a museum café pulsates with beats.

It is a reminder that the city of Mozart, Beethoven, Haydn, Schubert, Strauss, Brahms, Mahler and Schönberg is also the Vienna of Falco, who immortalised its urban textures in song. It's also a place where sushi and Austro-Asian fusion restaurants stand alongside the traditional *Beisl*. In this Vienna, it's okay to mention poetry slam and Stephansdom in one breath.

Throw in the mass of green space within the confines of the city limits (almost half the city expanse is given over to parkland), the 'blue' Danube cutting a path just to the east of the historical centre and the Wienerwald (Vienna Woods) creating much of Vienna's western border and you also have a capital with a great outdoors.

HIGHLIGHTS

- Scaling **Stephansdom** (p124), Vienna's glorious Gothic cathedral and beloved icon
- Savouring the bombastic pomp of **Schloss Schönbrunn** (p135) and the views from its gardens
- Immersing yourself in Vienna's textures on a night or day ramble along **Gumpendorfer Strasse** (p134)
- Hanging out in the **MuseumsQuartier** (p130), an art space spiked with bars and alive with urban energy
- Being provoked by naked bodies smeared with salad (among other modern art flourishes) at the Vienna's **MUMOK** (p130)

MuseumsQuartier & MUMOK ★ ★ Stephansdom
★ Gumpendorfer
Schloss ★ Strasse
Schönbrunn

■ POPULATION: 1.54 MILLION	■ AREA: 415 SQ KM
■ HIGHEST ELEVATION: HERMANNSKOGEL 542M	■ AREA CODE: 01

VIENNA

HISTORY

Vienna was probably an important trading post for the Celts when the Romans arrived around 15 BC. They set up camp and named it Vindobona, after the Celtic tribe Vinid. The settlement blossomed into a town by the 3rd and 4th centuries, and vineyards were introduced to the surrounding area.

In 881 the town, then known as 'Wenia', surfaced in official documents and over the ensuing centuries control of Vienna changed hands a number of times, before the Babenburgs gained the upper hand (see p30). The Habsburgs inherited it, but none of them resided here permanently until Ferdinand I in 1533; the city was besieged by Turks in 1529 (p37).

Vienna was a hotbed of revolt and religious bickering during the Reformation and Counter-Reformation and suffered terribly through plague and siege at the end of the 17th century. However, the beginning of the 18th century heralded a golden age for Vienna, with baroque architecture, civil reform and a classical music revolution.

Things turned sour at the beginning of the 19th century – Napoleon occupied the city twice, in 1805 and 1809 (p30). His reign over Europe was brief, and in 1814–15 Vienna hosted the Congress of Vienna in celebration. Vienna grew in post-Napoleon Europe and in 1873 hosted its second international event, the World Fair. The advent of WWI stalled the city's architectural and cultural development and, by the end of the war, the monarchy had been consigned to the past (p32).

The 1920s saw the rise of fascism, and by 1934 civil war broke out in the city streets. The socialists were defeated and Vienna's city council dissolved. Austria was ripe for the picking, and Hitler came a-harvesting; on 15 March 1938 he entered the city to the cries of 200,000 ecstatic Viennese.

Vienna suffered heavily under Allied bombing, and on 11 April 1945 advancing Russian troops liberated the city. The Allies joined them until Vienna became independent in 1955, and since then it has gone from the razor's edge of Cold War to the focal point between new and old EU member nations.

ORIENTATION

Vienna occupies 415 sq km in the Danube Valley, with the Wienerwald (Vienna Woods) forming a natural border to the north and west. The Danube (Donau) River flows northeast to southwest through the city. Vienna's heart, the Innere Stadt (inner city; 1st District), is south of the river on a diversion of the Danube, the Danube Canal (Donaukanal). It's encircled on three sides by the Ringstrasse, or Ring, a series of broad roads sporting an extravaganza of architectural delights. The Ring is at a distance of between 1.75km and 3km from the Gürtel (literally, 'belt'), a larger traffic artery that is fed by the flow of vehicles from outlying autobahns.

Stephansdom (St Stephen's Cathedral), with its slender spire, is in the heart of the Innere Stadt and is Vienna's principal landmark. Leading south from Stephansplatz station is Kärntner Strasse, an important pedestrian street that terminates at Karlsplatz, a major public transport hub.

The Danube runs down a long, straight channel, built between 1870 and 1875 to eliminate flooding. This was supplemented 100 years later by the building of a parallel channel, the Neue Donau (New Danube), creating the Donauinsel (Danube Island) recreational area. The original Alte Donau (Old Danube) loops north of the Neue Donau to enclose the Donaupark, Vienna International Center (UNO City, home to the UN), beaches and water-sports centres. Squeezed between the Danube Canal and the Danube is the Prater, a large park and playground of the Viennese.

Most hotels, pensions, restaurants and bars are in the Innere Stadt or west of the centre between the Ringstrasse and the Gürtel.

Maps

The free tourist office Vienna map shows bus, tram and U-Bahn routes, has a separate U-Bahn plan, and lists major city-wide sights. It also has a blow-up of the Innere Stadt. For a street index, Freytag & Berndt's 1:25,000 fold-out map (€7.99) is available at most bookshops.

INFORMATION
Bookshops

British Bookshop (Map pp120-1; www.britishbook shop.at; ⊙ 9:30am-6.30pm Mon-Fri, 9.30am-6pm Sat) Weihburggasse (☎ 512 19 45; 01, Weihburggasse 24); Mariahilfer Strasse (☎ 522 67 30; 07, Mariahilfer Strasse 4) The largest selection of English novels, guidebooks, reference and teaching books.

Freytag & Berndt (Map pp120-1; ☎ 533 86 85; www .freytagberndt.at; 01, Kohlmarkt 9; ⊙ 9am-7pm Mon-Fri,

9am-6pm Sat) For maps and travel guides; stocks its own and competitors' maps.

Shakespeare & Co (Map pp120-1; ☎ 535 50 53; www .shakespeare.co.at; 01, Sterngasse 2; ⊙ 9am-7pm Mon-Sat) Has a strong range of eclectic, literary, academic and art books; also literary and hard-to-find titles in English. Friendly staff.

Thalia (Map pp116-17; ☎ 595 45 50; 06, Mariahilfer Strasse 99; ⊙ 9.30am-7pm Mon-Wed, 9.30am-8pm Thu & Fri, 9.30am-6pm Sat) A good range of travel books, maps and a small range of English fiction.

Emergency

See Quick Reference on the inside front cover for nationwide emergency numbers for ambulance, doctor, fire and police.

Police station (Map pp120-1; ☎ 313 10; 01, Deutschmeisterplatz 3; ⊙ 24hr)

ViennaMed hotline ☎ 513 9595; ⊙ 24hr) Information in English and German on local doctors.

Women's Emergency Line (Frauennotruf; ☎ 71 719; ⊙ 24hr)

Internet Access

Vienna has dozens of places offering public access to online services. Free access is available at Flex (p153) and rhiz (p150; free after 9pm), which has a couple of terminals. Bücherei Wien (right) also has free internet access; rock up with your passport and log on.

Internet cafés charging around €2 to €4 per hour include:

BigNet (Map pp120-1; ☎ 533 2939; 01, Hoher Markt 8-9; ⊙ 9am-11pm) Centrally located in the Innere Stadt.

Speed Connect (Map pp120-1; ☎ 526 60 77; 01, Lerchenfelder Strasse 13; ⊙ 10am-midnight Mon-Fri, noon-midnight Sat & Sun) Smoky internet café and call centre.

Speednet Café (Map pp116-17; ☎ 892 56 66; 15, Europlatz, Westbahnhof; ⊙ 7am-midnight Mon-Sat, 8am-midnight Sun) Bustling internet café inside Westbahnhof with Skype.

Internet Resources

About Vienna (www.aboutvienna.org) General website with cultural and sightseeing information.

City of Vienna (www.wien.gv.at) Comprehensive government-run website.

Falter (www.falter.at, in German) Online version of the ever-popular *Falter* magazine (right).

Vienna Online (www.vienna.at, in German) Site with info on parties, festivals and news.

Vienna Tourist Board (www.wien.info) The first port of call for any visitor.

Left Luggage

Westbahnhof, Südbahnhof and Franz-Josef-Bahnhof have **left-luggage lockers** (per locker €2-3.50; ⊙ 24hr).

Libraries

Bücherei Wien (Map p122; ☎ 4000 84500; www.bue chereiwien.at; 07, Urban-Loritz-Platz; ⊙ 11am-7pm Mon-Fri, 11am-5pm Sat) The city library, straddling the U6 line.

Nationalbibliothek (Map pp120-1; ☎ 534 10 397; www.onb.ac.at; 01, Josefsplatz 1; ⊙ 10am-6pm Tue-Sun, till 9pm Thu) National library with huge reference and lending sections.

Media

For gay-specific publications see boxed text, p140.

City (in German) Like a downsized *Falter*; weekly paper with entertainment listings.

Falter (www.falter.at, in German) Weekly magazine; best resource for political commentary and entertainment listings in every genre imaginable.

Medical Services

The following s*Krankenhäuser* (hospitals) have emergency rooms open 24 hours a day, seven days a week.

Allgemeines Krankenhaus (Map p122; ☎ 404 00; 09, Währinger Gürtel 18-20)

Hanusch-Krankenhaus (Map pp114-15; ☎ 910 21-0; 14, Heinrich-Collin-Strasse 30)

Lorenz Böhler Unfallkrankenhaus (Map pp116-17; ☎ 331 10; 20, Donaueschingenstrasse 13)

Unfallkrankenhaus Meidling (Map pp116-17; ☎ 601 50-0; 12, Kundratstrasse 37)

If you require a *Zahnarzt* (dentist) after hours call ☎ 512 20 78 (recorded message in German only); likewise if you need an *Apotheken* (pharmacy) outside shop hours, dial ☎ 1550 (in German only).

Money

Banks and currency exchange offices are located around town, but compare commission rates before changing money. *Bankomats* (ATMs) are found everywhere, including at the train stations and airport; most shut down at midnight.

The money exchange and banking services office in Westbahnhof keeps hours from 7am to 10pm daily. The bank at Südbahnhof is open 8am to 6pm weekdays and 8am to 4pm Saturday.

(Continued on page 123)

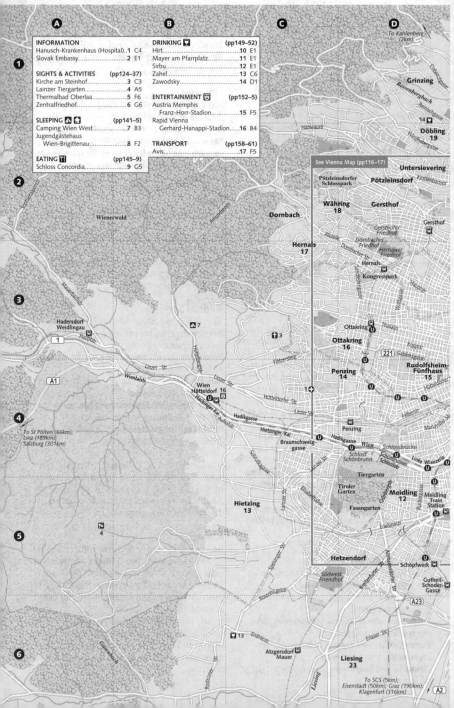

INFORMATION
Hanusch-Krankenhaus (Hospital)..**1** C4
Slovak Embassy..................................**2** E1

SIGHTS & ACTIVITIES   (pp124–37)
Kirche am Steinhof............................**3** C3
Lainzer Tiergarten.............................**4** A5
Thermalbad Oberlaa..........................**5** F6
Zentralfriedhof...................................**6** G6

SLEEPING   (pp141–5)
Camping Wien West...........................**7** B3
Jugendgästehaus
  Wien-Brigittenau............................**8** F2

EATING   (pp145–9)
Schloss Concordia..............................**9** G5

DRINKING   (pp149–52)
Hirt...**10** E1
Mayer am Pfarrplatz.........................**11** E1
Sirbu..**12** E1
Zahel..**13** C6
Zawodsky..**14** D1

ENTERTAINMENT   (pp152–5)
Austria Memphis
  Franz-Horr-Stadion........................**15** F5
Rapid Vienna
  Gerhard-Hanappi-Stadion......**16** B4

TRANSPORT   (pp158–61)
Avis..**17** F5

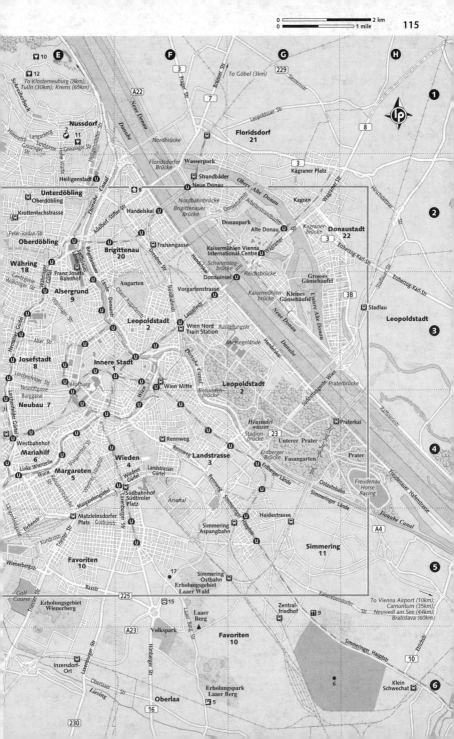

0   2 km
0   1 mile

E   **F**   **G**   **H**

□ 10
□ 12
To Klosterneuburg (8km);
Tulln (30km); Krems (65km)

A22

1

3

7

Leopoldauer Str

8

Nussdorf
2
11
Grinzinger Str
Sandgasse
Langackerg

Neue Donau

Nordbrücke

Floridsdorf
21

Nordbrücke

Danube

229

To Göbel (3km)

Brünner Str

Prager Str

Siemensstr

2

8

Heiligenstadt

Floridsdorfer
Brücke

Wasserpark

□ Strandbäder
Neue Donau

Obere Alte Donau

Kagraner Platz

3

Wagramer Str

Hochstädtstr

Unterdöbling
□ Oberdöbling

□ Krottenbachstrasse

Peter-Jordan-Str

Handelskai

Nordbahnbrücke
Brigittenauer
Brücke

Donaupark

Donaupark

Alte Donau

Kagran

Kagraner-
brücke

Donaustadt
22

3

Erzherzog-Karl-Str

2

Oberdöbling

Währing
18
Gentzgasse
Währinger Str

Gersthofer Str

Heiligenstädter Str

Billrothstr
Döblinger Hauptstr

Brigittenau
20

Traisengasse

Dresdner Str

Kaisermühlen Vienna
International Centre

Schüttaustr

Wagramer Str

Donaustadt

Grosses
Gänsehäufel

Kleines
Gänsehäufel

Erzherzog-Karl-Str

Leopoldstadt

3

3B

□ Stadlau

Alsergrund
9
Franz Josefs
Bahnhof

Augarten

Obere Augartenstr

Nordbahnstr

Leopoldstadt
2

Schwimmstegbrücke

Donauinsel

Kaisermühlen-
brücke

Reichsbrücke

Untere Alte Donau

Neue Donau

Josefstadt
8

Alser Str

Lerchenfelder Str

Innere Stadt
1

Hofburg

Neubau 7
Neustiftgasse
Burggasse

Wurt

Wien Mitte

Praterstr

Ausstellungsstr

Wien Nord
Train Station

Messegelände

Handelskai

Donaukanal

Leopoldstadt
2

Südosttangente Wien

Praterbrücke

Danube

3

Westbahnhof

Mariahilf
6

Linke Wienzeile

Neubaugürtel

Gumpendorfer Str

Rotundenbrücke

Rennweg

Rennweg

Landstrasse
3

Unterer Prater

Heustadel
wasser

Stadion-
brücke

23

Erdberger
Brücke

Fasangarten

Prater

Praterkai

4

Freudenau
Horse
Racing

Freudenauer Hafenstrasse

Raffineriestr

Wieden
4
Wiedner
Gürtel

Margareten
5

Margaretengürtel

Reinprechtsdorfer Str

Mariahilfer Str

Landstrasser
Gürtel

Erdberger Lände

Simmeringer Lände

Ostautobahn

Simmeringer Lände

Haidestraße

Simmering
11

A4

Danube Canal

Matzleinsdorfer
Platz

Südbahnhof
Südtiroler
Platz

Arsenal

Gudrunstr

Simmering
Aspangbahn

Simmeringer Hauptstr

To Vienna Airport (10km);
Carnuntum (35km);
Neusiedl am See (44km);
Bratislava (60km)

Str

Favoriten
10
Raxstr

Kundratstr
Triester Str
Eichenstr

Wienerbergstr

225

Erholungsgebiet
Wienerberg

Golf
Course

□ 15

17

Simmering
Ostbahn
Erholungsgebiet
Laer Wald

Laer
Berg

Laer Berg Str

Zentral-
friedhof

9

Str

Kaiserebersdorfer

Simmeringer Hauptstr

Etrichstr

10

Klein
Schwechat

5

6

Inzersdorf-
Ort

A23

Lastenstr
Himberger Str

Volkspark

Laer
Berg

Favoriten
10

Liesing

Oberlaer Str

16

Oberlaa

230

Erholungspark
Laer Berg

5

6

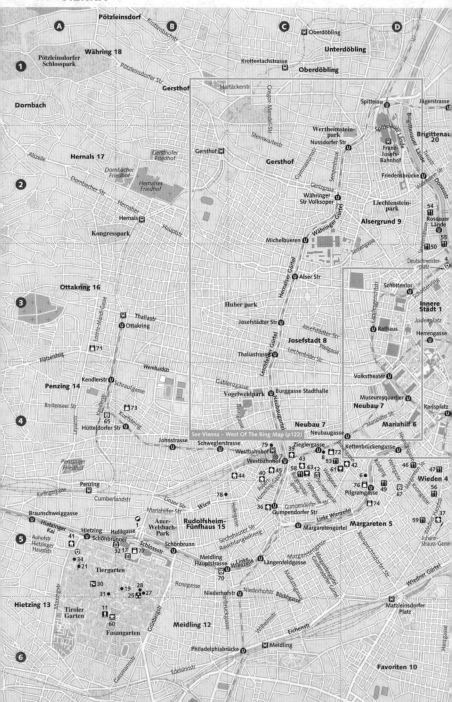

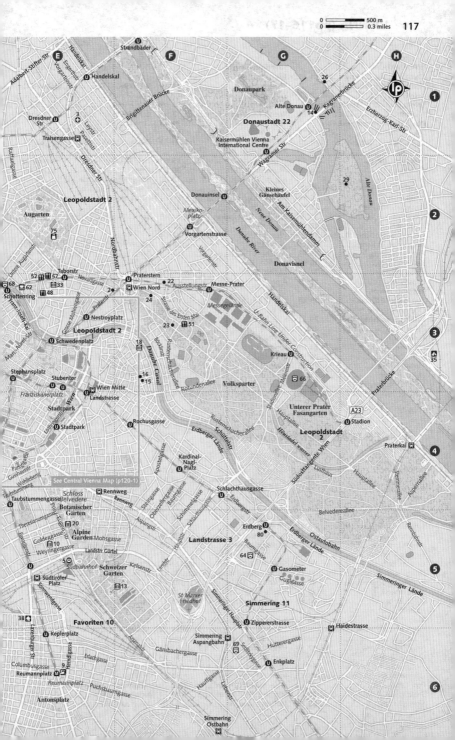

0 | 500 m
0 | 0.3 miles

E **F** **G** **H**

Adalbert-Stifter-Str
Handelskai
Strandbäder
1

Ennsgergasse
Vorgartenstr
Handelskai
Donaupark
26
Kagranerbrücke
Erzherzog-Karl-Str

Dresdner Str
3
Leystr
Pasettistr
Alte Donau
14

Traisengasse
Dresdner Str
Nordbahnstr
Donaustadt 22

Kaisermühlen Vienna
International Centre
Wagramer Str

Leopoldstadt 2
Augarten
75
Donauinsel
Mexiko-platz
Kleines
Gänsehäufel
29
2
Am Kaisermühlendamm
Alte Donau

Vorgartenstrasse
Neue Donau
Danube River
Donavisnel

52 57 Taborstr
Novargasse
33
Praterstern
Wien Nord
22
Ausstellungstr
Messe-Prater
Handelskai
U-Bahn Line Under Construction

68
62
48
Schottenring
Marc-Aurel-Str
Josef-Str
2
Praterstr
24
Strasse des Ersten Mai
Messegelände
3
35

Nestroyplatz
Leopoldstadt 2
Schwedenplatz
23 51
Böcklinstrasse
Rustenschacheralee
Krieau
Meiereistrasse

Stephansplatz
Stubentor
18
Danube Canal
16
15
Rotundenalee
Volksparter
66
Hauptallee
Hauptstrasse zur Wien
Unterer Prater
Fasangarten
A23
Stadion
4
Praterkai

Stadtpark
Wien Mitte
Landstrasse
Rochusgasse
Rustenschacher alee
Erdberger Lände
Schüttelstr
Leopoldstadt 2
Südosstangente Wien
Lusthaus
Hauptallee
Aspernallee

Ungargasse
Kardinal-Nagl-Platz
Apostelgasse
See Central Vienna Map (p120-1)
Schlachthausgasse
Erdbergstr
Belvederealee

Schloss Belvedere
Rennweg
Rennweg
Steingasse
Oberzellergasse
Baumgasse
Erdberg
80
Erdberger Lände
Ostautobahn
Simmeringer Lände

Taubstummengasse
Botanischer Gärten
20
Alpine Garden
Mohsgasse
Landstrasse 3
64
Gasometer
Guglgasse

Theresianumg
Goldeggasse
10
Weyringergasse
Landstr Gürtel
Aspangstr
Schimmelgasse
St Marxer
Friedhof

5
Südbahnhof
Schweizer Garten
Kelsenstr
Landstr Gürtel
Simmering 11
Simmeringer Hauptstr
Zippererstrasse
Haidestrasse
5

Südtiroler Platz
Sommerendgasse
13
Gudrunstr
6

38
Favoriten 10
Keplerplatz
Simmering
Aspangbahn
69
Hütteregasse
Enkplatz

Laxenburger Str
Herndlg
Arsenalstr
Gänsbachergasse
Hauffgasse

Columbusgasse
Reumannplatz
Reumannplatz
Puchsbaumgasse

Antonsplatz
Simmering
Ostbahn

CENTRAL VIENNA (pp120–1)

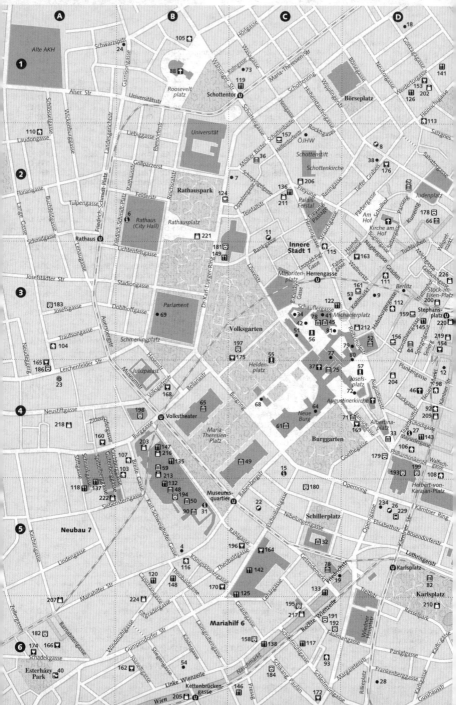

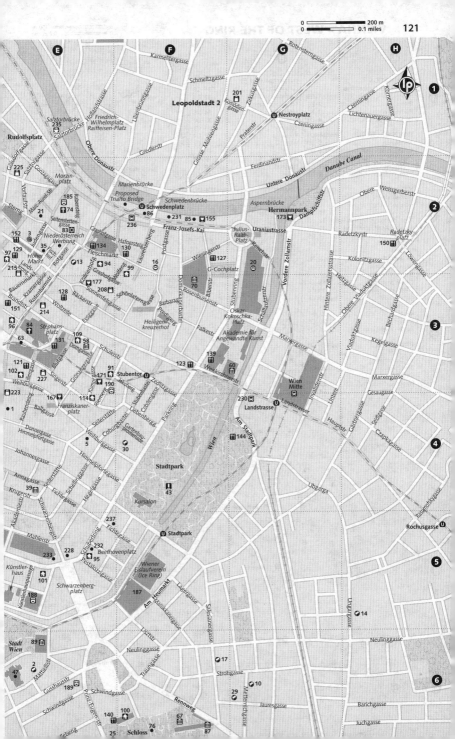

E · F · G · H

1 · 2 · 3 · 4 · 5 · 6

Karmelitergasse

Schmeltzgasse

Rotensterngasse

Leopoldstadt 2

201
Kohlgasse
Zirkusgasse

Nestroyplatz

Czeningasse

Czeningasse

Korniergasse

Lichtenauergasse

Rudolfsplatz

235
Salztorbrücke

Friedrich-
Wilhelmplatz
Raiffeisen-Platz

Lilienbrunngasse

Holandstrasse

Obere Donaustr

Gredlerstr

Grosse Mohrengasse

Ferdinandstr

Untere Donaustr

Danube Canal

225

Morzin-
platz

Marienbrücke

Proposed
Trialto Bridge

Schwedenbrücke

Aspernbrücke

Hermannpark

173

Obere Weissgerberstr

185
74

Schwedenplatz

86

231 · 85 · 155

Franz-Josefs-Kai

Julius-
Raab-
Platz

Uraniastrasse

Dampfschiffstr

Radetzkystr

Radetzky-
platz

150

236

3

Niederösterreich
Werbung

83

13

134

Hafnersteig

130

Laurenzerberg

Postgasse

Wiesingerstr

127

G-Cochplatz

20

Renngasse

Kolonitzgasse

Hintere Zollamtsstrasse

Löwengasse

152

35

Hoher
Markt

Rotgasse

16

Dominikanerbastei

Rosenbursenstr

Stubenring

Oskar-
Kokoschka-
Platz

Schanzelstr

Vordere Zollamtstr

Obere Viaduktgasse

Bechardgasse

97
129
215

177

94

99

128
208

Sonnenfelsgasse

Schönlaterngasse

Barbaragasse

Predigerg

Falkestr

Akademie für
Angewandte Kunst

Marxergasse

Viaduktgasse

Kegelgasse

214

Wollzeile

Backerstr

Essiggasse

Heiligen-
kreuzerhof

Marxergasse

Gesaugasse

151

96

84

63

Stephans-
platz

109
58

131

Domgasse

Schulerstr

91

139
70

60

123

Weiskirchnerstr

Wien
Mitte

Bauernmarkt

Kramergasse

Rotenturmstr

Brandstr

Blutgasse

Grünangergasse

471

190

Stubentor

Stubenbastei

Coburgbastei

Lechtizgasse

Parkring

Am Stadtpark

Landstrasser

Invalidenstr

Untere

Gärtnergasse

Seidlgasse

Czapkagasse

121
102
227
223

167

114

Singerstr

Kumpfgasse

Franziskaner-
platz

1

Ballgasse

Weihburggasse

5

30

Gartenbau-
promenade

230

Landstrasse

Hauptstr

Rochusgasse

Donnergasse
Himmelpfortgasse

Johannesgasse

39

Annagasse

Krugerstr

Akademiestr

Seilerstätte

Fichtegasse

Schellinggasse

Schwarzenbergstr

Sellerstätte

Weihburggasse

Himmelpfortgasse

Coburgbastei

Liebenberg

Seilerstätte

Heagasse

144

Stadtpark

Wien

Kursalon

43

Ubgarga

Mählerstr

237

Fichtegasse

Stadtpark

Canovagasse

Rasumofskygasse

228

232

95

Beethovenplatz

Pestalozzigasse

Wiener
Eislaufverein
(Ice Ring)

233

Künstler-
haus

101

Schwarzenberg-
platz

187

Am Heumarkt

Krakokanerg

Lagergasse

14

Neulinggasse

188

Ungargasse

Stadt
Wien

89

47
2

Martinstr

189

Gusshausstr

Schwindgasse

Prinz-Eugen-Str

140
100

Liebeng

25

Schloss

76

87

67

Neulinggasse

17

Strohgasse

10

29

Rennweg

Jauresgasse

Metternichgasse

Barichgasse

Juchgasse

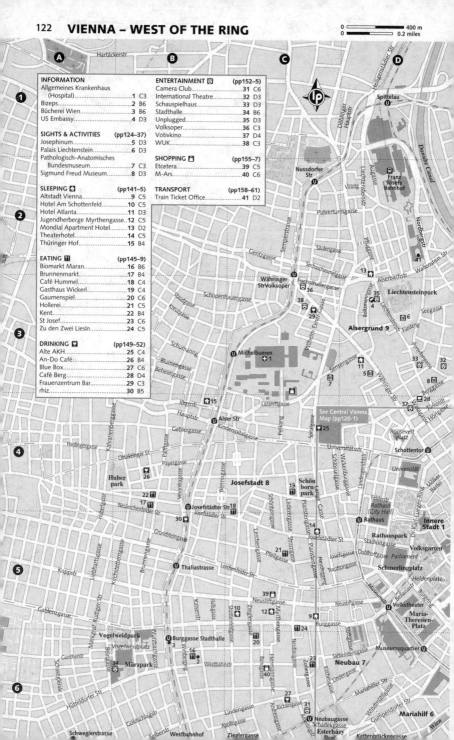

0 _____ 400 m
0 _____ 0.2 miles

INFORMATION
Allgemeines Krankenhaus
  (Hospital)...................................1 C3
Bizeps...2 B6
Bücherei Wien...............................3 B6
US Embassy...................................4 D3

SIGHTS & ACTIVITIES   (pp124–37)
Josephinum....................................5 D3
Palais Liechtenstein......................6 D3
Pathologisch-Anatomisches
  Bundesmuseum...........................7 C3
Sigmund Freud Museum...............8 D3

SLEEPING 🏠   (pp141–5)
Altstadt Vienna.............................9 C5
Hotel Am Schottenfeld...............10 C5
Hotel Atlanta..............................11 D3
Jugendherberge Myrthengasse....12 C5
Mondial Apartment Hotel............13 D2
Theaterhotel................................14 C5
Thüringer Hof.............................15 B4

EATING 🍴   (pp145–9)
Biomarkt Maran...........................16 B6
Brunnenmarkt.............................17 B4
Café Hummel...............................18 C4
Gasthaus Wickerl........................19 C4
Gaumenspiel................................20 C6
Hollerei......................................21 C5
Kent..22 B4
St Josef.......................................23 C6
Zu den Zwei Liesln.....................24 C5

DRINKING 🍷   (pp149–52)
Alte AKH....................................25 C4
An-Do Café..................................26 B4
Blue Box......................................27 C6
Café Berg.....................................28 D4
Frauenzentrum Bar......................29 C3
rhiz...30 B5

ENTERTAINMENT 🎭   (pp152–5)
Camera Club.................................31 C6
International Theatre....................32 D3
Schauspielhaus............................33 D3
Stadthalle....................................34 B6
Unplugged...................................35 D3
Volksoper.....................................36 C3
Votivkino.....................................37 D4
WUK...38 C3

SHOPPING 🛍   (pp155–7)
Etcetera.......................................39 C5
M-Ars..40 C6

TRANSPORT   (pp158–61)
Train Ticket Office.......................41 D2

(Continued from page 113)

Commissions on American Express cash and travellers cheque services vary; see the Directory (p389).

Post

Franz-Josefs-Bahnhof Post Office (Map p122; ☎ 0577 677 1090; 09, Althanstrasse 10; ☼ 7am-8pm Mon-Fri, 9am-2pm Sat & Sun)
Main post office (Map pp120-1; ☎ 0577 677 1010; www.post.at; 01, Fleischmarkt 19; ☼ 6am-10pm)
Südbahnhof post office (Map pp116-17; ☎ 0577 677 1103; 10, Wiedner Gürtel 1b; ☼ 7am-10pm Mon-Fri, 9am-2pm Sat & Sun)
Westbahnhof post office (Map pp116-17; ☎ 0577 677 1150; 15, Europlatz; ☼ 7am-10pm Mon-Fri, 9am-8pm Sat & Sun)

Tourist Information

Airport Information Office (☎ 6am-11pm) Located in the arrival hall.

ADDRESSES

ADDRESSES

Vienna is divided into 23 *Bezirke* (districts), fanning out in approximate numerical order clockwise around the Innere Stadt. Note that when reading addresses, the number of a building within a street *follows* the street name. Any number *before* the street name denotes the district. The middle two digits of postcodes correspond to the district. Thus a postcode of 1010 means the place is in district one, and 1230 refers to district 23.

City Hall Information Office (Map pp120-1; ☎ 525 50; www.wien.gv.at; 01, Rathaus; ☼ 8am-6pm Mon-Fri) Provides information on social, cultural and practical matters, and is geared as much to residents as to tourists.
Jugendinfo (Map pp120-1; ☎ 1799; www.jugendinfowien .at; 01, Babenbergerstrasse 1; ☼ noon-7pm Mon-Sat) Tailored to ages 14 to 26; tickets for a variety of events at reduced rates and tips on the young alternative scene in Vienna.

VIENNA IN...

Two Days
Start your day with a *melange* (coffee; specific to Austria) and *butter-semel* (butter-roll) at a traditional Kaffeehaus (coffee house). Jump on tram 1 or 2 and circle the **Ringstrasse** (p128) for a brief but rewarding informal tour of the boulevard's buildings. Get out at Kärntner Strasse and wander towards the heart of the city where the glorious Gothic **Stephansdom** (p124) awaits. Make your way to the **Hofburg** (p125) and its **Prunksaal** (p126) before crossing the Ringstrasse to the **Kunsthistorisches Museum** (p128), home to a breathtaking art collection. Recharge the batteries at one of the many **Innere Stadt restaurants** (p145) before attending a performance at the **Staatsoper** (p152).

Day two could begin with a visit to the imperial palace **Schönbrunn** (p135), before heading to the **MuseumsQuartier** (p130) and its **Leopold Museum** (p130), a treasure-chest of Austrian artists. Take an early dinner at Vienna's celebrated market, the **Naschmarkt** (p149), then cross the city for a ride on the **Riesenrad** (p131) in the **Prater** (p131). Finish the day with local wine and food at a **Heurigen** (p151).

Four Days
After fulfilling the two-day itinerary, start the third day with an exploration of the **Schloss Belvedere** (p132), an unequalled baroque palace, before lunching at **Zu den Zwei Liesln** (p147). Walk off that monstrous Wiener schnitzel in the **Ringstrasse Gardens** (p128) before viewing Klimt's sumptuous *Beethoven Frieze* in the **Secession** (p129). If there's time, make for **Kahlenberg** (p137) to beat the setting sun. End the night in one of the **Gürtel's progressive bars** (p150) or the plethora of night spots in and around the Naschmarkt.

If you're still up for unfathomable art collections in regal surroundings, a visit to the **Albertina** (p127) or **Palais Liechtenstein** (p132) is a must on the fourth day. This is a city where 'macabre' and 'imperial' comfortably exist in the same sentence, so an afternoon trip to the **Kaisergruft** (p127) should follow. Spend your last evening in one of the city's music houses, such as the **Konzerthaus** (p152) or **Musikverein** (p152), experiencing the music of Beethoven or Mozart where it was originally played.

Tourist Info Wien (Map pp120-1; ☎ 211 14-555; www.wien.info; 01, Albertinaplatz; ⏱ 9am-7pm) Vienna's main tourist office, with a ticket agency, hotel booking service, free maps and every brochure you could ever want for.

WienXtra-Kinderinfo (Map pp120-1; ☎ 4000 84 400; www.kinderinfowien.at; 07, Museumsplatz 1; ⏱ 2-7pm Tue-Thu, 10am-5pm Fri & Sat) This child-friendly tourist office has loads of information on kids activities and a small indoor playground.

Travel Agencies

American Express (Map pp120-1; ☎ 512 4004; 01, Kärntner Strasse 21-23; ⏱ 9am-5.30pm Mon-Fri; exchange office also 10am-1pm Sat) Travel section and financial services, and will hold mail (not parcels) free of charge for up to one month for Amex cardholders.

Österreichisches Verkehrsbüro (Map pp120-1; ☎ 588 00 100; www.verkehrsbuero.at, in German; 04, Friedrichstrasse 7; ⏱ 9am-5pm Mon-Fri) Major national agency that sells DDSG boat tickets and organises almost everything under the sun.

STA Travel Call Centre (Map 120-1; ☎ 401 48 60 00; 09, Garnisongasse 7; ⏱ 8.30am-7pm Mon-Thu, 8.30am-5.30pm Fri, 10am-5pm Sat) Call centre only, with ticket collection.

Travel Shop Rilkeplatz (Map 120-1; ☎ 502 43-0; www.statravel.at; 04, Rilkeplatz 2; ⏱ 9am-6pm Mon-Fri) STA has discounted flights for students and helpful staff that speak English. There are three other shops in the city.

SIGHTS

Most of Vienna's top attractions are inside the Innere Stadt or within 10 minutes' walk of its boundaries. The Innere Stadt is best tackled on foot as it's a maze of narrow one-way and pedestrian-only zones. The rest of the city is easily managed by public transport or, if you're feeling fit, by bicycle.

VIENNA'S MUSEUMS

Vienna's top museum spots for:

■ Contemporary art and Vienna Actionism – **MUMOK** (p130)

■ The dark side – **Pathologisch-Anatomisches Bundesmuseum** (p139)

■ European old masters and new – **Kunsthistorisches Museum** (p128)

■ Gesamtkunstwerk (quiet gardens, architecture and Austrian art) – **Schloss Belvedere** (p132)

■ Children – **Zoom** (p139)

■ Treasures and reliquaries – **Schatzkammer** (p126)

Innere Stadt

The Innere Stadt is a timeless and magical place where Vienna's past swirls and eddies in narrow ways and atmospheric cobblestone streets. The city centre district is a Unesco World Heritage site. Though well trodden, it rewards close exploration, and if crowds distract then try exploring the streets at night.

STEPHANSDOM

The most beloved and recognisable structure in all of Vienna is the Gothic masterpiece **Stephansdom** (Map pp120-1; ☎ 515 52-3520; www .stephanskirche.at; 01, Stephansplatz; admission free, guided tours adult/student & child €4/1.50; ⏱ 6am-10pm Mon-Sat, 7am-10pm Sun, tours in English 3.45pm Apr-Oct) or Steffl (little Stephen) as the Viennese call it.

The cathedral was built on the site of a 12th-century church, of which the surviving

---

MORE FOR YOUR MONEY

If you're planning on doing a lot of sightseeing in a short period, consider purchasing the **Wien-Karte** (Vienna Card; €18.50), which provides 72 hours of unlimited travel plus discounts at selected museums, attractions, cafés and shops. It comes with an information brochure and is available from hotels and ticket offices.

The Kunsthistorisches Museum and its associated museums are covered by Gold, Silver and Bronze tickets. The **Gold ticket** (€23) allows entry to the Kunsthistorisches Museum, Schatzkammer, Neue Burg museums, Museum für Völkerkunde, Wagenburg in Schönbrunn and the Theatermuseum. The **Silver ticket** (€21) covers everything the Gold ticket does, minus the Wagenburg. Third place **Bronze** (€19) will get you into the Kunsthistorisches Museum, Schatzkammer, Neue Burg museums and the Museum für Völkerkunde.

The City of Vienna runs some 20 **municipal museums** (www.museum.vienna.at) scattered around the city, all of which are included in a free booklet available at the Rathaus. Permanent exhibitions in all are free on Sunday.

Riesentor (Giant's Gate), main entrance and Heidentürme (Towers of the Heathens) are incorporated into the present building. These are Romanesque, but the cathedral's most distinctive features date from it being rebuilt in the Gothic style from 1359.

Dominating the cathedral is the skeletal **Südturm** (adult/student & child €3/1; ⏰ 9am-5.30pm), rising 136.7m and completed in 1433 after 75 years of work. Negotiating 343 steps brings you to a cramped viewing platform that's a stunning panorama of Vienna. Originally this should have been matched on the north side by a **companion tower** (adult/student €4/1.50; ⏰ 8.30am-5.30pm Apr-May & Sep-Oct, 8.30am-6pm Jul & Aug, 8.30am-7pm Nov-Mar), accessible by lift, but the imperial purse withered and when the Gothic style went out of fashion its incomplete tower was topped off with a Renaissance cupola in 1579. The **Pummerin** (boomer bell), Austria's largest bell and weighing in at a hefty 21 tonnes, was installed in 1952.

Look closely at decorations and statues on the exterior of the cathedral: at the rear the agony of the Crucifixion well captured, while the glorious **tiled roof** shows dazzling chevrons on one end and the Austrian eagle on the other.

Taking centre stage inside is the magnificent Gothic **stone pulpit**, fashioned in 1515 by Anton Pilgram. The expressive faces of the four fathers of the church (the saints Augustine, Ambrose, Gregory and Jerome) are at the centre of the design, but the highlight is Pilgram himself peering out from a window below. He also appears at the base of the organ loft on the northern wall, seemingly holding up the entire organ on his narrow shoulders. The baroque **high altar** in the main chancel depicts the stoning of St Stephen; the left chancel contains a winged altarpiece from Wiener Neustadt, dating from 1447; the right chancel houses the Renaissance-style red marble tomb of Friedrich III.

The cathedral's **Katakomben** (catacombs; adult/student €4/1.50; guided tour every 15 or 30min 10-11.30am & 1.30-4.30pm Mon-Sat, 1.30-4.30pm Sun) house the remains of plague victims, kept in a mass grave and a bone house. Also on display are rows of urns containing the organs of the Habsburgs. One of the many privileges of being a Habsburg was to be dismembered and dispersed after death: their hearts are in the Augustinerkirche in the Hofburg and the rest is in the Kaisergruft (p127).

HOFBURG

Nothing symbolises the culture and heritage of Austria more than its Hofburg (Imperial Palace; Map pp120–1). The Habsburgs were based here for over six centuries, from the first emperor (Rudolf I in 1273) to the last (Karl I in 1918). The Hofburg owes its size and architectural diversity to plain old one-upmanship; new sections were added by the new rulers, including the early baroque **Leopold Wing** (Map pp120–1), the 18th-century **Imperial Chancery Wing** (Map pp120–1), the 16th-century **Amalia Wing** (Map pp120–1) and the Gothic **Burgkapelle** (Royal Chapel; Map pp120–1).

The oldest section is the 13th-century **Schweizerhof** (Swiss Courtyard; Map pp120–1), named after the Swiss guards who used to protect its precincts. The Renaissance Swiss gate dates from 1553. The courtyard adjoins a larger courtyard, **In der Burg** (Map pp120–1), with a monument to Emperor Franz II adorning its centre. The palace now houses the offices of the Austrian president and a raft of museums.

Kaiserappartements

The **Kaiserappartements** (Imperial Apartments; Map pp120–1; ☎ 533 75 70; 01, Innerer Burghof, Kaisertor; adult/student/child €9.90/8.90/4.90; ⏰ 9am-5pm, 9am-5.30pm Jul & Aug), once occupied by Franz Josef I and Empress Elisabeth, are extraordinary for their opulence, fine furniture, tapestries and bulbous crystal chandeliers; only Schloss Schönbrunn (p135) matches the sheer extravagance of these apartments. The highlight of the adjoining **Hoftafel und Silberkammer** (Court Tableware and Silver Depot), a collection of porcelain and tableware, is a 30m long Mailänder Tafelaufsatz (Milan Table Piece). Admission to the apartments includes an audio guide plus entry to Hoftafel und Silberkammer and Sisi.

Sisi

Occupying the first six rooms of the Kaiserappartements and included in the entry price, **Sisi Museum** (Map pp120–1; ☎ 533 75 70; 01, Innerer Burghof, Kaisertor; ⏰ 9am-5pm, 9am-5.30pm Jul & Aug) is devoted to the life of Austria's Empress Elisabeth, often called 'Sisi'. A reconstruction of the luxurious coach that carried her on many a journey is one highlight, but it's the details that give a feel for the life of the empress: a reconstruction of the dress she wore on the eve of her wedding, plus her sunshade, fans and gloves.

Schatzkammer

The **Schatzkammer** (Imperial Treasury; Map pp120-1; ☎ 525 24-486; 01, Schweizerhof; adult/student/child/family €8.10/7.50/3.50/20; ☺ 10am-6pm Wed-Mon) is a spectacular collection of secular and ecclesiastical treasures. The sheer wealth on display is staggering: Room 7 alone contains a 2860-carat Colombian emerald, a 416-carat balas ruby and a 492-carat aquamarine; Room 11 holds the highlight of the Treasury, the 10th-century imperial crown with eight gold plates and precious gems; while Room 8 contains a 75cm-wide bowl carved from a single piece of agate, and a narwhal tusk, 243cm long and once claimed to have been a unicorn horn. The Sacred Treasury tops it off with rare religious relics, and the dubious claim to have fragments of the True Cross, one of the nails from the Crucifixion and one of the thorns from Christ's crown.

Lipizzaner Museum

The **Lipizzaner Museum** (Map pp120-1; ☎ 525 24-583; www.lipizzaner.at; 01, Reitschulestrasse 2; adult/student & child/family €5/3.60/10; ☺ 9am-6pm) focuses on the famous white stallions of the Spanische Hofreitschule (Spanish Riding School; below). A cross-breed of Spanish, Arab and Berber horses, the Lipizzaner were first imported from Spain (hence 'Spanish') by Maximilian II in 1562, and in 1580 a stud was established at Lipizza (hence 'Lipizzaner'), now in Slovenia. Text is in English, but the content is a little thin. Windows allow a view directly into the stallion stables, albeit obscured by thick glass and fine mesh.

Spanische Hofreitschule

For the real thing, cross the street to the **Spanische Hofreitschule** (Map pp120-1; ☎ 533 90 31; www.srs.at; 01, Michaelerplatz 1; admission €31-165; ☺ performances 11am Sun mid-Feb–Jun & Sep-Dec, extra performances Fri & Sat). These graceful stallions perform an equine ballet to a programme of classical music while chandeliers shimmer from above and the audience cranes to see from pillared balconies. Tickets can be ordered through the website, but be warned that performances are usually booked out months in advance. Unclaimed tickets are sold about two hours before performances, so you might try asking at the office about cancellations. Training or movement programmes are open to the public at various times. The most regular is the 'Morgenarbeit' **Morning Training** (adult/student & child/family €12/6/24; ☺ 10am-noon Tue-Sat Feb-Jun & mid-Aug–Dec) session. For these, tickets can be bought the same day at gate 2, Josefsplatz in the Hofburg. Queues are very long early in the day, but most people have disappeared by around 11am, when you can often get in quickly. It's a fairly dull affair, and photos aren't allowed at any sessions, so if you want one try waiting to see the horses cross between the school and the *Stallburg* (stables), which usually happens on the half-hour.

Nationalbibliothek

Austria's flagship library, the **Nationalbibliothek** (National Library; Map pp120-1; ☎ 534 10 397; www.onb.ac.at; 01, Josefsplatz 1; adult/student & child/family €5/3/9; ☺ 10am-6pm Tue-Sun, till 9pm Thu) contains an astounding collection of literature, maps, globes of the world and other cultural relics; its highlight, though, is the **Prunksaal** (Grand Hall), a majestic baroque hall built between 1723 and 1726. Commissioned by Karl VI (whose statue is under the central dome), it holds some 200,000 leather-bound scholarly tomes. Rare volumes (mostly 15th century) are stored within glass cabinets, with books opened to beautifully illustrated pages of text. The central fresco, by Daniel Gran, depicts the emperor's apotheosis.

Neue Burg Museums

An ensemble of three museums occupy part of the **Neue Burg** (Map pp120-1; ☎ 525 24-484; 01, Heldenplatz; adult/student & child/family €8/6/16, audio guide €3; ☺ 10am-6pm Wed-Mon). The **Sammlung Alter Musik Instrumente** (Collection of Ancient Musical Instruments) is the best of the bunch and contains instruments in all shapes, sizes and tones. The **Ephesos Museum** features artefacts from Ephesus and Samothrace donated (some say 'lifted') by the Sultan in 1900 after a team of Austrian archaeologists excavated Ephesus in Turkey. Last but not least is the **Hofjagd und Rüstkammer** (Arms and Armour), with a fine collection of ancient armour dating mainly from the 15th and 16th centuries.

Museum für Völkerkunde

The **Museum für Völkerkunde** (Ethnological Museum; Map pp120-1; ☎ 534 30-0; www.ethno-museum.ac.at; 01, Heldenplatz; adult/student & child/family €10/7.50/20; ☺ 10am-6pm Wed-Mon) has rotating exhibitions while being renovated (expected to finish in 2009). Its permanent collection of folk art from around the world includes an Aztec feather headdress once worn by Montezuma. (Note that entry to the Neue Burg museums and Museum für Völkerkunde have this combined price during exhibitions.)

ALBERTINA

Once used to house imperial guests, the **Albertina** (Map pp120-1; ☎ 534 83-544; www.albertina .at; 01, Albertinaplatz 3; adult/student/child €9.50/7/3.50; ⏰ 10am-6pm, to 9pm Wed) is now home to an astoundingly rich collection of graphic art. It contains 1½ million prints and 50,000 drawings, including 145 Dürer drawings (the largest in the world), 43 by Raphael, 70 by Rembrandt and 150 by Schiele. There are more by Leonardo da Vinci, Michelangelo, Rubens, Bruegel, Cézanne, Picasso, Klimt, Matisse and Kokoschka, and of course only a fraction of the collection is on display at any one time. Exhibitions, which normally follow a theme or artist, are changed every three months and also feature works from other collections.

HAUS DER MUSIK

The four floors of the **Haus der Musik** (House of Music; Map pp120-1; ☎ 516 48; www.hdm.at; 01, Seilerstätte 30; adult/student & child €10/8.50, half-price 5-9pm Tue; ⏰ 10am-10pm) are devoted in one form or another to music. All descriptions are in English and German. The 1st floor pays homage, rather briefly, to the Vienna Philharmonic.

The 2nd floor is where the fun begins; the **Sonosphere** section delves into the physics of sounds and uses touch screens and loads of hands-on displays to explain the mechanics of sound. Here you can test the limits of your hearing and play around with sampled sounds and record your own CD (€0.99 per song, plus €2 for CD and cover). The 3rd floor features the stars of Vienna's classical music – Haydn, Mozart, Beethoven, Schubert, Strauss and Mahler all receive a room apiece. Best of all is the 'virtual conductor', where a video of the Vienna Philharmonic responds to a conducting baton and keeps time with your movements. Floor 4 has experimental and electronic music, which you can also modify. Singing trees, sound sticks and beeping buttons are just some of the hands-on 'instruments' at your disposal.

KAISERGRUFT

The high-peaked **Kaisergruft** (Imperial Burial Vault; Map pp120-1; ☎ 512 68 53; www.kapuziner.at/wien; in German; 01 Neuer Markt; adult/student/child €4/3/1.50; ⏰ 10am-6pm), beneath the Kapuzinerkirche (Church of the Capuchin Friars), was instigated by Empress Anna (1585–1618), and her body and that of her husband, Emperor Matthias (1557–1619), were the first to be placed here. Since then, all but three of the Habsburg dynasty members found their way here (in bits and pieces), the last being Empress Ziti in 1989. The only non-Habsburg to be buried here is the Countess Fuchs.

The royals' fashion extends even to tombs: those in the vault range from the unadorned to the ostentatious. By far the most elaborate caskets are those in 18th-century baroque pomp, such as the huge double sarcophagus containing Maria Theresia and Franz I. The tomb of Charles VI has been expertly restored. Both were the work of Balthasar Moll (p54).

JÜDISCHES MUSEUM

The **Jüdisches Museum** (Jewish Museum; Map pp120-1; ☎ 535 04 31; www.jmw.at; 01, Dorotheergasse 11; adult/student & child €6.50/4; ⏰ 10am-6pm Sun-Fri), taking up three floors of Palais Eskeles, uses holograms and an assortment of objects to document the history of the Jews in Vienna, from the first settlements at Judenplatz in the 13th century up to the present. The ground floor is filled with the Max Berger collection – a rich compilation of Judaica mainly dating from the Habsburg era. Temporary exhibitions are presented on the 1st floor, with the 2nd floor dividing its space between more temporary exhibitions and 21 holograms depicting the history of the Jewish people in Vienna.

A combined ticket of €10/6 for adult/ student and child (bring ID) allows entry to the **Stadttempel** (Synagogue; Map pp120-1; ☎ 535 04 31; www.jmw.at; 01, Seitenstettengasse 4; adult/student & child €3/2; ⏰ guided tours 11.30am & 2pm Mon-Thu) and the Museum Judenplatz (below).

MUSEUM JUDENPLATZ

The **Museum Judenplatz** (Jewish museum; Map p120-1; ☎ 535 04 31; www.jmw.at; 01, Judenplatz 8; adult/student & child €4/2.50; ⏰ 10am-6pm Sun-Thu, 10am-2pm Fri) focuses on excavated remains of a medieval synagogue (1421) once situated on Judenplatz. The basic outline of the synagogue can still be seen and a small model of the building helps to complete the picture. Documents and artefacts dating from 1200 to 1400 are on display, and spacey interactive screens explain Jewish culture. On Judenplatz is Austria's first Holocaust memorial, the 'Nameless Library'.

VIENNA

This squat, boxlike structure pays homage to the 65,000 Austrian Jews who were killed during the Holocaust.

ANKERUHR

The picturesque **Ankeruhr** (Art Nouveau clock; Map pp120-1; Hoher Markt 10-11) was created by Franz von Matsch in 1911 and commissioned by the Anker Insurance Co. Over a 12-hour period, figures such as Josef Haydn and Maria Theresia slowly pass across the clock face – details of who's who are outlined on a plaque on the wall below. Join the mass of tourists at noon when all the figures trundle past in turn, and organ music from the appropriate period is piped out.

Other interesting sights in the Innere Stadt:

Beethovenhaus (Map pp120-1; ☎ 535 89 05; 01, Mölker Bastei 8; adult/student & child €2/1; ⏰ 10am-1pm & 2-6pm Tue-Sun) Beethoven's residence from 1804 to 1814 (he apparently occupied some 60 places in his 35 years in Vienna) where he composed Symphonies 4, 5 and 7 and the opera *Fidelio*, among other works. You can listen to works and view some memorabilia.

Mozarthaus Vienna (Map pp120-1; ☎ 512 1791; 01, Domgasse 5; adult/student/child €9/7/3; ⏰ 9am-6pm Tue-Sun) Three floors covering Vienna during Mozart's era, the musician himself and this former residence, where he penned *The Marriage of Figaro*.

Neidhart-Fresken (Map pp120-1; ☎ 535 90 65; 01, Tuchlauben 19; adult/child €2/1, free Sun; ⏰ 10am-1pm & 2-6pm Tue, 2-6pm Fri-Sun) The oldest extant secular murals in Vienna dating from 1398, retelling the story of the minstrel Neidhart von Reuental (1180–1240) in lively and jolly scenes.

Ruprechtskirche (St Rupert's Church; Map pp120-1; 01, Ruprechtsplatz) The oldest church in Vienna, first documented in 1137. Unfortunately it's rarely open to the public.

Ringstrasse

Emperor Franz Josef was largely responsible for the monumental architecture around the Ringstrasse (Ring). In 1857 he decided to tear down the redundant military fortifications and exercise grounds and replace them with grandiose public buildings in a variety of historical styles. Work began the following year and reached a peak in the 1870s. The stock market crash in 1873 put a major dampener on plans, and other grand plans were shelved due to lack of money and the outbreak of WWI. The Ring is easily explored on foot or bicycle; if you've not the time, jump on tram 1 or 2, both of which run the length of the boulevard and offer a snapshot of the impressive architecture.

PARLAMENT

The neoclassical façade and Greek pillars of **Parlament** (Map pp120-1; ☎ 40 110-2570; www.parlin kom.gv.at; 01, Dr-Karl-Renner-Ring 3; tours adult/student & child €4/2; ⏰ tours 10am, 11am, 2pm, 3pm & 4pm Mon-Fri, 10am, 11am, noon & 1pm Sat) are the work of Theophil Hansen in 1883 and make a striking impression; it's complemented by the beautiful **Athena Fountain** situated in front of the building. Athena is flanked by statues of horse breaking (though some would say horse punching).

RATHAUS

The neo-Gothic **Rathaus** (City Hall; Map pp120-1; ☎ 525 50; www.wien.gv.at; 01, Rathausplatz; ☎ tours 1pm Mon, Wed & Fri), which was modelled on Flemish city halls, steals the Ringstrasse show. Its main spire soars to 102m, if you include the pennant held by the knight at the top. You're free to wander through the seven inner courtyards but you must join a guided tour to catch a glimpse of the interior, with its red carpets, gigantic mirrors and frescoes.

KUNSTHISTORISCHES MUSEUM

The **Kunsthistorisches Museum** (Museum of Fine Arts; Map pp120-1; ☎ 525 240; www.khm.at; 01, Burgring 5; adult/student & child/family €10/7.50/20, audio guides in English €3; ⏰ 10am-6pm Tue-Sun, 10am-9pm Thu) ranks among the finest museums in Europe, if not the world, and should not be missed. The Habsburgs were great collectors, and the huge extent of lands under their control led to many important works of art being funnelled back to Vienna.

Rubens was appointed to the service of a Habsburg governor in Brussels, so it comes as no surprise that the museum has one of the best collections of his works. The collection of paintings by Pieter Bruegel the Elder (1525–69) is also unrivalled. In the building itself, the murals between the arches above the stairs were created by three artists, including a young Klimt (1862–1918; northern wall), painted before he broke with neoclassical tradition.

See the website for details of free tours on special topics.

Ground Floor

In the west wing is the Egyptian collection, including the burial chamber of Prince Kaninisut and mummified animal remains. The Greek and Roman collection here includes the Gemma Augusta cameo made from onyx in AD 10.

The east wing contains sculpture and decorative arts covering a range of styles and epochs. This is closed for renovation in 2008 and 2009; when it reopens the collection will include 17th-century glassware, ornaments and lavish clocks from the 16th and 17th centuries.

First Floor

The *Gemäldegalerie* (Picture Gallery) on this floor is the most important part of the museum and features Bruegel, Dürer, Rubens, Rembrandt and many others. All works are labelled in English and German.

The **East Wing** is devoted mainly to German, Dutch and Flemish paintings. The exact locations of paintings change somewhat, but one room is set aside for the Bruegel collection, amassed by Rudolf II. A recurrent theme in Bruegel the Elder's work is nature, as in *The Hunters in the Snow* (1565). A gallery also displays the warm, larger-than-life scenes of Flemish baroque. The motto in *The Celebration of the Bean King* by Jacob Jordaens (1593–1678), a rollicking painting depicting revellers raising their glasses, translates as 'None resembles a fool more than the drunkard'. Works by Albrecht Dürer (1471–1528) feature prominently among the German painters. His brilliant mastery of colour is perhaps best illustrated in *The Adoration of the Trinity*, originally an altarpiece.

The paintings by the mannerist Giuseppe Arcimboldo (1527–93), in rooms dedicated to Italian painting in the 15th and 16th century, use a device well explored later by Salvador Dalí (1904–89) – familiar objects arranged to be perceived in a new light. Dramatic baroque scenes of Peter Paul Rubens (1577–1640), who brought together northern European and Italian traditions, are showcased among the 17th-century Flemish painters, and several self-portraits by Rembrandt can be found among the 17th-century Dutch painters.

The **West Wing** contains evocative works by Titian (1485–1576), a member of the Venetian school. Never too far away is *The Three Philosophers* (1508), which is one of the few properly authenticated works by Giorgione (1478–1510). Also part of the 15th- and 16th-century Italian collection is Raphael's (1483–1520) harmonious and idealised *Madonna in the Meadow* (1505) –

its triangular composition and the complementary colours are typical features of the Florentine high Renaissance. It's interesting to compare this with Caravaggio's (1571–1610) *Madonna of the Rosary* (1606), housed in the collection of Italian paintings from the 17th and 18th century, in which the supplicants' dirty feet illustrate a new realism in early baroque. The 18th-century Italian painter Bernardo Bellotto (1721–80) was commissioned by Maria Theresia to paint scenes of Vienna. Several are on show here, and some of these landscapes, such as a view from Belvedere, break away from faithful representation of the landscape.

NATURHISTORISCHES MUSEUM

The **Naturhistorisches Museum** (Museum of Natural History; Map pp120-1; ☎ 52177-0 www.nhm-wien.ac.at; 01, Burg Ring 7; adult/senior/student & child €8/6/3.50; ⏰ 9am-6.30pm Thu-Mon, 9am-9pm Wed) is the scientific counterpart of the Kunsthistorisches Museum. Minerals, meteorites and animal remains are displayed in jars, while zoology and anthropology are covered in detail and there's also a children's corner. The 25,000-year-old *Venus of Willendorf* statuette is on display here (her 100th anniversary of discovery was celebrated in 2008), and also in room 11 is her older sister, the 32,000 BC statuette *Venus of Galgenberg* (the oldest figurative sculpture in the world).

AKADEMIE DER BILDENDEN KÜNSTE

The **Gemäldegalerie der Akademie der bildenden Künste** (Academy of Fine Arts; Map pp120-1; ☎ 588 16-0; www.akademiegalerie.at, in German; 01, Schillerplatz 3; adult/student/child under 10 €7/4/free, audio guide €2; ⏰ 10am-6pm Tue-Sun) has a small picture gallery, the highlight of which is *The Last Judgement* altarpiece by Hieronymus Bosch (1450–1516). Flemish painters are well represented in this building, which itself sports an elegant façade. As fate would have it, this was the academy that turned down would-be artist Adolf Hitler. A statue of Schiller takes centre stage in front of the academy.

SECESSION

The year 1897 was a fateful one for Austrian art. This was the year 19 progressive artists broke away from the conservative artistic establishment that met in the Künstlerhaus art gallery in Vienna and formed their own Secession movement. Their aim was to present new trends in contemporary art and depart from backward-looking historicism. Among their number were Gustav Klimt, Josef Hoffman (1871–1956), Kolo Moser (1868–1918) and Josef M Olbrich (1867–1908), a former student of Otto Wagner (1841–1918).

In 1898, Olbrich designed the movement's **Secession Building** (Map pp120-1; ☎ 587 53 07; www.secession.at; 01, Friedrichstrasse 12; admission exhibition & frieze adult/child & student €6/3.50, exhibition only €4.50/3; ☺ 10am-6pm Tue-Sun, 10am-8pm Thu); its most striking feature is the enormous golden sphere (prosaically described as a 'golden cabbage' by some Viennese) rising from a turret on the roof. Above the door are highly distinctive mask-like faces with dangling serpents instead of earlobes. The motto above the entrance postulates: 'Der Zeit ihre Kunst, der Kunst ihre Freiheit' (To each time its art, to art its freedom).

The 14th exhibition held in the building, in 1902, featured the famous *Beethoven Frieze* by Klimt. This 34m-long work was intended only as a temporary exhibit, but has been painstakingly restored and is permanently on show in the basement. The frieze shows willowy women with bounteous hair jostling for attention with a large gorilla, while slender figures float and a choir sings. The ground floor is still used for temporary exhibitions of contemporary art.

MUSEUMSQUARTIER

The **MuseumsQuartier** (Museum Quarter; Map pp120-1; ☎ 523 58 81-173, 0820-600 600; www.mqw.at; 07, Museumsplatz 1; ☺ information & ticket centre 10am-7pm) is a remarkable ensemble of museums, cafés, restaurants and bars inside former imperial stables designed by Fischer von Erlach. This breeding ground of Viennese cultural life is the perfect place to hang out and watch or meet people on warm evenings. With over 60,000 sq metres of exhibition space, the complex is one of the world's most ambitious cultural spaces.

Of the combined tickets on offer, the MQ Kombi Ticket (€25) includes entry into every museum (Zoom only has a reduction) and a 30% discount on performances in the TanzQuartier Wien; MQ Art Ticket (€21.50) gives admission into the Leopold Museum, MUMOK, Kunsthalle and reduced entry into Zoom, plus 30% discount on the TanzQuartier Wien; and MQ Duo Ticket

(€17) covers everything the Art ticket does, minus the Kunsthalle.

Leopold Museum

In 1994 the Austrian government acquired the enormous private collection of 19th-century and modern Austrian paintings amassed by Rudolf Leopold, paying €160 million for 5266 paintings (sold individually, the paintings would have made him €574 million). It then went about building a museum to display this important collection, and the **Leopold Museum** (Map pp120-1; ☎ 525 70-0; www.leopoldmuseum.org; 07, Museumsplatz 1; adult/child & student €9/5.50, audio guide €3; ☺ 10am-6pm, till 9pm Thu) was born.

Leopold began his art collection in 1950 with the purchase of his first Egon Schiele (1890–1918), so it comes as no surprise that the Leopold owns the largest collection of the painter's work in the world. Most are usually on the ground floor; his *Kardinale und Nonne – Liebkosung* (Cardinal and Nun – Caress) is a delightful oil on canvas depicting the two figures kneeled in furtive embrace, their eyes fixed on the onlooker. Also on the ground floor is a large collection of works by Gustav Klimt; his large *Tod und Leben* (Death and Life) is just one highlight. Simple yet highly emotional sketches by both artists are displayed in the basement.

Other artists well represented include Albin Egger-Lienz (1868–1922), Richard Gerstl (1883–1908) and, arguably Austria's third-greatest painter (after Klimt and Schiele), Oskar Kokoschka (1886–1980). Egger-Lienz had a knack for capturing the essence of rural life; this is seen in his stark *Pietá*, considered by Leopold to be the artist's best work. Some of the most exciting pieces by Kokoschka were done early in his long career; his *Selbstportrait mit ein Hand* (Self-Portrait with One Hand) from 1918 is just one fine example. Works by Hoffmann, Loos, Otto Wagner, Waldmüller and Romako are also housed here.

MUMOK

The dark basalt rock building that houses the **Museum moderner Kunst** (MUMOK, Museum of Modern Art; Map pp120-1; ☎ 525 00; www.mumok.at; 07, Museumsplatz 1; adult/student €8/6.50; ☺ 10am-6pm, to 9pm Thu) is alive inside with Vienna's premier collection of 20th-century art, centred on fluxus, nouveau realism, pop art and photorealism. The best of expressionism, cubism, minimal art and Viennese Actionism (p54) is represented in a collection of 9000 works that are rotated and exhibited on themes. On a visit you might glimpse in the following order: a wearily slumped attendant (not part of any exhibit), photos of horribly deformed babies, a video piece of a man being led by a beautiful woman across a pedestrian crossing on a dog leash, naked bodies smeared with salad and other delights, a man parting his own buttocks, flagellation in a lecture hall, and an ultra-close up of a urinating penis. The heavy stuff comes later. Be prepared.

Kunsthalle

The **Kunsthalle** (Arts Hall; Map pp120-1; ☎ 521 890; www .kunsthallewien.at; 07, Museumsplatz 1; Hall 1 adult/student €7.50/6, Hall 2 €6/4.50, combined ticket €10.50/8.50; ☒ 10am-7pm Fri-Wed, to 10pm Thu) showcases Austrian and international contemporary art. Programmes, which run for three to six months, tend to focus mainly on photography, video, film, installation and new media.

MUSEUM FÜR ANGEWANDTE KUNST

The **Museum für angewandte Kunst** (MAK, Museum of Applied Art; Map pp120-1; ☎ 711 36-0; www.mak.at; 01, Stubenring 5; adult/child & student €7.90/5.50, free Sat, tours €2; ☒ 10am-6pm Wed-Sun, 10am-midnight Tue, tours in English noon Sun) is devoted to craftsmanship and art forms in everyday life. Each exhibition room showcases a different style, which includes Renaissance, baroque, orientalism, historicism, empire, Art Deco and the distinctive metalwork of the Wiener Werkstätte. Contemporary artists were invited to present the rooms in ways they felt were appropriate, the effect of which is eye-catching and unique displays. The 20th-century design and architecture room is one of the most fascinating, and Frank Gehry's cardboard chair is a gem. The museum collection encompass tapestries, lace, furniture, glassware and ornaments, and Klimt's *Stoclet Frieze* is upstairs.

The basement Study Collection has exhibits based on types of materials: glass and ceramics, metal, wood and textiles. Here you'll find anything from ancient oriental statues to unusual sofas (note the red-lips sofa).

OTHER SIGHTS OF RINGSTRASSE

Parks Relax in one of the Ring's three parks; Stadtpark (Map pp120-1; note the gold statue of Johann Strauss), Burggarten (Map pp120-1) and Volksgarten (Map pp120-1).
Postsparkasse (Map pp120-1; ☎ 534 53-33088 www .ottowagner.at; 01, Georg-Coch-Platz; museum entry adult/student & child €5/3.50; ☒ 8am-3pm Mon-Fri, 8am-5.30pm Thu, 10am-5pm Sat) Celebrated Post Office Savings Bank designed by Otto Wagner, with a museum giving insight into the building.
Votivkirche (Map pp120-1; 09, Rooseveltplatz; ☒ 9am-1pm & 4-6pm Tue-Sat, 9am-1pm Sun) Commissioned by Franz Josef after he survived an assassination attempt, this neo-Gothic church has an impressive façade but its interior is rather bleak and unwelcoming.

Across the Danube Canal

The districts across the Danube Canal from the Innere Stadt are predominantly residential neighbourhoods, largely bereft of individual sights of interest to the average visitor. But this is Vienna's outdoor playground.

PRATER

This large park encompasses grassy meadows, woodlands, an amusement park known as the **Wurstelprater** and one of the city's icons, the **Riesenrad** (Ferris wheel; Map pp116-17; ☎ 729 54 30; www.wienerriesenrad.com; 02, Prater 90; adult/child/family €8/3.20/20; ☒ 9am-midnight May-Sep, 10am-10pm Mar, Apr, Oct, 10am-8pm Nov-Feb). Built in 1897, the wheel is 65m high and takes about 20 minutes to rotate its 430-tonne weight one complete circle, offering great views of Vienna. It achieved celluloid fame in *The Third Man* (p32) in a scene where Harry Lime is confronted by his friend Holly Martins and delivers one the film's most poignant lines.

DONAUINSEL & ALTE DONAU

Dividing the Danube from the Neue Donau is the svelte **Donauinsel** (Map pp116–17), which stretches some 21.5km from opposite Klosterneuburg in the north to the Nationalpark Donau-Auen in the south. The island features long sections of swimming areas, concrete paths for walking and cycling, and restaurants and snack bars. The **Alte Donau** (Map pp114–15) is a landlocked arm of the Danube, a favourite of sailing and boating enthusiasts, swimmers, walkers, fishermen and, in winter (when it's cold enough), ice skaters.

Inside the Gürtel

The districts that lie inside the Gürtel are a dense concentration of apartment blocks pocketed by leafy parks, with a couple of grand baroque palaces thrown in for good measure.

VIENNA

SCHLOSS BELVEDERE

Belvedere is a masterpiece of total art and one of the world's finest baroque palaces. Designed by Johann Lukas von Hildebrandt (1668–1745), it was built for the brilliant military strategist, Prince Eugene of Savoy, conqueror of the Turks in 1718. The Unteres (Lower) Belvedere was built first (1714–16), with an orangery attached, and was the prince's summer residence. Connected to it by a long, landscaped garden is the Oberes (Upper) Belvedere (1721–23), the venue for the prince's banquets and other big bashes.

The palace is now home to the **Österreichische Galerie** (Austrian Gallery; combined ticket for both sections adult/child/student €12.50/5/8.50), split between the Unteres Belvedere and Orangerie, which combine to house special exhibitions, and the Oberes Belvedere, housing primarily Austrian art from the Middle Ages to the present.

Oberes Belvedere

Pride and joy of **Oberes Belvedere** (Map pp116-17; ☎ 795 57-0; www.belvedere.at; 03, Prinz-Eugen-Strasse 27; adult/student/child/€9.50/6/3/, audio guide €3; ☺ 10am-6pm) are its paintings by Gustav Klimt, including his famous *The Kiss* (1908) and *Judith* (1901), which, with their rich gold tones and highly ornamental style perfectly embody Viennese Art Nouveau. Masterpieces by Egon Schiele and Oskar Kokoschka also feature in this collection, while the Viennese Biedermeier school figures strongly through the works of Ferdinand Georg Waldmüller (1793–1865), Friedrich von Amerling (1803–87) and Peter Fendi (1796–1842). The gallery is a staggeringly beautiful who's who of Austrian art, with works by other artists of the calibre of Hans Makart (1840–84), Friedensreich Hundertwasser (1928–2000), Fritz Wotruba (1907–75) and many more.

The west wing of Upper Belvedere goes beyond Austria's borders to showcase some stunning late-Gothic sculpture and panels, beginning from 1400 and culminating in the 16th century. Just one highlight here is the 15th-century Znaim Altar, probably originating from Znojmo in Czech Moravia.

The baroque era finds expression in the evocative and sometimes disturbing paintings of Johann Michael Rottmayr (1654–1730) and Paul Troger (1698–1762), and the bizarrely grimacing sculptured heads of Franz Xaver Messerschmidt (1736–83).

While visiting the Upper Belvedere, try to see the elaborately stuccoed and frescoed **Marmorsaal** (Marble Hall), offering superb views over the palace gardens and Vienna.

Unteres Belvedere

Construction of **Unteres Belvedere** (Map pp120-1; ☎ 795 57-0; www.belvedere.at; 03, Rennweg 6; adult/child/student €7.50/3/4.50; ☺ 10am-6pm) took from 1714 to 1716 and is remarkable for Prince Eugene's former residential apartment and ceremonial rooms, with grandiose interiors such as in the **Groteskensaal** (Hall of the Grotesque), the **Marmorgalerie** (Marble Gallery) and the **Goldenes Zimmer** (Golden Room). Temporary exhibitions are held in Lower Belvedere and the newly redesigned **Orangery** (Map pp120-1); the latter has a walkway offering views over Prince Eugene's private garden and to Oberes Belvedere.

Gardens

The long garden between the two Belvederes was laid out in classical French style and has sphinxes and other mythical beasts along its borders. South of the Oberes Belvedere is a small **Alpine Garden** (Map pp116-17; adult/child & student €4/3; ☺ 10am-6pm Apr-Jul), which has 3500 plant species and a bonsai section. North of here is the much larger **Botanischer Gärten** (Map pp116-17; Botanical Gardens; admission free; ☺ 9am-1hr before dusk) belonging to Vienna University.

PALAIS LIECHTENSTEIN

After many years collecting dust in depot vaults, the private collection of Prince Hans-Adam II of Liechtenstein is now displayed in the magnificent **Palais Liechtenstein** (Liechtenstein Museum; Map p122; ☎ 319 57 67-0; www.liechtenstein museum.at; 09, Fürstengasse 1; permanent exhibition adult/student/child €10/8/5, temporary exhibition €4, audio guide €1; ☺ 10am-5pm). It's a magnificent private collection consisting of some 200 paintings and 50 sculptures, dating from 1500 to 1700.

Built between 1690 and 1712, the palace illustrates the audacious folly and extravagance of baroque architecture. Frescoes and ceiling paintings by the likes of Johann Michael Rottmayer (1654–1730) and Marcantonio Franceschini (1648–1729) decorate the halls, staircases and corridors of this sumptuous palace.

The palace is in four sections. On the ground floor near the western staircase (left as you enter), is the **Gentlemen's Apartment**

Library, a magnificent neoclassical hall containing about 100,000 books, frescoes by Johann Michael Rothmayr and a temple-like empire clock dating from 1795. From the library you can enter galleries I–III, which have changing exhibitions. You can also enter these directly from alongside the eastern staircase (near the cloak room). After that, climb the eastern staircase, which, like its western counterpart, is decorated with Rothmayr frescoes uncovered during restoration work in 2003. Upstairs is the **Herkulessaal** (Hercules Hall) – so named for the Hercules motifs within its ceiling frescoes by renowned Roman painter Andrea Pozzo (1642–1709).

Surrounding the hall on three sides beginning from the eastern staircase (right) and culminating at the western staircase are galleries IV–X with the **permanent collection** of the palace. And what a collection this is! Seven galleries intertwine to provide a trip through 200 years of art history, starting in 1500 with early Italian panel paintings in Gallery IV. Gallery V is dedicated to late-Gothic and Renaissance portraits; Raphael's *Portrait of a Man* (1503) is a highlight here. The centrepiece of the upper floor is Gallery VII, which is home to Peter Paul Rubens' *Decius Mus* cycle (1618). Consisting of eight almost life-size paintings, the cycle depicts the life and death of Decius Mus, a Roman leader who sacrificed himself so that his army could be victorious on the battlefield. Gallery VIII is totally devoted to Rubens and Flemish baroque painting, and even more Rubens are on display in Gallery IX – this time his portraits – alongside Van Dyck and Fran Hals. The sheer exuberance and life captured by Rubens in his *Portrait of Clara Serena Rubens* (1616) is testament to the great artist's talent. Gallery X gives you a soft landing of ivory craftwork and Dutch still life.

From 2008 the palace plans to open only on Sundays, when concerts held between 2pm and 3pm in the Hercules Hall will provide the focal point of a visit to including the galleries. Check ahead for current times.

HEERESGESCHICHTLICHES MUSEUM

The superb **Heeresgeschichtliches Museum** (Museum of Military History; Map pp116–17; ☎ 795 61-60420; www.hgm.or.at; 03, Arsenal; adult/student/child under 11/family €5.10/3.30/free/7.30; ☼ 9am-5pm Sat-Thu) is housed in the Arsenal, a large neo-Byzantine barracks and munitions depot.

Spread over two floors, the museum works its way from the Thirty Years' War (1618–48) to WWII, taking in the Hungarian Uprising and the Austro-Prussian War (ending in 1866), the Napoleonic and Turkish Wars, and WWI. Highlights on the 1st floor include the Great Seal of Mustafa Pasha, which fell to Prince Eugene of Savoy in the Battle of Zenta in 1697.

On the ground floor, the room on the assassination of Archduke Franz Ferdinand in Sarajevo in 1914 – which set off a chain of events culminating in the start of WWI – steals the show. The car he was shot in (complete with bullet holes), the sofa he bled to death on and his rather grisly bloodstained coat are on show. The eastern wing covers the Republic years after WWI up until the Anschluss in 1938; the excellent displays include propaganda posters and Nazi paraphernalia, plus video footage of Hitler hypnotising the masses.

WIEN MUSEUM

The **Wien Museum Karlsplatz** (Map pp120–1; ☎ 505 87 47-0; www.museum.vienna.at, in German; 04, Karlsplatz 5; adult/student & child €6/4; ☼ 9am-6pm Tue-Sun) is the main building of the city museum and illustrates the development of the capital through a blend of art, illustrations and historic objects. Exhibits include maps and plans, artefacts and stunning paintings by Klimt and Schiele, while Biedermeier painters like Waldmüller are worth the entrance fee alone.

KARLSKIRCHE

Southeast of Ressel Park, **Karlskirche** (St Charles' Church; Map pp120–1; ☎ 712 44 56; www.karlskirche.at; 04, Karlsplatz; adult/student/child under 10 €6/4/free; ☼ 9am-12.30pm & 1-6pm Mon-Sat, noon-5.45pm Sun) was built between 1716 and 1739 to fulfil a vow made by Charles VI following the 1713 plague. The twin columns are modelled on Trajan's Column in Rome and show scenes from the life of St Charles Borromeo (who succoured plague victims in Italy), to whom the church is dedicated. The huge oval dome is 72m high and its interior is graced by cloud-bound celestial beings painted by Johann Michael Rottmayr; while the frescoes are being restored, it's possible to take a lift up the scaffolding to the dome for a close-up look (€2).

VIENNA

URBAN RAMBLING ON & OFF GUMPENDORFER STRASSE

Gumpendorfer Strasse is an odd street that is definitely worth exploring to get a feel for Vienna away from Hofburg and the big attractions. A good starting point is from the top end at the Gürtel near the Gumpendorfer U-Bahn station. If you're hungry, you could even begin with a meal 'off-Gumpendorfer' at the Russian restaurant **Wladimir** (Map pp116–17; ☎ 595 25 24; www.wladimir .at; 06, Bürgerspitalgasse 22; mains €9-19; ☒ 5-11pm Tue-Sun), where the homemade Siberian *pelmeni* (ravioli) is the best of its species in town. Two blocks to the east, also off Gumpendorfer, is **Tag/ Nachtasyl** (Map pp116–17; ☎ 5969 977; 06, Stumpergasse 53-55; ☒ 8pm-4am) one place in town where you will still hear Bob Dylan's 'Desolation Row' over the PA system and revolution hangs in the air. It grew out of the Charter 77 Czech dissident movement and these days mostly continues the tradition with Czech acoustic acts on stage (or occasional Gothic party).

Back on Gumpendorfer, continue past the small church at Kurt-Pint-Platz. Otto-Bauergasse, left off Gumpendorfer, is a weird street with niche stores. Good to his name, **Jimmy Gotik** (Map pp116–17; 06, Otto-Bauergasse 21) specialises in Gothic clothing. Jimmy's wife stitches much of it together, and Algerian Jimmy sells it off the racks. **Steman** (p148) and **Café Jelinek** (p151) are also just off Gumpendorfer here.

Going round the bend back on Gumpendorfer, you reach a concrete **flak tower** (*Flakturm*), a relic from WWII that was part of Vienna's defences. Inside this monstrosity is the **Haus des Meeres** (Map pp120–1; ☎ 587 14 17; www.haus-des-meeres.at; 06, Fritz-Grünbaumplatz 1; adult/student/child €10.30/7.90/4.80; ☒ 9am-6pm, till 9pm Thu), a small exhibition house replete with sea creatures and reptiles. Most interesting are its **piranha-feeding** (☒ 3pm Wed & Sun) and **snake-stroking** (☒ 2pm Wed) sessions. Those inclined towards alpine pursuits can scale a 37m face of the Flakturm, which has a **Kletterwand** (Map pp120–1; www.oeav-events.at/flakturm; adults/child per 2hr €12/8; ☒ 2-10pm Apr-Oct). It's serious climbing with clips, ropes and shoes.

Nearby Barnabitengasse is a slice of the Mediterranean, with a clutch of average restaurants. At the top of the street, where the arch crosses, is Mariahilfer Kirche. South of Gumpendorfer and along 100m, begins the **Naschmarkt** (pp120–1) and all this eating mile has to offer. Late-night crawlers can drop into the **Café Drechsler** (Map pp120–1), which *closes* for one hour each day. In Joanelligasse, you'll find the remarkable **Einhorn** (Map pp120–1; ☎ 586 32 12; 06, Joanelligasse 7; ☒ 4pm-4am Sun-Fri, 1pm-4am Sat), which used to be a jazz place but is now a relaxed, downbeat hangout with table football downstairs. Continuing along Gumpendorfer for the final leg, you reach **Café Sperl** (Map pp120–1), and across the road **Phil** (Map pp120–1; ☎ 581 04 89; 06, Gumpendorfer Strasse 10-12; ☒ 10-1am Tue-Sun, 5pm-1am Mon), another downbeat bar, also selling books and CDs; later come **Ra'mien** (Map pp120–1) and **Felixx** (Map pp120–1; ☎ 920 47 14; Gumpendorfer Strasse 5; mains €9-15; ☒ 7pm-3am), a mixed hetero and gay bar with a daily menu and some good wines.

Topping off the urban trek is **Top Kino Bar** (Map pp120–1; ☎ 208 30 00; Rahlgasse 1; ☒ 10-2am), which serves the Czech Kozel beer, has small balconies where you can loll in a warm breeze, and is part of an art-house cinema.

KUNSTHAUSWIEN

This **art gallery** (Map pp116–17; ☎ 712 04 91; www.kunst hauswien.com; 03, Untere Weissgerberstrasse 13; adult/ student & child €9/7, incl temporary exhibitions €12/9, half-price Mon; ☒ 10am-7pm) looks like something out of a toy shop. It was designed by Friedensreich Hundertwasser, whose highly innovative buildings feature uneven floors, coloured ceramics, patchwork decoration, irregular corners, and grass and trees on the roof. The permanent collection is something of a tribute to Hundertwasser, showcasing his paintings, graphics, tapestry, his philosophy on ecology, and architecture.

While you're in the area, walk down the road to see the exterior of **Hundertwasserhaus** (Map pp116–17; cnr Löwengasse & Kegelgasse), a block of residential flats also designed by the artist. Opposite is the **Kalke Village** (Map pp116–17; ☒ 9am-5pm, 9am-7pm summer), another piece of Hundertwasser handiwork housing cafés and souvenir and art shops.

Other attractions worth sniffing out: **Haydnhaus** (Map pp116–17; ☎ 596 13 07; 06, Haydngasse 19; adult/student & child €2/1; ☒ 10am-1pm & 2-6pm Wed & Thu, 10am-1pm Fri-Sun) Features a smattering of period furniture and memorabilia from Haydn, who lived here from 1796 till 1809; he composed *The Creation* and *The Seasons* under its roof. There are also rooms devoted to Brahms.

Majolikahaus (Map pp120-1; 06, Linke Wienzeile 40)
Art Nouveau masterpiece by Otto Wagner, so named for
the majolica tiles used to create the flowing floral motifs
on the façade.

Sigmund Freud Museum (Map p122; ☎ 319 15 96;
www.freud-museum.at; 09, Berggasse 19; adult/student/
child €7/4.50/2.50; ☽ 9am-5pm) Former house of the
famous psychologist, now housing a small museum
featuring some of his personal belongings.

Stadtbahn Pavillions (Map pp120-1; ☎ 505 87 47-84
059; 04, Karlsplatz; adult/student & child €2/1; ☽ 9am-
6pm Tue-Sun Apr-Oct) *Jugendstil* pavilions designed by
Otto Wagner for Vienna's first public transport system.

Outside the Gürtel

The districts that fall outside the Gürtel are
quite an unusual blend. Parts are rather dull
and uninviting (by Viennese standards) – in
particular towards the south – while others are
beautiful beyond belief and home to some of
Vienna's greatest treasures.

SCHLOSS SCHÖNBRUNN

The regal rooms of **Schloss Schönbrunn** (Map pp116-
17; ☎ 811 13-0; www.schoenbrunn.at; 13 Schloss Schönbrunn;
Imperial tour adult/student/child €9.50/8.50/4.90, grand tour
€12.90/11.40/6.90; ☽ 8.30am-6pm Jul-Aug, 8.30am-5pm
Apr-Jun & Sep-Oct, 8.30am-4.30pm Nov-Mar) are in a
league of their own in Vienna; the interior is
a majestic conflux of frescoed ceilings, crystal
chandeliers and gilded ornaments.

Commissioned by Leopold I, the palace
was completed by Johann Bernhard Fischer
von Erlach in 1700 but never quite reached
the grandeur he originally envisaged; it nevertheless has a startling 1441 rooms, of which
40 are open to the public. The full quota is
viewed in the Grand Tour, which takes in the
apartments of Franz Joseph I and Empress
Elisabeth, the ceremonial and state rooms,
and the audience chambers of Maria Theresia
and her husband Franz Stephan. The Imperial
Tour excludes the chambers of Maria Theresia
and Franz Stephan and takes in 22 rooms.

Both tours start in the west wing at the
bottom of the **Blauerstiege** (Blue Staircase) and
climb to the private rooms of Franz Joseph
I and Sisi. The ceremonial and state rooms
start with the **Spiegelsaal** (Hall of Mirrors)
where Mozart (then six) played his first royal
concert in the presence of Maria Theresia in
1762. The pinnacle of finery is reached in the
Grosse Galerie (Great Gallery), where gilded
scrolls, ceiling frescoes, chandeliers and huge
crystal mirrors are used to staggering effect.

Numerous sumptuous balls were held here,
including one for delegates attending the
Congress of Vienna (1814–15).

Near the Great Gallery is the **Round Chinese
Room**, which features a hidden doorway and
table that can be drawn up through the floor.
The Imperial Tour ends with the **Ceremonial
Hall**, while the Grand Tour continues onto the
Blue Chinese Room, where Charles I abdicated
in 1918, and the **Million Room**, named after the
sum that Maria Theresia paid for the decorations, which comprise Persian miniatures set
on rosewood panels and framed with gilded
rocaille frames. While not joined to the main
set of rooms, the **Bergl Rooms** are worth visiting for the paintings of Johann Wenzl Bergl
(1718–89); his exotic depictions of flora and
fauna quite successfully bring inside the palace's garden setting.

Gardens

The palace **gardens** (admission free; ☽ 6am-dusk
Apr-Oct, 6.30am-dusk Nov-Mar), arranged in the
French style, are a symphony of colour in
the summer and a fusion of demure greys
and browns in winter. The extensive grounds
reveal a number of attractions along tree-
lined avenues, including fake **Roman ruins**,
the **Neptunbrunnen** (Neptune Fountain) and
the Classical colonnaded **Gloriette** (adult/stu-
dent/child €1.99/1.50/1; ☽ 9am-6pm Apr-Sep, till 5pm Oct),
offering a stunning 360-degree panorama.
The original **Schöner Brunnen fountain**, from
which the palace gained its name, now pours
through the stone pitcher of a nymph near
the Roman ruins.

The **Palmenhaus** (Map pp116-17; ☎ 877 50 87-406;
adult/student & child €4/2.80; ☽ 9.30am-6pm May-Sep,
9.30am-5pm Oct-Apr) is a glorious glass and iron
construction still housing palms and hot-
house plants from around the world. Close
by is the **Wüstenhaus** (Desert House; Map pp116-17;
☎ 877 50 87-406; adult/student & child €6/4; ☽ 9am-6pm
May-Sep, 9am-5pm Oct-Apr), which makes good use
of the Sonnenuhrhaus (Sun Dial House) to
recreate arid desert scenes.

Behind both is the world's oldest zoo,
Tiergarten (Map pp116-17; ☎ 877 92 94; www.zoo
vienna.at; 13, Maxingstrasse 13b; adult/student/child €12/5/4;
☽ 9am-6.30pm Apr-Sep, 9am-5.30pm Mar & Oct, 9am-5pm
Feb, 9am-4.30pm Nov-Jan). Founded in 1752 as a
menagerie by Franz Stephan, the zoo now
houses some 750 animals of all shapes and
sizes; thankfully most of the original cramped
cages have been updated. The **Tirolerhof**, inside

the Tiergarten, is a real highlight both for adults and kids (see p138).

Wagenburg

The **Wagenburg** (Imperial Coach Collection; Map pp116-17; ☎ 877 32 44; 13; Schloss Schönbrunn; adult/student & child/family €4.50/3/9, audio guide €2; ✆ 9am-6pm Apr-Oct, 10am-4pm Tue-Sun Nov-Mar) displays carriages ranging from tiny children's wagons up to sumptuous vehicles of state, but nothing can compete with Emperor Franz I Stephen's (1708–65) coronation carriage. Weighing in at 4000kg, it is literally dripping in ornate gold plating and has Venetian glass panes and painted cherubs.

ZENTRALFRIEDHOF

Opened in 1874, the **Zentralfriedhof** (Central Cemetery; Map pp114-15; ☎ 760 41-0; 11, Simmeringer Hauptstrasse 230-244; admission free; ✆ information office 7.30am-3pm Mon-Sat; cemetery 7am-7pm May-Aug, 7am-6pm Mar, Apr, Sep & Oct, 8am-5pm Nov-Feb) has grown to become one of Europe's largest cemeteries – larger than the Innere Stadt and, with 2½ million graves, far exceeding the population of Vienna itself.

It contains the lion's share of tombs of Vienna's greats, including numerous famous composers: Gluck, Beethoven, Schubert, Brahms, Schönberg and the whole Strauss clan are buried here in the cold ground. A monument to Mozart has also been erected, but he was actually buried in an unmarked mass grave in the **St Marxer Friedhof** (Map pp116-17; 03, Leberstrasse 6-8; ✆ 7am-7pm Jun-Aug, 7am-6pm May & Sep, 7am-5pm Apr & Oct, 7am-dusk Nov-Mar). The Ehrengräber (Tombs of Honour) in the Zentralfriedhof are just beyond Gate Two and, in addition to the clump of famous composers, those pushing up daisies include Hans Makart, sculptor Fritz Wotruba, architects Theophil Hansen and Adolf Loos, and *the* man of Austrian Pop, Falco (Hans Hölzel; see boxed text, p49).

KIRCHE AM STEINHOF

Situated in the grounds of the Psychiatric Hospital of the City of Vienna, **Kirche am Steinhof** (Art Nouveau church; Map pp114-15; ☎ 910 60-11 204; 14, Baumgartner Höhe 1; tours €4; ✆ 3-4pm Sat) is the remarkable achievement of Otto Wagner from 1904 to 1907. Kolo Moser chipped in with the mosaic windows, and the roof is topped by a copper-covered dome that earned the nickname *Limoniberg* (lemon mountain) from its original golden colour. It's a bold statement in an asylum that has other Art Nouveau buildings, and it could only be pushed through by Wagner because the grounds were far from the public gaze.

ACTIVITIES

With its abundance of parks, waterways and woodlands, Vienna is a great city for fresh air and outdoor fun.

Boating

The Alte Donau is the main boating and sailing centre in Vienna, but the Neue Donau also provides opportunities for boating, windsurfing and water skiing. Places to rent boats include **Hofbauer** (Map pp116-17; ☎ 203 86 80; www.hofbauer.at, in German; 22, Wagramerstrasse 49; ✆ Apr–mid-Oct), which has electric boats for €13.50 for an hour, rudder boats (basically dinghies) for €7, and paddle boats for €11. You can also windsurf down the Danube for €11. The **sailing school** (Map pp114-15; ☎ 204 34 35; www.hofbauer.at; 22, An der Oberen Alten Donau 191; ✆ Apr-Oct) is on the eastern bank of the Alte Donau and has sailing boats for hire, and lessons in English.

Cycling

Vienna's layout and well-marked cycle lanes make cycling a pleasant and popular pastime, especially along the banks of the Danube, in the Prater and around the Ringstrasse. The Wienerwald is also popular for mountain biking; check the websites www.mbike.at and www.mtbwienerwald.at (both in German) for ideas and trails. For bike hire, see p159.

Swimming

The Donauinsel, Alte Donau and Lobau (all free bathing) are hugely popular places for taking a dip on steamy hot summer days. Topless sunbathing is quite the norm, as is nude sunbathing but only in designated areas; much of Lobau and both tips of the Donauinsel are *Frei Körper Kultur* (FKK, nude-bathing areas).

Complementing these natural swimming areas are numerous swimming pools owned and run by the city. In general, entry to these pools costs about €4.50/2.50 for adults/children. Some of the better ones are **Amalienbad** (Map pp116-17; ☎ 607 47 47; 10, Reumannplatz 23; ✆ 9am-6pm Tue & Sun, 9am-9.30pm Wed & Fri, 7am-9.30pm Thu, 7am-8pm Sat, 12.30-3.30pm Mon), a stunning *Jugendstil* bath (Monday sessions for seniors and people with disabilities only); **Strandbad Gänsehäufel** (Map pp114-15; ☎ 269 90 16; 22, Moissigasse 21; ✆ 9am-

7pm Mon-Fri, 8am-7pm Sat & Sun 2 May-13 May & 27 Aug-16 Sep, 9am-8pm Mon-Fri, 8am-8pm Sat & Sun 14 May-26 Aug), occupying a section of island in the Alte Donau; and the lovely **Thermalbad Oberlaa** (Map pp114-15; ☎ 6800 99600; 10, Kurbadstrasse 14; adult/child €9.60/6 for 2½hr; ⏱ 8.45am-10pm Mon-Sat, 7.45am-10pm Sun), a large thermal complex with both indoor and outdoor pools.

For a full list of pools call ☎ 60112 8044 between 7.30am and 3.30pm Monday to Friday or log on to www.wien.at/baeder (in German).

Walking

To the west of the city, the rolling hills and marked trails of the Wienerwald are perfect for walkers. A good trail heading in the woods to the north of Vienna starts in Nussdorf (take tram D from the Ring) and climbs Kahlenberg (484m), a hill offering views of the city. On your return to Nussdorf you can undo all that exercise by imbibing at a *Heuriger*. The round trip is around 11km, or you can spare yourself the leg-work by taking the Nussdorf-Kahlenberg 38A bus in one or both directions.

The Prater (p131) also has a wood with walking trails, and the densely forested Lainzer Tiergarten (Map pp114–15) animal reserve, a wild park in the west of Vienna, is perfect for roaming.

WALKING TOUR

This 1½- to two-hour walk (2.5km) takes you through some well-trodden tourist trails in Vienna. Some instantly recognisable sights (Stephansdom and the Hofburg) dominate this quarter of the Innere Stadt while Kärntner Strasse, Graben and Kohlmarkt attract shoppers by the busloads.

Start your walk heading north from the southern end of pedestrian-only Kärntner Strasse, a walkway of plush shops, trees, cafés and street entertainers. Detour left down the short Donnergasse to take a peek at the **Donnerbrunnen (1)** in Neuer Markt, a fountain with four naked figures representing the main tributaries of the Danube: the Enns, March, Traun and Ybbs. Across the square is the **Kaisergruft (2**; p127). Back on Kärntner Strasse, detour left again down Kärntner Durchgang. Here you'll find the **American Bar**

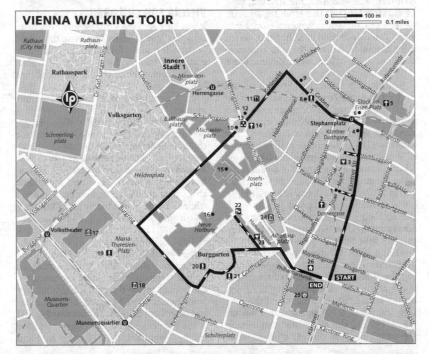

VIENNA WALKING TOUR

(3; p150), designed in 1908 by Adolf Loos, one of the prime exponents of a functional Art Nouveau style.

From Kärntner Strasse, the street opens out into Stock im Eisen Platz. Note the **nail-studded stump (4)**, said to have acquired its crude metal jacket in the 16th century from blacksmiths banging in a nail for luck when they left the city. Directly ahead is Vienna's symbol, Gothic **Stephansdom (5**; p124), offset by the unashamedly modern **Haas Haus (6)**. Many Viennese were rather unhappy about this curving silver structure crowding their beloved cathedral, but tourists seem happy enough to snap the spindly reflections of Stephansdom's spire in its rectangular windows.

Leading northwest from Stock im Eisen Platz is the broad pedestrian thoroughfare of **Graben**, another plush shopping street. It's dominated by the knobbly outline of the **Pestsäule (7)**, completed in 1693 to commemorate the 75,000 victims of the Black Death. Adolf Loos had a hand in the Graben's appearance, creating the **Schneidersalon Knize (8)** and the nearby **toilets (9)**. Turning left into Kohlmarkt, so named because charcoal was once sold here, the arresting sight of **Michaelertor (10)**, the Hofburg's northeastern gate on Michaelerplatz, comes into view. Towards the end of Kohlmarkt, on the right-hand side, is one of the most famous of the Konditorei-style cafés in Vienna, **Demel (11**; p151).

Reaching Michaelerplatz, keep an eye out for the **Loos Haus (12)**, a perfect example of the clean lines of Loos' work. Franz Josef hated it and described the windows, which lack lintels, as 'windows without eyebrows'. The **excavations (13)** in the middle of the square are of Roman origin. **Michaelerkirche (14)** on the square portrays five centuries of architectural styles, ranging from 1327 (Romanesque chancel) to 1792 (baroque doorway angels).

Cross Michaelerplatz and pass through the imposing Michaelertor and past the **Schweizertor (15)** to Heldenplatz and the impressive **Neue Burg (16**; p126), built between 1881 and 1908. Continue on past the line of *Fiakers* (horse-drawn carriages), noting the Gothic spire of the **Rathaus** (p128) rising above the trees to the right. Ahead, on the far side of the Ring, stand the rival identical twins, the **Naturhistorisches Museum (17**; p129) and the **Kunsthistorisches Museum (18)**; between them is a proud **statue of Maria Theresia (19)**, surrounded by key figures of her reign.

Turn left onto the Ring and, once past the Neue Burg, turn left again into the peaceful **Burggarten**, formerly reserved for the pleasure of the imperial family and high-ranking officials. It now contains **statues of Mozart (20)** and **Franz Josef (21)**, the **Schmetterlinghaus (22**; Butterfly House; ☎ 533 85 70; adult/senior/student/child €5/4.50/4/2.50; ☽ 10am-4.45pm Mon-Fri, 10am-6.15pm Sat & Sun Apr-Oct, 10am-3.45pm Nov-Mar) and the **Palmenhaus (23**; p150).

Only a hop, skip and a jump from the Burggarten is the newly renovated **Albertina (24**; p127) on Albertinaplatz. The square is home to a troubling work by sculptor and graphic artist Alfred Hrdlicka (1928–), created in 1988. This series of pale block-like sculptures commemorates Jews and other victims of war and fascism.

From here it's not far down Philharmonikerstrasse to the starting point of this walk. On your way you'll pass the rear of the grand **Staatsoper (25**; p152) and the frontage of **Hotel Sacher (26**; p143), a perfect spot to rest those weary legs.

VIENNA FOR CHILDREN

It was once said the Viennese love dogs more than they love children, and while this might be true for some folk, Vienna is actually quite child-friendly. Its museums, attractions and theatres, such as the Kunsthistorisches Museum and the Albertina, arrange children's programmes over the summer months.

The **Prater** (p131), with its wide playing fields, playgrounds and funfair, is ideal for children. **Praterfee** (Map pp116-17; ☎ 729 49 99-82; Prater 121, Prater Hauptallee; trampoline per 5 min €5, inflatable mountain €3.50, somersault trampoline €6; ☽ 11am-8pm, depending on weather) has a cool trampoline area where adults can enjoy a drink outside while the kids soar into the sky. One place that is just as fascinating for adults as kids (and adults can also relax here over a drink and sausage while the kids see the animals) is the **Tirolerhof** (Map pp116–17) inside the Tiergarten at Schloss Schönbrunn. Actually an historic farmhouse from Tyrol deconstructed and rebuilt inside the zoo, it holds ancient Noric horses, as well as goats, bulls, chickens and other farm animals. The **Donauinsel** (p131) is another place where kids can run off their energy. Swimming pools, located here and throughout Vienna, are free to children under 15 over the summer school holidays.

Aside from summer programmes and parks, two museums are aimed directly at kids. **Zoom** (Map pp120-1; ☎ 524 79 08; www.kindermuseum .at; 07, Museumsplatz 1; child €5, accompanying adult free; ⏰ 8.30am-4pm), next door to the WienXtra-Kinderinfo (p123) in the MuseumsQuartier, is a bonanza for kids, with a craft studio and ocean, lab, science and exhibition sections (some of these multimedia) for exciting sessions of about 1½ or two hours aimed at kids between the ages of zero and 14; book ahead. Schönbrunn's **Kindermuseum** (Map pp116-17; ☎ 811 13-239; www.schoenbrunn.at; 13, Schloss Schönbrunn; adult/child/family €6.50/4.50/17; ⏰ 10am-5pm Sat & Sun, 10am-5pm during school holidays) focuses quite understandably on the 16 children of Maria Theresa and the kids dress up in costume. But it's not all hob-nobbing – they'll also find out what aspects of life made the right royal Habsburgs different from mere lowlife mortals. The obvious – fortune, fame, pets you can ride – are a start.

The tourist office publishes a good brochure in English that covers things either of interest to kids or especially for kids – it's called *For heads of families and their parents*.

TOURS

Vienna has everything from bus tours to horse-drawn carriage rides, so if you're looking for a guided tour of the city you'll find something to suit your taste. Bus tours are good if you're very short on time and want to pack in as much as possible, while the walking tours are perfect if you're interested in learning more on a specific topic.

Cityrama (Map pp120-1; ☎ 534 130; www.viennasight seeing.at; 01, Börsegasse 1; adult €17-109, child €7-45) Half- and full-day bus tours of Vienna and attractions within a day's striking distance of the city, including Salzburg, Budapest and Prague. Some tours require an extra fee for admission to sights, such as training at the Spanish Riding School.

DDSG Blue Danube (Map pp120-1; ☎ 588 80; www .ddsg-blue-danube.at; 01, Schwedenbrücke; full-tour adult/child €16.80/8.40, half-tour €12/6, children under 10 free; ⏰ 2-5 times daily Apr-Oct) Boat trips circumnavigating the districts of Leopoldstadt and Brigittenau via the Danube and Danube Canal.

Fiaker (20min/40min/1hr tour €40/65/75) More of a tourist novelty than anything else, a *Fiaker* is a traditional-style open carriage drawn by a pair of horses. Drivers generally speak English and point out places of interest en route. Lines of horses, carriages and bowler-hatted drivers can be found at Stephansplatz, Albertinaplatz and Heldenplatz at the Hofburg.

QUIRKY VIENNA

Vienna has an unusually morbid side. Free-wheeling Viennese charm in a wine tavern, one expert on Viennese morbidity tells us, can easily deteriorate into 'profound death melancholia'. Worrying stuff. The abundance of crypts, the creation of the world's first crisis-intervention centre in Vienna – in 1948, incidentally, by a man with the unfortunate moniker Dr Suicide (the Romanian Dr Erwin Ringel, 1921–94) – and even the 'melancholy' waltz are held up as shining examples of Vienna's morbid side. An 'economy coffin' was even invented by Kaiser Joseph II in 1785 that allowed you to drop your relatives through a flap underneath and reuse it. Along with a bell placed inside coffins to alert relatives that your number was not quite up, this contraption and about 600 other exhibits are at the uplifting **Bestattungsmuseum** (Undertaker's Museum; Map pp116-17; ☎ 501 95-4227; 04, Goldeggasse 19; adult/student & child €4.50/2.50; ⏰ by prior arrangement noon-3pm Mon-Fri).

The **Pathologisch-Anatomisches Bundesmuseum** (Pathological-Anatomy Museum; Map p122; ☎ 406 86 72; 09, Spittalgasse 2; admission €2; ⏰ 3-6pm Wed, 8-11am Thu), housed in the Narrenturm (Fool's Tower), a former insane asylum, is possibly the most bizarre attraction. It's filled with medical oddities and abnormalities preserved in jars of formaldehyde, and the odd wax model with a grisly disease.

Also known as the Geschichte der Medizin (Museum of Medical History), the **Josephinum** (Map p122; ☎ 4277 63 422; 09, Währinger Strasse 25; adult/student €2/1; ⏰ 9am-3pm Mon-Fri, 9am-1pm 1st Sat every month) features ceroplastic and wax specimen models of the human frame, created over 200 years ago for the Academy of Medico-Surgery to improve the skills of army surgeons. Marginally tamer – until you reach the blow-up photographs of murdered and dismembered corpses – is the **Wiener Kriminalmuseum** (Map pp116-17; ☎ 214 46 78; Grosse Sperlgasse 24; ⏰ 10am-5pm Thu-Sun), covering all manner of crime in the capital.

VIENNA

GAY & LESBIAN VIENNA

Vienna is reasonably tolerant towards gays and lesbians, and things get better each year. Even the Vienna Tourist Board does their bit; their *Queer Guide* booklet has listings of bars, restaurants, hotels and festivals, while their *Vienna Gay Guide* is a city map with gay locations marked up. *Xtra* and *Night Life* (www.nightlifeonline.at, in German), two free monthly publications, are additional supplements packed with news, views and listings (in German only).

The best organisation in town is the **Rosa Lila Villa** (Map pp116–17; ☎ 586 8150; www.villa.at; 06, Linke Wienzeile 102), an unmissable pink house by the Wien River. Its **Lesbian Centre** (☎ 586 81 50; lesbenberatung@villa.at; 5–8pm Mon, Wed & Fri) is on the ground floor, while its **Gay Men's Centre** (☎ 585 43 43; schwulenberatung@villa.at; 5–8pm Mon, Wed & Sat) is on the 1st floor. **Homosexualle Initiative Wien** (HOSI; Map pp116–17; ☎ 216 66 04; www.hosiwien.at, in German; 02, Novaragasse 40), another helpful organisation, is politically minded and holds regular events.

Events to look out for on the gay and lesbian calendar include the **Regenbogen Parade** (Rainbow Parade), a colourful parade that takes over the Ring and MuseumsQuartier at the end of June, the **Life Ball** (www.lifeball.org), an AIDS-charity event around the middle of May, **Wien ist andersrum** (www.andersrum.at), a month-long extravaganza of gay and lesbian art in June, and **Identities – Queer Film Festival** (www.identities.at), a film festival showcasing queer movies, also in June.

Unfortunately there isn't much in the way of accommodation aimed at gay and lesbians; Hotel-Pension Wild (p143) is one option.

The Scene

Vienna has enough bars and clubs to entertain its gay and lesbian community, while some straight clubs, like U4 (p154), feature gay nights on a weekly basis. **Rainbow** (www.rainbow.at/guide) has a scene guide for large cities.

Café Berg (Map p122; ☎ 319 57 20; 09, Berggasse 8; 10am–1am) With some of the nicest staff in Vienna, a lovely, open layout and all-round friendly vibe, it's no wonder Café Berg is often full with a gay and straight crowd. Its bookshop, Löwenherz, stocks a grand collection of gay magazines and books.

Café Willendorf (Map pp116–17; ☎ 587 17 89; 06, Linke Wienzeile 102; 6pm–2am) This is one of Vienna's seminal gay and lesbian bars in Vienna, housed in the pink Rosa Lila Villa.

Frauencafé (Map pp120–1; ☎ 406 37 54; 05, Lange Gasse 8; 7pm–midnight Tue–Thu, till 2am Sat & Sun) A long-established strictly women-only café/bar.

Frauenzentrum Bar (Map p122; ☎ 402 87 54; 09, Währinger Strasse 59; 7pm–midnight Thu–Sat) Regular clubbing nights and more political events happen here in this lesbian woman-only venue.

Santo Spirito (Map pp120–1; ☎ 512 99 98; 01, Kumpfgasse 7; 6pm–2am) Attracting both a gay and straight crowd, Santo Spirito specialises in classical music at high decibels. In summer, customers spill out onto the cobblestone street to take a break from the noise.

Why Not? (Map pp120–1; ☎ 535 11 58; www.why-not.at; 01, Tiefer Graben 22; 10pm–6am Fri & Sat) Why Not? is small, very central and pops at the seams on weekends, when it fills quickly mainly with young gay guys.

Hop On-Hop Off Vienna Line (☎ 712 46 83; www.viennasightseeingtours.com; 01, Opernring; 1hr/2hr/all-day tickets adult €12/15/20, all tickets child €7; 10am–5pm) Bus tour passing 13 major sights. You can hop on and off the buses as many times as you wish. The main bus stop is outside the Staatsoper.

Music Mile Vienna (www.musikmeile.at; 3hr tour €5, extra hr €1.50) Audio-guided walking tour from Stephansdom to Theater an der Wien past some 70 stars embedded in the footpath commemorating musical geniuses related to Vienna in one way or another. Audio

guides and booklets are available between 10am and 7pm from **Musikmeile Wien Servicestelle** (Map pp120–1; ☎ reservations 588-300; 01, Stephansplatz), **Wien-Ticket Pavillon** (Map pp120–1; 01, Herbert-von-Karajan-Platz) and **Theater an der Wien** (Map pp120–1; 01, Linke Wienzeile 6).

Old Timer Trams (☎ 7909-105; www.wiener-tramwaymuseum.org; adult/child €15/5) On weekends and holidays from May to October, streetcars from 1929 trundle through Vienna on one-hour tours of the city. Departures from Stadt Pavilions at Karlsplatz (Map pp120–1).

Pedal Power (Map pp116-17; ☎ 729 72 34; www
.pedalpower.at; 02, Ausstellungsstrasse 3; tour with
own bike adult/child €19/10, with hired bike €23/12)
Half-day bicycle tours in and around Vienna from May
to September, starting at 10am. Five unguided tours are
offered: Innere Stadt and the Prater; Donau National Park
and Lobau; Donauinsel and Klosterneuburg; Donauinsel
and the *Heurigen* of Stammersdorf; and Classical Music
Memorials and the Zentralfriedhof.

Reisebuchladen (Map pp120-1; ☎ 317 33 84;
reisebuchladen@aon.at; 09, Kolingasse 6; tour €24;
🕐 10am-6pm Mon-Fri, 9.30am-12.30pm Sat) This travel
agency caters mainly for groups but will fit in individuals
on alternative bus tours, including tours of Red Vienna,
Jugendstil architecture and Hundertwasser creations.

Vienna Sightseeing Tours (☎ 712 46 830; www
.viennasightseeingtours.com; tour €35) Run by the same
company that organises the Hop On-Hop Off tours, Vienna
Sightseeing Tours offers a wide variety of half- and full-
day bus tours in English with free hotel pick-up.

Vienna Tour Guides (☎ 774 89 01; www.wienguide
.at; adult/child €13/6) Group of highly knowledgeable
guides who conduct 40 different guided walking tours,
11 of which are in English. Everything from Art Nouveau
architecture to Jewish traditions in Vienna is covered; one
of the most popular is the Third Man Tour. The monthly
Wiener Spaziergänge leaflet from the tourist office provides
details of all the walks.

FESTIVALS & EVENTS

Regardless of the time of year, there will be
something special happening in Vienna; pick
up a copy of the monthly booklet of events
from the tourist office. Tickets for many
events are available to personal callers at
Wien-Ticket Pavillon (Map pp120–1) in the
hut by the Staatsoper.

Christkindlmärkte Vienna's much-loved Christmas
market season runs from mid-November to Christmas Day.

Donauinselfest Free three-day festival of rock, pop,
hardcore, folk and country music on the Donauinsel in June.

ImPuls Tanz (☎ 523 55 58; www.impulstanz.com)
Vienna's premier avant-garde dance festival attracts an
array of internationally renowned troupes and newcomers
between mid-July and mid-August.

Jazzfest Wien (☎ 408 60 30; www.viennajazz.org) The
major jazz festival, held in June/July.

Jazzwerkstatt (www.jazzwerkstatt.at) Innovative jazz
festival organised by a musician collective each March.

Lange Nacht der Museen (langenacht.orf.at) On one
late-September/October evening some 500 museums
nationwide open their doors to visitors between 6pm and
1am. One ticket (adult/child €12/10; available at museums)
allows entry to all of them.

Musikfilm Festival (01, Rathausplatz) Screenings of
operas, operettas and concerts outside the Rathaus in July
and August.

Opernball (☎ 514 44-7880; 01, Staatsoper) Of the 300
or so balls held in January and February, the Opernball
(Opera Ball) is the ultimate. It's a supremely lavish affair,
with the men in tails and women in shining white gowns.

OsterKlang Festival (☎ 427 17; www.osterklang.at)
Orchestral and chamber music recitals in some of Vienna's
best music halls, the highlight of which is the opening
concert featuring the Vienna Philharmonic. Held at the
beginning of April.

Silvester The Innere Stadt becomes one big party zone
for Silvester (New Year's Eve), which features loads of
alcohol and far too many fireworks in crowded streets.

Viennale (☎ 526 59 47; www.viennale.at) The country's
biggest and best film festival, featuring fringe and
independent films from around the world in October.

Volksstimmefest (www.kpoe.at, in German) Communist
festival over a weekend around the end of August/
beginning of September in the Prater (p131); features
some 30 live acts and attracts a bizarre mix of hippies and
staunch party supporters.

Wiener Festwochen (☎ 589 22-22; www.festwochen
.or.at) Wide-ranging programme of arts from around the
world, from May to mid-June.

SLEEPING

Sleeping options in Vienna range from basic
youth hostels and student residences to hotels
where chandeliers, antique furniture and
original 19th-century oil paintings decorate
hallowed hallways and rooms. Between these
extremes are homy pensions and less ostentatious hotels, plus a small but smart range of
apartments for long-term rentals.

Prices given here are for the high season,
which is from June to September. Around
Christmas and New Year they can rise above
this. Except in winter, it's highly advisable to
book ahead. Always check for weekend or web
deals that might work out cheaper.

There are a handful of campsites on the
outskirts of Vienna; all are listed online at
www.wiencamping.at. Another cheap option
is student residences, which are converted to
seasonal hotels between July and September.

Accommodation Agencies

Tourist Info Wein (p124) can arrange accommodation, but charges a small commission
per reservation irrespective of the number
of rooms booked. Staff can help find private
rooms but don't provide lists. They have a
Jugendherbergen pamphlet detailing youth

VIENNA

hostels and campsites, and a booklet of hotels and pensions.

Viennese looking for apartments rely on word-of-mouth or turn to *Bazar* magazine. It's *the* paper if you're looking to buy, sell or rent anything, including flats or rooms. The time scale of places on offer may range from indefinite rental to occupation of a flat for a month or so while the resident is on holiday. *Falter*, *Kurier* and *Der Standard* also have accommodation ads.

Some short-term apartment rental outfits:

Appartement Pension Riemergasse (Map pp120-1; ☎ 512 72 200; www.riemergasse.at; 01, Riemergasse 8; apartments per night/month from €225/2707) Apartments (five minutes' walk from Stephansdom) all come with a kitchenette, telephone, cable TV, toilet and bath or shower.

Levante Laudon (Map pp120-1; ☎ 535 45 1551; 08, Laudongasse 8; apartments per day from €90, or €72 after 22 days) Small selection of fully furnished apartments in various sizes with washing machines and dryers in the basement and cleaning.

Singerstrasse Apartments (Map pp120-1; ☎ 514 49-0; www.singerstrasse2125.at; 01, Singerstrasse 21-25; weekly/monthly apartments from €609/2190, end cleaning €25-50) Apartments come complete with telephone, satellite TV, internet facilities for laptops (bring a network cable) and kitchenette.

Choosing a Location

Prices in the Innere Stadt are often higher than elsewhere; hotels and pensions between the Ring and the Gürtel can be good value but these are less convenient to major sights. If you have a car, leave it out in the suburbs and use public transport rather than pay the high parking fees (anything from €6 to €26).

Innere Stadt

BUDGET

Schweizer Pension (Map pp120-1; ☎ 533 81 56; www.schweizerpension.com; 01, Heinrichsgasse 2; s €36-65, d €58-87) Cheaper rooms here are without their own bathroom. This small, family-run pension is a superb deal, with homely touches and accreditation for being environmentally friendly. Book in advance, though, as it has only 11 rooms and is popular among those on squeezed budgets.

Pension Nossek (Map pp120-1; ☎ 533 70 41-0; www.pension-nossek.at; 01, Graben 17; s/d €73/115) Get in early here, too; Nossek's a strong choice not least because of its great Innere Stadt location, cosy feel and some nice rooms facing a courtyard.

MIDRANGE

Hotel-Pension Suzanne (Map pp120-1; ☎ 513 25 07; www.pension-suzanne.at; 01, Walfischgasse 4; s €78, d €98-119; 🖳) One of the nicest among the central places, Suzanne has a high comfort factor and a low-key, downbeat ambience; from here it's just a short hop to the Staatsoper.

Aviano (Map pp120-1; ☎ 512 83 30; 01, Marco-d'Aviano-Gasse 1; s €95, d €136-157) Aviano hangs out the window a long way when it comes to style: the precarious cream tones of period furniture and decoration here may not be to everyone's taste, but it rates highly for comfort.

Pertschy Pension (Map pp120-1; ☎ 534 49-0; www.pertschy.com; 01, Habsburgergasse 5; s €90-105, d €133-167) This gem of a pension has a peaceful inner courtyard, spacious rooms and toys for the toddlers. Here the very traditional furnishings of the rooms add nicely to the charm and old-world feel.

Hotel Amadeus (Map pp120-1; ☎ 533 87 38; www.hotel-amadeus.at; 01, Wildpretmarkt 5; s €93-129, d €172; 🗙 🖳) Maybe Wolfgang liked nothing better than a padded surface to bounce about on. Amadeus has carpeting on the ceiling of a lift and on the walls, and a padded lobby ceiling, making it a colourful, warm and very unusual place.

Hotel Austria (Map pp120-1; ☎ 515 23; www.hotel-austria-wien.at; 01, Am Fleischmarkt 20; s €97, d €139-149, apt €189; 🖳) Solid wood furnishings set the comfortable standard in this hotel with a summer terrace to the courtyard. The owners are continuously upgrading furnishings in the spacious rooms, some of which are also very quiet.

Hotel Kaiserin Elisabeth (Map pp120-1; ☎ 515 26; www.kaiserinelisabeth.at; 01, Weihburggasse 3; s €122, d €208-230) It's unusual to find a chandelier mounted in a skylight; you'll find one here. The likes of Mozart, Wagner and Liszt graced this hotel where rooms have a turn-of-the-century touch.

Hollmann Beletage (Map pp120-1; ☎ 96 11 960; www.hollmann-beletage.at; 01, Köllnerhofgasse 6; r €140-180; 🖳) Book early for this stylish and very popular choice in the Innere Stadt. Rooms have interesting design touches and are decked out in light styles and tones that lift; extras like a guest lounge well stocked with books make the difference.

our pick **Hotel am Stephansplatz** (Map pp120-1; ☎ 53 405-0; www.hotelamstephansplatz.at; 01, Stephansplatz 9; s €145-165, d €210-305, tr/ste €250/450) Someone has thought very hard about design elements while creating this charming hotel. Most rooms are lit by pairs of windows, some of these corner windows or ceiling to floor. Here your partner can lie in bed and admire the Gothic elegance of Stephansdom towering to your kneecaps. Rooms are tastefully appointed, quiet and surprisingly spacious for such a central location.

König von Hungarn (Map pp120-1; ☎ 515 84-0; www .kvu.at; 01, Schulerstrasse 10; s €145-165, d €208, apt €290-340; 🖳) The King of Hungary pulls off a tough act by balancing class with informality. Its inner atrium sets a wonderful mood, and the rooms, individually decorated with antique furniture, create a homy feel. Unusual and helpful for seniors is that bathrooms have telephones to reception.

Style Hotel (Map pp120-1; ☎ 22 780-0; www.stylehotel .at; 01, Herrengasse 12; r €265-285, ste €420-550; 🖳) This hotel lives up to its name admirably with mellow tones, a chilled-out feel and extras like a free minibar re-stocked daily; the sauna and fitness facilities might tip the scales if you find the price daunting.

TOP END

Hotel Ambassador (Map pp120-1; ☎ 961 610; www.ambas sador.at; 01, Kärntner Strasse 22/Neuer Markt 5; s €160-210, d €190-266) Prices vary by season and demand, but even in May and September you can find well-priced rooms in the historic Ambassador. Its gourmet restaurant Mörwald im Ambassador is a Vienna treat, making this a wonderful choice for weekend breaks.

Hotel Sacher (Map pp120-1; ☎ 51 456-0; www.sacher .com; 01, Philharmonikerstrasse 4; s €300-550, d €370-600) The elegant Sacher threw open its grand portals in 1876 and is not only home to the world-famous *Sacher Torte* but also revels in the sweet extravagance of the baroque epoch.

Ringstrasse
BUDGET & MIDRANGE

Hotel-Pension Wild (Map pp120-1; ☎ 406 51 74; www.pen sion-wild.com; 08, Lange Gasse 10; s €41-69, d €53-97, tr €90-114) This is a ultra-friendly pension embraces gays and straights alike. Wild, though, is the family name, not a description of the kind of nights you can expect here.

Hotel am Schubertring (Map pp120-1; ☎ 717 02-0; www.schubertring.at; 01, Schubertring 11; s €106-135, d €135-218) What an eccentric fish the graceful old 'Schubi' is! A maze of corridors, Biedermeier or Art Nouveau furnished rooms (some with views over the Vienna's rambling rooftops) and guests are usually

grouped among the warren of wings roughly according to generation.

Hotel Viennart (Map pp120-1; ☎ 523 13 45; viennart@ austrotel.at; 07, Breite Gasse 9; s/d/apt €140/200/245; 🖳) This four-star art hotel situated close to the MuseumsQuartier and Volkstheater has refreshing styles and a lobby that invites guests to meet and exchange stories. It's a period furnishing–free zone, with 56 ultra-modern rooms with an art edge.

Hotel Regina (Map pp120-1; ☎ 404 460; www.kremsleh nerhotels.at; 09, Rooseveltplatz 15; s €140, d €180-255; 🖳) After you wade through the impressive lobby, the size of the rooms do come as a letdown, but Regina's central location and rich decorative flavours make it a decent and convenient option, directly opposite the Votivkirche.

TOP END

Hotel Maria Theresia (Map pp120-1; ☎ 521 23; www .kkhotels.com; 07, Kirchberggasse 6; s €180-205, d €240-265; 🖳) Business travellers with buddies in their accounts department will harbour a soft spot for Maria Theresia. Advantages are its circular lobby bar, facilities that include a network cable for free internet in rooms (or terminals downstairs), a small fitness area and snugly styled rooms to relax in after doing deals.

Hotel Imperial (Map pp120-1; ☎ 501 10-0; www.luxury collection.com/imperial; 01, Kärntner Ring 16; d €760-860, ste €1460-4950, breakfast extra; 🖳 🅿) Originally the palace of the Prince of Württemberg, the Imperial re-invented itself as a hotel for the World Fair in 1873 while retaining the glory and majesty of a residence. It's a truly remarkable hotel: marble bathrooms, antiques and original oil paintings and silver service all help to re-create 19th-century Vienna.

Across the Danube Canal
BUDGET

Aktiv Camping Neue Donau (Map pp114-15; ☎ 202 40 10; 22, Am Kleehäufel; campsites per adult/tent €6.90/5.50; 🅥 mid-May–Sep; 🅿 🖳) This is the closest camping ground to the city centre and very handy to the popular swimming areas of Alte Donau and Donauinsel (p131). Rates subside outside July and August.

Jugendgästhaus Wien-Brigittenau (Map pp114-15; ☎ 332 82 94; jgh.1200wien@chello.at; 20, Friedrich-Engels-Platz 24; dm €17-20) With 410 beds, this is by far the largest of five HI hostels in Vienna. The neighbourhood is unappealing, and it's not really convenient to the Innere Stadt, but the hostel is modern, multi-storeyed and just a couple of minutes' walk from the Danube and Donauinsel.

Inside the Gürtel
BUDGET

Jugendherberge Myrthengasse (Map p122; ☎ 523 63 16; hostel@chello.at; 07, Myrthengasse 7; dm/tw €17/40) This well-run HI hostel on a quiet side street has a high convenience factor, gets busy and offers daytime check-in. Telephone reservations are strongly advised (only dorms can be reserved).

Pension Kraml (Map pp116–17; ☎ 587 85 88; www.pensionkraml.at; 06, Brauergasse 5; s/d/tr without bathroom €30/50/70, d €60-70, apt €95-125) Rooms are clean, cosy and surprisingly large in this family-run pension whose big plus is a location between Westbahnhof and the centre.

Westend City Hostel (Map pp116–17; ☎ 597 67 29; www.westendhostel.at; 06, Fügergasse 3; s €50, d €59-78, 12-/6-/8-/4-bed dm €18.50/20.50/20.50/22.10; ⌨) Handy to Westbahnhof and popular among young backpackers, Westend has very good facilities and offers guests a place to sleep rather than party and drop.

Hotel Fürstenhof (Map pp116–17; ☎ 523 32 67; www.hotel-fuerstenhof.com; 07, Europaplatz/Neubaugürtel 4; s/d without bathroom from €46/65, s €69-94, d/tr/q/ste €110/120/128/132). The Fürsty is a gem. To Vienna what the Chelsea Hotel is (or once was) to New York, it's the first choice for bands and artists. The single occupancy rooms and doubles are large and some are very quiet behind double doors. If you arrive tired, it can be reached almost on your knees from Westbahnhof.

MIDRANGE

Hotel Atlanta (Map p122; ☎ 405 12 30; www.hotelatlanta.at; 09, Währinger Strasse 33; s €79-104, d €89-144) Built in 1895, Atlanta has lost much of its original Art Nouveau sparkle, but brass chandeliers, creaking floors, leadlight windows and spacious rooms do add serious charm. The street is a dull shocker, but the best doubles are high up with bay windows.

Mondial Apartment Hotel (Map p122; ☎ 310 71 80; www.mondial.at/apt; 09, Pfluggasse 1; apt per night €70-110; ⓟ) This apartment hotel is a very stylish number with a three-day minimum stay (two, they say, when it's really quiet). The atmosphere is ultra-cosy, and helpful staff at reception are available round the clock. The intersection is busy, though, so ask for a room facing Pfluggasse. Monthly rates are significantly lower.

Attaché (Map pp116–17; ☎ 505 18 18; www.bestviennahotels.at; 04, Wiedner Hauptstrasse 71; s/d €85/120; ⓟ) Situated within a reasonable stroll of Naschmarkt, this hotel is clean and well run, with 26 rooms furnished with period furniture, including some in Art Nouveau style.

our pick Altstadt Vienna (Map p122; ☎ 526 33 99; www.altstadt.at; 07, Kirchengasse 41; s €109-139, d €129-189, ste €209-299; ⌨ ⓟ) Classic rooms or designer rooms tastefully composed by Italian star architect Matteo Thun, the architectural anomaly of a 120 sq metre roof garden attached to one room, and individual design touches are the outstanding highlights here. Altstadt Vienna offers respite in a part of town where the shopping is up-beat, the bars relaxed, and you feel a sense of arrival.

Tyrol (Map pp120–1; ☎ 587 54 15; www.das-tyrol.at; 06, Mariahilfer Strasse 15; s €109-209, d €149-259) This boutique hotel has 30 cosy rooms in lovely designs. Staff are friendly and helpful, and the location close to MuseumsQuartier is killer-bee.

Hotel Am Schottenfeld (Map p122; ☎ 526 51 81; www.falkensteiner.com/schottenfeld; 07, Schottenfeldgasse 74; s €133-144, d €169-185; ⌨) A sociably circular bar, a garishly coloured reception, but pretty apricot tones in comfortable rooms and very helpful staff – the Schottenfeld ranks highly as an address for business travellers. Add-ons like a fitness room with sauna, steam room and solarium add to its attraction.

Theaterhotel (Map p122; ☎ 405 36 48; chwien@cordial.at; 08, Josefstädter Strasse 22; s/d €184/196) Art Nouveau touches and friendly staff make this hotel one of the better 8th-district choices. But rooms are small and somewhat pricey unless you make good use of the kitchen niches.

TOP END

Das Triest (Map pp120–1; ☎ 589 18-0; www.dastriest.at; 04, Wiedner Hauptstrasse 12; s/d/ste €206/265/540) Business visitors will enjoy the enormous 95 sq metre suite with its own garden, while those seeking simple style and comfort will also feel snug in this refreshingly low-key hotel where everything – from the rooms through the lobby to the stairwells – fits effortlessly together in a mix of modern Italian and Viennese style.

Outside the Gürtel
BUDGET

Camping Wien West (Map pp114–15; ☎ 914 23 14; 14, Hüttelbergstrasse 80; campsites per adult/tent €6.90/5.50, 2-/4-person bungalows €27/37; ☽ Mar-Jan; ⓟ ⌨) This camping ground has cooking facilities and convenient transport from the Innere Stadt; take the U4 to Hütteldorf, then bus 148 or 152.

Wombat's (Map pp116-17; ☎ 897 23 36; www.wombats .at; 15, Grangasse 6; dm/r €21/50; ⌨) It's hard to find a more happening hostel than Wombat's – the atmosphere is more Gold Coast Australia than the Capital of Culture, staff are friendly and it's close to Westbahnhof.

Wombat's The Lounge (Map pp116-17; ☎ 897 23 36; 15, Mariahilfer Strasse 137; dm/r €21/50; ⌨) Sister hostel to the original Wombat's, it's even closer to the station.

Hostel Ruthensteiner (Map pp116-17; ☎ 893 42 02; www.hostelruthensteiner.com; 15, Robert-Hamerling-Gasse 24; dm/s/d €15.50/30/48; ⌨) Facilities at this hostel include a kitchen, laundry and a shady rear courtyard. Dorms range from two- to 10-bed rooms. The hostel is near Westbahnhof, one block south of Mariahilfer Strasse.

MIDRANGE

Altwienerhof (Map pp116-17; ☎ 892 60 00; www .altwienerhof.at; 15, Herklotzgasse 6; s/d/ste €87/129/185) Altwienerhof is a small, family-run, three-star hotel situated a stone's throw from the Gürtel. It offers style without walking all over your wallet in stilettos and is well-serviced by friendly and welcoming staff.

Thüringer Hof (Map p122; ☎ 401 79-0; www.thue ringerhof.at; 18, Jörgerstrasse 4-8; s/d €75/99; P ⌨) The exterior is rather off-putting, and inside the rooms are functional, but this hotel is well run and a good shot during a busy periods in Vienna. Rooms to the courtyard are surprisingly quiet. Kids aged six to 12 get a 50% discount and those under six stay free.

Favorita (Map pp116-17; ☎ 601 46; www.austria-trend .at/fav; 10, Laxenburger Strasse 8-10; s/d €120/150; ⌨ P) You'll find rooms modern and bright behind the striking yet simple façade of Favorita. There's also a sauna and free steam bath where you can rest those weary bones. Breakfast is available (€13).

Parkhotel Schönbrunn (Map pp116-17; ☎ 87 804-0; parkhotel.schoenbrunn@austria-trend.at; 13, Hietzinger Hauptstrasse 10-20; s €70-129, d €129-170; ⌨ ⌨) Partially built with money from Emperor Franz Josef, who treated it as his private guesthouse, today the four-star Parkhotel Schönbrunn is a more than welcoming abode. The façade is, of course, painted Schönbrunn yellow, the lobby and grand ballroom are opulent and majestic, and many rooms surround a large garden with sun lounges, trees and grass.

EATING

Vienna has thousands of restaurants covering all budgets and styles of cuisine, but dining doesn't stop there. *Kaffeehäuser* (coffee houses) and *Heurigen* (wine taverns; p151) are almost defining elements of the city, and just as fine for a good meal. The humble *Beisl*, Vienna's equivalent of a beer house or tavern, is normally a simple restaurant serving the best of Viennese cuisine in unhealthy portions.

If you've no time to sit around and wait, a *Würstel Stand* will suffice; sausage stands are conveniently located on street corners and squares, ready with sausages, bread and beer. Otherwise you could try the ubiquitous Schnitzelhaus chain, which serves up fast food Viennese-style.

Self-caterers will have no problem stocking up on provisions; Hofer, Zielpunkt, Billa, Spar and Merkur supermarkets are commonplace throughout the city. Some have well-stocked delis that make sandwiches to order – the perfect cheap lunch on the run. The city is also dotted with markets (see p157).

Innere Stadt
RESTAURANTS

Pasta…e Basta (Map pp120-1; ☎ 796 65 42; www.pasta ebasta.at; 01, Werdertorgasse 10; mains €6-7; ☷ 10am-11pm Mon-Fri, 10am-3pm Sat) Over 20 different sorts of pasta are made and sold on the premises, and several sorts are served to a loyal following at wooden tables in this stylish pasta house-cum-wine bar.

Figlmüller (Map pp120-1; ☎ 512 61 77; 01, Wollzeile 5; mains €7-14; ☷ 11am-10.30pm, closed Aug) Schnitzel of monumental proportions should be on your agenda here. The interior of Figlmüller has the look and feel of a village *Heuriger* and is a Vienna classic.

Rosenberger Markt Restaurant (Map pp120-1; ☎ 512 34 58; 01, Maysedergasse 2; mains €10; ☷ 10.30am-11pm, bistro from 7.30am) The meat and veg mains, starters, pulses and desserts are plentiful in this food-hall style place. You pay by plate size, so pack it on without guilt. The amenities are a big plus if you're in for the day or night – it has lockers, and to avoid having to use its nappy room at a later date there are condom machines in both toilets.

Expedit (Map pp120-1; ☎ 512 33 13-0; 01, Wie-singerstrasse 6; mains €8-18; ☷ noon-11pm Mon-Fri, 6-11pm Sat) Warehouse shelves, simple furnishing and an open kitchen are part of the elegant flourish of Expedit. The changing menu offers a

VIENNA

delightful mix of Austro-Italian classics like lamb with polenta, plus seasonal dishes.

Café Griensteidl (Map pp120–1; ☎ 535 26 92-0; 01, Michaelerplatz 2; lunch menu €8-10, mains €11-17; ☼ 8am-11.30pm) Situated in a prestigious corner between the splendour of the Hofburg and the eyebrow-less windows of the Loos Haus (p138), this coffee house crawls unashamedly with tourists but is a nice place to eat, linger and watch the world bustle on by.

Wrenkh (Map pp120–1; ☎ 533 15 26; www.wrenkh .at; 01, Bauernmarkt 10; lunch menu from €8, mains €9-16; ☼ lunch & dinner) Wrenkh can be uneven, but there's no denying its creative effort. On a 'miss' day, a gazpacho-like 'power soup' will be superb but a chicken main uninspiring. The creative dishes are complemented by workshops, 'cooking salons' and dashes of experimental group cooking (p64).

Lebenbauer (Map pp120–1; ☎ 533 55 56; 01, Teinfalt-strasse 3; mains €11-20; ☼ 11am-3pm & 5.30-10.30pm Mon-Fri) Sleek décor and quality upmarket vegetarian cuisine complemented by fish dishes are the highlights of Lebenbauer. The tables are a quite close together, though; here lone diners may not feel entirely at ease.

Griechenbeisl (Map pp120–1; ☎ 533 19 77; 01, Fleischmarkt 11; mains €15-24; ☼ 11am-1am) As much a chunky slice of Vienna for tourists as a restaurant, Griechenbeisl has been around since 1447 and was once frequented by musical greats Beethoven, Schubert and Brahms. Choose to dine on Viennese standards in one of the vaulted rooms or in the plant-fringed front garden.

En (Map pp120–1; ☎ 532 44 90; 01, Werdertorgasse 8; lunch menu €7.50-9.50, full meal plus wine about €25; ☼ lunch & dinner Mon-Sat) This rewarding slice of modern Japan in the back streets of Innere Stadt serves some of the best sushi in town. Its 16-piece flagship 'En sushi' is satisfying, and the atmosphere is relaxed even if you're eating alone.

Haas & Haas (Map pp120–1; ☎ 512 26 66; 01, Stephansplatz 4; light meals €8-13, breakfast €7-14; ☼ 8am-8pm Mon-Fri, 8am-6.30pm Sat) This tea house has the attraction of hefty breakfasts (served 8am to 11.30am) and a location that's the envy of town: Stephansdom to your left, a tranquil inner courtyard to your right.

QUICK EATS

Gelateria Hoher Markt (Map pp120–1; ☎ 533 32 97-1; 01, Hoher Markt 4; ice cream €1.80; ☼ 9am-11.30pm) Forget Zanoni on Rotenturmstrasse and wander a few steps west to this place on Hoher Markt for 30 varieties of homemade ice cream and a concoction of elaborate sundaes you can enjoy outdoors.

Würstelstand am Hohen Markt (Map pp120–1; 01, Hoher Markt; sausages from €3; ☼ 7am-4am) Possibly *the* Würstelstand in all of Vienna (which is truly saying something), this one attracts people from all walks of life who flock here for the best of the late-night Wurst.

Trzesniewski (Map pp120–1; ☎ 512 32 91; 01, Dorotheergasse 1; breads from €3; ☼ 8.30am-7.30pm Mon-Fri, 9am-5pm Sat) Even Franz Kafka frequented this Viennese deli bar. Choose your bread then select your spread, or pick from the ready-made sandwiches. They're quite tiny, though (two bites and they're gone).

SELF-CATERING

There's an Interspar (Map pp120–1) on the 1st floor on the corner of Rotenturmstrasse and Fleischmarkt, and a Billa (Map pp120–1) on Singerstrasse.

Freyung (Map pp120–1; 01, Freyung; ☼ 9am-6pm Fri & Sat 1st & 3rd weekend of month; U2 Schottentor) market exclusively sells fresh organic produce.

Ringstrasse
RESTAURANTS

Café Prückel (Map pp120–1; ☎ 512 61 15; 01, Stubenring 24; coffee €1.80-3.60, mains €6-11; ☼ 8.30am-10pm) In the best of Vienna's coffee houses, the past lingers like a stain on your living room carpet that brings back nice memories. Prückel is one of the best. The meals are hearty, the coffee is superb, the cakes irresistible and friendly waiters rule the world from here.

Vapiano (Map pp120–1; ☎ 581 12 12; 06, Theobaldgasse 19; pasta €6-9; ☼ 11am-midnight) Four categories of mains are offered in this cafeteria-style pasta chain whose young staff whip up your dish while you watch. Pick up a card at the door and let the chef swipe it when you order. Hold onto it and pay at the door when you leave. The pasta is made on the premises, and bonuses are its hours and a nappy-changing room.

Kantine (Map pp120–1; ☎ 523 82 39; 07, Museumsplatz 1; daily menu €6, pitta & mains €5-9; ☼ 9-2am Mon-Sat, 9am-midnight Sun) This upbeat café-cum-bar is replete with a disco ball and housed in former stables for the Emperor's horses. If the fresh daily menu – typically an Asian or Viennese dish with a vegetarian or fish choice thrown in – is sold out, settle for salad-filled pita bread.

ourpick Halle (Map pp120-1; ☎ 523 70 01; 07, Museumsplatz 1; lunch menu €7, mains €6-16; ❤ 10am-2am) With tempting food, groovy waiters and a warm, gay-friendly atmosphere, Kunsthalle's restaurant is the best of a good crop in the MuseumsQuartier. The small menu rotates weekly, but look out for its Styrian chicken salad with pumpkin seed oil. Antipasti, salads, pasta and tender meats are possible here, washed down by a good wine.

Una (Map pp120-1; ☎ 523 65 66; 07, Museumsplatz 1; mains €8-14; ❤ 9am-midnight Mon-Fri, 10am-midnight Sat, 10am-6pm Sun) Striking tiled walls, arched ceilings and massive windows complement a menu sporting upmarket salads and pasta through to goulash and seasonal specialities.

Österreicher im MAK (Map pp120-1; ☎ 714 01 21; 01, Stubenring 3-5; lunch menu €6.40, mains €10-19; ❤ 10am-11.30pm) The classic Viennese cuisine with a difference is a treat here. Chef Helmut Österreicher, one of Austria's stars, puts together delicious concoctions such as veal with prawns served on risotto at affordable prices inside the Museum für angewandte Kunst (p131). The garden in summer adds to the delicious pleasure.

Café Restaurant Landtmann (Map p120-1; ☎ 241 00; 01, Dr Karl-Lueger-Ring 4; lunch menu €10, mains €8-20; ❤ 7.30am-midnight) This elegant old dame has sidelong views of the Burgtheater (p153) from its lovely covered outdoor area. Staff bustle about taking orders for classic Austrian cuisine outside or in the lavish wood-panelled interior.

Vestibül (Map pp120-1; ☎ 532 49 99; 01, Dr Karl-Lueger-Ring 2; evening menu €39-45, mains €19-24; ❤ 11am-midnight Mon-Fri, 6pm-midnight Sat) The menu may be small at Vestibül but flavours run deep in this restaurant, which is very popular for dishes focused mainly on classic meat cuts. The interior is delightful, with marble columns, chandeliers and a mirrored bar; it's situated in the southern wing of the Burgtheater.

Across the Danube Canal
RESTAURANTS

Schöne Perle (Map pp116-17; ☎ 243 35 93; 02, Grosse Pfarrgasse 2; lunch menu €7, mains €6.50-12; ❤ noon-midnight Mon-Fri, 10am-midnight Sat & Sun) Schöne Perle uses organic eggs and cheeses in its delicious breakfasts and mains; the cuisine is Austro-international and you can enjoy it while the kids play with those toys up the front.

Schweizerhaus (Map pp116-17; ☎ 728 01 52 13; 02, Strasse des Ersten Mai 116; mains €10-15; ❤ 11am-11pm

mid-Mar–Oct) It's conceivable that your meal here will do you for three days: the house specialty, roasted *hintere Schweinsstelze* (pork hocks), is sold by the kilogram and you can wash it down with draught Budweiser (the Czech stuff) direct from the barrel while enjoying a rollicking Biergarten atmosphere.

Vincent (Map pp116-17; ☎ 214 15 16; 02, Grosse Pfarrgasse 7; a la carte €12-18, 3-10 course menus €29-98; ❤ 5.30-11.30pm Mon-Sat) There aren't a lot of Leopoldstadt options, but Vincent is a good one: Austrian flavours meet the rest of the culinary world here: *Tafelspitz* or freshwater crayfish in tempura batter; rich décor up the front is balanced by an atrium out the back.

SELF-CATERING

Karmelitermarkt (Map pp116-17; 02, Im Werd; ❤ 6am-6.30pm Mon-Fri, 6am-2pm Sat) Karmelitermarkt has fruit and vegetable stalls and butchers selling kosher and halal meats. On Saturday the square features a *Bauernmarkt* (farmers market).

Inside the Gürtel
RESTAURANTS

Aromat (Map pp116-17; ☎ 913 24 53; 04, Margareten Strasse 52; menus €5-7, mains about €5; ❤ 5-11pm Tue-Sun) Vegetarian and meat dishes are complemented by sweet and savoury crepes and galettes in this relaxed restaurant featuring a rotating menu. Much of it is concocted from whatever the cooks find fresh at the Naschmarkt. It's about the size of a living room, so get in early or reserve.

St Josef (Map p122; ☎ 526 68 18; 07, Mondscheingasse 10; small/large menu €5.80/6.70; ❤ 9am-7pm Mon-Fri, 8am-4pm Sat) This bustling vegetarian eatery is one of Vienna's favourites, and not just among the *Öko* (ecological) crowd. Everyone beats a trail here for a changing menu with 100% organic and vegetarian offerings. The kitchen is open all day. Take a seat upstairs or downstairs or get something to go.

Zu den Zwei Liesln (Map p122; ☎ 523 32 82; 07, Burggasse 63; mains €4.40-8; ❤ 11am-11pm) This thoroughly authentic *Beisl* is among the best in the business and its treed courtyard is a popular spot on warm summer days and evenings. If you're up for vast portions of Wiener schnitzel and drinking a refreshing beer or wine with a young-ish crowd, this is a fine place to do it.

Hollerei (Map p122; ☎ 406 25 69; 08, Pfeilgasse 2; mains €7-11; ❤ lunch & dinner Mon-Fri) The sleek wooden interior of Hollerei is the scene of some of the tastiest vegetarian dishes in town. Even the simple lentil soup is wonderfully spiced and fills a midday hole perfectly. A few tables are lined up outside when weather permits.

Zum Alten Fassl (Map pp116-17; ☎ 544 42 98; 05, Ziegelofengasse 37; lunch menu €5.70-7, mains €7-14; ☷ 5pm-1am Mon-Sat, noon-3pm & 5pm-1am Sun) Behind the unassuming façade on a residential street is one of Vienna's most esteemed *Beisl*. Locals cross town backwards on their knees for the desserts, and its rear garden is an absolute joy: overgrown with vines, you can sample a hidden garden in residential Vienna.

Steman (Map pp116-17; ☎ 597 85 09; 06, Otto-Bauer-Gasse 7; mains €7-13; ☷ 11am-midnight Mon-Fri) Run by the same people as Café Jelinek (p151), Steman serves traditional food for young and old in a nicely restored and unpretentious interior, with a few tables outside in summer.

Ra'mien (Map pp120-1; ☎ 585 47 98; 06, Gumpendorferstrasse 9; mains €6-15; ☷ 11am-midnight Tue-Sun) Picture a grey-white room, with an open, simple look, full of bright, young, hip things bent over bowls of piping hot noodles, and you have Ra'mien. The menu not only consists of noodles, but covers the spectrum of Asian delights, from Thai to Japanese. Arrive early or reserve a table.

Lux (Map pp120-1; ☎ 526 94 91; 07, Spittelberggasse 3; lunch menu €8.40, mains €8-15; ☷ 11-2am) This rambling restaurant and café-bar uses the French bistro as its role model, right down to the paper tablecloths; the atmosphere is convivial and the menu includes lamb and rabbit as well as vegetarian options.

Chang (Map pp116-17; ☎ 961 92 12; 04, Waaggasse 1; mains €6-16; ☷ lunch & dinner Mon-Sat) Noodles – absolutely oodles of them – and a couple of duck dishes are the strength of this eating house, prepared with expertise and flair in a relaxed atmosphere.

Wild (Map pp120-1; ☎ 920 94 77; 03, Radetzkyplatz 1; mains €9-20; ☷ 10am-1am) The building used to be a wine house peddling wares of a dubious quality, but today you can sit indoors or outdoors on Radetzkyplatz while enjoying genuine classics like veal roulade or schnitzel.

Motto (Map pp116-17; ☎ 587 06 72; 05, Schönbrunner Strasse 30; mains €8-21; ☷ 6pm-2am Sun-Thu, till 4am Fri & Sat) The culinary delights of Motto are legendary, right down to the steak with chocolate chilli sauce on mashed potato. If the fusion Asian, Austrian and Italian food doesn't get your pulse racing, linger and enjoy the vibe of the bar or get down at its regular music events. Reserve a table;

entrance is through the forbidding chrome door on Rüdigergasse.

Stomach (Map pp116-17; ☎ 310 20 99; 09, Seegasse 26; mains €10-17; ☷ 4pm-midnight Wed-Sat, 10am-10pm Sun) Stomach's been serving seriously good food for years, and getting better with age. The menu is a healthy mix of meat and vegetarian dishes and features plenty of game during the season. The interior is straight out of rural Austria, with an overgrown garden and cobblestones. Reservations are highly recommended.

Tancredi (Map pp116-17; ☎ 941 00 48; 04, Grosse Neugasse 5; lunch menu €7, mains €12-19; ☷ lunch & dinner Mon-Fri, dinner Sat) This ex-*Beisl* has stripped-back wooden floors, warm, pastel-yellow walls, fittings from yester-year and a lovely tree-shaded garden; its strengths are regional and fish specialities, organic products and its Austrian wines.

Gaumenspiel (Map p122; ☎ 526 11 08; 07, Zieglergasse 54; mains €15-20, midday menus around €8, full menus €35-42; ☷ lunch & dinner Mon-Fri, dinner Sat) Small and attracting a faithful following, Gaumenspiel has a bistro feel and serves up delicious Mediterranean-Austrian crossover cuisine – it's all chalked on a blackboard.

Amacord (Map pp120-1; ☎ 587 47 09; 05, Rechte Wienzeile 15; breakfast €5-8, mains €8-12; ☷ 10am-2am, breakfast till 6pm) Shoppers on a Saturday morning fill Amacord to bursting point, all fighting for a table and a chance to breakfast. Outside Saturday morning, the pace is more sedate, but the food – a mix of Viennese classics and Italian pastas – is still of the highest quality and the atmosphere is convivial and quirky, if a little smoky sometimes.

Gasthaus Wickerl (Map p122; ☎ 317 74 89; 09, Porzellangasse 24a; menu €5.80, mains €8-16; ☷ 9am-midnight Mon-Fri, 10am-midnight Sat) Wickerl's laurels are excellent Viennese home cooking served in a low-key ambience of bare wooden floors, simple furniture and summer street-side seating.

Scala (Map pp116-17; ☎ 310 20 79; 09, Servitengasse 4; mains €10-18.50; ☷ 11am-midnight Mon-Sat, 5pm-midnight Sun) Scala is one of those cosy Italian family places that makes for a great refuge on a rainy day for a plate of pasta and glass of wine, though it can get bustling at night for its antipasti, pizza and fish specialities.

Summer Stage (Map pp116-17; ☎ 315 52 02; 09, Rossauer Lände; mains €6-20; ☷ 5pm-1am Mon-Sat, 3pm-1am Sun May-Sep) A diverse range of restaurants set up shop over the summer months at Summer Stage, a covered area overlooking the Danube Canal near the Rossauer Lände U4 stop.

Amerlingbeisl (Map pp120-1; ☎ 526 16 60; 07, Stiftgasse 8; mains €6-9; ☺ 9am-2am) Amerlingbeisl in cobblestoned Spittelberg does a small selection of dishes like roasted pumpkin and salad for a young crowd who nosh from the changing menu. On balmy nights the roof slides back for those who are able to cram into the rear courtyard.

Ubl (Map pp120-1; ☎ 587 64 37; 04, Pressgasse 26; mains €9-14; ☺ lunch & dinner) Schnitzels as big as your boot and local classics such as *Tafelspitz* are the fare at this Viennese *Beisl* with bite.

Palais Schwarzenberg (Map pp120-1; ☎ 798 45 15-600; 03, Schwarzenbergplatz 9; ☺ closed for restoration until at least 2008) The grand baroque dining room and terrace with sweeping views of an 18-acre garden were being given a face-lift when we last looked in. Watch out for a re-opening, though, as the setting is wonderful.

Café Hummel (Map p122; ☎ 405 53 14; 08, Josefstädter Strasse 66; breakfast €5-10, mains €10-17; ☺ 7am-midnight Mon-Sat, 8am-midnight Sun) Unpretentious Hummel is a true locals' *Kaffeehaus*, with a decent schnitzel and chips, aloof waiters, outdoor seating, a huge range of Viennese dishes, top coffee and homemade cakes.

Café Sperl (Map pp120-1; ☎ 586 41 58; 06, Gumpendorfer Strasse 11; mains €6.50-9; ☺ 7am-11pm Mon-Sat, 11am-8pm Sun, closed Sun Jul & Aug) *Jugendstil* fittings, a cosy atmosphere, an honest goulash reminiscent of your grandmother's, topped off by a billiard table and the *Sperl Torte* – this is definitely one of Vienna's best coffee houses.

Naschmarkt (Map pp120-1; 06, Linke & Rechte Wienzeile; ☺ 6am-6.30pm Mon-Fri, 6am-5pm Sat) Vienna's biggest and boldest market is a food-lover's dream come true. Not only are there food stalls selling meats, fruits, vegetables, cheeses and spices, but there's also a wide variety of restaurants. Here's a couple:

Naschmarkt Deli (Map pp120-1; ☎ 585 08 23; 04, Naschmarkt 421; bagels €5, sandwiches €6-8, mains €7-9; ☺ 8am-11pm Mon-Sat) Wraps, baguettes, sandwiches and breakfasts and the perfect place to people-watch; don't turn up at 10am Saturday expecting to find a seat.

Indian Pavillon (Map pp120-1; ☎ 587 85 61; 04, Naschmarkt 74-75; mains €7-10; ☺ 11am-6.30pm Mon-Fri, 11am-5pm Sat) Serves dishes laden with spices from the subcontinent, including kebabs, samosas and rogan josh.

QUICK EATS

Bagel Station (Map pp120-1; ☎ 208 08 94; 06, Capistrangasse 10; bagels €3.50-4; ☺ 7am-9pm Mon-Fri, 9am-9pm Sat, 10am-6pm Sun) This European chain of bagel shops has garish orange, bright interiors. Another station can be found at Währinger Strasse 2-4.

SELF-CATERING

Biomarkt Maran (Map p122; ☎ 526 58 86-18; Kaiserstrasse 57-59) A whole-food supermarket with inexpensive fruit, vegetables and almost everything else needed to whip up a nutritious meal.

Outside the Gürtel
RESTAURANTS

Schloss Concordia (Map pp114-15; ☎ 769 88 88; 11, Simmeringer Hauptstrasse 283; mains €10; ☺ 10am-1am) Concordia's overgrown garden, bare wooden floors, gargantuan mirrors and stained-glass ceiling create a strange but highly appealing interior. The large stone Jesus statue adds to this. With 12 different types of schnitzel, its menu reads like a list from the abattoir; the house specialty – the Concordia schnitzel – is prepared with lentils; truly vegetarian options are also available.

Kent (Map p122; ☎ 405 91 73; 16, Brunnengasse 67; mains €5-9; ☺ 6am-2am) With a huge summer garden, excellent lamb kebabs, and good pizzas and Turkish-style breakfasts, Kent is one of our favourite Turkish restaurants in Vienna; its meats are *halal*.

SELF-CATERING

Brunnenmarkt (Map p122; 16, Brunnengasse; ☺ 6am-6.30pm Mon-Fri, 6am-2pm Sat) Brunnenmarkt is Vienna's largest street-market and totally reflects its ethnic neighbourhood; most stall-holders are of Turkish/Balkan decent. On Saturday nearby Yppenplatz features the best *Bauernmarkt* (farmers market) in the city.

DRINKING
Bars

Vienna is riddled with late-night drinking dens, but you will find concentrations of pulsating bars north and south of the Naschmarkt, around Spittelberg (many of these double as restaurants) and along the Gürtel (mainly around the U6 stops of Josefstädter Strasse and Nussdorfer Strasse). The Bermuda Dreieck (Bermuda Triangle), near the Danube Canal in the Innere Stadt, also has many bars, but they are more touristy. In summer, beach bars line the banks of the canal (see boxed text, p154).

VIENNA

Also during the summer months, party-goers congregate at Copa Kagrana and Sunken City, an area around the U1 Donauinsel U-Bahn station. It's quite a tacky affair, but it can be a lot of fun. Summer Stage (p148) and the **Alte AKH** (Map p122; ☎ 87 05 04; cnr Alser Strasse & Spitalgasse) also wage war against the threat of melting indoors.

Café Drechsler (Map pp120-1; ☎ 581 20 44; 06, Linke Wienzeile 22; ⏰ 3am-2am) This wonderful Vienna institution is a traditional coffee house that was recently refurbished by British architect Sir Terence Conran in an upbeat minimalist style; the food here is very good (€6 to €13), and it's a great place to begin, end or while away the night. At 2am you have to vacate while cleaners go through.

Palmenhaus (Map pp120-1; ☎ 533 10 33; Burggarten; ⏰ 10am-2am, closed Mon & Tue Jan & Feb) Relax in a splendidly restored palm house, replete with high, arched ceilings, glass walls and tempered steel. A well-to-do crowd eats, grooves and gets loud here till late.

Kleines Café (Map pp120-1; 01, Franziskanerplatz 3; ⏰ 10am-2am) What this small café lacks in size it makes up for with an off-beat atmosphere, tasty morsels from the kitchen and wonderful summer outdoor seating on Franziskanerplatz.

rhiz (Map p122; ☎ 409 25 05; www.rhiz.org; 08, Lerchenfelder Gürtel/Stadtbahnbogen 37-38; ⏰ 6pm-4am Mon-Sat, 6pm-2am Sun) With exposed brick walls that breathe the vibe and morph with the crowd, rhiz is one place that you can easily grow to love. It's the hippest of the Gürtel's bunch of bars situated inside the vaulting of the overground. Throw in friendly staff, a large outdoor seating area, large doses of electronic music and guest DJs and you've got the makings of a long night with a changing tempo (it shouldn't stop you exploring the other bars in the area, though!).

An-Do Café (Map p122; ☎ 408 15 89 08, 16, Yppenmarkt Stand 11-15; ⏰ 9am-10pm Mon-Sat, till midnight Sun) Situated on colourful Yppenplatz in a former market stall, this small bar and café has a set of scales on the floor that you walk over to reach the back section; it's a convivial place that fits in well with a visit to the nearby Kent (p149) for an evening of Turkish food and a drink, though it also does its own snacks.

Das Möbel (Map pp120-1; ☎ 524 94 97; 08, Burggasse 10; ⏰ 10-1am) Some sit with turbo-laptops free-surfing on wi-fi; others browse a catalogue for locally designed furniture you can sit on while drinking or breakfasting. Das Möbel is an odd joint much loved by a relaxed crowd that spends the day and night chatting over drinks – sometimes even about furniture.

ourpick Manolos (Map pp120-1; ☎ 526 20 82; 01, Volksgartenstrasse 1; ⏰ 6pm-2am Mon-Fri, 6pm-2am Sat) Deep in the shadows of the Natural History Museum, Manolos is a sleek Mexican restaurant and bar (the fusion food is OK, too, incidentally) with an art edge that can kick on in unusual ways. It's tequila selection will startle, and behind the bar a DJ wearing headphones tweaks a CD deck into the wee hours. Everyone rises to the occasion, dances on available surfaces, and one by one they usually fall off them.

Futuregarden Bar & Art Club (Map pp120-1; ☎ 585 26 13; 06, Schadekgasse 6; ⏰ 7pm-2am Mon-Sat, 9pm-2am Sun) A 30s to 40s crowd here soaks up the buzzing atmosphere while DJs spin vinyl. This basic bar's one piece of luxury – apart from the occasional art exhibition by local artists – is its rectangular disco 'ball' that floats from the ceiling.

Schikaneder (Map pp120-1; ☎ 585 58 88; 04, Margareten Strasse 22-24; ⏰ 6pm-4am) A cinema, club and bar merge in this art-house venue attracting a crowd with energy to burn. Movies are shown most nights.

Tanzcafé Jenseits (Map pp120-1; ☎ 587 12 33; 06, Nelkengasse 3; ⏰ 9pm-4am Mon-Sat) Rumour has it that Jenseits was formally a brothel, which is highly plausible considering the kitschy red velvet interior. DJs perform most nights and the place attracts a mainly alternative and arty crowd that quickly fills the tiny dance floor.

Blue Box (Map p122; ☎ 523 26 82; 07, Richtergasse 8; ⏰ 5pm-2am Mon, 10-2am Tue-Thu, till 4am Fri-Sun) This café and bar tucked away on back-street Richtergasse is enjoying a new lease of life. It has comfortable table seating and the atmosphere morphs at night when DJs take centre stage or events are held.

Volksgarten Pavillon (Map pp120-1; ☎ 532 09 07; 01, Burgring 1; €4-15; ⏰ 11am-2am May–mid-Sep) The larger garden of this 1950s-style pavilion is especially popular on warm evenings for stupendous views of Hofburg; events are held nightly, but the most popular is 'Techno Cafe' held Tuesdays from 7pm.

American Bar (Map pp120-1; ☎ 512 32 83; 01, Kärntner Durchgang 10; ⏰ noon-5am Tue-Sat, noon-4am Sun-Mon) Designed by Adolf Loos in 1908, the American Bar also goes by the name Loos-Bar. You can't swing a cat in this tiny salon; if the mirrors don't make you think otherwise, the excellent cocktails might – they're among the best in town.

Aera (Map pp120-1; ☎ 533 53 14; www.aera.at; 01, Gonzagagasse 11; mains €7.50-10; ☽ 10am-1am Sun-Thu, 10am-2am Fri & Sat) Aera is gay-friendly and it attracts a mixed art crowd who while away hours eating or drinking. You can descend into the cellar some nights for music and performance – from flamenco guitar to kid's theatre or even Austro-Latino choir sessions.

Coffee Houses & Cafés

The Vienna coffee houses are wonderful places for sipping a tea or coffee, imbibing a beer or wine, and catching up on gossip or news of the world. Most serve light meals, while most cafés have a good cake range.

Café Jelinek (Map pp116-17; ☎ 597 41 13; 06, Otto-Bauergasse 5; ☽ 9am-9pm) Walk in from the street here and everyone looks up as if keeping a secret of something shocking that happened 20 years ago. Newspapers fill a ledge near the doorway, the wood oven is fired up in winter and the cigarette smoke clings to you long after you've gone. There's food too, but drift across the street for Viennese nosh at Steman (p148), run by the same people.

Café Bräunerhof (Map pp120-1; ☎ 512 38 93; 01, Stallburggasse 2; snacks €3-6; ☽ 8am-9pm Mon-Fri, 8am-7pm Sat, 10am-7pm Sun) Not much has changed in this fine Viennese *Kaffeehaus* since the late great Thomas Bernhard once hung out here. There's classical music on weekends and holidays from 3pm to 6pm, and UK newspapers alongside Vienna's hallowed press.

Café Hawelka (Map pp120-1; ☎ 512 82 30; 01, Dorotheergasse 6; snacks €3-6; ☽ 8am-2am Mon & Wed-Sat, 10pm-2am Sun, closed late Jul-Aug) This is the perfect spot to people-watch and chat to complete strangers. It's a traditional haunt for artists and writers, and attracts the soaring figures of Viennese society; expect to be constantly shunted along to accommodate new arrivals at your table, though.

Café Central (Map pp120-1; ☎ 533 37 64-26; 01, Herrengasse 14; cakes €4; ☽ 7.30am-midnight) With its marble pillars, arched ceilings, cast-iron chandeliers, bustling waiters and live piano music from 4pm to 11pm, Central is a fascinating Viennese coffee house and restaurant. Trotsky came here to play chess and the writer-cum-regular Peter Altenberg (1859–1919) is still poised stoically at the entrance.

Café Sacher (Map pp120-1; ☎ 541 56-661; 01, Philharmonikerstrasse 4; Sacher Torte €4.80, food €11-25; ☽ 8am-midnight) Sacher is Vienna's coffee house where you can have your history as cake and eat it too; it is home to the infamous *Sacher Torte*. Meals are served here, borne by a battalion of waiters gliding among opulent furnishings.

Demel (Map pp120-1; ☎ 535 17 17-0; 01, Kohlmarkt 14; ☽ 10am-7pm) Demel is Sacher's *Torte* rival – the *Créme-Schnitte* here is to die for. You pay for quality, location and elegance.

Café Gloriette (Map pp116-17; ☎ 879 13 11; 13, Gloriette; snacks €6-8; ☽ 9am-1hr before dusk) This pleasant café occupies a neoclassical gem high on a hill behind Schloss Schönbrunn. Its sweeping views of the Schloss and magnificent gardens and the districts to the north make it arguably one of the best places in Vienna for a vista.

Heurigen

Vienna's *Heuriger* (wine tavern) tradition dates back to the Middle Ages. Identified by a *Busch'n* (a green wreath or branch) hanging over the door, many have outside tables in large gardens or courtyards, while inside the atmosphere is rustic. Some serve light meals, which in Vienna can be a hot or cold buffet.

Concentrations of *Heurigen* can be found in the wine-growing suburbs to the north, southwest, west and northwest of the city. Grinzing, in the northwest, is the best-known *Heurigen* area, but it is also the most touristy. It's generally avoided by the Viennese, but if you like loud music and busloads of rowdy tourists, then it's the place for you.

Esterházykeller (Map pp120-1; ☎ 533 34 82; 01, Haarhof 1; ☽ 11am-11pm Mon-Fri, 4-11pm Sat & Sun) Esterházykeller is one of the few city *Heurigen* gracing the Innere Stadt. Low ceilings and rural decorations blend to create a magnificent interior. Its wine comes from the Schloss Esterházy estate in Eisenstadt.

Zwölf Apostelkeller (Map pp120-1; ☎ 512 67 77; 01, Sonnenfelsgasse 3; ☽ 4.30pm-midnight) Even though Zwölf Apostelkeller plays it up big time to the tourists, it still retains plenty of rustic charm. This is mostly due to the premises themselves – a vast, dimly lit, multilevel cellar.

Hirt (Map pp114-15; ☎ 318 96 41; 19, Eisernenhandgasse 165; ☽ 3pm-late Wed-Fri, noon-late Sat & Sun Apr-Oct; noon-late Fri, Sat & Sun Nov-Mar) Hirt is a fantastic little *Heuriger* well hidden among the vineyards of Kahlenberg. Expect superb views, great food, friendly service and plenty of scrumptious wine.

Zawodsky (Map pp114–15; ☎ 320 79 78; 19, Reinischgasse 3; ☯ 5pm–midnight Mon, Wed & Thu, 2pm–midnight Fri–Sun Mar–Nov) The idyllic orchard and vineyard setting and the small selection of cold and hot meats make this Heuriger a wonderful retreat, far from the madding crowds.

Mayer am Pfarrplatz (Map pp114–15; ☎ 370 12 87; 19, Pfarrplatz 2; ☯ 4pm–midnight Mon–Sat, 11am–midnight Sun) Mayer is one of the few gems in Grinzing and also has a place in the history annals – in 1817 Beethoven called it home. Its large garden is particularly pleasant and there's live music from 7pm to midnight daily.

Göbel (Map pp114–15; ☎ 294 84 20; 21, Stammersdorfer Kellergasse 151; ☯ seasonal) About 80% of the output of this stylish Heuriger is red wine, served to complement warm and cold buffet dishes and traditional gourmet cuisine; the building was designed by owner-architect Peter Göbel.

Sirbu (Map pp114–15; ☎ 320 59 28; 19, Kahlenberger Strasse 210; ☯ 3pm–midnight Mon–Sat Apr–mid-Oct) Occupying a quiet spot up high among the vineyards on Kahlenberg, Sirbu is a far cry from the hustle and bustle of Vienna below. Its wines are award-winning, and the garden is perfect for whiling away a sunny afternoon.

Zahel (Map pp114–15; ☎ 889 13 18; 23, Maurer Hauptplatz 9; ☯ 3pm–midnight Tue–Sun) Zahel, housed in 250-year-old premises, is one of the oldest *Heurigen* in Vienna and the best on offer in the Mauer area (in the southwest of Vienna).

ENTERTAINMENT

Vienna is, and probably will be till the end of time, the European capital of opera and classical music. The programme of music events is never-ending, and as a visitor in the centre you'll continually be accosted by people in Mozart-era costume trying to sell you tickets for concerts or ballets. Even the city's buskers are often classically trained musicians.

The city also sports a number of great clubs, jazz bars and live-music venues. The tourist office produces a handy monthly listing of concerts and other events.

Opera & Classical Music

The list of venues below is certainly not complete, and many churches and cafés are fine places to catch a classical concert.

Tickets for the Akademietheater, Burgtheater, Schauspielhaus, Staatsoper and Volksoper can be purchased from the state ticket office, **Bundestheaterkassen** (Map pp120–1; ☎ 514 44-7881; www.bundestheater.at; 01, Operngasse 2; ☯ 8am–6pm Mon–Fri, 9am–noon Sat & Sun). The office charges no commission and tickets for the Staatsoper and Volksoper are available here one month prior to the performance. Credit card sales can be made by **telephone** (☎ 513 15 13; ☯ 10am–9pm), where English-speaking operators are available, or over the internet. The box office, **Info unter den Arkaden** (Herbert von Karajan-Platz; ☯ 9am–1hr before performance begins Mon–Fri, 9am–5pm Sat), handles tickets for the Staatsoper and Volksoper.

The **Wien-Ticket Pavillon** (Map pp120–1; 01, Herbert-von-Karajan-Platz; ☯ 10am–7pm) outside the Staatsoper sells tickets for Theater an der Wien, the Raimundtheater and various music acts. **Jirsa Theater Karten Büro** (Map pp120–1; ☎ 400 600; http://viennaticket.at; 08, Lerchenfelder Strasse 12; ☯ 9.30am–5.30pm Mon, Thu & Fri, till 1pm Tue & Wed, 10am–1pm Jul & Aug) covers most venues in town.

Staatsoper (Map pp120–1; ☎ 514 44 7880; www.wiener-staatsoper.at; 01, Opernring 2; tours adult/child €5/2; ☯ box office 9am–until 2hr before performance Mon–Fri, 9am–noon Sat, closed Jul & Aug) This is the premier opera and classical music venue in Vienna. Productions are lavish affairs and the Viennese take them very seriously and dress up accordingly. Standing-room tickets (€2 to €3.50) can only be purchased 80 minutes before the beginning of performances and any unsold tickets are available for €30 one day before a performance (call ☎ 514 44 2950 for more information).

Musikverein (Map pp120–1; ☎ 505 81 90; www.musik verein.at; 01, Bösendorferstrasse 12; ☯ box office 9am–8pm Mon–Fri, 9am–1pm Sat, closed Jul & Aug) The Musikverein, home to the Vienna Philharmonic Orchestra, is said to have the best acoustics of any concert hall in Austria. The interior is suitably lavish and can be visited on the occasional guided tour. Standing-room tickets in the main hall cost €4 to €6; there are no student tickets.

Konzerthaus (Map pp120–1; ☎ 242 002; www.konzert haus.at; 03, Lothringerstrasse 20; ☯ box office 9am–7.45pm Mon–Fri, 9am–1pm Sat, closed Jul & Aug) This is a major venue in classical music circles, but throughout the year ethnic music, rock, pop or jazz can also be heard in its hallowed halls. Regular tickets start at around €15; students can purchase tickets for €12, 30 minutes before the show.

Theater an der Wien (Map pp120–1; ☎ 588 85; www .musicalvienna.at; 06, Linke Wienzeile 6; ☯ box office 10am–7pm)

Once the host of monumental premiers such as Beethoven's *Fidelio*, Mozart's *Die Zauberflöte* and Strauss Jnr's *Die Feldermaus*, Theater an der Wien now showcases opera, dance and concerts. Tickets start from €7 for standing room, sold one hour before performances.

Volksoper (Map p122; ☎ 514 44 3670; www.volk soper.at; 09, Währinger Strasse 78; ⌚ box office 8am-6pm Mon-Fri, 9am-noon Sat) This is Vienna's second opera house and features operettas, dance and musicals. Standing tickets go for as little as €1.50, and there are discounts 30 minutes before performances.

Dating back to 1498, the Wiener Sängerknaben (Vienna Boys' Choir) is an institution of the city. The choir sings every Sunday (except during July and August) at 9.15am in the Burgkapelle (Royal Chapel; p125) in the Hofburg. Tickets (€5 to €29) should be booked around eight weeks in advance (☎ 533 99 27), otherwise try your luck for a last-minute ticket at the **Burgkapelle box office** (⌚ 11am-1pm & 3-5pm Fri) for the following Sunday or immediately before mass between 8.15am and 8.45am. Standing room is free and you need to queue by 8.30am to find a place inside the open doors, but you can get a flavour of what's going on from the TV in the foyer. The choir also sings a mixed programme of music in the Musikverein at 4pm on Friday in May, June, September and October. Tickets range from €36 to €63, and can be purchased from **Reisebüro Mondial** (Map pp120-1; ☎ 588 04 141; www.mondial.at; 04, Faulmanngasse 4) and hotels in Vienna.

Theatre & Dance

Theatrical performances in English can be seen at the **English Theatre** (Map pp120-1; ☎ 402 12 60-0; www .englishtheatre.at; 08, Josefsgasse 12; tickets €19.50-38; ⌚ box office 10am-5pm Mon-Fri) or the smaller **International Theatre** (Map p122; ☎ 319 62 72; www.internationaltheatre .at; 09, Porzellangasse 8; tickets €20-24; ⌚ box office 11am-3pm Mon-Fri, 6-7.30pm on performance days).

Of the German theatres around town, the best to visit is the **Burgtheater** (Map pp120-1; ☎ 514 44-4140; www.burgtheater.at; 01 Dr Karl-Leuger-Ring; tickets €1.50-48; ⌚ box office 8am-6pm Mon-Fri, 9am-noon Sat & Sun). Other theatres include **Schauspielhaus** (Map p122; ☎ 317 01 01-18; www.schauspielhaus.at; 09, Porzellangasse 19; tickets €16; ⌚ box office 4-6pm Mon-Fri, 2hr before performances) and **Volkstheater** (Map pp120-1; ☎ 52111-400; www.volkstheater.at, in German; 07, Neustiftgasse 1; tickets €3-40; ⌚ box office 10am-performance start Mon-Sat).

In 2001 Vienna opened its first dance institution, the **TanzQuartier Wien** (Map pp120-1; ☎ 581 35 91; www.tqw.at; 07, Museumsplatz 1; tickets €9.50-155; ⌚ box office 10am-7pm Mon-Sat). Located in the newly completed MuseumsQuartier, it hosts an array of local and international performances with a strong experimental nature.

Nightclubs

Goodmann (Map pp120-1; ☎ 967 44 15; www.goodmann .at; in German; 04, Rechte Wienzeile 23; €5-10; ⌚ 4am-10am Mon-Sat) Who cares that Goodmann keeps the strangest opening hours of any establishment in Vienna? This is where clubbers go when the clubs close; most come for a snack (food is served till 8am) before heading downstairs to dance till closing.

Camera Club (Map p122; ☎ 523 30 63; www.camera -club.at, in German; 07, Neubaugasse 2; €5-10; ⌚ 2pm-6am Thu-Sat) Decked out with orange-walled seating inherited from the 1970s, the Camera Club gets Vienna's top DJs and has even morphed into the wintering ground for one of the country's most innovative – DJ Tibcurl and the Icke Micke Club. A live band usually plays the first Wednesday of each month from about 10pm.

Flex (Map pp116-17; ☎ 533 75 25; www.flex.at; 01, Donaukanal, Augartenbrücke; €4-10; ⌚ 6pm-4am) Change is afoot at Vienna's most celebrated low-life club, with a new pavilion being built out the front. Flex still looks like a complete dive, but it has one of the best sound systems in Europe, puts on great shows and features the top DJs from Vienna and abroad. The Dub Club on Monday and London Calling (alternative and indie) on Wednesday are among the most popular. Live bands also take the stage, and there's free internet access.

Roxy (Map pp120-1; ☎ 961 88 00; www.sunshine.at; 04, Operngasse 24; €5-10; ⌚ 10pm-late Thu-Sat) Roxy's tiny dance floor reaches bursting point when DJs from the electronic scene guest here, though everything from Brazilian to jazzy grooves can be heard.

Volksgarten (Map pp120-1; ☎ 532 42 41; 01, Burgring 1; free-€15; ⌚ 8pm-2am Mon-Wed, 9.30pm-late Thu-Sat) This club attracts a well-dressed crowd, keen to strut their stuff and scan for talent from the long bar. The quality sound system pumps out an array of music styles, which changes from night to night.

Ost Klub (Map pp120-1; ☎ 505 62 28; 04, Schwarzenbergplatz 10; price varies; ⌚ 7pm-4am Thu-Sat) Ost Klub hooks right into the wave of European

VIENNA

MORE BRACKISH THAN BLUE (BUT WHO CARES?)

Much ado is made about the romantic Danube, but what about its canal? At first glance the Danube Canal seems no great shakes. It slurps through town brown and disturbingly opaque. There's more to its 'flowing upside down' appearance, though. From this small stretch of water you can jump on a boat on a Friday or Saturday summer evening, zip downstream to Bratislava for dinner, and back upstream to Vienna in time for a nightcap or some clubbing (p400; book early though!).

Sometime after 2008 the converted cargo vessel, **MS Supamira** (www.supamira.com), should swing into life as a floating culture platform modelled on similar ships in Paris and Belgrade. Visual arts, film, theatre and performance will be the focus. The idea is that the ship will spend part of the year moored in Vienna and at other times cruise the Danube to culturally hook up cities along the river. Original plans were to moor it in front of Strandbar Herrmann, but that hit a hitch and the location is still undecided.

Speaking of that nightlife devil: **Strandbar Herrmann** (Map pp120-1; www.strandbarherrmann.at, in German; 01, Donaukanal/Wienfluss; ☼ 10-2am May-Sep), regarded as one of the world's hottest venues, looks set to pack up its deck chairs in 2015 (time enough for a few more cocktails, anyway) to make room for some canal construction work. No-one knows where Herrmann will be or what form he'll take after that. There's always space upriver, where a few other beach bars are situated on the canal, a stone's throw from the Bermuda Triangle nightlife zone.

Meanwhile, the club **Flex** (p153) is getting a dazzling glass pavilion and roof terrace that is tipped to attract a less feral clientele. It'll be interesting to see what happens to the grunge when it's exposed to all those rays of light and good manners. The word around town is also that a second Badeschiff (Bathing Ship) with a pool will moor here (run by Flex), so look out for that. The original is the **Badeschiff Wien** (Map pp120-1; ☎ 51307-44; www.badeschiff.at; 01, btwn Schwedenbrücke & Aspernbrücke; €5 for pool; ☼ 11am-midnight), which contains the club **Laderaum** (☼ 10pm-4am Mon-Sat; free or about €5-6) within its bowels, with regular DJs and electronic sounds.

Another new attraction is **Surfwelle** (www.surfwelle.at, in German), a large polystyrene wave with a water film that you can surf on boards. But if hanging 10 in the canal is not your thing, upstream the historic **Otto-Wagner-Schützenhaus** (Map pp116-17; Obere Donaustrasse 59) is getting an overhaul and will be an Art Nouveau café from 2009.

The 'mother of all projects', the **Trialto Bridge** (Map pp116-17; btwn Marienbrücke & Schwedenbrücke) is a new bridge development with shops, restaurants and bars. At the time of publication, though, approval was being held up due to some political issues that need talking through. The year 2011 could be the time for unveiling the new bridge.

---

clubs with an Eastern European and Balkan flavour; you can see a Georgian choir going through its paces one night and hear kletzmer, turbo folk, world music or lounge and electronic the next in a mixture of turntable and live sounds in its 'Klub' and 'Kantine' rooms.

U4 (Map pp116-17; ☎ 817 11 92; www.u-4.at; 12, Schönbrunner Strasse 222; €6-25; ☼ 10pm-late) Once the cutting edge of techno in Vienna, these days U4 pulls a young, studenty crowd – the edge has blunted somewhat but it's still very popular.

Live Music

Porgy & Bess (Map pp120-1; ☎ 512 88 11; www.porgy.at; 01, Riemergasse 11; about €15 ☼ 8pm-4am Mon-Sat, 7pm-4am Sun) This is the place to catch home-grown

and international jazz acts. Its jam sessions have recently been revived on Friday night after the scheduled performance.

WUK (Map p122; ☎ 40 121-0; www.wuk.at; 09, Währinger Strasse 59; free-€10) WUK is a space as much as a venue. You can catch Mieze Medusa & Tenderboy hip-hopping one night and classical concerts, film evenings, theatre or even children's shows another.

Szene Wien (Map pp116-17; ☎ 749 33 41; www.szene wien.at; 11, Hauffgasse 26; €8-20; ☼ from 7.30pm) Good things happen in small places – this small venue hauls out a mixed bag that includes rock, reggae, funk, jazz and world music.

Arena (Map pp116-17; ☎ 798 85 95; www.arena.co.at, in German; 03, Baumgasse 80; price varies; ☼ 2pm-late summer, 4pm-late winter) Arena normally hosts hard rock, metal and rock, which is well suited to its industrial location. The former slaughterhouse also shows films outdoors in summer and it holds once-a-month all-night parties; 'Iceberg', a German/British 1970s new wave bash, is popular.

Jazzland (Map pp120-1; ☎ 533 25 75; www.jazzland.at; 01, Franz-Josefs-Kai 29; price varies; ✆ 7pm-2am Mon-Sat) Jazzland has been an institution of Vienna's jazz scene for the past 30 years. The music covers the whole jazz spectrum and the brick venue features a grand mixture of local and international acts.

Unplugged (Map pp120-1; ☎ 5; www.vienna-unplugged .at, in German; 09, Liechtensteinstrasse 61; €2-8; ✆ from 8pm) This live venue has sporadic acts and provides a platform for local bands to perform live. Musos of all styles unpack their instruments here: punk, pop and rock – it's raw, small and back to the roots of the live gig.

Cinemas

Vienna has a fine mix of cinemas, featuring Hollywood blockbusters to art-house films, in both German and English. *Falter, City* and *Der Standard* (daily newspaper) all contain film listings. Monday is *Kinomontag*, when many seats are discounted. Expect to pay about €8 for tickets.

Artis International (Map pp120-1; ☎ 535 65 70; www .cineplexx.at; 01, Schultergasse 5) Mainstream films in English.

Breitenseer Lichtspiele (Map pp116-17; ☎ 982 21 73; 14, Breitenseer Strasse 21) Opened in 1905; still contains the original fittings and plays old B&W classics and independents.

Burg Kino (Map pp120-1; ☎ 587 84 06; www.burgkino .at; 01, Opernring 19) English films; has regular screenings of *The Third Man*.

English Cinema Haydn (Map pp120-1; ☎ 587 22 62; www.haydnkino.at; 06, Mariahilfer Strasse 57) Features mainstream Hollywood-style films in their original language.

Film Casino (Map pp116-17; ☎ 581 39 00-10; www.film casino.at; 05, Margareten Strasse 78) Art-house cinema with a mix of Asian and European independent films.

Österreichisches Filmmuseum (Map pp120-1; ☎ 533 70 54; www.filmmuseum.at; 01, Augustinerstrasse 1; ✆ Sep-Jun) Monthly retrospectives on directors or genres.

Top Kino (Map pp120-1; ☎ 208 30 00; www.topkino.at; 06, Rahlgasse 1) Cinema showing European independent films. Also hosts the Vienna Short Film Festival each May and has a great bar.

Votivkino (Map p122; ☎ 317 35 71; www.votiv kino.at; 09, Währinger Strasse 12) Hollywood and art-house films in their original language.

Sport

Football is easily the largest spectator sport in Vienna. Catch Rapid and Austria Memphis, Vienna's local teams, at the **Austria Memphis Franz-Horr-Stadion** (Map pp114-15; ☎ 688 01 50; 10, Fischhofgasse 12) and the **Rapid Vienna Gerhard-Hanappi-Stadion** (Map pp114-15; ☎ 914 55 10; 14, Keisslergasse 6). International games are normally played at the **Ernst Happel Stadion** (Map pp116-17; ☎ 728 08 54; 02, Meiereistrasse 7).

Stadthalle (Map p122; ☎ 98 100-0; 15, Vogelweidplatz) hosts a diverse array of events, including tennis, indoor football, horse shows and ice hockey.

SHOPPING

Vienna is one place where the glitz and glamour of shops selling high-end brands stand in stark contrast to some weird and idiosyncratic local stores. Specialities include porcelain, ceramics, handmade dolls, wrought-iron work and leather goods, and there are many shops selling *Briefmarken* (stamps), *Münze* (coins) and *Altwaren* (secondhand odds and ends).

The bustling Mariahilfer Strasse and Kärntner Strasse are lined with global High St names and chain stores. Off Mariahilfer Strasse in Mariahilf itself and in Neubau are where some of the more interesting shops are located. Otto-Bauer-Gasse is a freak's paradise, while Neubaugasse is good for secondhand hunters and collectors, and Josefstädter Strasse is an old-fashioned shopping street filled with quaint shops selling anything from flowers to tea. Not to be forgotten, too, is the Flohmarkt (p157).

Antiques

Dorotheum (Map pp120-1; ☎ 515 60-0; www.dorotheum .com; 01, Dorotheergasse 17) Founded in 1707 by Joseph I, the Dorotheum ranks among the largest auction houses in Europe. The range of objects is quite extraordinary, but stick to the categories of art, antiques and collectables. Some of it is reasonably priced, especially household ornaments.

Glasfabrik (Map pp116-17; ☎ 494 34 90; 16, Lorenz-Mandl-Gasse 25; ✆ 2-7pm Tue-Fri, 10am-4pm Sat) Glasfabrik specialises in antiques dating from 1670 to 1970, so the range on offer is eclectic to say the least.

Art

M-ARS (Map p122; ☎ 890 58 03; 07, Westbahnstrasse 9) The driving idea is that art can be bought

VIENNA

THE VOLATILE VOLANT – VIENNA DESIGN

Anyone into the international designer scene will be familiar with Vienna design brands like Wendy & Jim and Petar Petrov & Co. In keeping with the times, Vienna's design scene is prickling with talent; here's a few tips. In 2007 **Martina Rogy & Marcel Ostertag** (Map pp120-1; ☎ 532 3054; www.martinarogy.com; 1, Landskrongasse 1-3) released a summer collection with some *volant* designs that would make a sex goddess out of Wilma Flintstone. On a more casual note, **PiaMia** (Map pp116-17; ☎ 890 44 72; www.piamia.at; 05, Schönbrunnerstrasse 65) cuts the stuff for men as well as women in dress-down styles that look smart. **Ninali** (Map pp120-1); ☎ 699 1044 46 41; www.ninali .at; 07, Neustiftgasse 21; ⏱ noon-7pm Thu, Fri & Sat) is the label of Nina Kepplinger and Ali Rabbani, whose 2007 women's summer streetwear (it also has men's collections) crossed over into the occasional gather or volant.

---

without the artist having to sell his or her soul, here in Vienna's 'supermarket' for contemporary art. Some key figures in Austria's art world are behind this project, which got off the ground in 2007.

Ceramics, Glass & Crystal

Woka (Map pp120-1; ☎ 513 29 12; www.woka.at; 01, Singerstrasse 16) Accurate re-creations of Wiener Werkstätte lamps are the hallmark of Woka, using designs from the likes of Adolf Loos, Koloman Moser and Josef Hoffmann.

J&L Lobmeyr (Map pp120-1; ☎ 512 05 08; www.lob meyr.com; 01, Kärntner Strasse 26) Around since the late-19th century and supplying the imperial court with glassware, Lobmeyr now focuses on Werkstätten pieces.

Österreichische Werkstätten (Map pp120-1; ☎ 512 24 18; www.oew.at; 01, Kärntner Strasse 6) The best Austrian crafts and design is found upstairs here, including Kisslinger, a family glassware company since 1946, with Klimt- and Hundertwasser-styled designs.

Porzellan Manufactur Augarten Schloss Augarten (Map pp116-17; ☎ 211 24-200; www.augarten.at; 02, Obere Augartenstrasse 1, Schloss Augarten; ⏱ 9.30am-5pm Mon-Fri); Stock-im-Eisen-Platz (Map pp120-1; ☎ 512 14 94; 01, Stock-im-Eisen-Platz 3) Exquisite, albeit very traditional, porcelain ornaments and gifts are sold at the well-established factory and its city outlet.

Clothes, Leather & Jewellery

Kaufhaus Schiepek (Map pp120-1; ☎ 533 15 75; 01, Teinfaltstrasse 3) If you're looking for inexpensive, colourful jewellery or beads to create your own, look no further than Kaufhaus Schiepek.

Combinat (Map pp120-1; ☎ 699 1200 8920; 01, Museumsplatz 1; ⏱ noon-7pm Tue-Sat) Four designers have pooled resources in this fashion shop and have one guest each month to present

five labels for handbags, textiles and other art or accessories.

Loden-Plankl (Map pp120-1; ☎ 533 80 32; 01, Michaelerplatz 6) Loden-Plankl is a specialist in *Trachten*, traditional folk wear like *Lederhosen* (leather trousers) and *Dirndl* (traditional women's dress). It's been in operation for over 170 years, but the prices for quality stuff are less folkloric.

Lederwaren-Manufaktur Thomas Hicker (Map pp116-17; ☎ 982 82 06; 14, Schanzstrasse 55) The favoured address of Austria's prominence for briefcases and handcrafted leather accessories for business and the office.

Etcetera (Map p122; ☎ 524 56 37; 07, Neubaugasse 77; ⏱ 10am-noon & 3-6pm Mon-Fri, closed afternoon Wed) One of the best secondhand shops in Vienna for women's clothing – lots of retro stuff on the racks here, some of it prestigious labels. Stroll along Neubaugasse for more of this ilk.

See also boxed texts, above and p134.

Confectionary

Altmann & Kühne (Map pp120-1; ☎ 533 09 27; 01, Graben 30) Altmann & Kühne have been producing their handmade bonbons for over 100 years using a well-kept secret recipe. The packaging is designed by Wiener Werkstätten.

Demel (Map pp120-1; ☎ 535 17 17; www.demel.at; 01, Kohlmarkt 14) Demel produces stunning cakes, which are lovingly prepared – and lovingly devoured. Cakes can also be ordered over the internet.

Manner (Map pp120-1; ☎ 513 70 18; 01, www.manner .com; 01, Stephansplatz 7; ⏱ 10am-9pm Mon-Sat) The concept store of Vienna's favourite for sweet teeth since 1898. The peachy pink is hard to ignore, but so too are the confectionery delights available in a variety of packaging and combinations.

Department Stores

Gerngoss (Map pp120-1; ☎ 521 80; 07, Mariahilfer Strasse 38-40) Five floors of shops at Gerngoss cover most shopping genres, although the selection is very mainstream.

Steffl (Map pp120-1; ☎ 514 31-0; 01, Kärntner Strasse 19) Steffl is the most upmarket of Vienna's department stores, filled with designer labels and cosmetics.

Markets

Flohmarkt (flea market; Map pp116-17; 05, Ketten-brückengasse; ⊙ dawn-4pm Sat) This atmospheric flea market, in the mould of an Eastern European market, shouldn't be missed, with goods piled up in apparent chaos on the walkway. You can find anything you want (and everything you don't want): books, clothes, records, ancient electrical goods, old postcards, ornaments, carpets…you name it. Bargain for prices here.

From around the middle of November, *Christkindlmärkte* (Christmas Markets) start to pop up all over Vienna. Ranging from kitsch to quaint in style and atmosphere, the markets all have a few things in common: plenty of people, loads of Christmas gifts to purchase, mugs of *Glühwein* (mulled wine) and hotplates loaded with *Kartoffelpuffer* (hot potato patties) and *Maroni* (roasted chestnuts). Most close a day or two before Christmas day. Some of the best include:

Freyung market (Map pp120-1) Austrian arts and crafts and an old-worldly feel.

Heiligenkreuzerhof market (Map pp120-1) Oft-forgotten market which is arguably the most authentic and quaint of all the *Chrsitkindlmärktes*.

Karlsplatz market (Map pp120-1) Mainly sells arty gifts and is situated close to the Karlskirche.

Rathausplatz market (Map pp120-1) Easily the biggest and most touristy Christmas market in Vienna, held on the square in front of the Rathaus, but most of the Christmas gifts on sale are kitschy beyond belief unfortunately.

Schönbrunn market (Map pp116-17) Circle of upmarket stalls, loads of events for the kids and daily classical concerts at 6pm (more on weekends).

Spittelberg market (Map pp120-1) Traditional market occupying the charming cobblestone streets of the Spittelberg quarter. Stalls sell quality arts and crafts, but not at the cheapest prices.

Music

Black Market (Map pp120-1; ☎ 533 24 58; www.soul seduction.com; 01, Gonzagagasse 9; ⊙ noon-7pm Mon-Fri, 11am-6pm Sat) This is Vienna's house, techno and electronic specialist. The vinyl selection is enormous and the staff are highly knowledgeable.

MP3 (Map pp120-1; ☎ 526 47 15; www.musiktank stelle.at, in German; 01, Museumsplatz 1; ⊙ 1-7pm Tue-Sun) There's only one other place in the world where you'll find another of these – inside the Haus der Musik (p127). Zillions of Austrian pop, rock and electronic beats in one place for downloading. You can listen on the computer and have your selection burnt onto a CD for €0.99 per song plus €2 for the CD.

Rave Up (Map pp116-17; ☎ 596 96 50; 06, Hofmühlgasse 1) Friendly staff, loads of vinyl and a massive collection covering every genre of music in the world makes a trip to Rave Up a real pleasure.

Teuchtler (Map pp120-1; ☎ 586 21 33; 06, Wind-mühlgasse 10; ⊙ 1-6pm Mon-Fri, 10am-1pm Sat) This second-hand shop buys, sells and exchanges records and CDs, including rare and discontinued titles.

Photography

Lomoshop (Map pp120-1; ☎ 523 70 16; 07, Museumsplatz 1; ⊙ 11am-7pm) What began in the '80s as a bit of fun for a handful of Lomo fanatics in Vienna has now turned into a worldwide cult, and the Lomoshop is considered the very heart of the global Lomo movement. Here you'll find Lomo cameras, gadgets and accessories for sale, including original Russian-made multiple lens and fisheye Lomos.

Wine

Wien & Co (Map pp120-1; ☎ 535 09 16-12; www.weinco .at; 01, Jasomirgottstrasse 3-5) Wein & Co is arguably the best place to buy wine in Vienna; prices are extremely competitive, the selection hard to beat and the concentration of New World wines is impressive.

Bernthaler + Bernthaler (Map pp120-1; ☎ 216 37 57; 02, Komödiengasse 3; ⊙ 3-7pm Tue, Thu & Fri) This small Burgenland winemaker from Gols sells (mostly) his own wines at cellar door prices. Those with a deep appreciation of chocolate will gravitate towards his wine-spiked variety.

Unger und Klein (Map pp120-1; ☎ 532 13 23; www .ungerundklein.at; 01, Gölsdorfgasse 2; ⊙ 3pm-midnight Mon-Fri, 5pm-midnight Sat) Austrian wines make a great show at this wine bar/shop, with the best the country has to offer – whether expensive boutique varieties or bargain-bin bottles.

GETTING THERE & AWAY

Air

Vienna is the main centre for international flights. Flying domestic routes offers few benefits over trains. Although there are frequent flights to Graz, Klagenfurt, Salzburg and Linz with Austrian Airlines from Vienna (from about €78 each way), Innsbruck in Tyrol is the one place where flying is considerably faster than train (from about €93, one hour, five times daily). Book early for the cheapest fares. See p395 for more information.

Boat

Steamers head west (mostly from Krems) and fast hydrofoils head east – see p400 and p164.

Bus

Vienna currently has no central bus station and national Bundesbuses arrive and depart from several different locations, depending on the destination – many routes south (eg Eisenstadt) go from Südtiroler Platz. The Eurolines Bratislava service makes a stop here. For information, call ☎ 711 01 (open 7am to 8pm).

Car & Motorcycle

All the major car rental companies are represented in Vienna.

Avis (Map pp114-15; ☎ 587 6241; www.avis.at; 10, Laaer-Berg-Strasse 43; ⏱ 7am-6pm Mon-Fri, 8am-2pm Sat, 8am-1pm Sun)

Denzeldrive (Map pp116-17; ☎ 0501 054190; www .denzeldrive.at; 15, Europlatz (Westbahnhof); ⏱ 8am-5pm Mon-Fri, 8am-1pm Sat)

Europcar (Map pp120-1; ☎ 714 67 17; www.europcar .at; 01, Schubertring 9; ⏱ 7.30am-6pm Mon-Fri, 8am-1pm Sat, 8am-noon Sun)

Hertz (Map pp120-1; ☎ 512 86 77; www.hertz.at; 01, Kärntner Ring 17; ⏱ 7.30am-6pm Mon-Fri, 9am-4pm Sat & Sun)

LaudaMotion (Map pp116-17; ☎ 0900 240 120; www .laudamotion.com; 15, Europlatz; ⏱ 9am-6pm Mon-Fri, 9am-noon Sat, 4-6pm Sun) Cheap deals and (almost) free city sponsor cars.

Train

Vienna has excellent rail connections with Europe and the rest of Austria. Not all destinations are served by one station, and schedules are subject to change. The following stations (except Meidling) have lockers, currency exchange, *Bankomats* and places to eat and buy provisions for your journey.

WESTBAHNHOF

Trains to the west and north depart from Westbahnhof. Hourly services head to Salzburg (€43, 3½ hours) and four travel to Munich (€72, five hours). Seven daily direct trains run to Zürich (€88, six hours), frequent direct trains go to Frankfurt (€112, 7½ hours), one night train goes to Berlin (€155, 12 hours) and six go to Budapest (Keleti; €34, 2¾ hours). Westbahnhof is on U-Bahn lines U3 and U6, and many trams stop outside.

SÜDBAHNHOF

From Südbahnhof trains travel to Italy, the Czech Republic, Slovakia, Hungary and Poland. One direct train leaves each evening for Rome (€100, 13½ hours; via Klagenfurt, Venice and Florence); more services require a change at Venice. Hourly trains go to Bratislava (€13, one hour); there's six a day to Prague (€47, 4½ hours) and one each morning to Berlin (€98, nine hours).

Trams D (to the Ring and Franz-Josefs-Bahnhof) and O (to Wien Mitte and Praterstern) stop outside. Transfer to Westbahnhof in about 20 minutes by taking tram 18, or the S-Bahn to Meidling and then the U6.

FRANZ-JOSEFS-BAHNHOF

This station handles regional and local trains, including to Tulln (p174), Krems an der Donau (p170), and the Wachau region. From outside, tram D goes to the Ring, and tram 5 goes to Westbahnhof (via Kaiserstrasse) in one direction and Praterstern (Wien Nord) in the other.

OTHER STATIONS

The smaller stations Wien Mitte (Map pp120-1), Wien Nord (Map pp116-17) and Meidling (Map pp116-17) all have U-Bahn stops and the former two have connections to the airport.

GETTING AROUND

To/From the Airport

Getting to/from the airport is possible using the following transport options:

Bus Link (☎ 05 17 17, 7007 32300; www.oebb.at; adult one way/return €6/11, child 6-15 €3/5.50, child under 6 free; ⏱ from Westbahnhof every 30 min 5am-11pm, ⏱ from Schwedenplatz 5am-11.30pm, every 20 min (U1 and U4)). The Westbahnhof service takes 35 minutes and calls at Wien Südbahnhof station; the Schwedenplatz service is direct and takes 20 minutes.

OUT FOR THE RIDE

With its network of over 30 tram lines, Vienna is ideal for exploration by tram. Just to spice up one possible ride, here's a 'mystery tour'. Set aside a half day to do it with stops.

Board the tram N at Schwedenplatz going east. After a few stops you cross the lovely bridge of a famous general (p30) who helped keep the Habsburg monarchy in power with a stunning win. Get off here if you like and try something Wild (p148). Look or ask someone for a house where no line runs straight (the boxed text, p53, will help). Board again in the same direction, get out once you've reached the terminus and walk towards *the* major attraction here. It'll take you about 20 minutes. Along the way, there's a trampoline centre (in good weather). If it's open, tell the person at the booth you've got a brother who weighs 100kg and ask whether that's OK on the trampolines. ('Mein Bruder wiegt Einhundert Kilo, geht das überhaupt?'). There are places to snack, eat or drink all along the way if your brother needs upsizing, or you can rent a bike to downsize him.

Press on until you reach the train station. Jump on tram 5 towards Westbahnhof and immediately look out for the lovely little bar named after a famous 1970s kitsch film (we don't really recommend this one). After a while, you cross the bridge Friedensbrücke. On the right is another masterpiece from our 'Straight is not great' fellow. It was completed in 1971, and our architect wrote a famous manifesto called…? (Time you read that 'Architecture' section, isn't it?) You've crossed the canal now and are weaving towards Westbahnhof through the districts of Alsergrund and Josefstadt (Vienna's smallest district in terms of area). You might get off at Blindengasse to explore the neighbourhood, if it's evening try one of the bars beneath the Josefstädter U-Bahn station, or continue on to Westbahnhof.

C&K Airport Service (☎ 444 44; one way €27) C&K car service is a better and cheaper option than a taxi as its rates are fixed. On arrival at the airport, head to its stand to the left of the exit hall; when leaving Vienna, call ahead to make a reservation.

City Airport Train (☎ 252 50; www.cityairporttrain .com; return adult/child 6-14 €15/free if accompanied by adult; ☉ 5.38am-11.08pm, every 30 min) Departs from Wien-Mitte and takes 16 minutes; luggage check-in facilities and boarding card issuing service.

Schnellbahn 7 (☎ 05 17 17; www.oebb.at; one way €3, with city transport passes €1.50; ☉ 1.09am, 2.09am, 3.09am, 4.32am & 4.56am-11.22pm, every 30 min from Wien-Mitte) Cheapest way to get to the airport; also departs Wien-Nord.

Eurolines buses (see p398) run between Bratislava airport in Slovakia and Schwechat five times daily (departing Schechat between 8.15am and 8.45pm, departing Bratislava airport between 7.30am and 10.30pm). The trip takes 1½ hours and costs €10 return.

Bicycle

With a cycle track network of over 700km, Vienna is great for a bike ride on a warm day. Bikes can be rented from **Pedal Power** (Map pp116-17; ☎ 729 7234; 02, Ausstellungsstrasse 3; 1hr/half-/full-day rental €5/17/27; ☉ 8am-6pm Mar-Apr & Oct, 8am-7pm May-Sep; bring a passport or credit card) or from **Vienna City**

Bike (☎ 0810-50 05 00; www.citybikewien.at; 1st hr free, 2nd/3rd/4th hr €1/2/4), which has blue and yellow bike racks across the city. International MasterCard or Visa credit cards can be used, but unfortunately only an Austrian bank Maestro card; buying a city bike card is easiest. This is available from some hotels and pensions, or from **Royal Tours** (Map pp120-1; ☎ 710 4606; www.royaltours .at; 01, Herrengasse 1-3; ☉ 8-11.30am & 1-6pm) for €2 per day. But make sure you don't lose the bike, or €600 will be deducted from your card.

Bicycles can be carried on carriages marked with a bike symbol on the S-Bahn and U-Bahn (9am to 3pm and after 6.30pm Monday to Friday, after 9am Saturday, and all day Sunday) for half the adult fare. It's not possible to take bikes on trams and buses.

Car & Motorcycle

Due to a system of one-way streets and expensive parking, you're better off using the excellent public transport system. If you do plan to drive in the city, take special care of the trams; they always have priority and vehicles must wait behind trams when they stop to pick up or set down passengers.

Districts one to nine and 20 are pay zones and display *Kurzparkzone* (short-stay parking zones) where a *Parkschein* (parking voucher) is required. These come in colour-coded

30-/60-/90-minute lots (€0.60/1.20/1.80) and can be purchased from most *Tabaks* (tobacconist shops), banks, train stations and Wiener Linien ticket offices. A free 10-minute voucher is also available. To validate a voucher, just cross out the appropriate time, date and year and display it on your dashboard.

Public Transport

Vienna has one of Europe's best integrated public transport networks. Flat-fare tickets are valid for trains, trams, buses, the underground (U-Bahn) and the S-Bahn regional trains. Services are frequent, and you will rarely have to wait more than five or 10 minutes.

Public transport kicks off around 5am or 6am. Buses and trams finish between 11pm and midnight, and S-Bahn and U-Bahn services between 12.30am and 1am. Twenty-one Nightline bus routes crisscross the city from 12.30am to 5am. Schwedenplatz, Schottentor and the Oper are starting points for many services; look for buses and bus stops marked with an 'N'. All tickets are valid for Nightline services.

Transport maps are posted in all U-Bahn stations and at many bus and tram stops. Free maps and information pamphlets are available from **Wiener Linien** (☎ 7909 100; www.wienerlinien.at; ⏲ information line 6am-10pm Mon-Fri, 8.30am-4.30pm Sat & Sun), located in nine U-Bahn stations. The Karlsplatz, Stephansplatz and Westbahnhof information offices are open from 6.30am to 6.30pm Monday to Friday and 8.30am to 4pm Saturday and Sunday. Those at Erdberg, Floridsdorf, Landstrasse, Philadelphiabrücke, Praterstern and Schottentor are closed on weekends.

TICKETS & PASSES

Tickets and passes can be purchased at U-Bahn stations – from automatic machines (with English instructions and change) and occasionally-staffed ticket offices – and in *Tabaks*. Once bought, tickets need to be validated before starting your journey (except for weekly and monthly tickets); look for small blue boxes at the entrance to U-Bahn stations and on buses and trams. Just pop the end of the ticket in the slot and wait for the 'ding'. It's an honour system and ticket inspection is infrequent, but if you're caught without a ticket you'll be fined €60, no exceptions.

Tickets and passes are as follows:

8-Tage-Karte (Eight-day Ticket; €27.20) Valid for eight days, but not necessarily eight consecutive days; punch the card as and when you need it.

24-Stunden Wien-Karte (24hr Ticket; €5.70) Unlimited travel for 24 hours from time of validation.

Die Wien-Karte (The Vienna Card) See p124.

Fahrschein (Single Ticket; €1.70) Good for one journey, with line changes; costs €2.20 if purchased on trams and buses (correct change required).

Monatskarte (Monthly Ticket; €49.50) Valid from the 1st of the month to the last day of the month and transferable.

Streifenkarte (Strip Ticket; €6.80) Four single tickets on one strip.

Wiener Einkaufskarte (Vienna Shopping Card; €4.60) For use between 8am and 8pm Monday to Saturday; only good for one day after validation.

Wochenkarte (Weekly Ticket; €14) Valid Monday to 9am Monday.

Children aged six to 15 travel for half-price, or free on Sunday, public holidays and during Vienna school holidays (photo ID necessary); younger children always travel free. Senior citizens (women over 60, men over 65) can buy a €2 ticket that is valid for two trips; inquire at transport information offices.

Taxi & Pedal Taxi

Taxis are reliable and relatively cheap by West European standards. City journeys are metered; expect a flagfall of €2.50 from 6am to 11pm Monday to Saturday and €2.60 any other time, plus a small per kilometre fee. A small tip is expected; add on about 10% to the fare. Taxis are easily found at train stations and stands all over the city, or just flag them down in the street. To order one call ☎ 31 300, ☎ 60 160, ☎ 40 100 or ☎ 81 400. Don't count on taxis taking credit cards.

Pedal taxis (called Faxi) will set you back €2.50 per kilometre if you flag one down. Expect to pay €40 for a short spin of 20 minutes in a *Fiaker* (see p139).

AROUND VIENNA

KLOSTERNEUBURG

Realistically, much of Lower Austria can be visited as a day trip from Vienna. Klosterneuburg, a small town only 12km north of the Innere Stadt, is an easy half-day trip.

Without doubt the biggest attraction is Klosterneuburg's **Stift Klosterneuburg** (☎ 02243-

411 212; www.stift-klosterneuburg.at; Stiftplatz 1, Klosterneuberg; tours adult/student/child/family €7/6/5/4/14; tours 10am-5pm hourly). Founded in 1114, the abbey's baroque facelift didn't begin until 1730, and wasn't completed until 1842. The plans actually called for something much more grand, but fortunately these were not realised, leaving large sections intact in their original medieval style. The abbey's **museum** (9am-6pm Tue-Sun May–mid-Nov) contains an eclectic mix of religious art from the Middle Ages to the present. It closes in winter to individual visitors, but tours of are conducted almost hourly all year (tours in English require advanced notice). The highlight of the 'Der Sacrale Weg' tour is the **Verdun Altar** in St Leopold's Chapel, an annexe of the church. Made in 1181 by Nicholas of Verdun, it is an unsurpassed example of medieval enamel work and is gloriously adorned with 51 enamelled panels showing biblical scenes.

Not far from the abbey, but light years away in its displays, is **Sammlung Essl** (02243-370 50; www.sammlung-essl.at; Kunst Der Gegenwart, An der Donau-Au 1, Klosterneuburg; adult/student & child €7/5/3.50, free Wed 7-9pm; 10am-6pm Tue-Sun, 10am-9pm Wed). This gallery houses the extensive contemporary art collection of the Essl family, and includes the likes of Gerhard Richter, Hermann Nitsch, Georg Baselitz and Elke Krystufek.

Getting There & Away

Klosterneuburg's on the S-Bahn route from Vienna (Franz-Josef-Bahnhof) to Tulln. The station closest to the abbey is Klosterneuburg-Kierling (€4.40; 15 minutes; evey 30 minutes).

Lower Austria

Surrounding Vienna on all sides, the fertile valleys and plains of Lower Austria are the 'cradle' of Austrian culture, and it has one of the country's richest cultural landscapes. The Viennese often come out here to paddle its rivers, sup its wines and scale its mountains, but the cultural aspect of Lower Austria is what stands out most.

The north is an often neglected region of rich pastures, forested glens and pretty vineyards set upon gentle, rolling hills. Poppy fields deliver one of the country's most interesting culinary aspects (foods brimming with poppy seed), while the town of Drosendorf near the Czech border is an isolated fortress town with Austria's only intact town wall. The south is sprinkled with mountains rising up to about 2000m on the doorstep of Vienna; here you also find the moderately interesting towns of Baden bei Wien and Wiener Neustadt, and one of the nicest ways to travel between Lower Austria and Styria – the Semmering Pass and spectacular *Semmeringbahn* (Semmering Railway). Carnuntum, a small region between Vienna and the Slovakian border, has some fascinating remnants of the Roman period in Austria, dating from about 15 BC.

Most famous of all regions in Lower Austria, however, is the Danube River (Donau) and its valley, a place of magnificent natural beauty and cultural achievement. The Wachau, which stretches from Melk to Krems an der Donau, is the prettiest section and is truly a European highlight for its wines, castles, abbeys and medieval villages. Elsewhere, towns such as St Pölten, Lower Austria's largest town and the provincial capital, and Tulln offer a feel for provincial urban texture, and both have a couple of good museums and art spaces.

HIGHLIGHTS

- Hiking through the vineyards and forest around **Spitz** (p172) and exploring the historical **Danube Valley** (p164)

- Meandering through **Stift Melk** (p172), a magnificent baroque monastery on the banks of the Danube

- Indulging in the rustic pleasures of wine and *Wurst* (sausage) in one of the *Heurigen* (wine taverns) in **Krems an der Donau** (p169) or **Dürnstein** (p171)

- Riding the **Semmering railway** (p187), a remarkable engineering feat and Unesco World Heritage site

- Getting caught in the 'mother of all rainstorms' while hiking **Schneeberg** (p187), Lower Austria's highest peak

| POPULATION: 1.5 MILLION | AREA: 19,178 SQ KM | HIGHEST ELEVATION: SCHNEEBERG 2076M |

HISTORY

Settlement of Lower Austria can be traced back to prehistoric times; some of the earliest archaeological finds in Europe, such as the 25,000-year-old *Venus of Willendorf*, come from the region. The Romans had a strong presence here, particularly in the area south of the Danube, and built fortifications at Ybbs, Melk, Mautern and Carnuntum (p178).

Lower Austria's borders were drawn in the 13th century under Babenberg rule, but in 1278 the region fell to the Habsburgs. Lower Austria's flat plains to the north were a favourite of marauding foreigners; it was often overrun with Bohemian Hussites in the early 15th century, the Turks in the 16th century and the Swedes during the Thirty Years' War.

Following WWII, the region was occupied – and plundered – by the Russians. With independence acheived in 1955, the situation improved, and in 1986 Lower Austria gained its own provincial capital, St Pölten (Vienna had played the role until then).

CLIMATE

Lower Austria has a mix of climates; to the north and east you'll find a Pannonian climate and to the south more alpine weather, with rapid changes in temperature common. The Danube Valley is marked by a continental climate.

GETTING THERE & AWAY

Much of Lower Austria has great connections to the rest of the country. The A1 autobahn, running from Upper Austria to Vienna, splits the province into two unequal halves to the south of the Danube (which also connects Upper Austria and Vienna by boat). The A2 runs south from Vienna to Graz through its lower region; off this branches the A3 towards Eisenstadt and Hungary and the S6 to northern Styria. Passing through Lower Austria's eastern fringe is the A4, which links Vienna with northern Burgenland and eventually Budapest.

Shadowing most of the major roads is an extensive rail system.

GETTING AROUND

Train connections are some of the best in Austria, *Postbus* (Post Bus) services are also good on weekdays, and well-maintained autobahn and *Bundesstrasse* (alternative routes) make it simple and safe to explore the entire region by car.

THE DANUBE VALLEY

The Danube, which enters Lower Austria from the west near Ybbs and exits in the east near Bratislava, Slovakia's capital, carves a winding path through the province's hills and fields. The dramatic stretch of river between Krems an der Donau and Melk is known as the Wachau and is Austria's most spectacular section of the Danube. Here the landscape is characterised by vineyards, forested slopes, wine-producing villages and imposing fortresses at nearly every bend. In 2000 the Wachau became a Unesco World Heritage site due to its harmonious blend of natural and cultural beauty.

Tourismusverband Wachau-Nibelungengau (☎ 02713-300 60 60; www.wachau.at; Schlossgasse 3, Spitz an der Donau; ☯ 9am-4.30pm Mon-Thu, 9am-2.30pm Fri) can help with information on the Wachau and its surrounds.

GETTING AROUND

A popular way of exploring the region is by boat, particularly between Krems and Melk, but it's also possible to travel from Passau to Vienna; see p208 for more details. The most popular time to take a boat trip on the Danube is between May and September, when a several companies service the route.

DDSG Blue Danube (☎ 01-588 80; www.ddsg-blue-danube.at; 01, Friedrichstrasse 7, Vienna; Vienna-Dürnstien one way/return €19.50/26, Melk-Krems one way/return €17.50/22.50, Melk-Spitz & Spitz-Krems one way/return €10/13.50) does the routes Melk–Krems, Spitz–Melk, and Spitz-Krems from early April to October up to three times daily, and between Vienna and Dürnstein every Sunday from May till September.

Brandner (☎ 07433-25 90-21; www.brandner.at; Ufer 50, Wallsee; Krems-Melk return adult/child €22.50/11.50, one way adult/child €17.50/9) operates boats between Krems and Melk one to two times daily from mid-April to late October.

More popular is exploring the region by bicycle. A wonderfully flat cycle path runs along both sides of the Danube from Vienna to Melk, passing through Krems, Dürnstein, Weissenkirchen and Spitz (these are all on the northern bank). Many hotels and pensions (B&Bs) are geared towards cyclists and most towns have at least one bike-rental shop. For more information pick up a free copy of *The Donauradweg – Von Passau bis Bratislava* (from tourist offices and some hotels), which provides details of distances, hotels and information offices along the route.

The roads on both sides of the Danube between Krems and Melk, where the B3 and the B33 hug the contours of the river, lend themselves well to a driving tour (see below). Vehicle bridges cross the river at Krems, Melk, Pöchlarn and Ybbs. A rail track runs along the Danube's northern bank and while it's a scenic trip, it's slow.

DRIVING TOUR OF THE DANUBE VALLEY

If you plan to take in just a few of the Danube Valley sights in Lower Austria, train and bus connections are adequate, but visiting many sights in one grab will, unfortunately, require having your own vehicle. See p170 for details on car rental.

This road trip is almost all-weather and needs little preparation. It follows the Danube for almost all of the 150km, taking in towns and sights on a circuit between Krems an der Donau and Maria Taferl (both on the north bank) and Melk and other significant sights on the south bank. The junctions only get tricky around Melk; but even if you only have limited experience driving on the right-hand

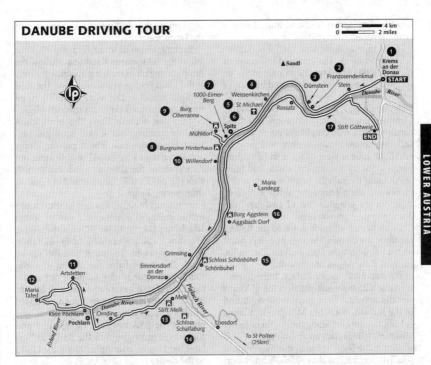

side of the road, these shouldn't present a huge problem.

The best time to do the trip is on a Monday or Tuesday, when traffic is light. Allow about four hours, or a full day with stops.

From the **Krems-Stein roundabout (1)** take the B3 southwest towards Spitz. About 3km from Krems-Stein you approach the small settlement of Unterloiben, where on the right you can see the **Franzosendenkmal (2;** French Monument), erected in 1805 to celebrate the victory of Austrian and Russian troops here over Napoleon. Shortly afterwards the lovely town of **Dürnstein (3;** p171), 6km from Krems, comes into view and you can see the blue-towered Chorherrenstift (p171) backed by Kuernringerburg (p171), the castle where Richard the Lionheart was imprisoned in 1192.

The valley is punctuated by picturesque terraced vineyards as you enter the heart of the Wachau. In **Weissenkirchen (4)**, 12km from Krems, you'll find the pretty hilltop fortified **parish church** (☎ 02715-2203; Weissenkirchen 3; ✆ 8am-7pm Easter-Oct, 8am-5pm Sat & Sun Nov-Easter), whose front doors are approached by a labyrinth of

covered pathways. This Gothic church was built in the 15th century and has a baroque altar and a garden terrace with good views of the Danube. Below the church is the charming Teisenhoferhof arcaded courtyard, with a covered gallery and lashings of flowers and dried corn. The **Wachau Museum** (☎ 02715-2268; Weissenkirchen 32; adult/senior/concession & child €5/3.50/2.50; ✆ 10am-5pm Tue-Sun Apr-Oct, closed Nov-Mar) is also here and houses work by artists of the Danube school. Close to the river is the **Raffelsberger Hof** (☎ 02715-22 01; www.raffelsbergerhof .at; s €72-85, d €104-124, ste €130-154; P), a four-star hotel in a small but beautifully renovated Renaissance castle.

A couple of kilometres on, just after Wösendorf, you find the church of **St Michael (5)**, in a hamlet with 13 houses. If the kids are along for this ride, now's the time to ask them to count the terracotta hares on the roof (seven, in case they're not reading this!).

Some 17km from Krems, the pretty town of **Spitz (6;** p172) swings into view, surrounded by vineyards and lined with quiet, cobblestone streets. There are some good trails leading across hills and into *Heurigen* (wine taverns) here (p109).

Turn right at Spitz onto the B217 (Otten-schläger Strasse). The terraced hill on your right is **1000-Eimer-Berg (7)**, so-named for its reputed ability to yield a thousand buckets of wine each season. On your left, high above the valley opening, is the castle ruin **Hinterhaus (8)**. Continue along the B217 to the mill wheel and turn right towards **Burg Oberranna (9; ☎ 02713-8221; www.tiscover.at/burg-oberranna, in German; s/d €68/122; Ⓟ)**, 6km west of Spitz in Mühldorf. Surrounded by woods, this castle and hotel overlooking the valley is furnished with period pieces and has a refreshing old-worldly feel. Tours of the grounds cost €2 and run from 3pm to 6pm every weekend.

From here, backtrack down to the B3 and continue the circuit. The valley opens up and on the left, across the Danube, you glimpse the ruins of Burg Aggstein (opposite).

Willendorf (10), located 21km from Krems, is where a 25,000-year-old figurine of Venus was discovered. The original is today housed in the Naturhistorisches Museum in Vienna (p128). Continuing along the B3, the majestic Stift Melk (p172) rises up across the river. This section of the Danube has a power station and you'll notice that just above Melk-Emmersdorf the river slows to a placid pace. There's some decent swimming in the backwaters here if you're game to dip into the Danube.

At Klein Pöchlarn a sign indicates a first turn-off on Artstettner Strasse (L7255), which you can follow for 5km to **Artstetten (11; ☎ 07413-80060; Artstetten 1; adult/senior/student/child €6.50/5.80/4.70/3.60; Ⓨ 9am-5.30pm Apr-Nov)**, unusual for its many onion domes. The castle has endured lots of modifications over the past 700 years but gained fame through a former owner, the one and only Archduke Franz Ferdinand. Inside is a museum devoted to the luckless heir, displaying photos and stories of his and his wife's time at the castle and their fateful trip to Sarajevo where his murder there triggered WWI. Their tomb is in the church.

From here, a minor road L7257 winds 6.5km through a sweeping green landscape to **Maria Taferl (12; ☎ 07413-278; Maria Taferl 1; admission free; Ⓨ 7am-7pm)** high above the Danube Valley. Created by Jakob Prandtauer (of Melk fame), this baroque church is notable for its two onion domes and dark dome-frescoes. Its altar is a complicated array of figures in gold. You'll find lots of hotels and pensions,

and some of the most spectacular views across the Danube here.

Backtrack 6km down towards the B3. Turn left at the B3 towards Krems and follow the ramp veering off to the left and across the river at the Klein Pöchlarn bridge. Follow the road straight ahead to the B1 (Austria's longest road) and turn left onto this towards Melk.

This first section along the south bank is uninteresting, but it will soon get better. Unless the weather isn't playing along, across the river you should be able make out Artstetten in the distance, and shortly **Stift Melk (13; p172)**, will rise up ahead in a golden shimmering heap.

From Stift Melk, a 7km detour leads south to the splendid Renaissance castle, **Schloss Schallaburg (14; ☎ 02754-6317; www.schallaburg.at; Schallaburg 1; adult/concession/child/family €8/7/3.50/16; Ⓨ 9am-5pm Mon-Fri, 9am-6pm Sat & Sun Apr-Oct)**. To reach the castle from the abbey in Melk, follow the signs to the *Bahnhof* (train station) and Lindestrasse east, turn right into Hummelstrasse/Kirschengraben (L5340) until it changes name to Roggendorf and reaches the B3A near the railway line and highway. Turn right onto the B3A and 2km later right again, continuing along the L5342 to the castle.

In a region packed with gems, this is one of the highlights. Just beyond the entranceway is the castle's architectural centrepiece, a two-storey arcaded Renaissance courtyard with magnificent terracotta arches and rich red-brown carvings. There are some 400 terracotta images, completed between 1572 and 1573; the largest figures support the upper-storey arches, of which the court jester sniggering in the corner is the most intriguing. Below these are pictorial scenes and a series of mythological figures and masks. The castle is host to an annual prestigious exhibition, based on different cultural themes. Combined tickets with nearby attractions, which change yearly, are usually on offer.

Backtrack to the B33. Be careful here that you stay on the south side of the river. When you reach Hummelstrasse you need to go one block beyond Lindestrasse to Abt-Karl-Strasse and back down to the Stift. Follow the B1 for 4km to **Schloss Schönbühel (15; admission free; Ⓨ dawn-dusk)**, a 12th-century castle standing high on a rock some 5km northeast of Melk. Continue along this lovely stretch of the B33 in the direction of Krems. About 10km from

Schloss Schönbühel the ruins of **Burg Aggstein** (**16**; ☎ 02753-82281; www.ruineaggstein.at; admission €2; ⊙ 9am-6pm Apr-May & Sep-Oct, till 7pm Jun-Aug) swing into view. This 12th century hilltop castle was built by the Kuenringer family and now offers a grand vista of the Danube. The 'robber barons' of both Schloss Schönbühel and Burg Aggstein are said to have imprisoned their enemies on a ledge of rock (the Rosengärtlein), where the hapless captives faced starvation (unless they opted for a quicker demise by throwing themselves into the abyss below).

From the right bank of the Danube you now get a bird's-eye view of the towns and ruins you passed earlier. One of the exquisite pleasures of the region is its famous *Marillen* (apricots), and you'll see lots of orchards among the vineyards. Shops in the region also sell a variety of liqueurs made from apricots. The section of the B33 between Aggstein and Mautern (across from Krems) is dotted with *Heurigen* for those who are not at the wheel.

About 27km from Melk some pretty cliffs rise up above the road. From Mautern it's a detour of about 6km to **Stift Göttweig** (**17**; p170). To reach it, at the roundabout near the bridge follow the road right from the B33 to Mautern and right again immediately afterwards towards Fürth. Stift Göttweig is signposted at the next roundabout on the L7071. From there it's a short drive back to Krems.

This road trip can also be done from St Pölten, situated 36km south of Krems an der Donau. If you do set out from there, be sure to include **Stift Herzogenburg** (p176).

KREMS AN DER DONAU
☎ 02732 / pop 23,900

Krems an der Donau is the prettiest of the larger towns on the Danube and marks the beginning of the Wachau. It has a small university and some good eating and drinking, and if the circus of history that can be Vienna in summer has not sated the appetite for past glories, Krems offers a very attractive historical aspect too. It rests on the northern bank of the Danube, surrounded by terraced vineyards, and has been a centre of the wine trade for most of its history.

Orientation & Information

Krems has three parts: Krems to the east, the smaller settlement of Stein (formerly a separate town) to the west, and the connecting suburb of Und. Hence the local witticism:

Krems und Stein sind drei Städte (Krems and Stein are three towns).

The centre of Krems stretches along a pedestrian-only street, Obere and Untere Landstrasse. The **tourist office** (☎ 826 76; www .tiscover.com/krems; Undstrasse 6; ⊙ 9am-6pm Mon-Fri, 9am-5pm Sat, 9am-4pm Sun May-Oct, 9am-5pm Mon-Fri Nov-Apr) has an excellent walk-by-numbers *Krems Stadtrundgang* (Krems city walk; in German) map with route descriptions. It also stocks a *Heurigen* calendar and culinary guide and for those with their own car a *Weinstrasse Kremstal* map (in German) showing vineyards.

The **main post office** (☎ 677-3500; Brandströmstrasse 4-6) is near the *Hauptbahnhof* (main train station). The boat station is near Donaustrasse, about 2km west of the train station.

Sights

A walk through the cobblestone streets of Krems and Stein, especially at night, is one of the delights of a visit. Some of the most atmospheric parts to explore are on and behind **Schürerplatz** and **Rathausplatz** in Stein (don't miss these two wonderful squares), dominated by the baroque **Mazzettihaus** and the 18th-century **Steiner Rathaus** respectively; here you could be forgiven for thinking you had stumbled upon an isolated Adriatic village.

If you've picked up the tourist office's walking map, it leads you there via 20 stops, beginning at the imposing **Steiner Tor** on Obere Landstrasse, constructed in the 15th century and refashioned into a baroque gate in the 18th century. Another highlight along the way is the **Pfarrkirche St Veit** (☎ 832 85; Pfarrplatz 5; ⊙ dawn-dusk), a baroque parish church resurrected from earlier Gothic and Romanesque forms. Its colourful frescoes are by Martin Johann Schmidt, an 18th-century local artist who was also known as Kremser Schmidt and occupied a house from 1756 near the Linzer Tor in Stein. Behind this is the **Piaristenkirche** (☎ 820 92; Frauenbergplatz; ⊙ dawn-dusk), with Gothic vaulting, huge windows and baroque altars.

Just west of here is the **Weinstadt Museum** (☎ 801 567; www.weinstadtmuseum.at; Körnermarkt 14; adult/student/child €4/3/2; ⊙ 10am-6pm Tue-Sun Mar-Nov), housed in a former Dominican monastery; inside you'll find displays on the town's pride and joy (wine) and its production, and paintings by our friend, Kremser Schmidt.

LOWER AUSTRIA

KREMS AN DER DONAU

INFORMATION	
Main Post Office	1 E2
Tourist Office	2 C3

SIGHTS & ACTIVITIES	
Karikaturmuseum	3 C3
Kloster Und	(see 2)
Kunsthalle	4 C3
Mazzettihaus	5 A4
Pfarrkirche St Veit	6 E1
Piaristenkirche	7 E1
Rathausplatz	8 B4
Schürerplatz	9 A4
Steiner Rathaus	10 B4
Steiner Tor	11 D2
Weingut der Stadt Krems	12 D1
Weinstadt Museum	13 E1

SLEEPING	
Gästehaus Einzinger	14 A4
Gästehaus Freisleben	15 B4
Hotel Alte Poste	16 D2
Hotel Unter den Linden	17 D3
Jugendherberge	18 D3
ÖAMTC Donau Camping	19 D4
Steigenberger Avance Hotel	20 B2

EATING	
Filmbar im Kesselhaus	21 C2
Gasthaus zum Elefanten	22 A4
Jell	23 E1
m.kunst.genuss	(see 4)
Mörwald Kloster Und	(see 2)
Spar	24 A4
Spar	25 E2

DRINKING	
Piano	26 B4

TRANSPORT	
Boat Station	27 C4
City Buses	28 F2
Postbus Departures	29 F2
Postbus Departures	30 F2

Further west of here, along Steiner Landstrasse, you reach the **Kunstmeile** (Art Mile), the section of Steiner Landstrasse with museums and space for art and media. The rather forbidding building nearby is the local prison, and behind that is the leafy university.

The **Karikaturmuseum** (☎ 908 020; www.karikaturmuseum.at, in German; Steiner Landstrasse 3a; adult/student/child/family €9/8/3.50/18; combined ticket for 3 Kunstmeile museums €11; 🕑 10am-6pm Apr-Oct, 10am-5pm Nov-Mar) features changing exhibitions and a large permanent collection of caricatures of prominent Austrian and international figures. Directly opposite is the town's arts centre, the **Kunsthalle** (☎ 908 010-19; Steiner Landstrasse 3; adult/student/child/family €9/8/3.50/18; combined ticket for 3 Kunstmeile museums €11; 🕑 10am-6pm Apr-Oct, 10am-5pm Nov-Mar). Small but often unusual changing exhibitions are held here.

Krems is a wine-making heartland and **Weingut der Stadt Krems** (☎ 801 441; Stadtgraben 11; 🕑 9am-noon & 1-5pm Mon-Sat) is the city-owned vineyard, yielding 200,000 bottles per year (90% is Grüner Veltliner and Riesling), some of which you can sample free and buy.

Sleeping

Krems is fairly well-supplied with hotels, pensions and private rooms, but booking ahead in summer is always advisable. Many private rooms, especially in Stein, are marked with signs; the tourist office can also help.

ÖAMTC Donau Camping (☎ 844 55; donaucampingkrems@aon.at; Wiedengasse 7; campsites per person with tent €5.30; 🕑 Easter–mid-Oct; P) This campsite is conveniently close to town.

Jugendherberge (☎ 834 52; oejhv.noe.krems@aon.at; Ringstrasse 77; dm €18.50; 🕑 Apr-Oct; P) This popular Hostelling International (HI) hostel close to the tourist office is well geared for cyclists; it features a garage, an onsite bicycle repair service and packed lunches.

Gästehaus Einzinger (☎ 823 16; gaestehaus.einzinger@aon.at; Steiner Landstrasse 82; s €33, d €54-64) The courtyard in this 16th-century guesthouse will blow away even the most history-hardened: blackbirds buzz and chirp, budgies taunt them from a cage, and one portico after another opens up around a courtyard spilling with foliage. Rooms are a little basic but some have views to night-lit Stift Göttweig.

Hotel Alte Poste (☎ 822 76; www.altepost-krems.at, in German; Obere Landstrasse 32; s €30-45, d €55-75; P) This friendly guesthouse in a historic 500-year-old building has comfortable rooms, an enchanting courtyard and a good traditional restaurant.

Gästehaus Freisleben (☎ 851 69; www.gaestehaus-freisleben.at, in German; Steiner Landstrasse 16; s €37-49, d €60-84) Freisleben is bright and tastefully furnished, with sparkling tiled surfaces, large rooms and a small table in each room where you can catch up on writing your travel journal.

Hotel Unter den Linden (☎ 821 15; www.udl.at; Schillerstrasse 5; s €45-70, d €66-92; P) This big, yellow, family-run hotel has knowledgeable and helpful owners, bright comfortable rooms and a convenient location in Krems itself. Book ahead as it gets bus groups and is arguably the best deal in town.

Gourmet-Hotel Am Förthof (☎ 833 45; www.hotel-foerthof.at; Förthofer Donaulände 8; s €60-80, d €100-130; P 🍴) This country-style mansion about 500m west of Stein combines cosy rooms, romantic ambience, a pretty garden and a superb gourmet restaurant (mains €15, menus €22 to €44) serving Austrian classics such as *Tafelspitz* (boiled beef with apple and horseradish sauce), lamb, and fried liver with slices of apple.

Steigenberger Avance Hotel (☎ 710 10; www.krems.steigenberger.at; Am Goldberg; s €108-113, d €176-186; P 🍴) It's a stiff walk up the hill here but well worth it for a splurge in comfortable modern rooms. Views are across town and the valley, or over to the vineyards from the twin-level wellness/spa area with its infinity pool and panorama windows (it also has an outdoor pool and bar area). Reserve to get the best views from the outdoor restaurant patio.

Eating & Drinking

Filmbar im Kesselhaus (☎ 893 3599; www.filmbar.at, in German; Dr.-Karl-Dorreck-Strasse 30; mains €5-10; 🕑 11am-6pm Sun-Tue, 11am-11pm Wed-Sat) This sleek student restaurant and bar is the hub of eating and drinking activity on the university campus. Beyond that, it also shows art-house films usually related to the theme of shows in its associated exhibition space (www.filmgalerie.at). If the vegetarian offerings, salads, pasta and meats don't get you up here, then the lively indoor and outdoor bar or the cinematic aspect might.

m.kunst.genuss (☎ 908 010-21; Steiner Landstrasse 3; lunch buffets €8-15; 🕑 10am-6pm) Another eatery in the Toni Mörwald stable – excellent for breakfast, buffet or a quick coffee beside the Kunsthalle.

Gasthaus zum Elefanten (☎ 850 16; Schürerplatz 10; mains €8.50-14.50; ☷ lunch & dinner Wed-Sun) Situated on a romantic baroque town square, 'the Elephant' serves classics such as Styrian chicken with beans and pumpkin oil, schnitzel and lamb in a cosy atmosphere indoors or at outdoor tables.

Jell (☎ 823 45; Hoher Markt 8-9; mains €16-24; ☷ lunch & dinner Tue-Fri, lunch Sat & Sun) Occupying a gorgeous stone house, Jell is hard to beat for a rustic atmosphere and fine wine from its own vineyard. The game goulash is a bit rich, but Jell has good food on the whole. It's friendly staff also adds to a great regional experience.

our pick **Mörwald Kloster Und** (☎ 704 930; Undstrasse 6; mains €20-33, menus €39-56; ☷ 10am-10pm Tue-Sat) Mörwald is most central of a crop of restaurants run by Toni Mörwald outside Vienna; it offers exquisite delights ranging from roast pigeon breast to beef, poultry and fish dishes with French influences. A lovely yard and an impressive wine selection round off one of the best restaurants in the Wachau.

You'll find one **Spar** (Obere Landstrasse 15) supermarket in Krems, and a second **Spar** (Schürerplatz) in Stein.

Don't omit a *Heurigen* visit; most are out of the centre and provide an authentic eating and drinking experience. They're only open for two- or three-week bursts during the year; get the schedule from the tourist office.

Piano (☎ 858 09; Steiner Landstrasse 21; ☷ 5pm-2am Mon-Thu, 5pm-3am Fri & Sat, 5pm-midnight Sun) A crossover crowd of students, young workers and mellow jazz types gathers at this lively and off-beat pub. It does a couple of local sausage snacks to go with its great selection of beer; a few other decent bars and restaurants are on this street.

Getting There & Away

Frequent daily trains depart from Krems for Vienna's Franz Josefs Bahnhof (€13.50, one hour). The quickest way to Melk is by train to Spitz and continue by bus (€4.40, five times daily, one hour).

Autovermietung Becker (☎ 82433; www.rent.becker .at, in German; Wachauer Strasse 30) rents cars from €49 per day and minibuses from €120.

Getting Around

From the train station, bus 1 does a long loop through Stein and back into the centre of Krems for the cost of €1.70. Bikes can be

hired at ÖAMTC Donau Camping (p169) and some hotels.

AROUND KREMS
Stift Göttweig

It's difficult *not* to notice **Stift Göttweig** (Göttweig Abbey; ☎ 02732-85581-231; Furth bei Göttweig; adult/student & child €7/6.50, full/part-guided tour €3/2; ☷ 10am-6pm Oct-May, 9am-6pm Jun-Sep, tours 11am & 3pm), not least because of its brooding hilltop presence. Founded in 1083, the abbey you see today is mostly baroque due to restoration after a devastating fire in the early 18th century. Aside from the grand view back across the Danube Valley from its garden terrace and restaurant, the abbey's highlights include the **Imperial Staircase** with a heavenly ceiling fresco painted by Paul Troger in 1739, and the over-the-top baroque interior of the **Stiftskirche** (which has a Kremser Schmidt work in the crypt). Fully guided tours take in the abbey's Imperial Wing, church and summer vestry; shorter tours explore either the Imperial Wing or the church and vestry.

Only three direct buses on weekdays travel between Krems train station and Göttweig (€1.70, 25 minutes). The train is another possibility, but it's a steep walk up hill from the Klein Wien station (€2.90, 10 minutes).

Schloss Grafenegg

About 10km east of Krems near the road to Tulln is **Schloss Grafenegg** (☎ 02735-220 522; www .grafenegg.com; Haitzendorf; adult/senior/family €5/3/7.50; ☷ 10am-5pm Tue-Sun mid-Apr–Sep), a castle with the look and feel of an ornate Tudor mansion set in English woods. Built in a revivalist (neo-gothic) style by Leopold Ernst in the mid-19th century it is now a venue for exhibitions and concerts, but you can explore the interior, which includes a chapel and decadent state rooms, weighed down with plenty of wood, period furniture, carpets and fireplaces.

The castle's manicured gardens are perfect for a picnic, but for fine dining don't pass up **Restaurant & Hotel Schloss Grafenegg** (☎ 02735-2616-0; grafenegg@moerwald.at; Grafenegg 12; 3-/5-course menu €45/60; ☷ 10am-10pm Wed-Sun Easter-Oct; Ⓟ) owned by celebrity chef and winemaker Toni Mörwald. Accommodation costs are €89 to €103 for a single, and €118 to €138 for a double. Two kilometres away in Feuersbrunn is his **Hotel Villa Katharina** (☎ 02738-229 80; rezeption@moerwald.at; Kleine Zeile 10; s €81-96, d €108-128; Ⓟ), with its **Restaurant zur**

Traube (☎ 02738-229 80; Kleine Zeile 13-17; 3-/8-course menu €29/69; ⊗ 10am-10pm).

To get to Schloss Grafenegg, catch one of the six daily trains to nearby Wagram-Grafenegg (€4.40, 18 minutes) and walk 2km northeast to the castle.

DÜRNSTEIN
☎ 02711 / pop 1000

The pretty town of Dürnstein, on a supple curve in the Danube, is not only known for its beautiful buildings but also for the castle above the town where Richard I (the Lionheart) of England was once imprisoned.

Orientation & Information

The train station and **tourist office** (☎ 200; www .duernstein.at; Dürnstein Bahnhof; ⊗ 1-6pm mid-Apr–mid-May & late Sep–mid-Oct, 11am-6pm mid-May–late Sep) are about five minutes' walk east of Hauptstrasse, the town's main street. The **Rathaus** (town hall; ☎ 219; Hauptstrasse 25; ⊗ 8am-noon & 1.30-4pm Mon-Fri), near the centre of the town, also offers information.

Sights

Kuenringerburg, the castle high on the hill above the town, is where Richard the Lionheart was incarcerated from 1192 to 1193. His crime was to have insulted Leopold V; his misfortune was to be recognised despite his disguise when journeying through Austria on his way home from the Holy Lands; his liberty was achieved only upon the payment of an enormous ransom of 35,000kg of silver (which partly funded the building of Wiener Neustadt). It was also here that the singing minstrel Blondel attempted to rescue his sovereign. There's not a lot to see but a heap of rubble, but the view is worth the 15- to 20-minute climb.

Of the picturesque 16th-century houses and other prominent buildings lining Dürnstein's streets, the meticulously restored **Chorherrenstift** (☎ 375; Stiftshof; admission adult/concession & child €2.40/1.50; ⊗ 9am-6pm Apr-Oct) is the most impressive. It's all that remains of the former Augustinian monastery originally founded in 1410; it received its baroque facelift in the 18th century (overseen by Josef Munggenast, among others). Kremser Schmidt did many of the ceiling and altar paintings. Entry includes access to the porch overlooking the Danube and an exhibition on the Augustinian monks who once ruled

the roost here (up until the monastery was dissolved by Joseph II in 1788).

Sleeping & Eating

The tourist office can supply a list of private rooms, pensions and *Gasthöfe* (inns) in Dürnstein and neighbouring Oberloiben and Unterloiben.

Pension Böhmer (☎ 239; pension.boehmer@i-one.at; Hauptstrasse 22; s €35, d €60-70) This small pension in the heart of town has comfortable rooms at very reasonable prices. It's only a hop, step and a crawl to the castle from here.

Hotel Sänger Blondel (☎ 253; www.saengerblondel .at; Klosterplatz/Dürnstein 64; s €64, d €92-98; **P**) One of the nicest options in town, this hotel has good-sized rooms furnished in light woods, some with sofas. A couple have views to the Danube and others look out onto the castle or garden. Meals are served in a fine tree-shaded garden restaurant (mains €9 to €17).

Richard Löwenherz (☎ 222; www.richardloewenherz .at; Dürnstein 8; s €96-116, d €166-191, apt €250; **P** 🖵 🕿) One of the best hotels in town, the 'Lionheart' has midsized rooms right on the Danube in a former monastery. These days the monastic side has been thrown overboard and there's no reason to do without comforts. The walled garden is superb, and the restaurant (mains €10.50 to €23) serving the Austrian classics such as seasonal baked calf's head or *Tafelspitz* is also very good.

our pick **Hotel Schloss Dürnstein** (☎ 212; www .schloss.at; Dürnstein 2; s €153-165, d €166-253, apt €338-365; **P** 🕿) This castle is the last word in luxury in town and has a high-end restaurant. Most rooms are furnished tastefully in antiques, a massage can be arranged for your arrival, and it has a sauna and steam bath. Stay five nights and you will be treated to a free 'surprise menu' in the terrace restaurant (mains €16 to €25) with staggering views over the river. Stay 10 and you get a night on the house (which might be useful if you happen to be broke by that stage).

Alter Klosterkeller (☎ 378; Anzuggasse 237; mains €5-15; ⊗ 3-11pm Mon-Fri, noon-11pm weekends Apr-Nov) This attractive *Heuriger* is just outside the village walls (on the eastern side) and overlooks the vineyards close to the town. It's the perfect place to sample the local cuisine and wines.

Restaurant Loibnerhof (☎ 828 90; Unterloiben 7; mains €13-25, 4-course menu €37; ⊗ 11.30am-9.30pm Wed-Sun) Situated 1.5km east of Dürnstein in Unterloiben, this family-run restaurant inside a 400-year-old building has a lovely garden where you can enjoy delicious local specialties such as *Kalbsbeuschel* (veal lights), which traditionally uses the lung and heart of the calf.

Getting There & Away

Dürnstein's train station is called Dürnstein-Oberloiben. Krems and Weissenkirchen are both about 20 minutes away by Brandner boat (€10, twice daily May to September); it's cheaper and quicker by train though (€2.90, 11 minutes to Krems, seven minutes to Weissenkirchen, hourly).

SPITZ
☎ 02713 / pop 1800
Situated 17km west of Krems on the north bank of the Danube, Spitz is a pleasant town that doesn't get as clogged with visitors as Dürnstein, has a picturesque old town centre, and offers some good hiking in the surrounding forests and vineyards.

The train station is near the B3 and river. To reach the old town, turn left after leaving the station and right up Markstrasse to Kirchenplatz. The **tourist office** (☎ 02713-2363; www.spitz-wachau.at, in German; Mittergasse 3a; 🕙 9.30am-1pm & 2-7.30pm Mon-Sat, 2-6pm Sun May-Oct, 2-4pm Mon-Fri Nov-Apr) is situated 400m west of the station. It has free maps of the town and hiking trails, including a good *Naturerlebnis Wachau* map (€1).

Spitz's major sight is its Gothic **parish church** (☎ 02713-2231; Kirchenplatz 12; 🕙 8am-6pm), unusual for its chancel, which is out of whack with the main body of the church. Other noteworthy features are the 15th-century statues of the 12 apostles lining the organ loft.

Many of the local hiking trails begin from the former medieval city gate, **Rotes Tor**, which offers nice views over the Danube, and if you're energetic even better views are had from the castle ruins of the 13th-century **Burgruine Hinterhaus** (see p109).

If you decide to stay in town, the tourist office can help with accommodation, or look for signs advertising private rooms. **Hotel Wachauer Hof** (☎ 2303; www.wachauerhof-spitz.at, in German; Hauptstrasse 15; s/d €39/62; 🅿) is very centrally located, with comfortable rooms and a restaurant with outside seating in summer. **Hotel Garni Weinberghof** (☎ 2939; www.weingut-lagler.at, in German; Am Hinterweg 17; s €45-48, d €70-80; 🅿) is situated above the centre among the

pretty vineyards and is geared more to hikers and cyclists.

Regular trains run between Spitz and Krems (€4.40, 30 minutes), and frequent buses and less frequent train services connect Spitz and Schwallenbach (€2.90, three minutes). See opposite and p164 for bus and boat services. Bicycles can be rented from the train station (see opposite).

MELK
☎ 02752 / pop 5200
With its sparkling and majestic abbey-fortress, Melk is a high point for tourists visiting the Danube Valley. And they arrive here in hoards – either by the busload, by train or wearily trudging with bikes through the cobblestone streets.

The **tourist office** (☎ 523 07-410; www.tiscover.com /melk; Babenbergerstrasse 1; 🕙 9am-noon & 2-6pm Mon-Fri, 10am-noon & 4-6pm Sat & Sun May, Jun & Sep, 9am-7pm Mon-Sat, 10am-noon & 5-7pm Sun Jul & Aug, 9am-noon & 2-6pm Mon-Fri, 10am-noon Sat Apr, 9am-noon & 2-5pm Mon-Fri, 10am-noon Sat Oct) east of Rathausplatz has maps and plenty of useful information.

Stift Melk
Of the many abbeys in Austria, **Stift Melk** (Benedictine Abbey of Melk; ☎ 555-232; www.stiftmelk.at; Abt Berthold Dietmayr Strasse 1; adult/student & child/family €7.50/4.10/15, with guided tour €9.30/5.90/18.60; 🕙 9am-5.30pm May-Sep, 9am-4.30pm mid-Mar–Apr & Oct-Nov) is the best known. Historically, Melk was of great importance to both the Romans and the Babenbergs, who built a castle here. In 1089 the Babenberg margrave Leopold II donated the castle to Benedictine monks, who converted it into a fortified abbey. Fire destroyed the original edifice, which was completely rebuilt between 1702 and 1738 according to plans by Jakob Prandtauer and his disciple, Josef Munggenast.

The huge **monastery church** is enclosed by the buildings, but dominates the complex with its twin spires and high octagonal dome. The interior is baroque gone barmy, with endless prancing angels and gold twirls. The theatrical high-altar scene, depicting St Peter and St Paul (the two patron saints of the church), is by Peter Widerin. Johann Michael Rottmayr did most of the ceiling paintings, including those in the dome.

Other highlights include the **Bibliothek** (Library) and the **Marmorsaal** (Marble Hall); both have painted tiers on the ceiling (by

Paul Troger) to give the illusion of greater height, and ceilings are slightly curved to aid the effect. Eleven of the **Imperial rooms**, where dignitaries (including Napoleon) stayed, are now used to house a **museum**.

From around November to mid-March, the monastery can only be visited by guided tour. Always phone ahead, even in summer, to ensure you get an English-language tour.

Sleeping & Eating

There is no shortage of hotels, but you're actually better off doing a day trip and staying in more attractive Dürnstein, Spitz or Krems.

If you do stay, **Hotel Restaurant zur Post** (☎ 523 45; www.post-melk.at, in German; Linzer Strasse 1; s €55-62, d €90-99, apt €138-198; P ⃰) is a bright and pleasant hotel in the heart of town and has the attraction of large, comfortable rooms in plush colours with additional nice touches such as brass bed lamps. There's a sauna, facilities for massages and free bike use for guests (€10 per day for nonguests). The restaurant is also very decent for Austrian classics.

Tom's Restaurant (☎ 524 75; mains €20, 4/9-course menu with wine €90/135; ⏰ lunch & dinner Thu-Tue) is gourmet quality and changes its menu each week; it has an extensive wine cellar and a list as thick as a book!

Getting There & Away

Boats leave from the canal by Pionierstrasse, 400m north of the abbey; see p164 for more information. Almost hourly trains travel direct to Melk from Vienna's Westbahnhof (€15.50, 1¼ hours). To get to Schloss Schallaburg from Melk, **Taxi Türke** (☎ 523 16) runs a minibus from the Melk train station (€4 one way, leaving 10.25am, 1.15pm and 4pm daily). You might be able to negotiate other trips between runs, but expect to pay about €1 per kilometre (the going rate in summer for a driver).

Wachau Touristik Bernhardt (☎ 02713-2222; office@wachau-touristik.at; Laaben 1a in Spitz; €12 per day) rents out bicycles from the ferry station in Melk and from the train station in Spitz. Book ahead.

TULLN
☎ 02272 / pop 14,000

Tulln, the home town of painter Egon Schiele and situated 30km northwest of Vienna, has several interesting attractions and has recently put a lot of energy into pulling in visitors by staging world-class exhibitions and upgrading its museums.

Orientation & Information

The **tourist office** (☎ 675 66; www.tulln.at, in German; Minoritenplatz 2; ⏰ 9am-7pm Mon-Fri & 10am-7pm Sat May-Sep, 8am-3pm Mon-Fri Oct-Apr) is one block north of Hauptplatz (the fountain end) and a 15-minute walk northwest from the main train station. Tulln Stadt, an S-Bahn station (for suburban trains from Vienna), is just five minutes' walk south of Hauptplatz along Bahnhofstrasse.

Sights & Activities

The **Egon Schiele Museum** (☎ 645 70; Donaulände 28; adult/concession/child €5/3.50/3; ⏰ 10am-noon & 1-5pm Tue-Sun Apr-Oct), housed in a former jail near the Danube, vividly presents the story of the life of the Tulln-born artist. It contains 100 of his paintings and sketches and a mock-up of the cell he was briefly imprisoned in (he was however jailed in Neulengbach). He fell foul of the law in 1912 following the seizure of 125 erotic drawings; some were of pubescent girls, and Schiele was also in trouble for allowing children to view his explicit works. Schiele fans should also make sure they visit the Leopold Museum in Vienna (p130).

Alongside the tourist office, the rococo **Minoritenkirche** (☎ 623 380; Minoritenplatz 1; ⏰ 8am-7pm) from 1739 is decorated with a magnificent series of ceiling frescoes dedicated to St Johannes Nepomuk, culminating in one depicting his fall from a bridge at the hands of Bohemia's King Wenceslaus IV; the angel trying to save him is tumbling out of the frame. Also not to be missed is the **Pfarrkirche St Stephan** (☎ 623 380; Wiener Strasse 20; admission free; ⏰ 7.30am-7.30pm summer, 7.30am-5pm winter) with its perfectly preserved 13th-century frescoed Romanesque funerary chapel.

The **Museum im Minoritenkloster** (☎ 690 442; Minoritenplatz 1; hr & price vary) adjoins the church. This city-promoted art space features excellent changing exhibitions such as one in 2007 of erotic art with works by Picasso, Warhol, Richard Lindner and Viennese artist Gottfried Helnwein among the many on show.

The town and its tourist office are well set up for cyclists as the Danube cycle-way cuts between the river on the town's northern border; to encourage green tourism, the city provides six free city bicycles, which you can pick up just off Hauptplatz from **2Rad Wegl** (☎ 626 95; Jasomirgottgasse 4). Bikes can also be hired from Donaupark Camping (see p174).

Sleeping & Eating

The tourist office can help with a list of accommodation options (including private rooms), and also provide a map of the town.

Donaupark Camping (☎ 652 00; www.campingtulln.at; Hafenstrasse 4; campsites per person/tent €6.50/4.50; ☾ Apr-Oct; ℗) This campsite is located just east of the centre on the river and alongside a pretty forest.

Jugendherberge Tulln (☎ 651 65 10; jugendherberge-tulln@aon.at; Marc-Aurel-Park 1; dm €18.90-28.90; ℗) This youth hostel near the Danube caters for seminar guests as well as tourists. All the dorms have their own showers, and there is table tennis, table football, a café, plus a handy ATM.

Zum Schwarzen Adler (☎ 626 76; Rathausplatz 7; s/d/tr €42/64/78; ℗) In a town short on midrange or upmarket options, this hotel in the centre of town is the best choice; rooms are clean, the furnishings are modern, and it has a restaurant downstairs that brews its own dark and light beer and serves up honest Austrian nosh at very reasonable prices (menus €5 to €7, mains €6 to €13).

Verdi (☎ 0676/40 84 841; Hauptplatz 25; mains €8-19; ☾ lunch & dinner Wed-Mon) Verdi is a refreshing, all-round eating option with a range from fish through Austrian classics to Mediterranean flavours; there's a terrace for warm summer evenings.

Getting There & Away

Tulln is reached hourly by train (€7.60, 25 minutes) or S-Bahn (line 40; €7.60, 45 minutes) from Vienna's Franz Josefs Bahnhof. The train is quicker, but only stops at the main Tulln station, while the S-Bahn stops at Tulln Stadt. Heading west, trains go to Krems (€9.30, 30 to 45 minutes, hourly) or St Pölten (€9.30, one hour, hourly).

ST PÖLTEN

☎ 02742 / pop 51,000

St Pölten, a destination few may even notice as they scream through on their way from Vienna to Salzburg, may be Lower Austria's capital but it retains a very sleepy atmosphere. While it's not all that attractive or exciting, it does have a nice *Altstadt* (old town), with pedestrian-only cobblestone streets, juxtaposed by a new Landhaus

Viertel (Landhaus Quarter) with contemporary architectural delights.

HISTORY

In a strange twist of fate – first an ailing economy in the 1920s stalled the decision to give Lower Austria its own capital, and later the Nazis favoured making Krems the capital – St Pölten became capital of Lower Austria only in 1986, ending an anomaly in which Lower Austria was administered geographically from Vienna, but was in fact a separate province. This prompted the catch-cry, 'A province without a capital is like a goulash without juice'. Ironically, it happens to have the oldest known municipal charter – granted in 1159. The *Altstadt* is noted for its baroque buildings: baroque master Jakob Prandtauer lived and died in the city.

ORIENTATION & INFORMATION

The centre of town is a compact, mostly pedestrian-only area to the west of the Traisen River. Rathausplatz, is home to the *Rathaus* (town hall) and **tourist office** (☎ 353 354; tourismus@st-poelten.gv.at; Rathausplatz 1; ☾ 8am-5pm Mon-Fri, 9am-5pm Sat, 10am-5pm Sun Apr-Oct, 8am-5pm Mon-Fri Nov-Mar). Ask for the *Übernachten in St Pölten* booklet (in German, but with useful listings). The main post office is near Herrenplatz, and internet access is available in Cinema Paradiso (see p176). The Landhaus Viertel is 700m east of Rathausplatz.

SIGHTS

Pick up the tourist office's *Your Personal City Guide* brochure (in English) that outlines two walking tours of the city which can be complemented by an audio guide (€1.45).

Rathausplatz is lined with eye-catching pastel-coloured buildings and dominated by the **Rathaus** and **Franziskanerkirche** (☎ 352 6211; Rathausplatz 12; ☾ dawn-dusk), which was completed in 1770 and has a grandiose altar offset by side altar paintings by Kremser Schmidt. Between the two is the tall **Dreifaltigkeitssäule** (Trinity Column).

Not far south and west of Rathausplatz is the **Institut der Englischen Fräulein** (☎ 352 188-0; Linzer Strasse 11; admission free; ☾ 8am-noon & 3-5pm Mon-Sat, 10am-noon & 3-6pm Sun), a convent founded in 1706, which has a classic baroque façade, black-and-gold organ and several frescoes by Paul Troger in the chapel. At the time of publication the **Stadtmuseum** (☎ 333-26 43;

Prandtauerstrasse 2) was receiving a facelift and upgrade, but when this museum reopens it should have a permanent section on Art Nouveau and changing exhibitions on town history.

To the east of Rathausplatz is Domplatz, which hosts a **morning market** every Thursday and Saturday and is home to the **Domkirche** (☎ 353 402-0; Domplatz 1; ☉ dawn-dusk); its interior, with lashings of fake marble and gold, was designed by Jakob Prandtauer and is easily the most impressive in St Pölten.

From Domplatz walk down Lederergasse to the Landhaus Viertel, passing the town's former **synagogue** (Dr. Karl Renner-Promenade 22; admission free; ☉ 9am-3pm Mon-Fri). The building, which contains Art Nouveau frescoes,

dates from 1912; it was ravaged by the Nazis and restored to become an institute for Jewish history. The Jewish community itself couldn't be re-established. The **Landesmuseum** (☎ 90 80 90-153; Franz Schubert-Platz 5; adult/concession/child/family €8/7/3.50/16; ☉ 9am-5pm Tue-Sun) is devoted to the history, art and environment of Lower Austria. A wave made from glass, frozen in movement above the entrance, sets the mood, and indeed water is a theme throughout. Its highlight in an art collection spanning the Middle Ages to the present is the 13th-century Lion of Schöngrabern.

For a bird's-eye view of the quarter take the lift to the top of the **Klangturm** (☎ 90 80 50; Landhausplatz; adult/child €7.50/3.50; ☉ 8am-7pm Mon-Sat, 9am-5pm Sun).

LOWER AUSTRIA

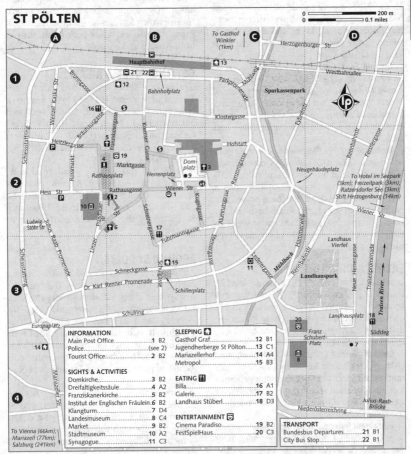

ST PÖLTEN

0 — 200 m
0 — 0.1 miles

INFORMATION	
Main Post Office	1 B2
Police	(see 2)
Tourist Office	2 B2

SIGHTS & ACTIVITIES	
Domkirche	3 B2
Dreifaltigkeitssäule	4 A2
Franziskanerkirche	5 B2
Institut der Englischen Fräulein	6 B2
Klangturm	7 D4
Landesmuseum	8 B2
Market	9 B2
Stadtmuseum	10 A2
Synagogue	11 C3

SLEEPING	
Gasthof Graf	12 B1
Jugendherberge St Pölten	13 C1
Mariazellerhof	14 A4
Metropol	15 B3

EATING	
Billa	16 A1
Galerie	17 B2
Landhaus Stüberl	18 D3

ENTERTAINMENT	
Cinema Paradiso	19 B2
FestSpielHaus	20 C3

TRANSPORT	
Bundesbus Departures	21 B1
City Bus Stop	22 B1

SLEEPING

The tourist office has a list of accommodation, including private rooms.

Hotel im Seepark (☎ 251 510; www.hotel-seepark.at; Am Ratzerdorfer See; campsite per single-person tent €15.50, extra person €7.50, s/d €45/66; Ⓟ) This lakeside pension, 3km to the northeast of the centre in the Freizeitpark, doubles as a camping ground and is a fine place to spend the day sunning and swimming.

Jugendherberge St Pölten (☎ 321 96; office3100@ hostel.or.at; Bahnhofplatz 1; dm €17.50) The youth hostel is about as convenient to the train station as it gets – it's virtually in the same building.

Mariazellerhof (☎ 769 95; www.pension-maria zellerhof.at, in German; Mariazeller Strasse 6; s €33-42, d €52-64; Ⓟ) The pink façade of family-owned Mariazellerhof faces a busy intersection, but double-glazing keeps the noise down. Many of the good-sized rooms come with kitchen facilities.

Gasthof Graf (☎ 352 757; www.hotel-graf.at, in German; Bahnhofplatz 7; s €55, d €76; Ⓟ) This pleasant *Gasthof* directly across from the *Hauptbahnhof* is very good value for the price: it's clean and its modern rooms are pleasant. Furnishings, though veneer, include a coffee table and desk.

Metropol (☎ 707 00-0; www.austria-trend.at/met; Schillerplatz 1; s €250, d €300; Ⓟ ▣) Cosy, upmarket and aimed at a business and culture clientele, the Metropol is not cheap (low season prices are 20% less), but for these prices, you get free use of the sauna, steam bath and infrared lamps. Its restaurant (mains €14 to €22) serves up steak and good business-type meals.

EATING & DRINKING

Landhaus Stüberl (☎ 245 24; Landhausboulevard 27; breakfast €3.50-5, mains €5.50-12; Ⓥ breakfast, lunch & dinner Mon-Fri) Aimed at office workers in the quarter, Landhaus has good, cheap lunchtime dishes, including pasta; a terrace overlooks the Traisen River.

Gasthof Winkler (☎ 364 944; Mühlweg 64; mains €7-18; Ⓥ lunch & dinner Tue-Sat, lunch Sun) This upmarket restaurant has been serving delicious local and Austrian seasonal specialties for over a century. You'll find it about 1km north of the *Hauptbahnhof*.

Restaurant Galerie (☎ 351 305; Fuhrmannsgasse 1; mains €12.50-25.50, 4 courses €29.50; Ⓥ lunch & dinner Mon-Fri) Galerie serves delicious Viennese cuisine and has a great wine list, especially for Italian and French vintages. Although Wiener schnitzel isn't on the menu, it's always available for the asking.

Cinema Paradiso (☎ 214 00; www.cinema-paradiso .at, in German; Rathausplatz 14; Sun breakfast buffet €6; Ⓥ 9-1am) This is one of the best centrally located places in town for a coffee or drink. It also does an all-you-can eat breakfast buffet on Sunday and, true to its name, is an art-house cinema.

Self-caterers should head for **Billa** supermarket on the corner of Brunngasse and Bräuhausgasse.

ENTERTAINMENT

The **FestSpielHaus** (☎ 90 80 80-222; www.festspiel haus.at, in German; Franz Schubert-Platz 2) is a modern theatre which features an impressive array of music, theatre and dance performances from both Austria and abroad.

GETTING THERE & AWAY

Trains run about every half hour from Vienna to St Pölten (€11, 40 to 75 minutes), continuing on to Linz (€20, one hour) and Salzburg (€34, 2½ hours). Hourly direct trains run to Krems (€7.60, 45 minutes) and several each day to Mariazell (€14.50, 2½ hours).

St Pölten has equally good road connections: the east–west A1/E60 passes a few kilometres south of the city and the S33 branches north from there, bypassing St Pölten to the east, and continuing to Krems.

AROUND ST PÖLTEN

Although the region around Lower Austria's capital won't bowl you over, the baroque Augustinian abbey **Stift Herzogenburg** (☎ 02782-831 12; Herzogenburg; adult/student/child €7/5.50/3/2; Ⓥ tours 9.30am, 11am, 1.30pm, 3pm, 4.30pm Apr-Oct) is a highlight. Admission is on a guided tour (in English, arrange in advance), which includes the **Stiftskirche** and a late Gothic collection of paintings by the Danube School of artists.

Herzogenburg lies on the main train line between Krems (€4.40, 30 minutes) and St Pölten (€4.40, 15 minutes); at least a dozen trains pass through the town's train station (which is 10 minutes' walk from the abbey) daily.

MOSTVIERTEL

The Mostviertel, in Lower Austria's southwestern corner, takes its name from apple cider which is produced and consumed in the area. By Lower Austrian standards, the landscape is spectacular, with the eastern Alps ever-present in its southern reaches. It's largely ignored by international tourists and is certainly an area off the beaten track.

One town not to be missed is **Waidhofen an der Ybbs**, with historic gabled houses, arcaded courtyards and dramatic onion domes. Staff at its **tourist office** (☎ 07442-511 255; www.waidhofen.at; Schlossweg 2; ☺ 9am-6pm) have information on the town and the eight **mountain bike trails** of varying degrees of difficulty around Waidhofen. Mountain bikes are available free of charge between 10am and 6pm, Thursday to Sunday from May to October (maximum period one week). Pick up the key to the lock and the tour map from the tourist office, and then the bike from the *Sporthalle* (sport hall) on Oskar-Czeija-Strasse.

From Gstadt, Bundesstrasse 31 leads through some lovely mountainous country and a string of pretty little villages such as **Göstling**, **Lunz am See** and **Gaming**.

In the eastern fringes of the Mostviertel, and only 23km south of St Pölten, is the **Cistercian monastery** (☎ 02762-524 20; www.stift-lilienfeld.at; Klosterrotte 1; tours adult/student & child €7/4, admission without tour €3/1; ☺ 8am-noon & 1-5pm, tours 10am & 2pm Mon-Sat, 2pm Sun) of Lilienfeld. Founded in 1202, the foundations of the monastery are Romanesque, but have received Gothic and baroque make-overs.

GETTING THERE & AWAY

Frequent daily trains go to Waidhofen an der Ybbs (€15.50, one hour, change at Amstetten) from St Pölten; only a couple of services run to Göstling (€9.30, 1¼ hours), daily services to Lunz (€11, 1½ hours) are more frequent. You'll need your own wheels for Gaming, which is 30km from Waidhofen.

WALDVIERTEL & WEINVIERTEL

Between them, the Waldviertel (Woods Quarter) and Weinviertel (Wine Quarter) take up most of the land north of the Danube in Lower Austria. The Waldviertel to the northwest is a region of rolling hills and rural villages, and while there isn't actually much forest to speak of, there are a number of fine attractions. The Weinviertel, north and northeast of Vienna, is flat and agricultural, and has little of interest for the average tourist (unless you're crazy about Austrian wine). Both regions are places to escape the madding crowds.

Waldviertel's central **tourist office** (☎ 02822-54109-0; info@waldviertel.or.at; www.waldviertel.or.at, in German; Sparkasseplatz 4; telephone & email only) is located in Zwettl, a small town near a baroque **Cistercian Abbey** (☎ 02822-550; Stift Zwettl 1; tours adult/child €6/3; tours 10am, 11am, 2pm, 3pm & 4pm Mon-Sat, 11am, 2pm, 3pm & 4pm Sun May-Oct), which has one-hour tours in German with English description sheets. The B217 south of Zwettl leads through the heart of poppy country, a booming industry in Lower Austria.

Some 40km east of Zwettl are a group of interesting sights. First up is the Benedictine **Stift Altenburg** (☎ 02982-3451; www.stift-altenburg.at, in German; Stift 1; adult/child & student/family €9/4.50/16, includes English audio guide; ☺ 10am-5pm Apr-Oct), which can trace its foundations back to 1144. The abbey library (which has ceiling frescoes by Paul Troger) and the crypt (with frescoes by Troger's pupils) are highlights. The abbey's church, which is free to enter, contains some of Troger's best frescoes (you'll find them in the central dome, and above the high and side altars).

A few kilometres southeast of Altenburg is **Schloss Rosenburg** (☎ 02982-2911; www.rosenburg.at, in German; Rosenburg am Kamp; tours adult/child & student/family €10/8.50/24, extra €3 for falconry & pageantry; ☺ 9.30am-4.30pm Tue-Sun Mar, Apr & Oct, 9.30am-5pm May-Sep), a Renaissance castle where splendid falconry shows take place at 11am and 3pm.

A further 18km east of Rosenburg, the quaint town of **Eggenburg** comes into view. It's still surrounded by much of its original defensive walls, but more intriguing is its **Österreichisches Motorradmuseum** (Motorbike Museum; ☎ 02984-2151; www.motorradmuseum.at, in German; Museumgasse 6; adult/student/child €6/5/3; ☺ 8am-4pm Mon-Fri, 10am-5pm Sat & Sun mid-Jan–mid-Dec). This masterpiece of motorbike dedication has over 320 immaculately restored bikes on show. More unusual models include the NSU Max Sportversion, with its sharp angles, and the Böhmerland 600, the longest bike in the world.

GETTING THERE & AWAY

Zwettl is best reached by bus from Krems (€9, 45 minutes to 1½ hours). Services are frequent but only a couple run on Sunday. Several direct trains travel from Krems to Horn daily (€9.30, one hour), stopping at Rosenburg (€7.60, one hour). From Horn, very irregular buses run to Altenburg (€2.20, 10 minutes). Eggenburg has plenty of daily train connections to Tulln (€9.30, 40 minutes).

DROSENDORF

☎ 02915 / pop 1280

Situated on the extreme northern fringe of the Waldviertel, hard on the Czech border, the lovely fortressed town of Drosendorf is often overlooked by the Viennese – it's simply too far-flung. Yet, with a completely intact town wall, it is a unique and beautiful town.

An **information service** (☎ 232 10; 8am-4.30pm Mon-Fri) is located inside the castle, and an **information stand** with a useful walk-by-numbers brochure (in German) as well as an accommodation list is situated on Hauptplatz, inside the walls.

The **fortress walk** also begins here, passes the **Schloss**, a mostly baroque structure on top of Romanesque foundations, and exits through the **Hornertor**, the main gate in the southeast dating from the 13th to the 15th century. Cross the moat and follow the wall clockwise.

If you're staying overnight in town, there are several good options, but the most atmospheric is **Schloss Drosendorf** (☎ 232 10; schloss-drosendorf@drosendorf.at; Schlossplatz 1; s €34-50, d €60-70; P).

Poppies – or rather poppy-seed specialities – are a big local industry in the Waldviertel. **MOKA** (☎ 22 27; www.moka.at, in German; Hauptplatz 5; cake & coffee €6; 9am-7pm Thu-Mon Apr-Oct) does a delicious poppy-seed cake and coffee, and also has a few comfortable rooms right on Hauptplatz (single/double €35/70).

To reach Drosendorf from Vienna (Floridsdorf station), take the frequent train to Retz (€12.50, one hour), making sure it connects with one of several buses weekdays (€5.90, one hour).

NATIONALPARK THAYATAL

Straddling the border of Austria and the Czech Republic in the northwestern reaches of the Weinviertel is Austria's smallest national park, Thayatal. This unique stretch of land is actually two parks; its other half, Podyjí

National Park, is located across the border. Of the 3000 plant species found in Austria, about 1300 occur in Thayatal. Thayatal's landscape consists of a deep canyon cut by the Thaya river, numerous rock formations and steep slopes. Walking is the most popular activity in the park.

The **Nationalparkhaus** (☎ 02949-7005-0; www .np-thayatal.at, in German; exhibition adult/student & child €3.80/2.20; 9am-6pm Apr-Sep, 10am-4pm Mar, Oct & Nov), near Hardegg, has loads of information and an exhibition on the park's ecology. Hardegg, the natural jump-off point for the park, is not easy to get to without your own transport; it's best approached by train from Vienna to Retz (€12.50, one hour), from where the occasional bus runs to the town (€3.60, 20 minutes).

MARCH-DONAULAND

The March-Donauland stretches from the eastern border of Vienna to the Slovakian border, an area dominated by the Danube and its natural flood plains. It's an area rich in history and natural wonder – Carnuntum, an important Roman camp, and Nationalpark Donau-Auen are found here.

CARNUNTUM

The Roman town of Carnuntum was the most important political and military centre in the empire's northeast; with a population of 50,000 people at its peak, it made Vienna look like a village in comparison. The town developed around AD 40 and was abandoned some 400 years later. Today it exists as a relic of Roman civilisation in Upper Pannonia, and is integrated into two modern-day settlements set 4km apart: Petronell-Carnuntum and the larger spa town of Bad Deutsch-Altenburg.

Orientation & Information

Carnuntum consists of three parts: an open-air museum and nearby ancient victory arch in Petronell-Carnuntum, an amphitheatre halfway between Bad Deutsch-Altenburg and Petronell, and a museum in Bad Deutsch-Altenburg. Petronell's *Bahnhof* (train station) is 1km south of the main street, Hauptstrasse, which is home to the open-air museum, its **information office** (☎ 02163-337 70; www.carnuntum.co.at; Hauptstrasse 1; 9am-5pm mid-Mar–mid-Nov) and the **Regionalbüro Auland-Carnuntum** (☎ 02163-3555-10; www.aulandcarnuntum .com, in German; Hauptstrasse 3; 🕑 9am-4.30pm Mon-Thu, 9am-2.30pm Fri).

Bad Deutsch-Altenburg also has its own **tourist office** (☎ 02165-629 00-11; www.baddeutsch -altenburg.at, in German; Erhardgasse 2; 🕑 7am-noon, 12.30-5pm Mon-Thu, 7am-1pm Fri May-Oct, 7am-noon & 12.30-4pm Mon-Fri Nov-Apr).

Sights

All four local attractions are covered by the one ticket (adult/student and concession/child €8/6/3, tours extra €3/2), including transport in the archaeological park bus on weekends (see right).

The **open-air museum** (☎ 02163-3377-16; www .carnuntum.co.at; Hauptstrasse 1; 🕑 9am-5pm mid-Mar–mid-Nov, tours 10am, 11.30am, 2pm & 3.30pm) lies on the site of the old civilian town. It includes ruins of the public baths and a reconstructed temple of Diana. Actors lead tours in tunics and togas, and you can buy replicas of Roman sandals and clothing here for your next toga party. The museum is enclosed and very touristy, but is interesting and good fun; descriptions everywhere are in English. The **Heidentor** (Heathen Gate; admission free) was once the southwest entrance to the city and now stands as an isolated anachronism amid fields of grain.

About 2km on from the park towards Bad Deutsch-Altenburg is the grass-covered **amphitheatre** (Wienerstrasse 52; 🕑 9am-5pm mid-Mar–mid-Nov) that formerly seated 15,000. It now hosts a theatre festival over summer.

Bad Deutsch-Altenburg's **Museum Carnuntinum** (Badgasse 40-46; 🕑 noon-5pm Mon, 10am-5pm Tue-Sun mid-Mar–mid-Nov, tours 1.30pm & 3.30pm Sat & Sun) is the largest of its kind in Austria, having amassed over 3300 Roman treasures in its 100-year existence. The museums highlight, *Tanzende Mänade* (Dancing Maenad), a marble figure with a perfect bum, is usually here. The town is also a health spa, with 28°C iodine sulphur springs and a wonderful **Kurpark** (spa gardens) on the Danube.

Hainburg, 3km further east, has the depot for Museum Carnuntum, housed in the **Kulturfabrik** (☎ 02163-33 770; www.kulturfabrik-hain burg.at; Kulturplatz 1; adult/child €5/3; 🕑 10am-6pm). The depot can be toured with an advance booking and special exhibitions on archaeological themes are also held here. On top of this, it has splendid views over the Danube and **fenestra** (☎ 02165-63844; Kulturplatz 1; mains €8-16, 🕑 10am-

TAKING IN THE ROMANS

Getting from one Roman site to the next in Carnuntum can be difficult during the week. If you feel energetic, your best option on a weekday is either to hire a bike in Vienna and ride the 50km along the Danube (see p159 for bike hire in Vienna) or take the train out and hire a bike locally in Bad-Deutsch-Altenburg (see below). On weekends from mid-March to mid-November a free bus meets the Vienna train hourly from 10am and does the circuit of sites (the last bus from Museum Carnuntum is 4.30pm).

10pm), a café and gourmet restaurant with a changing seasonal menu. Hainburg itself is a pretty town with hilltop ruins. **Bratislava**, the Slovakian capital, is also an easy day trip from Carnuntum.

Sleeping & Eating

Bad Deutsch-Altenburg, with its pretty *Kurpark*, spa facilities and location near the Danube, is far more appealing than Petronell for overnighting. Much of the accommodation is found on Badgasse.

Gasthof Hotel zum Amphitheater (☎ 02165-627 37; Wienerstrasse 51; s/d/tr €28.60/45.20/66.60; **P**) Rising up from the road opposite the amphitheatre, this friendly, family-run hotel is packed with local atmosphere; rooms are spacious and some have views over the fields or amphitheatre.

Pension Riedmüller (☎ 02165-62473-0; www .tiscover.at/riedmueller.hotels; Badgasse 28; s/d €27/54; **P**) This hotel has massage facilities, free bike use for guests and organises tours or helps with bike tours to Bratislava (€40 each way). Rooms are fine, though not as good as their delicious apple strudel downstairs in the café.

Hotel König Stephan (☎ 02165-624 73-0; Badgasse 34; s/d €27/54; **P**) Run by the same people who operate Pension Riedmüller. This place also has a good restaurant (mains €7 to €17).

A nice place to relax and sip a beer while watching the Danube flow is the **Wirtshaus an der Donau** (🕑 10am-11pm) in the *Kurpark*.

Getting There & Around

From Vienna, the S7 train (direction Wolfsthal) departs Wien Floridsdorf hourly, via Wien Nord and Wien Mitte to Petronell (€9.30, 55 minutes), Bad Deutsch-Altenburg

(€9.30, one hour) and Hainburg (€10.90, 66 minutes).

The cycle path from Vienna goes along the north bank of the Danube, crosses to the south at Bad Deutsch-Altenburg, and continues into Slovakia. See p179 for information about buses and bikes.

NATIONALPARK DONAU-AUEN

Nationalpark Donau-Auen is a thin strip of natural floodplain on either side of the Danube, running from Vienna to the Slovakian border. Established as a national park in 1997, it was the culmination of 13 years of protest and environmentalist action against the building of a hydroelectric power station in Hainburg. You'll find plentiful flora and fauna, including 700 species of fern and flowering plants, and a high density of kingfishers (feeding off the 50 species of fish). Guided tours by foot or boat are available; for more information contact **Nationalpark Donau-Auen** (☎ 02212-355 55; www .donauauen.at, in German; Schlossplatz 1, Orth an der Donau; 🕑 9am-6pm mid-Mar–Sep, till 5pm Oct & 8am-1pm Mon-Fri Nov–mid-Mar).

From Vienna, the Nationalpark Donau-Auen is best explored either by bicycle (see p159 for details of bicycle hire in Vienna), or on summer Nationalpark-run 4½ hour tours leaving from the **Salztorbrücke** (☎ 01-4000 494-80; adult/child €10/4, booking necessary; 🕑 departs 9am May-Oct).

WIENERWALD

The Wienerwald (Vienna Woods) encompasses gentle wooded hills to the west and southwest of Vienna, and the wine growing region directly south of the capital. For the Viennese, it's a place for walking and mountain biking, but it is often overlooked by tourists. Numerous walking and cycling trails in the area are covered in the *Wienerwald Wander und Radkarte*, available free from local tourist offices and the region's main office, **Wienerwald Tourismus** (☎ 02231-621 76; www.wienerwald.info; Hauptplatz 11, 3002 Purkersdorf; 🕑 9am-5pm Mon-Fri).

Attractive settlements, such as the grape-growing towns of **Perchtoldsdorf** and **Gumpoldskirchen**, speckle the Wienerwald. Picturesque **Mödling**, only 15km south of Vienna, was once favoured by the artistic elite: Beethoven's itchy feet took him to Hauptstrasse 79 from 1818 to 1820, and Schönberg stayed at Bernhardgasse 6 from 1918 to 1925. More information is available from the **Tourismus-Information Mödling** (☎ 02236-267 27; tourismus@moedling.at; Elisabethstrasse 2; 🕑 9am-5pm Mon-Fri).

About 20km from Mödling is **Heiligenkreuz** and the 12th-century Cistercian abbey **Stift Heiligenkreuz** (☎ 02258-8703; www.stift-heiligenkreuz .at, in German; Heiligenkreuz 1; tours adult/student & child €6.40/3.20; 🕑 tours 10am, 11am, 2pm, 3pm & 4pm Mon-Sat, 11am, 2pm, 3pm & 4pm Sun). The chapter house is the final resting place of most of the Babenberg dynasty, which ruled Austria until 1246. The abbey museum contains 150 clay models by Giovanni Giuliani (1663–1744), a Venetian sculptor who also created the Trinity column in the courtyard. Note that tours in English are by request only.

Mayerling, which lies 6km southwest of Heiligenkreuz, has little to show now, but the bloody event that occurred there (see the boxed text opposite) still draws people to the site. The **Carmelite convent** (☎ 02258-2275; Mayerling 1; admission €1.50; 🕑 9am-5pm) can be visited, but it's not really worth the effort; all you see is a chapel and a couple of rooms of mementos.

GETTING THERE & AWAY

To explore this region, it's best if you have your own transport. Trains skirt either side of the woods and the bus service is patchy. The Baden–Alland bus passes through Heiligenkreuz (€1.70, 35 minutes) and Mayerling (€3.40, 45 minutes) on an hourly basis Monday to Friday, but this drops to a trickle on weekends. From Mödling (reached on the Vienna Südbahnhof–Baden train route), there are frequent buses going to Hinterbrühl (€1.70, 11 minutes) which sometimes continue on to Alland via Heiligenkreuz (€3.40, 30 minutes).

The main road through the area is the A21 that loops down from Vienna, passes by Heiligenkreuz, then curves north to join the A1 just east of Altlengbach.

BADEN BEI WIEN

☎ 02252 / pop 25,200

With its sulphurous mineral springs (giving it an egg-like smell in parts) and its lush green parks, gardens and woods, this spa town on the eastern fringes of the Wienerwald is a picturesque anomaly. Baden has a long his-

MYSTERY AT MAYERLING

It's the stuff of lurid pulp fiction: the heir to the throne found dead in a hunting lodge with his teenage mistress. It became fact in Mayerling on 30 January 1889, yet for years the details of the case were shrouded in secrecy and denial. Even now a definitive picture has yet to be established – the 100th anniversary of the tragedy saw a flurry of books published on the subject, and Empress Zita claimed publicly that the heir had actually been murdered.

The heir was Archduke Rudolf, 30-year-old son of Emperor Franz Josef, husband of Stephanie of Coburg, and something of a libertine who was fond of drinking and womanising. Rudolf's marriage was little more than a public façade by the time he met the 17-year-old Baroness Maria Vetsera in the autumn of 1888. The attraction was immediate, but it wasn't until 13 January the following year that the affair was consummated, an event commemorated by an inscribed cigarette case, a gift from Maria to Rudolf.

On 28 January, Rudolf secretly took Maria with him on a shooting trip to his hunting lodge in Mayerling. His other guests arrived a day later; Maria's presence, however, remained unknown to them. On the night of 29 January, the valet, Loschek, heard the couple talking until the early hours, and at about 5.30am a fully dressed Rudolf appeared and instructed him to get a horse and carriage ready. As he was doing his master's bidding, he reportedly heard two gun shots; racing back, he discovered Rudolf lifeless on his bed, with a revolver by his side. Maria was on her bed, also fully clothed, also dead. Just two days earlier Rudolf had discussed a suicide pact with long-term mistress Mizzi Caspar. Apparently he hadn't been joking.

The official line was proffered by Empress Elisabeth, who claimed Rudolf died of heart failure. The newspapers swallowed the heart failure story, though a few speculated about a hunting accident. Then the rumours began: some believed Maria had poisoned her lover, that Rudolf had contracted an incurable venereal disease, or that he had been assassinated by Austrian secret police because of his liberal politics. Even as late as 1982, Empress Zita claimed the heir to the throne had been killed by French secret agents. Numerous books have been written on the subject, but no-one can say what exactly occurred on that ill-fated morning.

Through all the intrigue, the real victim remains Maria. How much of a willing party she was to the suicide will never be known. What has become clear is that Maria, after her death, represented not a tragically curtailed young life but an embarrassing scandal that had to be discreetly disposed of. Her body was left untouched for 38 hours, after which it was loaded into a carriage in such a manner as to imply that it was a living person being aided rather than a corpse beyond help. Her subsequent burial was a rude, secretive affair, during which she was consigned to the ground in an unmarked grave (her body was later moved to Heiligenkreuz). Today the hunting lodge is no more – a Carmelite nunnery stands in its place.

---

tory of receiving notable visitors; the Romans came here to wallow in the medicinal waters, Beethoven blew into town in the hope of a cure for his deafness, and in the early 19th century it flourished as the favourite summer retreat of the Habsburgs. Much of the town centre is in the 19th-century Biedermeier style, resulting from rebuilding after Turkish invasions and severe fires. Note that Baden goes into hibernation between October and March.

Orientation & Information

The town is centred on pedestrian-only Hauptplatz; the *Lokalbahn* (tram) station is just south of the Hauptplatz, while the *Hauptbahnhof* is 500m southeast. A couple of minutes' walk west of Hauptplatz is **Baden**

Tourismus (☎ 226 00-600; www.baden.at; Brusattiplatz 3; ☏ 9am-6pm Mon-Fri, 10am-2pm Sat May-Sep, 9am-5pm Mon-Fri Oct-Apr); ask about the VIP Card (free if you stay two nights or more in any type of accommodation), which gives very useful benefits such as discounts on entry prices and free walking tours. In the centre, **Andrea Kreuter EDV Services** (☎ 444 22 22; Frauengasse 10; per hr €5; ☏ 9am-10pm Mon-Fri, 9am-noon Sat) has internet access. The post office is squeezed between the Schwechat River and Kaiser Franz Josef Ring, 150m south of Hauptplatz.

Sights & Activities

Baden's prime attraction is its 14 **hot springs**, with a daily flow of 6.5 million litres. The waters emerge at a temperature of 36°C and are

LOWER AUSTRIA

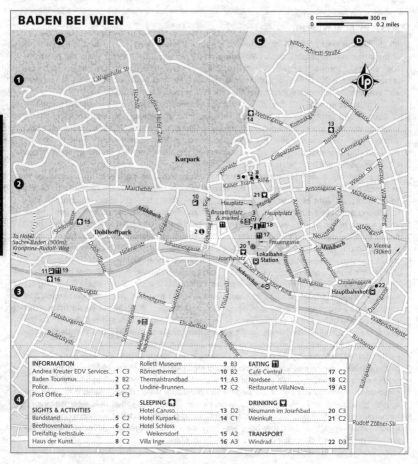

BADEN BEI WIEN

0 — 300 m
0 — 0.2 miles

INFORMATION
Andrea Kreuter EDV Services...	**1** C3
Baden Tourismus.................	**2** B2
Police................................	**3** C2
Post Office.........................	**4** C3

SIGHTS & ACTIVITIES
Bandstand.........................	**5** C2
Beethovenhaus..................	**6** C2
Dreifaltig-keitssäule...........	**7** C2
Haus der Kunst..................	**8** C2

Rollett Museum..................	**9** B3
Römertherme.....................	**10** B2
Thermalstrandbad..............	**11** A3
Undine-Brunnen.................	**12** C2

SLEEPING
Hotel Caruso.....................	**13** D2
Hotel Kurpark....................	**14** C1
Hotel Schloss	
Weikersdorf..................	**15** A2
Villa Inge.........................	**16** A3

EATING
Café Central......................	**17** C2
Nordsee...........................	**18** C2
Restaurant VillaNova..........	**19** A3

DRINKING
Neumann im Josefsbad.......	**20** C3
Weinkult...........................	**21** C2

TRANSPORT
Windrad...........................	**22** D3

enriched with sulphates. Its largest pool complex, the **Thermalstrandbad**, is actually dedicated to good old-fashioned fun (see opposite). The **Römertherme** (Roman baths; ☎ 450 30; www.roem ertherme.at, in German; Brusattiplatz 4; 2hr/all-day entry €8.90/13.10, 3hr family card €19.10-27.30; ☼ 10am-10pm) offers the same health benefits albeit without the fun.

The **Kurpark** is a magnificent setting for a stroll or as a place to repose on the benches in front of the **bandstand**, where free concerts are held from May to September. The tourist office can tell you about these and others held in winter in the **Haus der Kunst** (€3); an operetta festival takes place from June to September. Attractive flower beds complement monuments to famous artists (Mozart, Beethoven,

Strauss, Grillparzer etc). Near the southern entrance to the park, the **Undine-Brunnen** (fountain) is a fine amalgam of human and fish images.

Back in the town centre, one of the houses Beethoven stayed in has inevitably been turned into the **Beethovenhaus** (Rathausgasse 10; adult/child €3/1.50; ☼ 4-6pm Tue-Fri, 10am-noon & 2-4pm Sat & Sun) with little to actually see; though, is the **Dreifaltig-keitssäule**, dating from 1714, dominating the Hauptplatz.

The **Rollett Museum** (☎ 482 55, Weikersdorfer Platz 1; adult/child €2.50/1; ☼ 3-6pm Wed-Mon), southwest of the town centre, covers important aspects of the town's history. The most unusual exhibit is the collection of skulls, busts and death masks amassed by the founder of phrenology,

EGGS BENEDICT IN THE BATH

Because of the sulphur content in its healing waters, Baden bei Wien has a distinctive 'poached egg' smell in parts of town. All the more unusual, therefore, when an outdoor swimming pool used for recreation and fun has this ubiquitous 'eggy' scent. If you've got a finely tuned nose, the egg smell is very in your face at the **Thermalstrandbad** (☎ 486 70; Helenenstrasse 19-21; all day entry with locker or cabin €5.30-8.20, child/student €3.80/2.70; ⏱ 8am-6.30pm May–mid-Sep). With its dubious brownish stretch of sand backed by a functionalist building from 1926, the pool complex is a sulphurous Hades-meets-Majorca. Originally, the designers wanted to import sand from the Adriatic (not exactly known for sandy beaches, but anyway); in the end they settled for sand from Melk in the Danube Valley.

Josef Gall (1752–1828), who sparked the craze of inferring criminal characteristics from the shape of one's cranium.

Though interesting, the museums won't knock you over if you have seen those in Vienna, so **cycling** or **hiking** the 12-km long Kronprinz-Rudolf-Weg along the Schwechat River to Mayerling (see p180) is a good summer alternative. The tourist office has a free trail description (in German) and bikes can be hired in town (see p184). The trail can be combined with a 6km northern trail leading to Heiligenkreuz (see p180) to make a loop.

Sleeping

It's possible to visit Baden on a day trip from Vienna, and in summer the hotels can get very full. The tourist office has a good accommodation brochure.

Villa Inge (☎ 431 71; Weilburgstrasse 24-26; s/d €36/58; P) This large villa is set alongside the river and close to the Thermalstrandbad. Although the furnishing is rather long in the tooth, it's spacious and run by a friendly family. It offers good value for Baden.

Hotel Kurpark (☎ 891 04; www.hotel-kurpark.at; Welzergasse 29; s €49-52, d 74-84, apt €96-130; P ⚑) This small hotel backing onto the *Kurpark* has a large garden, indoor and outdoor pools and bright, spacious, rooms.

Hotel Caruso (☎ 88 662-0; www.hotelcaruso.at, in German; Trostgasse 23; s €80-135, d €115-170, ste €166-210; P ⚑ 🖥) One advantage of this four-star hotel is that it's large enough to cope with busy periods; facilities are excellent, rooms have modern furnishings, and it is situated in its own grounds. It caters for business people as well as tourists.

Hotel Schloss Weikersdorf (☎ 48 301-0; www.hotelschlossweikersdorf.at; Schlossgasse 9-11; s €135-155, d €170-190; P ⚑) For a weekend of pampering look no further. This hotel with modern rooms has massage services, relaxation coves and lounges and other wellness facilities; it's also set in beautiful gardens.

Eating & Drinking

Baden is no great shakes when it comes to eating and drinking; nor is it really a town where the nightlife has a wild call. A few practical or very decent places are to be found, however.

Nordsee (☎ 441-65; Hauptplatz 17; fish snacks €5, mains €10; ⏱ 9am-6.30pm Mon-Fri, 9am-4pm Sat) This fast-seafood chain is very convenient. The standard of freshness and hygiene is high, and the fish rolls are tasty.

Restaurant VillaNova (☎ 209 74 5; Helenenstrasse 19; mains €17-25; ⏱ 5.30-11pm Tue-Sat) Veal roulade with carrot, ginger and polenta was on the ticket when we visited. The menu is changing, but the standard is consistently high – food often features Austrian cuisine with Asian influences.

Café Central (☎ 48 454; Hauptplatz 19; coffee €2.40-3; ⏱ 7am-9pm Tue-Sat, 8am-9pm Sun) Central takes pride of place on the Hauptplatz. It's a '60s-style café that's a bit on the dark side but dripping with character.

Weinkult (☎ 699 1280 65 46; Pfarrgasse 7; antipasto plate €9; ⏱ 1-8pm Mon-Wed, till 10pm Thu & Fri, 10am-5pm Sat) This wine shop sells almost 150 Austrian wines and serves 10 (mostly) Austrian wines by the glass, rotating the selection on a weekly basis. Antipasto is served to prime the palate.

Neumann im Josefsbad (☎ 252 212; Josefsplatz 2; ⏱ 8am-2am Mon-Sat, 10am-1am Sun) This all-rounder serves light dishes such as chicken wings but is better known as a café and the hub of nightlife in town, with a DJ spinning on Friday and Saturday.

Getting There & Around

Frequent regional and S-Bahn trains run to Baden from Vienna's Südbahnhof (€4.50, 20 to 30 minutes). The *Lokalbahn* tram (€4.50, one hour, every 15 minutes) and buses (€4.50, 40 minutes, hourly) from Karlsplatz in Vienna do the same. Frequent trains run to Wiener Neustadt (€6, 20 minutes).

The north–south road routes, Hwy 17 and the A2, pass a few kilometres to the east of the town.

Bikes can be rented from **Windrad** (☎ 0664-511 37 38; Bahnhof; hire half day/day €6/9; ☯ 8-11.45am & 1-6pm Mon-Fri). Bus 362 runs between the Thermalstrandbad and Bahnhof (€1.50) via the centre.

SÜD-ALPIN

This southern corner of Lower Austria, known as the Süd-Alpin (Southern Alps), has some of the province's most spectacular landscapes. Here the hills rise to meet the Alps, peaking at Schneeberg (2076m), a mountain popular with the Viennese for its skiing and hiking possibilities. Nearby Semmering has long been a favourite of the capital's burghers, due mainly to its crisp alpine air. One of the greatest highlights of the area though is the journey there; the winding railway over the Semmering Pass has been designated a Unesco World Heritage site.

WIENER NEUSTADT

☎ 02622 / pop 39,650

Wiener Neustadt used to be known simply as Neustadt (New City) or Nova Civitas and was built by the Babenbergs in 1194 with the help of King Richard the Lionheart's ransom payment (see p171). It became a Habsburg residence in the 15th century during the reign of Friedrich III. His famous AEIOU (*Alles Erdreich Ist Österreich Untertan*; Austria rules the world) engraving can be found throughout the city. The town was severely damaged in WWII (only 18 homes were left unscathed), so the historic buildings of Wiener Neustadt needed careful reconstruction.

Orientation & Information

Wiener Neustadt is centred on the large Hauptplatz, where you'll find the **tourist office** (☎ 373-311; Hauptplatz 3; ☯ 8am-5pm Mon-Fri, 8am-noon Sat) which provides the free booklet, *Cultural Promenade*, describing the central sights and giving their locations on a map. Parts of the centre are pedestrian-only.

The *Hauptbahnhof* is about 750m southwest of the Hauptplatz; regional buses also stop here. It has bike rental, a travel agency and an ATM. The main post office is next door.

Sights

While the **Hauptplatz** is too big to be truly charming, it is lined with elegant buildings, not least of which are the three parts of the **Rathaus** (first built in 1401), featuring an arcade and colourful crests. East of Hauptplatz is **Neukloster** (☎ 231-02; Ungargasse; admission free; ☯ dawn-dusk), a 14th-century Gothic church with striking baroque fittings and a dark-wood pulpit. A finely carved tomb of Empress Eleonore, wife to Friedrich III, is behind the high altar.

To the north of Hauptplatz is the Romanesque **Dom** (☎ 373-440; Domplatz; admission free; ☯ dawn-dusk), erected in 1279 but subsequently rebuilt. It has a rather bare and grey exterior, two severe-looking square towers, and the interior has an unbalanced look, caused by the chancel being out of line with the nave as well as an asymmetric arch connecting the two. Fifteenth-century wooden apostles peer down from pillars and there's a baroque high altar and pulpit. At the Dom's southwest corner is the **Turmmuseum** (☎ 373-441; admission €2; ☯ 10am-5pm Tue & Wed, 10am-8pm Thu, 10am-noon Fri, 10am-4pm Sun May-Oct), a free-standing tower that provides grand views over the city's rooftops. The key for the Turmmuseum is available from the **Stadtmuseum** (☎ 373-950; Petergasse 2a; adult/student & child €3/1.50; ☯ 10am-5pm Tue & Wed, 10am-8pm Thu, 10am-noon Fri, 10am-4pm Sun), housed in the former St Peter's monastery. Its displays include artefacts from the Dom and photos of the devastation Allied bombing wrought on the town.

Heading south from the Hauptplatz, the imposing **Militärakademie** (Military Academy; ☎ 381-0; Burgplatz 1; admission free) soon comes into view. The four towers and walls of this former castle date from the 13th century, though it was completely rebuilt after WWII bombing. Since the mid-18th century it has housed a military academy (founded by Empress Maria Theresia) which at one time was commanded by the young Rommel

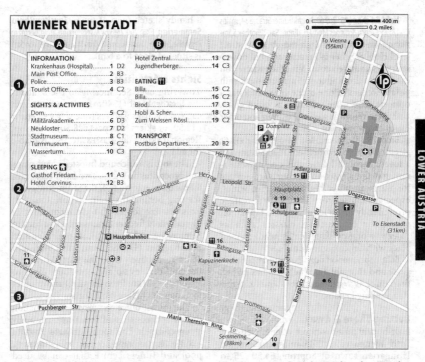

WIENER NEUSTADT

INFORMATION	
Krankenhaus (Hospital)............	1 D2
Main Post Office......................	2 B3
Police.....................................	3 B3
Tourist Office..........................	4 C2

SIGHTS & ACTIVITIES	
Dom..	5 C2
Militärakademie......................	6 D3
Neukloster..............................	7 D2
Stadtmuseum.........................	8 C1
Turmmuseum..........................	9 C2
Wasserturm............................	10 C3

SLEEPING	
Gasthof Friedam.....................	11 A3
Hotel Corvinus.......................	12 B3

| Hotel Zentral......................... | 13 C2 |
| Jugendherberge..................... | 14 C3 |

EATING	
Billa..	15 C2
Billa..	16 C2
Brod.......................................	17 C3
Hobl & Scher..........................	18 C3
Zum Weissen Rössl.................	19 C2

TRANSPORT	
Postbus Departures................	20 B2

LOWER AUSTRIA

from his pre-'desert fox' days. Visits are by appointment only, or register at the gate. Within the complex is **St-Georgs-Kathedrale** (admission free; ⏰ 10am-5pm), with a fine late-Gothic interior. Maximilian I, who was born in the castle, is buried under the altar. On the outside wall is the **Wappenwand** (Heraldic Wall) comprising 15th-century carvings of 107 coats of arms. This wall was all that survived the bombing during WWII (the stained glass had already been previously removed to the Altaussee salt mines in the Salzkammergut). The statue below the window is Friedrich III, whose AEIOU motto also appears on the wall.

Further south, rising between the convergence of two busy roads, is the town's **Wasserturm** (water tower) from 1910. Its shape intentionally apes the gilded goblet donated to the townsfolk by King Matthias Corvinus of Hungary after he took the town in 1487.

Sleeping

Jugendherberge (☎ 296 95; oejhv-noe@oejhv.or.at; Promenade 1; dm/s/d €12.50/16/32; P) This HI hostel is situated in the Stadtpark, near the *Wasserturm*. Phone ahead as reception is not always open and it's often full.

Hotel Zentral (☎ 23 169; www.hotel-zentral.tos .at; Hauptplatz 27; s €40-43, d €73.50, tr €98, 4-bed €110; 🖥) Situated right in the heart of town, all 45 rooms of Zentral are renovated, comfortable and decked out with modern furnishings. Some front the Hauptplatz.

Hotel Corvinus (☎ 24 134; www.hotel-corvinus.at; Bahngasse 29-33; s/d/tr €75/118/147; 🖥 P) Catering to business and seminar guests as well as tourists, the Corvinus has bright rooms sweetened with extras such as a wellness area, a bar and a leafy terrace. The cube-like exterior may not appeal to all, but this four-star hotel is very comfortable inside.

Eating

Zum Weissen Rössl (☎ 233 04; Hauptplatz 3; mains €7-11; ⏰ 7am-8pm Mon-Fri, 7am-5pm Sat) This *Gasthaus* may look a little dusty from the outside, but it's cosy and welcoming and serves solid Austrian food, including a choice of a small or large goulash. It has outdoor seating on the Hauptplatz.

LOWER AUSTRIA

Hobl & Scher (☎ 269 69; Neunkirchner Strasse 34; mains €7-18; ☙ lunch & dinner Mon-Fri, dinner Sat, Vinothek 5pm-midnight Mon-Fri, 11am-2pm & 6pm-midnight Sat) At street level Hobl & Scher is a restaurant, but downstairs it's a vaulted cellar Vinothek where you can enjoy a drink after, say, a hearty steak with potato wedges or one of the vegetarian pasta options. The wine selection is quite good, with New World as well as Austrian and other European wines.

Brod (☎ 281 07; Bahngasse 1; 3-6 course menus €33-49; à la carte €10-20; ☙ lunch & dinner Tue-Sat) Situated in a lovely baroque house, this quality restaurant has the attraction of courtyard seating for warm summer nights. Austrian wines, especially those from Burgenland, feature prominently on its long wine list. Upmarket renditions of Austrian classics such as *Tafelspitz* or *Kalbskopf* (calf's head) share a place with delicious new cuisine.

Billa supermarkets can be found on Bahngasse and Hauptplatz, which also has no less than three *Würstel* (sausage) stands and one stand selling kebabs.

Getting There & Away
Half-hourly trains connect Wiener Neustadt with Vienna (€9.30, 45 minutes) and the Hungarian town of Sopron (€4.50, 25 to 45 minutes) daily. Postbus services depart from the northern end of Wiener Neustadt train station.

SEMMERING
☎ 02664 / pop 750

With its clean air and grandiose peaks rising out of deeply folded valleys, Semmering is a popular alpine resort for the Viennese, especially among a slightly older crowd who come to this spa town in summer for peaceful walks or to ride the railway; a younger set hits the ski pistes.

Orientation & Information
Semmering sits on a south-facing slope above the Semmering Pass. There's no real centre to the resort: it's mostly ranged along Hochstrasse, which forms an arc behind the train station.

Railway enthusiasts at the train station run an **Infostelle Bahnhof** (☎ 845 20; www.semmeringbahn .at, in German; ☙ 9-11.30am & 1.30-4.30pm May-Oct), with material on the Semmeringbahn as well as a good stock of the town's brochures. The *Semmering* booklet has useful addresses and

a handy sketch map of town. **Tourismusbüro Semmering** (☎ 200 25; www.semmering.at, in German; Passhöhe 248; ☙ 8am-noon & 1-4pm Mon-Fri, 9am-noon Sat) is situated close to a bank.

Sights & Activities
Towering over Semmering to the south is the **Hirschenkogel** (1340m), where a modern cable car whisks walkers (one way €9, return €12.50) or skiers (day pass €28.50) to the top. Regional skiing day passes are also available for €31.

The tourist office and Infostelle have maps and brochures on walks. Two fairly easy trails follow the scenic route of the Semmeringbahn, starting behind the train station. One follows the line for 17km to Mürzzuschlag in Styria, where frequent trains chug you back to Semmering, and a second leads to Breitenstein and Klamm (Lower Austria), 9.5km and 15km respectively from the start. At Klamm the trail divides up and one route leads to Payerbach (21km from the start) and another to Gloggnitz (23km from the start).

The tourist office can provide information on ski schools or golf (on a horrendously steep course). The four-star **Hotel Panhans** (☎ 818 10; Hochstrasse 32) has a swimming pool and fitness centre that can be used by nonguests (day cards €9 weekdays, €14 weekends).

Sleeping & Eating
Most sleeping options are situated on Hochstrasse. Many have their own restaurants, which means there's only a short hobble between table and bed.

Gasthof Edelweiss (☎ 2284; edel-weiss@aon.at; Hochstrasse 57; s/d €32/64; **P**) This quaint wooden chalet is set back from the road in a grove of trees; it has a children's playground, a lovely secluded garden, and also rents bikes and organises skiing as well as airport shuttle services.

Pension-Restaurant Löffler (☎ 23 04; Hochstrasse 174; s/d €39/72; **P**) Löffler is a fresh, colourful and modern pension with a restaurant (mains €8 to €18) serving classic meat and fish dishes, including baby lamb, pepper steaks and trout.

Hotel-Restaurant Belvedere (☎ 22 70; hotel.bel veder@telecom.at; Hochstrasse 60; s €40, d €80-96; **P**) The family-run Belvedere has alpine décor, rooms with balconies, and features such as a swimming pool, sauna and large garden and

---

SEMMERING PASS BY TRAIN

For its time, it was an incredible feat of engineering, something which took more than 20,000 workers years to complete. Even today, it never fails to impress with its switchbacks, 15 tunnels and 16 viaducts. This is the **Semmering railway** (www.semmeringbahn.at, in German), a 42km stretch of track that begins at Gloggnitz and rises 455m to its highest point of 896m at Semmering Bahnhof.

Completed in 1854 by Karl Ritter von Ghega, the Semmering line was Europe's first alpine railway, and due to its engineering genius, gained Unesco World Heritage status in 1998. It passes through some impressive scenery of precipitous cliffs and forested hills en route; the most scenic section is the 30-minute stretch between Semmering and Payerbach (€6). If you're leaving from Vienna, there are four direct IC/EC services daily to Semmering (€19, 1¼ hours), a few regional direct services, and others trains with a change at Wiener Neustadt.

---

patio area. The restaurant has a regional and seasonal focus (mains €6 to €18).

Panorama Hotel Wagner (☎ 25 12-0; www.panoramahotel-wagner.at, in German; Hochstrasse 267; s €106-215, d €158-300; P ✗) Body and mind are catered for here: rooms have wood furniture, natural cotton bedding and grand views of the valley. Yoga, meditation and Qi Gong courses are offered and there are sauna, spa and massage facilities. Its highly rated restaurant (mains €8 to €16) uses organic products.

There is a **Billa** supermarket between Hotel Belvedere and the main highway.

Getting There & Away

At least once-daily direct EC/IC trains between Graz (€18, 1½ hours) and Vienna Südbahnhof (€19, 1½ hours) stop at Semmering. For trains from Vienna, see the boxed text (above).

If you're under your own steam, consider taking the small back road northwest of Semmering to Höllental via Breitenstein; the road winds its way down the mountain, passing under the railway line a number of times and taking in the spectacular scenery you see on the train trip.

SCHNEEBERG, RAXALPE & HÖLLENTAL

To the north of Semmering are two of Lower Austria's highest points, Schneeberg (2076m) and the Raxalpe (2007m). The area is easily reached by train from Vienna, making it popular for hiking (see p107).

The trailhead for hiking or taking the cogwheel railway is Puchberg am Schneeberg, where the **tourist office** (☎ 02636-2256; www.puchberg.at; Sticklergasse 3; ✆ 9am-6pm & 1-4pm Mon-Thu, 9amnoon Fri Oct-late May, 9am-noon & 1-5pm Mon-Thu, 9am-noon & 3-5pm Fri, 9.30-11.30am Sat late May-Sep) can tell you about hiking conditions on Schneeberg. The

Schneebergbahn (☎ 02636-3661-20; www.schneebergbahn.at, in German; Salamander one way/return €21/29.60, steam train €27/36.60; ✆ late Apr-Oct) leaves from Puchberg am Schneeberg and takes about an hour on the Salamander and around 1¼ hours on the steam train; check the website for the train timetable.

A hotel and several huts are situated on the mountain if you want to stay overnight here (see p107), whereas in Puchberg itself **Gasthof Pension Schmirl** (☎ 2636-2277; www.schmirl.at; Muthenhofer Strasse 8; s €30, d €60-68; P) has comfortable rooms on the edge of town near the railway. Some have balconies, in others you can psyche yourself for the stiff climb ahead with window views of Schneeberg.

On the southern side of Schneeberg is the scenic **Höllental** (Hell's Valley), a deep, narrow gorge created by the Schwarza River. Rising to the south of Höllental is the **Raxalpe**, another place for walkers; from Hirschwang, a small village in Höllental, the **Raxseilbahn** (☎ 02666-524 97; www.raxseilbahn.at, in German; return adult/child €17.60/15.70; ✆ year-round) cable car ascends to 1547m and hiking trails. The Raxseilbahn is the site of Austria's first cable car, built in 1926.

In Höllental, the **Hotel Marienhof** (☎ 02666-529 95; www.marienhof.at, in German; Hauptstrasse 71-73, Reichenau; s/d from €76/104; P 🛉), a grand old dame with a restaurant (mains €11 to €14), is not far from the Raxseilbahn.

Getting There & Away

There are hourly direct trains daily from Vienna to Puchberg am Schneeberg (€13.50, 1½ hours), going via Wiener Neustadt (€6, 45 minutes). Hirschwang (€7.60, 50 minutes) is only a little harder to get to; a train must first be taken to Payerbach, from where regular buses run up the Höllental valley.

LOWER AUSTRIA

Burgenland

Often given a wide berth by tourists, Burgenland is all but the typical Austria you hear of or read about. It has neither bombastic architecture nor deep lakes and soaring mountains. On the contrary, it is small and sleepy, and in large sections a flat province situated on the border with Hungary. Even the jewel in its crown – Neusiedler See – has dried up and disappeared several times in its natural history – most recently in the mid-19th century.

This is the kind of place where everyday life takes precedence, but it is precisely this 'every-day' aspect that makes it interesting. The province receives a reputed 300 days of sunshine a year; couple this with a rich soil base and a wine history dating back to pre-Roman times, and you have Austria's best wine-producing region. What better way to spend an afternoon than sampling local *Weine* (wines) in a *Heuriger* (wine tavern) under a warm sun? Throw in the shallow Neusiedler See and a section of it that is now the Neusiedler See-Seewinkel National Park, tack on a bike path that leads into the park and through Hungary before re-emerging in Austria, and add a swampy, medieval town such as Rust, and you might find yourself fascinated by Burgenland's charms.

Stork-spotters will be in their element here in summer, when feathered friends populate the roofs of several towns near the lake – including Rust, one of the nicest places to observe them. Although it does have a handful of interesting cultural sights, such as Schloss Ester-házy in Eisenstadt, the province's small capital, Burgenland is more a place where people are content to enjoy good wine and food, and relax in the great outdoors.

BURGENLAND

HIGHLIGHTS

- Sipping golden wines and supping in one of Burgenland's pretty **Heurigen** (p194), dotted across Burgenland
- Swimming, splashing or sailing in the **Neusiedler See** (p193), Austria's slurping steppe lake
- Cycling at a leisurely pace through the **Neusiedler See- Seewinkel National Park** (p197), a haven for birdlife
- Staring into the face of the mummified Roman legionnaire Constantine on a grand tour of **Schloss Esterházy** (p191) in the capital, Eisenstadt
- Revelling in views from Eisenstadt's **Bergkirche** (p191) after completing the Stations of the Cross

Eisenstadt ★   ★ Neusiedler See
                    ★ Neusiedler See -
                    Seewinkel
                    National Park

■ POPULATION: 279,300   ■ AREA: 3966 SQ KM   ■ HIGHEST ELEVATION: GESCHRIEBENSTEIN 884M

BURGENLAND

0 ——— 20 km
0 ——— 12 miles

SLOVAKIA

LOWER AUSTRIA

A22

Klosterneuburg

VIENNA

BRATISLAVA

Schwechat

Danube

Perchtoldsdorf

Mödling

Schwechat Airport

A21

Baden

Traiskirchen

A4

Breitenbrunn

Bad Vöslau

A3

Purbach am See

Neusiedl am See

B10

A2

Eisenstadt

Wiener Neustadt

Wulkaprodersdorf

Rust

Podersdorf am See

To Semmering (20km); Bruck an der Mur (73km)

Mörbisch am See

Illmitz

Apetlon

Neunkirchen

Forchtenstein

Burg Forchtenstein

St Margareten

Seewinkel

S6

S31

Sopron

HUNGARY

Raiding

A2

Oberpullendorf

B50

B61

Lockenhaus

Klostermarienberg

Bernstein

Geschriebenstein (884m)

Bad Tatzmannsdorf

Oberwart

Hartberg

Szombathely

To Graz (45km)

Gerersdorf

Güssing

STYRIA

Fürstenfeld

SLOVENIA

History

Burgenland is the youngest of Austria's provinces, arising after the collapse of the Austrian empire at the end of WWI. It's so named for the 'burg' suffix of the four western Hungarian district names at that time – Pressburg (Bratislava), Wieselburg (Moson), Ödenburg (Soporn) and Eisenburg (Vasvär).

The region was first settled some 7000 to 12,000 years ago, and over the ensuing millennia many peoples tried their hand at settling permanently, including the Illyrians, Celts and Romans. However, the arrival of the Hungarians in the 10th century changed the face of Burgenland forever. The region soon became a buffer zone between the Hungarians and the Austrian-Germans, who traded uneasy peace with outright war throughout the centuries.

The arrival of marauding Turks in the 16th century quashed both the Hungarians and the Austrian-Germans, and devastated the local population. Landlords, without anyone to tend their farms, invited substantial numbers of Croats to settle. Their presence is still felt today – around 10% of the population is Croatian, Croatian is a recognized local language and a few small towns in middle Burgenland bear Croat signs.

With the defeat of the Turks at the gates of Vienna in 1683 (p37), relative peace settled over the area. With the demise of the Habsburg empire after WWI Austria lost control of Hungary, but managed to retain the German-speaking western region of Hungary under the Treaty of St Germain. The new province of Burgenland was born, but Hungary was loath to lose Ödenburg (Sopron) to Austria, and a plebiscite held in December 1921 (under controversial circumstances) resulted in the people of Ödenburg opting to stay in Hungary. Burgenland lost its natural capital, and Eisenstadt became the new *Hauptstadt* (capital).

Climate

The Pannonian microclimate of hot summers and mild winters is perfect for wine production. The Neusiedler See, to the north of the province, consistently records some of the highest summer temperatures in Austria, but the large expanse of water ensures high humidity.

Language

With its close proximity to Hungary, it's no surprise that some Burgenlanders speak German with a slight Hungarian accent. Burgenland is the only province to include Croatian and Hungarian alongside German as official languages.

Getting There & Away

Eisenstadt and the northern extension of Neusiedler See are easily reached by train from Vienna and Lower Austria. Lower and middle Burgenland are less accessible by train; here the bus is often your best option. The A2 autobahn, heading south from Vienna towards Graz and Carinthia, runs parallel to the western border of Burgenland.

BURGENLAND

Its many off-ramps provide quick, easy access to much of the province.

Getting Around

Like the rest of Austria, destinations not connected to the country's train network are covered by bus. From late April to October, ferries ply the Neusiedler See, linking Podersdorf with Rust and Breitenbrunn, and Illmitz with Mörbisch (p193).

Burgenland is a cyclist's dream – much of the landscape is flat or has gentle rolling hills – and is crisscrossed with well-marked cycle paths. Local tourist offices can supply cycle maps, or simply log on to www.bikeburgenland.at, in German.

EISENSTADT

☎ 02682 / pop 12,000

The small capital of Burgenland is perhaps best known for its most famous former resident, 18th-century musician and composer Josef Haydn. Although it doesn't have a large number of attractions for visitors, it does have a wonderful palace, a couple of good museums and a rather bizarre church. Its nightlife hums rather than buzzes, but taking in its sights can easily be done on a day trip from Vienna or as an excursion from pretty, lakeside Rust.

History

Eisenstadt was first mentioned in 1264 (although archaeological digs have confirmed settlement since the Stone Age). At the time, the town was under control of the Hungarians, but it wasn't until 1371 that it gained its charter from the ruling nobility. In the ensuing centuries the Hungarians and the Habsburgs fought for control of Eisenstadt, but it was the Turks who decided the town's fate, by neutralising the Hungarian threat at the 1526 Battle of Mohács. In 1622 Eisenstadt became the residence of the Esterházys, a powerful Hungarian family, and in 1648 the town was granted the status of *Freistadt* (free city) by Ferdinand III. In 1925 it became the capital of Austria's newest province.

Orientation

Eisenstadt's pretty *Altstadt* (old town), centred on the pedestrian-only Hauptstrasse and Schloss Esterházy, is surrounded by a mod-

EISENSTADT

0   300 m
0   0.2 miles

INFORMATION	
Burgenland Tourismus	1 B1
Eisenstadt Tourismus	2 C1
Hospital & Pharmacy	3 A1
Main Post Office	4 B2
Ricky's Cafe	5 C2

SIGHTS & ACTIVITIES	
Bergkirche	6 A2
Haydn-Haus	7 C1
Jüdisches Museum	8 B1
Landesmuseum	9 B1
Schloss Esterházy	10 B1

SLEEPING	
Haus der Begegnung	11 A2
Hotel Burgenland	12 C1
Hotel Ohr	13 C3
Hotel-Pension Vicedom	14 C2

EATING	
Bodega La Ina	15 C1
Haydnbräu	16 C2
im esterházy	17 B2
Spar	18 C1

TRANSPORT	
Main Bus Station	19 C1

ern, uninteresting urban sprawl. It's about a 10-minute walk north along Bahnstrasse from the train station. The main bus station is on Domplatz, one block south of the Hauptstrasse. The tourist office's brochure map is useful for getting around town.

Information

INTERNET ACCESS

Ricky's Cafe (☎ 65 88 1; Pfarrgasse 18; ☷ 9.30am-2pm)

MEDICAL SERVICES

Hospital & Pharmacy (☎ 601; Esterházystrasse 26)

MONEY

There are a number of banks with ATMs on the Hauptstrasse and along its side streets.

POST

Main Post Office (☎ 62 27 10; Ignaz-P-Semmelweis-Gasse 7)

TOURIST INFORMATION

Burgenland Tourismus (☎ 0633 84-0; www.burgen land.info; Schloss Esterházy, Eisenstadt; ☷ 8.30am-5pm Mon-Fri)

Eisenstadt Tourismus (☎ 673 90; www.eisenstadt.at, in German; Hauptstrasse 37; ☷ 8am-5pm Mon-Fri, 9am-1pm Sat & Sun Apr-Oct, 8am-4pm Mon-Thu, 8am-1pm Fri Nov-Mar) Situated in the Rathaus, provides a useful brochure listing hotels, private rooms, restaurants, festivals and details of museums.

Sights & Activities

Eisenstadt's most significant attraction is **Schloss Esterházy** (☎ 719 3000; www.schloss-esterhazy.at; adult/student & child/family €6/5/14, grand tours €7.50/7/16, combined ticket palace & Haydn-Haus €8/7/19; ☷ tours 10am & 2pm Tue-Fri Jan-Mar & mid-Nov–Dec, noon, 2pm & 4pm Mon-Fri, hourly 10am-5pm Sat & Sun Apr & Oct–mid-Nov, hourly 10am-5pm May-Jun & Sep, hourly 10am-6pm Jul-Aug), a giant, Schönbrunn-yellow castle-cum-palace that dominates Esterházyplatz. Dating from the 14th century, the *Schloss* (castle) received a makeover in baroque, and later in neoclassical, style. Many of the 256 rooms are occupied by the provincial government, but 25 can be viewed on tours.

The regular tour covers 13 rooms and is very interesting in itself, but you need to take the grand tour to view the true highlights, culminating in the spectacularly frescoed **Haydn Hall**. The hall's original marble floor has been replaced by an aesthetically inferior but acoustically superior wooden floor (it's

rated the second-best concert hall in Austria, after Vienna's Musikverein). During Haydn's employment by the Esterházys from 1761 to 1790, he conducted an orchestra on a near-nightly basis in this hall.

After that you view the **palace chapel**, completed in 1740 and now containing the remains of Constantine 'Conny' the Martyr, a mummified Roman legionnaire who converted to Christianity and was given to the Esterházys by Pope Innocent XI for services in fighting the Turks. (He's in a glass case and looks like he could do with a stiff Turkish coffee.)

Josef Haydn said that Eisenstadt was 'where I wish to live and to die'. He achieved the former, being a resident for 31 years, but it was in Vienna that he finally tinkled his last tune. He also rather carelessly neglected to give any directive about his preferred residence after death. His skull was stolen from a temporary grave shortly after he died in 1809, after which it ended up on display in a Viennese museum. The headless cadaver was subsequently returned to Eisenstadt (in 1932), but it wasn't until 1954 that the skull re-joined it.

The white marble tomb that now contains Haydn's reunited parts can be viewed in the **Bergkirche** (☎ 626 38; www.haydnkirche.at, in German; Haydnplatz 1; adult/student €3/1; ☷ 9am-noon & 1-5pm Apr-Oct). This unusual church began life as a small chapel and in 1701 was transformed into a bizarre representation of Calvary, the mountain outside Jerusalem upon which Christ is thought to have been crucified. Manage all the dungeon-like rooms and you'll quite literally be feeling the Stations of the Cross in your feet; get to the top of the 'mountain', though, and not a gaggle of stone-throwing sinners awaits you but a fantastic view over town.

For more on Haydn, visit **Haydn-Haus** (☎ 719 3900; www.haydnhaus.at; Josef Haydn Gasse 21; adult/student & child/family €3.50/2.50/8; ☷ 9am-5pm Apr–mid-Nov), the great composer's former residence to the east of the *Schloss*. The recently revamped museum has a strong permanent exhibition documenting Haydn's life and work.

Just west of the *Schloss* are two other interesting museums: the **Landesmuseum** (☎ 600 1234; www.burgenland.at/landesmuseum, in German; Museumgasse 1-5; adult/student & child/family €5/3/9; ☷ 9am-5pm Tue-Sat, 10am-5pm Sun) and the **Jüdisches Museum** (☎ 651 45; Unterbergstrasse 6; adult/student & child €3.70/2.90; ☷ 10am-5pm Tue-Sun May-Oct). The Landesmuseum plunges you deep into the local history of the region, and includes a collection of Roman mosaics, ancient artefacts, wine-making equipment and some interesting propaganda posters from the 1920s. There's also a room devoted to Franz Liszt, replete with a warty death mask of the Hungarian composer. The latter museum primarily hosts temporary and permanent exhibitions on Jewish culture, and includes one of the few synagogues to survive the *Reichskristallnacht* (p36) of 1938.

Festivals & Events

The high point on Eisenstadt's cultural calendar is, of course, associated with Haydn. The **Internationale Haydntage**, staged through much of September, attracts both local and international acts and features anything from chamber pieces to full-scale orchestral performances. Most events take place in the Haydn Hall or the Bergkirche; for more information contact the **Haydnfestspiele Büro** (☎ 618 66-0; www.haydnfestival.at).

Behind the palace is the **Schlosspark**, a picturesque park and the setting for the **Fest der 1000 Weine** (Festival of 1000 Wines) in late August.

Sleeping

Staff at the tourist office have a complete list of accommodation.

Hotel-Pension Vicedom (☎ 642 22; www.vicedom.at; Vicedom 5; s/d €44/72; 🖵) This bright and breezy pension has quite simple but very clean and comfortable rooms in a new building located in the heart of town.

Haus der Begegnung (☎ 632 90; www.hdb-eisenstadt .at; Kalvarienbergplatz 11; s/d €44/74; P) This church-affiliated pension is spotless, very quiet and well run. Rooms are simple but comfortable and it has its own grassed café area. It's open to everyone, but obviously not the place to stay if you want to party all night.

Hotel Ohr (☎ 624 60; www.hotelohr.at; Ruster Strasse 51; s €68-78, d €105-115, tr €150 P ; restaurant mains €8-16; 🕑 lunch & dinner, closed Mon Sep-Apr) The Ohr is a family-run hotel with nicely styled modern rooms and within walking distance of the centre. Its rustic restaurant is one of the best around: there's leafy outdoor/undercover seating on decking and it serves seasonal dishes often on a theme, such as goose around St Martin's day (late October & early November).

Hotel Burgenland (☎ 6960; www.hotelburgenland .at; Franz Schubert-Platz 1; s €85-100, d €110-140, ste from €195; P 🔊) This centrally located business and seminar hotel is the best of the crop, and defies its ugly exterior with comfortable modern rooms. The kitchen in the midrange restaurant downstairs is open all day.

Eating

Bodega La Ina (☎ 623 05; Hauptstrasse 48; tapas €3-8, menus €44-65; 🕑 10am-midnight Tue-Sat) Tapas and full-course menus featuring *Kalbsrücken* (saddle of veal) are the speciality in this up-market Austro-Andalusian restaurant with a quiet courtyard.

Haydnbräu (☎ 639 45; Pfarrgasse 22; mains €6.50-16; 🕑 8am-11pm) Duck into this microbrewery and restaurant for some of the best-value eating in town; culinary classics like schnitzel and goulash to seasonal lamb with polenta plus steaks are a treat here.

im esterházy (☎ 628 19; Esterházyplatz 5; mains €17-20, menus €25-45; 🕑 9am-midnight Mon-Thu & Sun, to 2am Fri & Sat) This stylish eatery directly opposite the *Schloss* is a wonderful spot for coffee or a drink outside in summer, as well as a full meal from its international cuisine.

A **Spar** (Hauptstrasse 13) supermarket on the main street is handy for self-caterers.

Getting There & Away

Bus is one option for travel between Eisenstadt and Vienna; frequent direct buses leave from Vienna's Südtiroler Platz daily (€6, 1¼ hours). Frequent trains make the same trip daily (from Südbahnhof), but a change is required at either Neusiedl am See or Wulkaprodersdorf (€14, 1¼ hours).

AROUND EISENSTADT
Burg Forchtenstein

Straddling a dolomite spur some 20km southwest of Eisenstadt, **Burg Forchtenstein** (☎ 02626-812 12; www.burg-forchtenstein.at, in German; Melinda Esterházy-Platz 1; guided tour of castle & arsenal adult/ student & child/family €7/6/20, treasury €9/8/27; 🕑 10am-6pm Apr-Oct) is another of Burgenland's imposing castles. This stronghold was built in the 14th century and enlarged by the Esterházys (who still own it today) in 1635. Apart from a grand view from its ramparts, the castle's highlights include an impressive collection of armour and weapons, portraits of regal Esterházys in the **Ahnengalerie** (Ancestral Gallery; adult/student & child/family €6/5/18) and spoils from the Turkish wars (the castle curators will proudly tell you Forchtenstein was the only castle in the area not to fall to the Turks). Its

Schatzkammer (treasury) contains a rich collection of jewellery and porcelain.

GETTING THERE & AWAY

On weekdays four buses run directly from Eisenstadt (€5.10, 40 minutes) and three from Wiener Neustadt (€4.40, 30 minutes) to Forchtenstein.

Wiesen

About 5km north of Forchtenstein lies the small town of Wiesen which, during summer, morphs into Austria's version of Glastonbury. The series of summer festivals hosted here are the biggest in the country and range from jazz to reggae. For more information, log on to www.wiesen.at, in German.

Wiesen can be reached by bus or train from Vienna's Südbahnhof (€12, 1½ hours) on a regular basis Monday to Saturday.

NEUSIEDLER SEE

Neusiedler See, Europe's second-largest steppe lake, is the lowest point in Austria. But what it lacks in height, it makes up for in other areas. Ringed by a wetland area of reed beds, it's an ideal breeding ground for nearly 300 bird species and its Seewinkel area is a particular favourite for **bird-watching**. The lake's average depth is 1.5m, which means the water warms quickly in summer. Add to this prevailing warm winds from the northwest and you have a water enthusiast's dream come true. Thousands of tourists flock to the lake for **windsurfing** and **sailing** during the summer months. The best swimming beaches are on the eastern side of the lake, as the western shore is thick with reed beds. The lake's shallowness also attracts many families – the only drawback is that the water has a slightly saline quality, as there is no natural outlet.

The area is also perfect for **cycling**; a flat cycle track winds all the way round the reed beds, the ferries crisscrossing the lake carry bikes and most hotels and pensions cater well to cyclists. It's possible to do a full circuit of the lake but as the southern section stretches into Hungary, remember to take your passport (path open April to November).

To top it all off there are acres upon acres of vineyards, producing some of Austria's best wines. Rust, on the western shore of the lake, is a perfect place to sample wine in a *Heuriger*.

Much of the Neusiedler See closes down from October to late March. If you're overnighting, ask whether the place you're staying at issues the free *Neusiedler See Gästekarte* (most do), which provides free admission to swimming areas and museums (including many in Sopron), the national park, free use of public transport (travel on ferries is half-price) and other perks.

Neusiedler See Tourismus (☎ 02167-8600; www .neusiedlersee.com; Obere Hauptstrafe 24, in Neusiedl am See; ☼ 8am-5pm Mon-Fri) is the information centre for the lake region for telephone, post and email enquiries.

Getting Around

There is at least one *Radverlieh* (bike hire) shop in every town on the lake; rental costs around €10 to €15 per day. Pick up a copy of the *Radtouren* map, available from tourist offices, which lists all *Radverlieh* and marks out cycle routes around the lake.

Ferry services across the Neusiedler See are provided by a number of companies from around 9am to 6pm from May to the beginning of October; it costs €6 for ferries between Podersdorf and Breitenbrunn, Podersdorf and Rust, and between Mörbisch and Illmitz.

Bus connections are frequent; see the separate towns below for specific details.

RUST

☎ 02685 / pop 1700

Rust, 14km east of Eisenstadt, is one of the prettiest towns along the Neusiedler See. It brims with *Heurigen,* has a reed seashore and hidden boatsheds, giving it a sleepy, swampy feel on a steamy day, and in the summer months storks glide lazily overhead, make out with each other, and clack their beaks agitato from rooftop roosts. Dozens of storks roost on chimneys in town, although it's wine, not storks, that has made Rust prosperous. In 1524 the emperor granted local vintners the right to display the letter 'R' (a distinctive insignia as a mark of origin from Rust) on their wine barrels and today the corks still bear this insignia. It's best to sample this history in one of the town's many *Heurigen*.

BURGENLAND

Orientation & Information

Postbus services stop at the post office, 100m from Conradplatz, a small square that leads to the town hall and Rathausplatz, the focal point of the village.

The **tourist office** (☎ 502; www.rust.at; Conradplatz 1, Rathaus; ☻ core hr 9am-noon & 1-4pm Mon-Thu all year, also 9am-noon Fri Jan-Feb & Nov-Dec, 9am-noon & 1-4pm or later Fri Apr-Oct, 9am-noon & 1-4pm Sat Apr-Oct, 9am-noon Sun Aug & Sep) has a list of wine growers offering tasting, plus hotels and private rooms in the town.

Sights & Activities

Rust's affluent past has left a legacy of attractive burgher houses on and around the main squares. **Storks**, which descend on the town from the end of March to rear their young, take full advantage of these houses (and their kindly owners, who have erected metal platforms on chimneys to entice the storks). The clacking of expectant parents can be heard till late August. A good vantage point is from the tower of the **Katholische Kirche** (Haydengasse; ☻ dawn-dusk Apr-Oct) at the southern end of Rathausplatz. The **Fischerkirche** (☎ 502; Rathausplatz 16; ☻ dawn-dusk Apr-Oct), at the opposite end of Rathausplatz, is the oldest church in Rust, built between the 12th and 16th centuries.

Access to the **lake** and **bathing facilities** (☎ 591; Seebad; adult/child per day €4/; ☻ 9am-7pm May–mid-Sep) is 1km down the reed-fringed Seepromenade. The swimming is very reedy.

Sleeping

Storchencamp (☎ 595; office@gmeiner.co.at; Ruster Bucht; campsite per adult/tent/car €5.20/4/4; ☻ Apr-Oct) With a large children's playground, cheap bike rental, close proximity to the lake and free access to the bathing area, this campsite is a great place for families.

Ruster Jugendgästehaus & Pension (☎ 591; www .seebadrust.at; Ruster Bucht 2; dm/s/d €17/33/60; ☻ year-round) This HI hostel is right on the harbour, forms part of the bathing complex and has modern, clean rooms.

Alexander (☎ 301; www.pension-alexander.at, in German; Dorfmeistergasse 21; s €55, d 76-110; P ☲) Though situated on the northern outskirts of town and more suitable if you have your own bike or car, Alexander is a great deal for comfortable three- and four-star rooms; take advantage of its sauna, garden and outdoor swimming pool.

Hotel Sifkovits (☎ 276; Am Seekanal 8; s/d €68/104; mains €10-17; P) Close to the centre of town, Sifkovits is a fine family-run hotel with large rooms and extras, like a downstairs lounge for reading and relaxing, a fruit bowl and a refrigerator stocked with free mineral water. It also has one of the finest restaurants in town.

Eating

When in Rust, do as the locals do and head for one of the many *Heurigen*. They're easy to spot – just look for the *Buschen* (small bush) hanging in front of doorways. Some operate under restaurant licenses and are therefore open throughout the summer.

ourpick Weingut Gabriel (☎ 236; www.weingut -gabriel.at; Hauptstrasse 25; cold platter about €10; ☻ from 4pm Thu & Fri, from 2pm Sat & Sun Apr-Oct) Not only is the pay-by-weight buffet brimming with delicious sausage and cold cuts (plus one warm), the wine is a treat, and in season the idyllic cobblestone courtyard is a wonderful vantage point to observe storks.

Peter Schandl (☎ 265; Hauptstrasse 20; mains €6-12; ☻ 4pm-midnight Mon & Wed-Fri, from 11am Sat & Sun Apr-Oct) With more of a restaurant feel, here you can enjoy game goulash and other warm dishes just off Rathausplatz.

Inamera (☎ 64 73; Oggauer Strasse 29; mains €9-22, menus €44-69; ☻ dinner Wed & Thu, lunch & dinner Fri-Sun) With its lovely stone interior, tiled floor and the small pond in the charming garden, Inamera is packed with atmosphere. It rates among the best restaurants in the Neusiedler See region.

Bla Bla (☎ 379; Hauptstrasse 18; ☻ from 9pm) It's easy to overlook this tiny champagne bar – until it opens up and the night owls move in for some bubbly and fun.

Getting There & Away

One to two hourly buses connect Eisenstadt and Rust (€3.40, 25 minutes). For Neusiedl am See (€6.80, one to 1½ hours), a change is required in Eisenstadt. Ferries cross the lake to Podersdorf from mid-May to September (€6).

MÖRBISCH AM SEE

☎ 02685 / pop 2350

Mörbisch am See, a quiet town 6km south of Rust and only a couple of kilometres from the Hungarian border, is pleasant for soaking

---

THE WINES OF BURGENLAND

The wine produced throughout this province is some of the best in Austria, due in no small part to the 300 days of sunshine per year, rich soil and excellent drainage. Although classic white varieties have a higher profile, the area's reds are more unusual, and the finest of the local wines is arguably the red Blaufränkisch, whose 18th-century pedigree here predates its arrival in the Danube region and Germany.

Sweet dessert wines are currently enjoying a renaissance in Austria. *Eiswein* (wine made from grapes picked late and shrivelled by frost) and selected late-picking for sweet or dessert wines are being complemented by *Schilfwein*, made by placing the grapes on reed (*Schilf*) matting so they shrivel in the heat. The guru of *Schilfwein* is Gerhard Nekowitsch from **Weingut Gerhard Nekowitsch** (☎ 02175-2039; www.nekowitsch.at, in German; Urbanusgasse 2, Illmitz).

Middle Burgenland, especially around the villages of Horitschon and Deutschkreutz, has a long tradition of Blaufränkisch, which is also at home in southern Burgenland, although this area is better known for Uhudler, a wine with a distinctly fruity taste.

One of the easiest ways to experience wine in the Neusiedler See region is to hire a bicycle in Neusiedl am See and pedal south through the vineyards towards the national park (p197). Along the way you'll pass vineyards and places where you can taste the local wine.

---

up a relaxed atmosphere and taking in quaint whitewashed houses with hanging corn and flower-strewn balconies.

The town's sleepy mood changes dramatically during the evening from mid-July to August with the **Seefestspiele** (www.seefestspiele -moerbisch.at), a summer operetta festival that attracts some 200,000 people each year. Its biggest competitor is the **Opern Festspiele** (www.ofs.at, in German; ☺ early Jul–late Aug), an opera festival held in an old Roman quarry near St Margareten, around 7km northwest of Mörbisch.

The local **tourist office** (☎ 8430; www.moerbisch .com; Hauptstrasse 23; ☺ 9am-5pm Mon-Fri, to noon Sat & Sun Mar-Jun & Sep-Oct, to noon & 1-6pm Jul & Aug, to 3pm Mon-Thu Nov-Feb) can advise on accommodation and what's available, the festivals, lakeside facilities and give you a list of *Heurigen*.

Frequent buses pass through Rust on their way to Mörbisch from Eisenstadt (€3.40, 40 minutes). A foot- and cycle-only **border crossing** (☺ 6am-10pm Jun-Sep, 8am-8pm Apr, May & Oct) into Hungary, 2km south of Mörbisch, is handy for those circumnavigating the lake. If you've forgotten your passport, or don't have the energy, jump on the ferry.

PURBACH AM SEE
☎ 02683 / pop 2500

Purbach am See, 17km north of Rust, is another pretty town along the lake. Its small, compact centre is filled with squat houses and it is still protected by bastions and three gates – reminders of the Turkish wars.

While there isn't a lot to see in the town – nor has it direct access to Neusiedler See – it's nice to soak up the slow pace of life and wander from one **wine cellar** (☺ from 4pm 1st Sat in month Apr-Oct) to the next along historic Kellergasse and Kellerplatz, both outside the town's walls.

The **tourist office** (☎ 5920-4; www.tiscover.at /purbach; Hauptgasse 38; ☺ 9am-noon & 3-6pm Mon-Sat, to noon Sun Apr-Sep, to noon & 3-6pm Mon-Fri Oct-Mar) has information on accommodation and wine. If you need a place to stay, look no further than **Camping Purbach & Jugendberge** (☎ 51 70; office@gmeiner.co.at; Türkenhain; campsite per adult/child/tent/car €4.50/3/2.60/2.40, dm €19) on the edge of the reed beds, or **Purbachhof** (☎ 55 64; www.tiscover.com/purbachhof; Schulgasse 14; d/tr/q €80/99/112), a converted wine-maker's house that could easily double as a folk museum.

our pick **Weingut & Weingasthof Kloster am Spitz** (☎ 5519; www.klosteramspitz.at, in German; Waldsiedlung 2; s €63-70, d €96-130; 6-course menu €75 with wine, mains €13-21; ☺ dinner Wed, lunch & dinner Thu-Sun Mar-Dec), on the northwest fringe of town located among vineyards (follow Fellnergasse), is a small former monastery with a modern hotel. Wines from the vineyard are produced organically and served in its very highly rated restaurant. Roast venison with ginger couscous and a pumpkin-plum chutney is one dish you may find on its seasonal menu.

Frequent daily trains heading for Neusiedl am See from Eisenstadt pass through Purbach (€4.40, 20 minutes).

BURGENLAND

NEUSIEDL AM SEE

☎ 02167 / pop 5900

Neusiedl am See is the region's largest town, the most accessible from Vienna, and a good springboard into the region.

Neusiedl's city **tourist office** (☎ 2229; www.tis cover.at/neusiedl.see; Hauptplatz 1; ☽ 8am-noon & 1-4.30pm Mon-Thu, 9am-1pm Fri Oct-Apr, 8am-noon & 1-4.30pm Mon-Fri May, Jun & Sep, 8am-6pm Mon-Fri, 10am-noon & 2-6pm Sat, 3-6pm Sun Jul & Aug) has a map of the town and the lake, as well as information on other towns. If you do stay in town, **Rathausstüberl** (☎ 2883; www.rathausstueberl.at; Kirchengasse 2; s €42-67, d €84-104; P) has bright rooms and a lovely midrange restaurant.

Neusiedl has good train connections from Vienna's Südbahnhof (€11, 40 minutes). Hourly buses travel down the eastern side of the lake, passing through Podersdorf (€3.40, 15 minutes) and Illmitz (€5.10, 30 minutes). Regular trains to Eisenstadt (€6, 35 minutes) pass through Purbach (€4.40, 15 minutes). For Rust, change to the bus in Eisenstadt.

Fairly regular city buses (€1) go to town from the train station, or call a **taxi** (☎ 5959). **Fahrräder Bucsis** (☎ 207 90; train station, Neusiedl am See; ☽ Apr–mid-Oct) rents bikes (with seven to 24 gears) for €15 per day at the station, where the Neusiedler See bike trail leads south.

PODERSDORF AM SEE

☎ 02177 / pop 2050

Podersdorf am See, on the eastern shore, is the only town which can truly claim to be *Am See* (on the lake). It's the most popular holiday destination in the Neusiedler See region (and Burgenland), largely due to good wind conditions and a reed-free location by the lake.

The town's **tourist office** (☎ 2227; www .podersdorfamsee.at; Hauptstrasse 2; ☽ 8am-noon & 1-4pm Mon-Fri, 9am-noon & 2-4pm Sat, 9am-noon Sun Jun-Sep, 8am-noon & 1-4pm Mon-Fri, Oct-May) can help find accommodation.

Sights & Activities

Podersdorf offers the most convenient bathing on Neusiedler See, with a long grassy **beach** (adult/child €4/2; ☽ 7.30am-6pm Apr-Sep) for swimming, boating and windsurfing. Windsurfing costs an extra €3.50, even with your own board, and paddle/electric boat hire is €6/10 per day. Wind and water enthusiasts can head for the Südstrand (South Beach), where **Fun & Sail** (☎ 0676-407 23 44; www.fun-and-sail.at, in German; boards per hr/day €9/45, 2-day kite surfing courses €199) has

equipment for hire and offers kite-surfing courses; **Surf- & Segelschule Nordstrand** (☎ 23 20; www.nordstrand.at, in German; Seeufergasse 17; boats per hr €14) rents out sailing boats and holds weekday sailing courses (from €160).

If you haven't already picked up a bicycle – the perfect way to see the Seewinkel wetlands, which start about 5km south of town – six places around town rent for between €7 and €15 per day, depending on the category of bike.

Sleeping & Eating

Book ahead for July and August. Seestrasse, the street leading from the tourist office to the lake, has many small places to stay.

Strandcamping (☎ 2279; Strandplatz 19; campsite per adult/child/tent/car €6.80/4/4.80/4.90; ☽ end-Mar-Oct) Right by the beach, this popular camping ground is one of the largest around and has plenty of shade from sweltering heat.

Steiner (☎ 2790; www.steinergg.at; Seestrasse 33; s/d €26.50/53; P) This *Gästehaus* has friendly staff, a quiet, homy atmosphere and super clean rooms with modern bathrooms and balcony. Don't let the cat out, though.

Hotel-Restaurant Pannonia (☎ 2245; www.pannonia-hotel.at, in German; Seezeile 20; s €54-57, d €77-114; P ☐ ☜) Set back from the waterfront, this recently renovated hotel has a New World feel, ultra-modern furnishings (including glass doors to the bathroom) and a large grassed area where children can play. The owners run a second hotel across the road. The restaurant (meals €10 to €20, open lunch and dinner) has an enormous wine list and seasonal dishes such as venison carpaccio served on bear's garlic pesto with tomatoes.

Seewirt (☎ 2415; www.seewirtkarner.at; Strandplatz 1; s €72-84, d €99-162; P) Four-star Seewirt is especially popular because it occupies a prime spot right next to the ferry terminal and beach. Its restaurant (€12 to €14, open lunch and dinner) serves uncomplicated Austrian cuisine.

Zur Dankbarkeit (☎ 22 23, Hauptstrasse 39, Podersdorf; mains €8-19; ☽ lunch & dinner Mon, Tue, Fri, 11.30am-9pm Sat & Sun) Zur Dankbarkeit is a lovely old restaurant that serves some of the best regional cooking around. The inner garden, with its mature trees and country ambience, is perfectly complemented by a glass of wine.

Weinklub 21 (☎ 21 170, Seestrasse 37; tastings €10; ☽ 9am-noon & 4-9pm May, Aug & Sep, 2-7pm Fri-Sun Oct–mid-Dec & mid-Feb–Apr) This excellent Vinothek represents 21 wine producers in town and the region; it holds regular tastings and events.

Getting There & Away

Hourly buses make the journey between Neusiedl and Podersdorf on weekdays but are infrequent on the weekend (€3.40, 15 minutes). Ferries connect Podersdorf with Rust (€6) and Breitenbrunn (€5.50) on the western shore.

SEEWINKEL
☎ 02175

Seewinkel is the heart of the Neusiedler See–Seewinkel National Park, and a grassland and wetland of immense importance to birds and other wildlife. The vineyards, reed beds, shimmering waters and constant birdsong make this an enchanting region for an excursion. This is an excellent area for **bird-watching** and explorations on foot or by bicycle.

The protected areas cannot be directly accessed by visitors, so to really get into the bird-watching you need a pair of binoculars. There are viewing stands along the way.

The park has its own information centre on the northern fringes of Illmitz, the **Nationalparkhaus** (☎ 344 20; www.nationalpark-neusiedlersee.org, in German; ☼ 8am-5pm Mon-Fri, 10am-5pm Sat & Sun Apr-Oct, 8am-4pm Mon-Fri Nov-Mar). It has a small display on the ecology and staff can tell you the best places to spot local wildlife.

The town of **Illmitz**, 4km from the lake, is surrounded by the national park and makes for a good base. Staff at its **tourist office** (☎ 2383; www.tiscover.at/illmitz; Obere Hauptplatz 2-4; ☼ 8am-noon & 1-5pm Mon-Fri, 9am-noon & 1-5pm Sat, 9am-noon Sun Jul & Aug, 8am-noon & 1-4pm Mon-Fri Sep & Nov-Jun, 8am-noon & 1-4pm Mon-Fri, 9am-noon Sat & Sun October) can provide information on the region. **Arkadenweingut-Gästehaus** (☎ 3345; www.tiscover.at/arkadenweingut-fam.heiss; Obere Hauptstrasse 20; s/d €29/50) is a lovely arcaded homestead in the centre of Illmitz.

Illmitz is connected with Mörbisch by ferry (€6) and Neusiedl am See by one-to-two hourly buses (€5.10, 30 minutes).

MIDDLE & SOUTHERN BURGENLAND

Heading south, the flat expanse of the Neusiedler See is soon forgotten as you enter an undulating landscape replete with lush hills, forested glens and castles that rise up in the distance. It's a region often overlooked by visitors and a place where life is still very much connected to the land; the influence of long-resident Hungarian and Croatian settlers can be felt here.

LOCKENHAUS & AROUND

Lockenhaus, in the centre of Burgenland, is famous for its **castle** (☎ 02616-23 94; www.tiscover.com/burg.hotel.lockenhaus; adult/student/child €5/4/2.50; ☼ 8am-4pm Sat & Sun Mar, to 4pm Apr, to 6pm May-Oct, to 4pm Nov-Christmas, closed late-Dec–Feb), or more accurately, for its former resident Elizabeth Báthory. Better known as the 'Blood Countess', she has gone down in history for her reign of terror early in the 17th century, when she reputedly tortured and murdered over 600 mainly peasant women for her own sadistic pleasure. The castle has long been cleansed of such gruesome horrors but still contains an impressive torture chamber, complete with an Iron Maiden.

If you want to sleep inside a castle, the **Burghotel Lockenhaus** (☎ 02616-23 94; www.tiscover.com/burg.hotel.lockenhaus; s/d €65/100) has antique-furnished rooms and a sauna.

Some 13km east of Lockenhaus is the tiny village of **Klostermarienberg**, home to a now-defunct monastery housing the only dog museum in Europe, the **Europäisches Hundemuseum** (☎ 2611-22 92; www.kulturimkloster.at, in German; Klostermarienberg; adult/student/child/family €4/3/2/8; ☼ 2-5pm Sat & Sun May-Oct). The odd collection of dog paraphernalia includes paintings, statues and intriguing photos of dogs dressed for war during WWI and WWII, complete with gas masks. Take a few minutes to visit the monastery's crypt, a chamber containing archaeological finds dating from the 13th and 14th centuries.

Bernstein, 15km west of Lockenhaus, is another town dominated by an impressive **castle** (☎ 03354-63 82; www.burgbernstein.at; r €150-190; ☼ end Apr–mid-Oct; Ⓟ). Ten of the castle's rooms, all of which are tastefully decorated with period furniture, are now used to accommodate guests. The castle, whose foundations date from 1199, is a delightful retreat from the stress of modern-day living and a time warp back to more rustic days. In the town centre is a small **Felsenmuseum** (☎ 03354-66 20-14; www.felsenmuseum.at, in German; Hauptplatz 5; adult/child €5/2; ☼ 9am-6pm Jul & Aug, 9am-noon & 1.30-6pm Mar-Jun & Sep-Dec), which concentrates its displays on the gemstone serpentine and its local mining (it was first mined in the town in the mid-19th century).

If your body needs some TLC, stop in at the spa-town of **Bad Tatzmannsdorf**, 15km south of Bernstein. Aside from taking the waters at the **Burgenland Therme** (☎ 03353-89 90; www.burgenlandtherme.at; Am Thermenplatz 1; daycard adult/child €17.50/12; ☼ 9am-10pm), you can visit the **Südburgenländisches Freilichtmuseum** (☎ 03353-83 14; Bahnhofstrasse; admission adult/child €2/1; ☼ 9am-6pm May-Oct), a small but rewarding open-air museum filled with thatched buildings from 19th-century Burgenland. The local **tourist office** (☎ 03353-70 15; www.bad.tatzmannsdorf.at; Joseph-Haydn-Platz 3; ☼ 8am-5.30pm Mon-Fri, 9.30am-2.30pm Sat, 9.30-11.30am Sun Apr–mid-Oct, 8am-4.30pm Mon-Fri, 9.30-11am Sat mid-Oct–Mar) helps with accommodation.

Getting There & Away

You're better off with your own transport in this region, as bus connections can be thin. A couple of direct buses connect Lockenhaus and Eisenstadt (€12.30, 1½ hours), but just one on Sunday. Taking a direct bus north from Oberwart (where there's a train station) to Bad Tatzmannsdorf (€2.20, 5 minutes; every two hours), Bernstein (€4.30, 30 minutes, every one to three hours) or Lockenhaus (€5.90, one hour, twice each weekday) is manageable on weekdays.

GÜSSING & AROUND

If you're not castled-out by this stage, head 40km south of Bad Tatzmannsdorf to Güssing, a peaceful town on the banks of the Strembach river. Here the arresting **Burg Güssing** (☎ 03322-434 00; www.burgguessing.info, in German; adult/child & student €5.50/3.50; ☼ 10am-5pm Tue-Sun Easter Mon-Oct) rises dramatically over the river and town. The castle, which is a mix of ruins and renovations, contains plenty of weapons from the Turks and Hungarians, striking portraits from the 16th century and a tower with 360-degree

views. Also on display is an iron safe with a tiny statue of a dog at the bottom – a sign that the owner was *auf den Hund gekommen* (had gone to the dogs). A modern 100m **funicular railway** (tickets €1; ☼ same hr as castle) helps those with weary legs reach the castle.

A visit to the **Auswanderer Museum** (☎ 03322-425 98; Stremtalstrasse 2; adult/child €2/1; ☼ 2-6pm Sat & Sun May-Oct), to the north of the castle, is also worthwhile; it relays the story of the mass exodus of *Burgenlander* (including Fred Astaire's father) to America before and after WWI. Most emigrated due to lack of work or poor living conditions.

If you missed the open-air museum in Bad Tatzmannsdorf, head 5km west of Güssing to the **Freilichtmuseum** (☎ 03328-322 55; Gerersdorf bei Güssing 66; adult/child & student €4.50/2; ☼ 9am-5pm Mon-Fri, 10am-6pm Sat & Sun Apr-Oct) at **Gerersdorf**. An hour or two could easily slip by while you explore the 30-odd buildings and their traditional furniture and fittings, which capture the rural culture of Burgenland in the 18th and 19th centuries.

The **tourist office** (☎ 03322-440 03; www.tiscover.at/guessing; Hauptplatz 7; ☼ 9am-noon Mon-Fri Jan-Jun & Sep-Dec, 8am-noon & 1-4pm Mon-Fri Jul & Aug) in Güssing can help with private rooms, otherwise try **Landgasthof Kedl** (☎ 03322-42 40 30; www.tiscover.at/gasthof.kedl; Urbersdorf 33; s/d €34/52; **P**), 3km north of Güssing in Urbersdorf. The castle's restaurant, **Burg Güssing** (☎ 03322-444 74; mains €8-17, menu €25; ☼ 10am-10pm Tue-Sun May-Oct), has a filling six-course Knight's menu (with chicken in barley juice) and a terrace with extensive views over the countryside.

Getting There & Away

Two to four direct buses daily connect Güssing (€6.50, 50 minutes) with Oberwart. On weekdays and Saturday several direct buses connect Güssing and Geresdorf (€1.70, 10 minutes).

Upper Austria

While Upper Austria may not exactly leap off the map as a holiday destination, it revels in the unexpected. Its cutting-edge cityscapes, Gothic architecture and glorious countryside aren't yet well known, but they will be. The capital, Linz, is a bit of a rebel by Austrian standards. Once considered an industrial backwater, the city is now catapulting into the 21st century: where there was dull concrete now there are flagship museums – high-tech temples of glass, steel and clean lines. With its edgy bars, boutique hotels and mushrooming avant-garde arts scene, this is clearly a city on the move.

Venture south from Linz and the countryside takes on a dreamlike quality, with rambling *Vierkanter* (four-sided) farmhouses and cornfields fading off into a watercolour distance. Pick a random spot on the map to explore on foot or by bike, or go straight for the biggies: St Florian's striking Augustine abbey, Steyr's knot of medieval lanes, the radon-laced waters of Bad Hall and the limestone pinnacles of the Nationalpark Kalkalpen grazing the border to Styria. Winding along scenic country lanes, the landscape switches from thick evergreen forests to undulating hills in the Traunviertel, where earthy locals and a pitcher of *Most* (cider) are never far away.

The northern stretch of the Mühlviertel strikes an entirely different chord – Gothic churches, mist-enshrouded forests and an air of Bohemian melancholy are evidence that the Czech Republic is close by. Stepping slightly east, the Innviertel is where, in the space of a day, you can roam the banks of the Inn River in Braunau, soak in Geinberg's Caribbean lagoon and sleep sweetly above the treetops in Kofing. Upper Austria boring? We think not.

UPPER AUSTRIA

HIGHLIGHTS

- Flying high above Linz's rooftops at the futuristic **Ars Electronica Center** (p203)
- Marvelling at the golden Tassilo Chalice in Kremsmünster's sublime **Benedictine Abbey** (p213)
- Quaffing potent brews and staggering around centuries-old fortifications in **Freistadt** (p215)
- Wandering cobblestone lanes in medieval **Steyr** (p211), squeezed between the Enns and Steyr Rivers
- Sipping cider in the orchards and soaking in the thermal baths of **Bad Hall** (p213)

★ Freistadt

★ Linz

Kremsmünster ★
Bad Hall ★ ★ Steyr

| POPULATION: 1.3 MILLION | AREA: 9480 SQ KM | HIGHEST ELEVATION: GROSSE PRIEL 2515M |

UPPER AUSTRIA

Climate

The temperate climate of the Mühlviertel is characterised by long summers and harsh winters. Heading south, milder temperatures are more prevalent until the Alps rise from the east.

Getting There & Away

Upper Austria has good connections; the A1 autobahn runs east–west to Vienna and Salzburg, the A8 north to Passau and the rest of Germany and the A9 south into Styria. Express trains between Vienna and Salzburg pass through Linz and much of southern Upper Austria, and there are also express trains heading south from Linz to St

Michael in Styria, from where connections to Klagenfurt and Graz are possible.

Getting Around

Upper Austria's excellent bus and train services are covered by **Oberösterreichischer Verkehrsverbund tickets** (☎ 0810-240 810; www .ooevv.at, in German). Prices depend on the number of zones you travel (one zone is €1.60, 10 zones cost €8.10). As well as single tickets, daily, weekly, monthly and yearly passes are available.

LINZ

☎ 0732 / pop 203,000

Linz dares to defy the braces-and-breeches image of Austria; a city with an urban edge, a thriving youth culture and its feet firmly in the 21st century. It may not have old-world architecture to rival the giddy heights of Vienna or Salzburg, but it comes up trumps in the modern art and new technology stakes, with crystalline venues like Lentos and the Ars Electronica Center.

And who would have thought that this industrial powerhouse had it in it to become European Capital of Culture 2009? By injecting life into the centre in recent years, the city has successfully reinvented itself: where people once diverted their gaze from unsightly smoke stacks, they now crane their necks to ogle glass-walled galleries displaying Kokoschka or daring public art installations. This sleeping city has finally awoken, even though she may not be a classic beauty.

While Linz takes contemporary design seriously, it has not become a soulless space. Alongside the modernist cubes are snug cafés where you can indulge in a slice or two of scrumptious *Linzer Torte*, hip bars lining the narrow streets of the *Altstadt* (old town) and a creaking railway that has crept into the Guinness Book of Records. So next time you're passing through this corner of Austria, hop off the train to see why this city is worth more than a cursory glance.

History

Linz was a fortified Celtic village by the time the Romans arrived, who took over and named it Lentia. By the 8th century, when the town came under Bavaria's thumb, its name had changed to Linze, and by the 13th century it had mushroomed into an important trading town for raw material out of Styria. In 1489, Linz became the imperial capital under Friedrich III until his death in 1493.

Like much of Upper Austria, Linz was at the forefront of the Protestant movement in the 16th and 17th centuries. However, the Counter-Reformation made a spectacular comeback, knocking the stuffing out of the place for the following century. Its resurgence in the 19th century was largely due to the development of the railway, when Linz became an important junction.

Adolf Hitler may have been born in Braunau am Inn (p217), but Linz was his favourite (he spent his school days here), and his (largely unrealised) plans for the city were grand. His Nazi movement built massive iron and steel works, which still employ

many locals. After WWII, Linz was at the border between the Soviet- and the US-administered zones. Since 1955, Linz has flourished into an important industrial city, port and provincial capital.

Orientation

Linz straddles both sides of the Danube (Donau), with the *Innenstadt* (city centre) and most attractions huddling on the south bank. Most sights on the north bank cluster in the district of Urfahr, squatting in the shadow of 537m-high Pöstlingberg. The main hub is Hauptplatz, an elongated square that is mostly car-free and abuts Landstrasse, the main shopping thoroughfare with a long pedestrian-only section. The *Hauptbahnhof* (main train station) is about 1km south of Hauptplatz.

MAPS

A free map, with information in both German and English and an enlargement of the *Innenstadt*, is available from Tourist Information Linz.

Information
BOOKSHOPS
Thalia (☎ 76 15-0; Landstrasse 41; ⊠ 9am-7pm Mon-Fri, to 6pm Sat) A small selection of English-language books.

INTERNET ACCESS
Atlas Media (☎ 78 10 05; Graben 17; per hr €2.40; ⊠ 9.30am-11pm Mon-Sat, 1-11pm Sun) Internet access, discount international calls, Skype and copying available.
Hotspot Linz Offers free wi-fi at 120 hotspots in the city centre; details are given online at www.hotspotlinz.at, in German.

INTERNET RESOURCES
Linz.info.at (in German) Links to the city's prominent cultural venues, firms and transport providers.
www.linz-termine.at Listings of cultural events and exhibitions throughout the year.

MEDICAL SERVICES
Krankenhaus der Stadt Linz (☎ 78 06-0; Krankenhausstrasse 9) The main hospital, 1km east of the centre.
Unfallkrankenhaus (☎ 69 20-0; Garnisonstrasse 7) Emergency hospital.

MONEY
There are a number of banks with ATMs in the *Innenstadt*; the airport also has a bank. The *Hauptbahnhof* has an ATM and

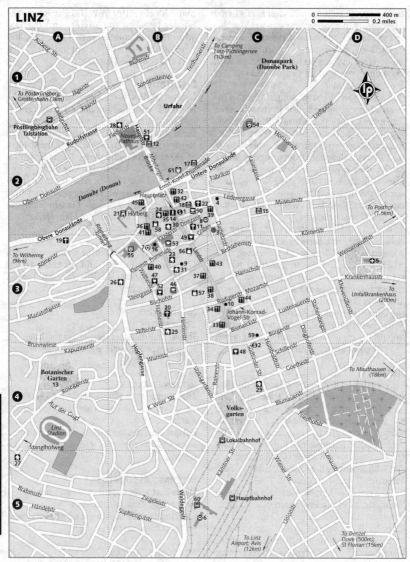

LINZ

a **money exchange office** (7.30am-4pm Mon-Thu, 7.30am-1.30pm Fri).

American Express (☎ 66 90 13; Bürgerstrasse 14; 9am-5.30pm Mon-Fri) Financial and travel services under one roof.

POST
Main Post Office (Bahnhofplatz 11; 7am-9pm Mon-Fri, 9am-6pm Sat) Near the *Hauptbahnhof*; has an ATM.

Post Office (Domgasse 1; 8am-6pm Mon-Fri) This post office is handier to the centre.

TOURIST INFORMATION
Tourist Information Linz (☎ 7070 1777; www.linz .at; Hauptplatz 1; 8am-7pm Mon-Fri, 10am-7pm Sat & Sun May-Oct, 8am-6pm Mon-Fri, 10am-6pm Sat & Sun Nov-Apr) Brochures, accommodation listings, free room

reservation service and a separate Upper Austria information desk can be found here.

TRAVEL AGENCIES

STA Travel (☎ 77 58 93; Herrenstrasse 7; ⏰ 9am-5.30pm Mon-Fri)

Sights & Activities

Before setting off, consider purchasing the Linzer Museumskarte (€12) for entry to 12 museums, or the Linzer City Ticket (€20) for entry to all museums, a €10 restaurant voucher and a return trip on the Pöstlingbergbahn. The Junior Linz Ticket (€8, for ages six to 14) is also available. All three tickets are valid the entire year.

In preparation for Linz seizing the reigns of European Capital of Culture in 2009, many sights are undergoing renovation, including the Pöstlingbergbahn. The Ars Electronica Center is moving to a temporary home (Graben 15) until early 2009.

LENTOS KUNSTMUSEUM

The gleaming **Lentos Kunstmuseum** (☎ 7070 3614; www.lentos.at; Ernst-Koref-Promenade 1; adult/child €6.50/4.50; ⏰ 10am-6pm Wed-Mon, to 10pm Thu) stops you dead in your tracks. Defined by razor-sharp lines, this glass-and-steel landmark was designed by Zurich architects Weber & Hofer, who decided to leave a large gap in the base of its rectangular shape. The gallery showcases a world-class collection of contemporary art,

including works by Warhol, Schiele, Klimt and Kokoschka, which is complemented by rotating exhibitions.

Next to Lentos onto the southern bank of the Danube is the **Donaupark** (Danube Park), the city's green escape vault. Modern sculptures rise above the bushes in the well-tended gardens, which are a magnet to walkers, joggers, skaters, picnickers and city workers seeking fresh air in summer.

ARS ELECTRONICA CENTER

On the opposite side of the Danube is the **Ars Electronica Center** (☎ 72 72-0; www.aec.at; Hauptstrasse 2; adult/child €6/3; ⏰ 9am-5pm Wed-Fri, 10am-6pm weekends), where virtually anything is possible – from diving to the depths of the Danube to flying high above Linz. This temple of interactive wizardry is devoted to the evolving world of technology (the lift projects graphics and a remote-controlled robotic arm tends to the entrance-hall flower garden). The must-do attractions are Humphrey II, a flight simulator that (literally) sweeps you off your feet, and Gulliver's World, where you can redesign the planet by shaping landscapes, moving mountains and putting yourself in the picture.

LANDESGALERIE

Housed in a sumptuous 19th-century building, the **Landesgalerie** (☎ 77 44 82-0; www.landesgalerie.at; Museumstrasse 14; adult/child €4/2.20; ⏰ 9am-6pm Tue-Fri, 10am-5pm Sat & Sun) exhibits

20th-century paintings, photography and installations that bear some relation to Upper Austria. Alongside masterpieces by Dürer and Kokoschka, you'll find a peerless collection of fantastical works by the Austrian expressionist Alfred Kubin. The open-air **Skulpturenpark** juxtaposes modern sculpture with the gallery's classic architecture.

BOTANISCHER GARTEN

Rest beside the rhododendrons and orchids in Linz's **botanical garden** (☎ 7070 8160; Roseggerstrasse 20-22; adult/child €2/1; ☑ 8am-5pm Nov-Feb, to 6pm Mar & Oct, to 7pm Apr & Sep, 7.30am-7.30pm May-Aug). This peaceful pocket of greenery south of the centre nurtures 10,000 species, from native alpine plants to tropical palms and one of Europe's largest cacti collections.

PÖSTLINGBERG

Linz spreads out beneath you atop **Pöstlingberg** (537m), which affords bird's-eye views over the city and the snaking Danube. It's a gentle hike to the top or a precipitous 15-minute ride aboard the narrow-gauge **Pöstlingbergbahn** (adult/child €4/2, combined ticket with Tram 3 €6.20/3.10; ☑ every 20-30min 5.40am-8.20pm Mon-Sat, 7.15am-8.20pm Sun). This gondola features in the Guinness Book of Records as the world's steepest mountain railway – quite some feat for such a low-lying city!

At the summit is the turn-of-the-century **Grottenbahn** (☎ 3400 7506; Am Pöstlingberg 16; adult/child €4.50/2.30; ☑ 10am-6pm Jun-Aug, to 5pm Sep-Nov & Mar-May), where families – and anyone that loves a bit of cult kitsch – can board the dragon train to trundle past gnomes, glittering stalactites and scenes from Grimms' fairytales.

Walking Tour

Kick off your one-hour walk of Linz's *Innenstadt* at the effervescent **Hauptplatz (1)**, where street performers wow the crowds and locals chill in pavement cafés. Pause to admire the pastel-coloured baroque houses framing the square and its centrepiece, the **Dreifaltigkeitssäule (2)** (trinity column), a striking 20m pillar of Salzburg marble carved in 1723 to commemorate the town's deliverance from war, fire and plague. Opposite is the **Altes Rathaus (3)** housing **Linz-Genesis** (☎ 7070 1920; Hauptplatz 1; admission free; ☑ 9am-1pm & 2-6pm Mon-Fri), unravelling the city's history and celebrating famous sons such as Johannes Kepler and Anton Bruckner.

Turning into Klosterstrasse, you'll spy the sleek grey-and-white façade of the 13th-century **Minoritenkirche (4)**, famed for its rococo stuccowork and frescoes (the brushwork of Bartlomeo Altomonte). Next door is the **Landhaus (5)**; wander into the arcaded courtyard to see the **Planet Fountain** (1582), which predated the arrival of the great astronomer Johannes Kepler, who taught here for 14 years. Across the way, appreciate the Renaissance architecture of **Mozarthaus (6)**, where Amadeus composed the *Linzer Sinfonie* in 1783, before soaking up the ambience in the *Altstadt*'s maze of cobbled streets.

Crossing the Alter Markt, take the steps up the Hofberg to medieval **Schloss Linz (7)** for great views of the Danube. Time permitting, pop into the **Schlossmuseum** (☎ 77 44 19; Tummelplatz 10; adult/child €3/1.70; ☑ 9am-6pm Tue-Fri, 10am-5pm Sat & Sun) to glimpse a fine collection of Gothic art. From here, follow Römerstrasse to the 8th-century **Martinskirche (8)**. This humble little church is one of Austria's oldest, as the Roman oven inside confirms.

Head back along Römerstrasse towards Promenade, presided over by the mighty **Landestheater (9)**, then onto Herrenstrasse, where you'll be forced to look up at the **Neue Dom (10)**, a neo-Gothic giant with a riot of skinny spires and fabulous stained glass windows depicting Linz's history. The cathedral's height was apparently restricted to 134m, so as not to outshine Stephansdom (p124) in Vienna. Veer onto Bichofstrasse for a peak at Michael Pruckmayer's handiwork – the baroque **Bischofshof (11)** residence.

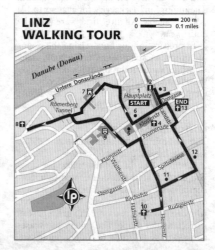

LINZ WALKING TOUR

Continue along Landstrasse, the city's main artery dominated by the twin onion-domed towers of former nunnery **Ursulinenkirche (12)**, then nip down Domgasse to admire the 17th-century **Alter Dom (13)** (☎ 770 866-0; Domgasse 3; ☯ 7am-7pm), where Anton Bruckner served as church organist. Step inside to admire the interior – the architectural equivalent of a wedding cake, with its theatrical pink marble altar and lavish white stuccowork. Bearing left on Domgasse brings you back to the *Hauptplatz*.

Tours

If you'd prefer to explore the city with a group, Tourist Information Linz organises 1½-hour **walking tours** (tour €8; ☯ 11am & 2.30pm May-Sep), which go ahead regardless of the weather or the number of people.

Festivals & Events

Linz's most celebrated festival is the **Brucknerfest** (☎ 7612 2170; www.brucknerhaus.at; tickets €11-92) in September, when the Brucknerhaus or the Stiftskirche in St Florian (p209) stage world-class concerts. It's preceded by the **Ars Electronica Festival**, an innovative art and technology event held in early September. Both festivals coincide with free **Klangwolke** concerts in Donaupark.

The **Linz Fest**, a huge shindig in late May or early June, runs for three or four weeks and brings free rock, jazz and folk concerts to the city. In July, musicians, jugglers and acrobats from across Europe take to the city's streets for the three-day **Pflasterspektakel** street festival.

Sleeping

Besides traditional pensions, the city has a growing crop of no-nonsense hostels and designer boutique hotels. Tourist Information Linz offers a free accommodation booking service for visitors, but only face-to-face and not over the phone.

BUDGET

Camping Linz-Pichlingersee (☎ 30 53 14; Wienerstrasse 937; campsites per adult/child/tent €4/2.60/4.50; P) Escape to the country at this tree-shaded site, where you can wake up with a swim in Pichlingersee lake. There is a playground, kitchen and a restaurant serving Portuguese food. Hop on bus 2051 from the *Hauptbahnhof*.

Herberge Linz (☎ 0699-1180 7003; herberge.linz@aon .at; Kapuzinerstrasse 14; dm/s/d €15/22/36) Within staggering distance of the big sights, this bright yellow hostel has a friendly vibe. The spacious dorms all have lockers, fridges and showers. Chill over drinks in the leafy garden.

Jugendgästehaus (☎ 66 44 34; jgh.linz@oejhv.or.at; Stanglhofweg 3; dm/s/d €19.50/29.50/44; P) This modern HI hostel is 1.5km from the centre. The rooms won't win any design awards, but the above-par facilities include a tennis court and common room.

Wilder Mann (☎ 65 60 78; wilder-mann@aon.at; Goethestrasse 14; s/d €35/60; P) Don't be put off by the '70s wallpaper in the corridors at this simple pension, the high-ceilinged rooms are quiet, spacious and a bargain, given the central location.

MIDRANGE & TOP END

Goldenes Dachl (☎ 77 58 97; goldenesdachl@gmx.de; Hafnerstrasse 27; s/d €45/85) Few can beat this place for price and proximity to the centre. Rooms aren't flash but they're comfy, with wooden floors, sofas and loads of space. There's a restaurant and beer garden downstairs.

Goldener Anker (☎ 77 10 88; Hofgasse 5; s/d €55/90) Set in a 17th-century inn, this family-run place just off Hauptplatz is a superb deal, with cosy rooms, a beer garden and a vaulted tavern serving Austrian staples and monastic brews.

Zum Schwarzen Bären (☎ 77 24 77; baer@linz-hotel .at; Herrenstrasse 9-11; s/d €68/90; P 🖳) Modern art glams up this three-star hotel, offering free wi-fi throughout. The warm-hued rooms are quiet and comfy, but bathrooms are a bit poky. You can upgrade to a room with a waterbed if the mood takes you.

Wolfinger (☎ 77 32 91; www.hotelwolfinger.at; Hauptplatz 19; s/d €87/126; P 🖳) The scent of fresh-cut flowers hits you upon entering this ever-so-posh hotel. One of the top addresses in Linz, its historical feel is accentuated by archways, stuccowork and period furniture. Ask for one of the back rooms with a balcony.

Drei Mohren (☎ 77 26 26-0; www.drei-mohren .at; Promenade 17; s/d €108/142; P 🖳) Anton Bruckner tops the list of famous past guests at this grand 16th-century hotel with plush touches like marble floors, chandeliers and gold drapes. Its 25 Biedermeier-style rooms are individually furnished.

our pick **Spitz Hotel** (☎ 73 64 410; www.spitzhotel .at; Fiedlerstrasse 6; r €120-250; P 🖳) Isa Stein is the brainchild of the Spitz Hotel's futuristic design. The wow factor is there from the moment you enter the lobby, decked out with pod-shaped stools, sphere lighting and a wall screening clips from the Prix Ars Electronica. Clean lines, open-plan bathrooms and hardwood floors define minimalist chic in the rooms, where free wi-fi and flat-screen TVs are standard.

Eating

Linz's cuisine is a melting pot of Austrian classics, world flavours and fusion cuisine. The city has recently jumped on the organic bandwagon, so you'll find plenty of healthy vegetarian and fair-trade options. The *Linz is(s)t gut* booklet, available from the tourist office, lists most restaurants in town.

RESTAURANTS

Gragger (Hofgasse 3; snacks €2-5; 7.30am-8pm Mon-Thu, to 11pm Fri & Sat) Antipasti, chunky soups and organic breads are served at a communal wooden table in this little gem of a café.

Ikaan (☎ 77 19 40; Altstadt 16; mains €5-12; lunch & dinner Mon-Fri, dinner Sat) Zesty lime walls and bamboo set the scene at this ethnic restaurant blending organic Asian and European flavours. Create-your-own salads and stir-fries top the menu. The chilli-chocolate mousse and mango lassis are divine.

Pius (☎ 070-77 05 70; Hauptplatz 2; mains €6-10; 11am-8pm Mon-Fri, to 5pm Sat) Health-conscious locals pack into this home-grown shop and café to fill up on organic salads, handmade pasta and vegetarian dishes. The freshly squeezed juices pack a punch.

p'aa (☎ 070-77 64 61; Altstadt 28; mains €7-11; lunch & dinner Mon-Sat) p'aa dishes up vegan and organic dishes, from feisty curries to pumpkin schnitzel, in a trendy lounge setting with low seating and mellow music.

Tom Yam (☎ 94 69 69; Johann-Konrad-Vogel-Strasse 11; mains €7-15; lunch & dinner Mon-Sat, dinner Sun) The King of Thailand beams down from the wall and Thai pop plays at this funky little restaurant with a terrace the size of a postage stamp. Breathe fire with a green papaya salad or the house special – tom yam prawn soup.

Mia Cara (☎ 78 57 28; Pfarrplatz 13; mains €8-16; lunch & dinner Mon-Sat) Mario cooks up a storm in the kitchen at this buzzing Italian *osteria*. Sample antipasti from the counter or homemade penne with a nice glass of Chianti. The patio is popular in summer.

Niu (☎ 78 67 78; Klammstrasse 1; mains €8-15; lunch & dinner Tue-Fri) Zen-style minimalism and Asian fusion cuisine draw foodies to this hole-in-the-wall restaurant. The aromatic yellow porcini mushroom curry and chilli beef noodles come recommended.

Alte Welt (☎ 77 00 53; www.altewelt.at, in German; Hauptplatz 4; mains €9-16; lunch & dinner Mon-Fri, dinner Sat) Opening onto an inner courtyard, Alte Welt is a bit of a Jekyll and Hyde: by day it serves hearty fare such as crispy roast pork and potato gnocchi, while by night it becomes a haunt for students, artists and musicians (the cellar hosts jam sessions, live jazz and plays).

Klosterhof (☎ 77 33 73; Landstrasse 30; mains €9-18; 9am-midnight) Klosterhof's tree-shaded beer garden is arguably the best in Linz, with space for 1500. If this isn't enough to tempt you, tasty *Knödel* (dumplings) with Stiegl beer in the vaulted tavern at the front should.

Los Caballeros (☎ 77 89 70; Landstrasse 32; mains €10-19; 11am-2am) Decked out with fake cacti and sombreros, this Mexican place is cheesy but a good laugh for a group. Potent shark shots (tequila and Tabasco) help wash down T-bone steaks and enchiladas.

Zum Kleinen Griechen (☎ 78 24 67; Hofberg 8; mains €13-26; lunch & dinner Mon-Sat) Close to Schloss Linz, this classy little number tempts with well-prepared Greek specialities such as octopus, stuffed vine leaves and ouzo-drenched figs. The award-winning cuisine is definitely worth it.

SELF-CATERING

Self-caterers will have no problem finding a supermarket; there are two Billas and a Spar on Landstrasse. For fresh local produce, head to the *Bauernmärkte* (farmers markets) on Hauptplatz (9am to 2pm Tuesday and Friday) and outside the Neuen Rathaus (8am to noon Saturday). Cheap *Würstel* (sausage) stands line the Volksgarten.

Drinking

Linz's young, fun-loving population ensures plenty of after-dark action. The tourist office hands out *Linzer Nacht Meile* with nightlife listings, but it's fairly easy to pinpoint the main drag; the glut of watering holes around Landstrasse, Hauptplatz and the area nicknamed the 'Bermuda Triangle', one block west, are safe bets for a night out on the tiles.

BARS

Thüsen Tak (Walterstrasse 21; 5pm-4am) This spit 'n' sawdust pub is pure rock 'n' roll, with loud music and walls smothered in posters of Led Zeppelin, Thin Lizzy and Deep Purple. Enjoy a beer and natter with Mike at the bar, or surf the web for free.

Strom (73 12 09; Kirchengasse 4; 2pm-2am Sun-Thu; to 4am Fri & Sat) DJs spin hip-hop, electro and funk at this lively bar. Upstairs is rough and ready, while downstairs is more laid-back, with partygoers spilling out onto Kirchengasse. Next door is Stadtwerk, which hosts clubbing events.

Cheeese (79 28 27; Waltherstrasse 11; 6pm-4am Tue-Sat) A grinning Cheshire cat welcomes you to this party-hearty bar, reeling in a young crowd with wacky events – from Latino parties and all-you-can-eat spaghetti feasts to ear-splitting karaoke nights on Thursdays.

Divino (070-94 74 73; Domgasse 20; 2-10pm Mon-Fri, to 10pm Sat) Pillar-box red walls, gleaming wine bottles and huge hunks of Serrano ham set the scene in this Spanish *vinoteca*, where flamenco music plays and glasses tinkle.

Count Davis (0664-1984 732; Landstrasse 71-75; 6pm-4am Mon-Sat) Sounds of the sax fill this uber-cool jazz club; the place to sip a mojito and see up-and-coming homegrown talent perform.

CAFÉS

While in Linz, it would be rude not to try the famous *Linzer Torte*, an almond pastry and redcurrant (not raspberry!) tart. The recipe has been around since the 17th century, and it's the greatest rival to Vienna's own *Sacher torte*.

k.u.k. Hofbäckerei (78 41 10; Pfarrgasse 17; coffee & cake €3-6; 6.30am-6pm Mon-Fri, 7am-12.30pm Sat) Fritz Rath (below) pours passion into creating *the* best *Linzer Torte* in the city's oldest café (first mentioned in 1371). Whiffs of sugar and butter permeate the wood-panelled café, crammed with Sissi portraits and Habsburg curios.

Café Jindrak (77 92 58; Herrenstrasse 22; lunch menus €5-7; 8am-6pm Mon-Sat) Join the old dames for sticky cakes at this celebrated café. You would need a huge appetite (and fork) to tackle the legendary *Linzer Torte* that set a Guinness World Record in 1999, measuring 4m high and weighing 650kg.

Traxlmayr (77 33 53; Promenade 16; coffee & cake €2.50-6; 8am-10pm Mon-Sat) A blast from

---

VOICES: FRITZ RATH, LINZ BAKER

Fritz Rath has known the secret of the *Linzer Torte* since he was knee-high. He runs the k.u.k Hofbäckerei in Linz, where he can often be seen flitting to and fro with a wagon-wheel-sized *Linzer Torte*. Here he reveals his lifelong passion for baking cakes according to age-old family recipes.

Did you always want to continue the family baking tradition? I felt tied to the kitchen as a teenager and needed to get out and experience the world – spread my wings a bit. So I worked in Sweden and the Midlands for a while in the late '60s. It was quite an eye-opener, but eventually you always come back to your roots.

What does baking mean to you? Baking holds up a mirror up to culture: Austria is the king of cakes, Germany rye bread, France baguettes…

What is the key ingredient in Linzer Torte? I recently met a lady in Berlin who insisted *Linzer Torte* is made with raspberry jam. My god, raspberry! It's redcurrant! But she was right in a way. The tart is world famous and each country interprets the recipe differently. It just tastes better in Linz because that's where it comes from.

So what's the secret to baking Linzer Torte? You need the right balance of ingredients (almonds, flour, butter, spices, redcurrant jam) and I usually add a dash of milk to the dough. But a lot boils down to instinct. My father used to say baking cakes is like playing music: if you take the same piano, sheet of music and 10 musicians the mixture is the same, but each one produces a slightly different result.

the 1920s, Traxlmayr is a Viennese-mould coffee house with a buzzing atmosphere, high ceilings and dickie-bow-tied waiters carrying trays piled high with dainty sandwiches and strudel.

Both the Lentos Kunstmuseum and Ars Electronica Center have ultramodern cafés that afford fine views over the Danube and city.

Entertainment

Brucknerhaus (☎ 76 12-0; www.brucknerhaus.linz.at, in German; Untere Donaulände 7) The Brucknerhaus is the city's premier music venue, staging regular classical and jazz concerts, plus a dedicated programme for kids ('mini' and 'midi' music).

Posthof (☎ 77 05 48-0; www.posthof.at, in German; Posthofstrasse 43) This venue near the docks headlines Linz's avant-garde events with an eclectic line-up of music, dance and theatre. Raves are occasionally held here.

Landestheater (☎ 76 11-0; www.landestheater-linz.at, in German; Promenade 39) Opera, ballet and musicals take to the stage of Linz's main theatre, which hosts largely classic productions. The u/hof team keeps kids amused with plays aimed at a young audience.

Shopping

Antique shops, galleries and musty bookshops line Bischofstrasse; this is a great street to rummage for handcrafted jewellery, paintings and kooky gifts. If you've got the spare change and a well-padded suitcase, check out the designer glasswork in the **Glas Galerie** (☎ 77 10 11; Bischofstrasse 11; ☒ 11am-5pm Tue-Fri, 10am-1pm Sat).

At the other end of the scale, the city's *Flohmärkte* (flea markets) spring forth in front of the **Neues Rathaus** (☒ 7am-2pm Sat Nov-Mar) and on the **Hauptplatz** (☒ 6am-2pm Sat Mar-Oct).

The glass-roofed **Arkade** (☎ 79 38 07; Landstrasse 12; ☒ 9.30am-6pm Mon-Fri, 9am-5pm Sat) mall is the place to hibernate when it rains. Alongside high-street names like Boss and Agatha, you'll find a smattering of boutiques, speciality shops and a juice bar.

Honey you can eat, drink and bathe in (including chestnut and acacia tree varieties) fills the shelves at the **Imkerhof** (☎ 77 17 09; Altstadt 15; ☒ 9am-6pm Mon-Fri, to noon Sat).

Getting There & Away

AIR

Austrian Airlines, Lufthansa, Ryanair and Air Berlin are the main airlines servicing the **Blue Danube Airport** (☎ 07221-600-0; www.linz-airport .at). There are flights to Vienna, Salzburg and Graz, as well as Berlin, Frankfurt, Düsseldorf, Stuttgart and Zürich. Ryanair has daily flights to London Stansted; see p397

BOAT

The **Schiffsstation** (Untere Donaulände 1) is on the south bank next to the Lentos Kunstmuseum. **Wurm + Köck** (☎ 78 36 07; www.donauschiffahrt .de, in German) sends boats westwards to Passau (one-way/return €22/25, six to seven hours, 9.45am and 2.20pm Tuesday to Sunday May to October) and east to Vienna (€52/64, 11½ hours, 9am Saturday May to September).

BUS

Regional buses depart from stands at the main bus station adjacent to the *Hauptbahnhof*. Information can be obtained from the **bus information counter** (☎ 61 71 81; ☒ 7.50am-5.30pm Mon-Fri).

TRAIN

Linz is on the main rail route between Vienna (€27.90, two hours) and Salzburg (€19.90, 1⅓ hours), and express trains run twice hourly in both directions. Slower trains also service this route and others. At least three trains depart daily for Prague (€58, five hours). Aside from the obligatory **information desk** (☒ 8am-6.50pm), there are also some snack bars and an ATM at the *Hauptbahnhof*.

Getting Around

TO/FROM THE AIRPORT

Linz airport is located 12km southwest of the town. A direct airport bus service connects the *Hauptbahnhof* (€2.30, 20 minutes) with the airport hourly.

BICYCLE

Bikes are available for hire at **Donau Touristik** (☎ 20 80 38; Lederergasse 4-12; bike per day/week €10/63; ☒ 8am-5.30pm Mon-Thu, to 4.30pm Fri).

CAR

One-way systems, congested roads and pricey parking make public transport preferable to driving in central Linz, although a car is a definite plus if you're keen to explore more of Upper Austria. There are some free car parks along Obere Donaulände. Linz has offices for all the major car hire firms:

Avis (☎ 0722-1600 6300; Flughafenstrasse 1)
Denzel Drive (☎ 0501-0541 70; Bahnhofplatz 3-6)
Hertz (☎ 78 48 41; Bürgerstrasse)
LaudaMotion (☎ 0900 240 120) Has an office at the *Hauptbahnhof*.

PUBLIC TRANSPORT

Linz has an extensive bus and tram network (☎ 3400 7000, www.linzag.at), but by early evening some services stop or become infrequent. Single tickets (€1.60), day passes (€3.20) and weekly passes (€10.70) are available from pavement dispensers and *Tabak* (tobacconist) shops. Drivers don't sell tickets – buy and validate your tickets before you board.

AROUND LINZ

ST FLORIAN

☎ 07224 / pop 5600

Unassuming St Florian, a market town 15km southeast of Linz, hides one of the best abbeys in Upper Austria, if not the whole country. St Florian was a Roman who converted to Christianity and was drowned in the Enns River (in AD 304) for his pains. In many Austrian churches he is represented wearing Roman military uniform and dousing flames with a bucket of water.

The centre of town is Marktplatz, just below the abbey. Here you'll find a small **tourist office** (☎ 56 90; st.florian@oberoesterreich.at; Marktplatz 2; ☿ 9am-1pm Mon-Fri), a few guesthouses and the post office.

Sights & Activities

AUGUSTINER CHORHERRENSTIFT

Rising like a vision above St Florian, the **Augustinian Abbey** (☎ 89 02; www.stift-st-florian.at; Stiftstrasse 1; tours adult/concession €6/5; ☿ tours 10am, 11am, 2pm, 3pm & 4pm Apr-Oct) dates at least to 819 and has been occupied by the Augustinians since 1071. The main entrance is flanked by statues and is particularly striking when bathed in afternoon sunlight.

You can only visit the abbey's interior by guided tour, which takes in the lavish apartments, resplendent with rich stuccowork and emotive frescoes. They include 16 emperors' rooms (once occupied by visiting popes and royalty) and a galleried library housing 145,000 volumes. The opulent **Marble Hall** pays homage to Prince Eugene of

Savoy, a Frenchman who frequently led the Habsburg army to victory over the Turks. Prince Eugene's Room contains an amusing bed featuring carved Turks, which gives a whole new meaning to the idea of sleeping with the enemy!

A high point of the tour is the **Altdorfer Gallery**, displaying 14 paintings by Albrecht Altdorfer (1480–1538) of the Danube School. The sombre and dramatic scenes of Christ and St Sebastian reveal an innovative use of light and dark. Altdorfer cleverly tapped into contemporary issues to depict his biblical scenes (for example, one of Christ's tormentors is clearly a Turk).

The **Stiftskirche** (admission free; ☿ approx 7am-10pm) is almost overpowering: its altar is shaped from 700 tonnes of pink Salzburg marble and the huge 18th-century organ, which is literally dripping with gold, was Europe's largest at the time it was built. To hear the organ in full song, catch one of the **concerts** (adult/concession with tour €8/7; ☿ 2.30pm Mon, Wed-Fri & Sun mid-May–mid-Oct).

Anton Bruckner was a choirboy in St Florian and church organist from 1850 to 1855; he is buried in the **crypt** below his beloved organ. Also in the spooky crypt are the remains of 10,000 people believed to be Roman, which were unearthed in the 13th century. Stacked in neat rows behind a wrought iron gate, their bones and skulls create a spine-tingling work of art.

Every little boy's dream is the **Historisches Feuerwehrzeughaus** (Fire Brigade Museum; ☎ 42 19; Stiftstrasse 2; adult/concession €2.50/1.50; ☿ 9am-noon & 2-4pm Tue-Sun May-Oct) opposite the *Stiftskirche*, housing historic fire engines, hoses, buckets and other firefighting paraphernalia.

Sleeping & Eating

The tourist office hands out a useful accommodation booklet listing hotels and private rooms in and around St Florian.

Gästehaus Stift St Florian (☎ 0664-1358 243; Stiftstrasse 1; s/d €40/78) An oasis of calm, this guesthouse within the abbey's walls overlooks the cloisters and groomed gardens. The design is sleek and simple, but antique furniture and candlelight add character. The light-flooded rooms feature solid wood floors and Art Nouveau touches.

Landgasthof zur Kanne (☎ 42 88; www.gasthof -koppler.at; Marktplatz 7; s/d €52/86; Ⓟ) This yellow fronted, 14th-century guesthouse on the main square scores points for its clean, snug rooms and restaurant serving fresh produce from the Koppler family's farm.

Zum Goldenen Löwe (☎ 89 30; Speiserberg 9; mains €7-13; ☺ lunch & dinner Thu-Tue) The sound of the chef pounding humungous schnitzels welcomes you to this wood-panelled restaurant opposite the abbey gates. The sunny terrace out the back overlooks rolling countryside.

Getting There & Away

St Florian (officially Markt St Florian) is not accessible by train. There are a zillion buses departing from the main bus station at Linz's *Hauptbahnhof* Monday to Friday (€2.40, 22 minutes), but only five on Sunday.

MAUTHAUSEN
☎ 07238 / pop 4850

Nowadays Mauthausen is an attractive small town on the north bank of the Danube east of Linz, but its status as a quarrying centre prompted the Nazis to site **KZ Mauthausen** (☎ 22 69; Erinnerungsstrasse 1; adult/concession €2/1; ☺ 9am-5.30pm) concentration camp here. Prisoners were forced into slave labour in the granite quarry and many died on the so-called *Todesstiege* (stairway of death) leading from the quarry to the camp. Some 100,000 prisoners died or were executed in the camp between 1938 and 1945.

The camp, about 3km northwest of the centre, has been turned into a museum, retelling its history, and the history of other camps such as those at Ebensee and Melk.

Visitors can walk through the remaining living quarters (each designed for 200, but housing up to 500) and the see the cramped and disturbing gas chambers. The former Sick Quarters now shelters most of the camp's harrowing material – charts, artefacts and many photos of both prisoners and their SS guards. It is a stark and incredibly moving reminder of human cruelty.

Getting There & Away

From Linz the quickest way to Mauthausen is by train (€4, 30 minutes). You can rent a bike from the station, which eases the 5km journey to the camp (follow the KZ Mauthausen signs).

THE TRAUNVIERTEL

Punctuated with apple orchards and sprawling *Vierkanter* farmhouses, the Traunviertel is a swathe of green and pleasant countryside; the perfect place to kick back, twiddle your thumbs and enjoy the view after a few days in Linz. Gentle hills rise slowly above fields of ripening corn as they roll south towards the Nationalpark Kalkalpen. If the thought of mingling with the locals over *Most* (cider) and drinking fresh-from-the-cow milk at breakfast appeals, overnight in one of the region's farms that offer private rooms. When you tire of all that *Gemütlichkeit* (cosiness), picture-perfect villages, spa towns and cities with cultural clout like Steyr and Wels beckon.

SMALL PLEASURES

Getting on your bike to village-hop through Upper Austria's unspoilt countryside reveals plenty of wee treasures. In the Traunviertel, take a detour to **Adlwang**'s orchards, where tonnes of ripe apples go into making juice, *Most* (cider) and schnapps. At farmhouse **Gangl** (☎ 07258-40 18; Mandorferstrasse 28), Leopold Höllhuber sells award-winning stuff that will knock your socks off.

Pedalling through the gently rolling fields of the Mühlviertel, pause in **Hirschbach** to follow a steep 13km trail up to a high-altitude herb garden, which grows 150 different types of herbs, some famed for their healing properties. Organic peppermint and melissa are among hundreds of varieties for sale at **Bergkräuter-Genossenschaft** (☎ 07948-87 02; Thierberg 32; ☺ 8am-noon & 1-5pm Mon-Fri).

Further west in the misty hills of the Böhmerwald, stop off in sweet-toothed **Bad Leonfelden** for yummy homemade gingerbread. **Kastner** (☎ 07213-63 26-0; Lebzelterstrasse 243; ☺ 8.30am-6pm Mon-Fri, 9am-5pm Sat) has been guarding a secret recipe since 1599; sample freshly baked fruit, nut, honey and chocolate varieties at the bakery shop.

STEYR

☎ 07252 / pop 40,100

Undoubtedly one of the prettiest cities in Upper Austria, Steyr grew fat on the riches of the iron industry in the Middle Ages and it shows: cobbled squares fan out into a warren of alleyways stacked with houses in sweet-shop colours. When the weather warms, the locals pile into gelaterias or spill out onto pavement terraces. The turquoise Enns and Steyr rivers converge here and create a spectacular backdrop for walking and cycling along willow-fringed banks.

Orientation & Information

The pedestrianised town centre is caught between the ice-cold Enns and Steyr, while the *Hauptbahnhof* is situated on the eastern bank of the Enns, eight minutes' walk from the pivotal Stadtplatz. The **tourist office** (☎ 532 29-0; www.steyr.info; Stadtplatz 27; ☺ 8.30am-6pm Mon-Fri, 9am-noon Sat) is on the main square in the Rathaus.

Close to the *Hauptbahnhof* is the **main post office** (Dukartstrasse 13; ☺ 7.30am-6.30pm Mon-Fri, 8am-11pm Sat); the other **post office** (Grünmarkt 1; ☺ 8am-5.30pm Mon-Fri) is more handy to the Stadtplatz.

Sights & Activities

Steyr's compact centre is best explored on foot, with most sights clustering on the Stadtplatz. First up is the 18th-century **Rathaus**, with its church-like belfry and rococo façade. Opposite is the steep-gabled, late-Gothic **Bummerlhaus**

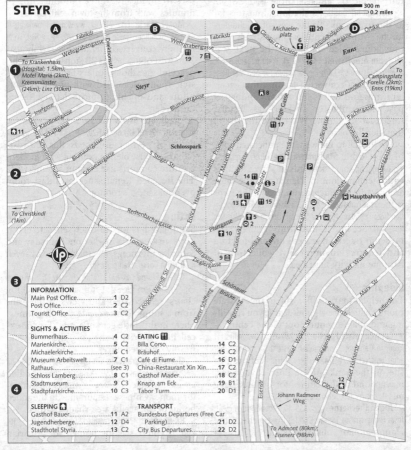

STEYR

```
0          300 m
0          0.2 miles
```

UPPER AUSTRIA

(Stadtplatz 32). In the 19th century, blurry-eyed punters to this former inn called the golden lion on the sign *Bummerl* (small, fat dog) and the name stuck. Also worth a peek is **Franz Schubert's house** (Stadtplatz 16), where he found inspiration to pen the *Trout Quintet*. The southern end of Stadtplatz is dominated by the peaches-and-cream **Marienkirche** (☎ 531 29; Stadtplatz 41; ☾ daylight hr).

Next to the Bummerlhaus, a steep passageway with overhanging arches squeezes through the old city walls and climbs up to **Berggasse**. This narrow street weaves past crumbling frescoes and sculptures to baroque-style **Schloss Lamberg**, towering high above the Steyr River and backing onto the shady **Schlosspark** gardens.

Further north, across the Steyr River, the tall steeple of **Michaelerkirche** (Michaelerplatz; ☾ daylight hr) casts its shadow almost as far as the river bank. To the west of Michaelerkirche – through cobblestoned streets with one house piled on top of the next – is **Museum Arbeitswelt** (☎ 773 51; Wehrgrabengasse 7; adult/concession €5/3.50; ☾ 9am-5pm Tue-Sun Mar-Dec). Housed in a converted factory, this excellent museum delves into Steyr's industrial past with exhibits on working-class history, forced labour during WWII and the rise of the Socialist party.

Up the hill to the west, the punctured spire of the Gothic **Stadtpfarrkirche** (Brucknerplatz 4; ☾ daylight hr) soars skywards. It shares features with Stephansdom in Vienna and the same architect, Hans Puchsbaum. Down the steps is the **Stadtmuseum** (☎ 575 348; Grünmarkt 26; admission free; ☾ 10am-4pm Tue-Sun Apr-Oct, to 4pm Wed-Sun Nov-Mar). Set in a 17th-century granary, the museum traces Steyr's culture and folklore and features an impressive collection of baroque nativity figurines.

Sleeping

The helpful tourist office can arrange private rooms, which are a good deal if you're willing and able to venture out of the centre.

Campingplatz Forelle (☎ 780 08; www.forellesteyr .com, in German; Kematmüllerstrasse 1a; campsites per adult/tent/car €4.70/3/4.40; P) This leafy campsite on the banks of the Enns River has a playground and facilities for cyclists (take bus 1 from the centre).

Jugendherberge (☎ 455 80; jugend@steyr.gv.at; Josef Hafnerstrasse 14; dm €12-15) Just behind the *Hauptbahnhof* (bus 3 runs close), this HI

hostel is bang in the middle of suburbia, but the dorms are totally fine.

Gasthof Bauer (☎ 544 41; Josefgasse 7; s/d €35/62; P) Situated on an island in the Steyr River, this family-run *Gasthof* has a homy ambience, comfy rooms and a chestnut tree-shaded garden. The restaurant (mains €7.50 to €9.50) uses fresh, locally sourced produce. It's 10 minutes' walk from the town centre.

Motel Maria (☎ 710 62; www.motel-maria.at, in German; Reindlgutstrasse 25; s/d €35/70; P) Set in a lovingly converted *Vierkanthof* farmhouse, 2km west of town (bus 2B stops nearby), this peaceful guesthouse offers bright, country-style rooms decorated with pinewood furniture and opening onto balconies facing the garden.

Stadthotel Styria (☎ 515 51; www.stadthotel.at; Stadtplatz 40; s/d €81.60/121.20; P ▣) The grandaddy of Steyr's plush hotels, this 400-year-old townhouse blends vaulting with modern creature comforts like a hammam and wi-fi. The frescoed Renaissance breakfast room overlooks Steyr's rooftops.

Eating

Stadtplatz has lots to offer self-caterers; it hosts an open-air market on Thursday and Saturday mornings, has snack stands, as well as a **Billa Corso** (Stadtplatz 30).

Café di Fiume (☎ 871 21; Michaelerplatz 11; lunch menu €5; ☾ 8am-7pm Tue-Sat, 1-7pm Sun) Mismatching chairs, relaxed staff and views of the Enns from a sunny terrace create a chilled atmosphere in this little gem of a café. Try the excellent vegetarian dishes, organic coffee and freshly squeezed juices.

China-Restaurant Xin Xin (☎ 470 34; Enge Gasse 20; lunch menu €6, mains €7-12.50; ☾ lunch & dinner) Adding a touch of spice to Steyr's mix is this value-for-money Chinese restaurant with the added bonus of a peaceful, tree-shaded garden.

Bräuhof (☎ 420 00; Stadtplatz 35; mains €8-18; ☾ 10-1am) If you're seeking homemade Austrian fare, this lantern-lit restaurant delivers with favourites like gooey *Kasnocken* (cheese noodles). The contemporary wine bar is the place to nibble antipasti with a glass of Rioja.

Gasthof Mader (☎ 533 58; Stadtplatz 36; mains €8-18; ⏰ 10.30am-midnight Mon-Sat) Delicious smells waft out of the kitchen at Mader, where you can nurse a glass of wine in the cellar's red-brick vaults, or feast on fresh seabass in the arcaded inner courtyard.

our pick **Knapp am Eck** (☎ 762 69; www.knappameck.at; Wehrgrabengasse 15; mains €11-19; ⏰ lunch & dinner Tue-Sat, lunch Sun) Down the cobbled lane and beside the fast-flowing Steyr River is this gorgeous tavern with a boho feel. The menu places emphasis on seasonal, local produce; flavours like sage-stuffed pork and lamb with polenta are served at chunky wooden tables. By night, candles and lanterns illuminate the ivy-covered walls, trailing roses and chestnut trees in the secluded garden.

Tabor Turm (☎ 729 49; Taborweg 7; mains €16-24; ⏰ 10.30am-midnight Wed-Sun, to 5pm Mon) A steep climb up to this gourmet haunt (occupying a former church) works up an appetite for specialities such as breast of pigeon with gnocchi. There are panoramic views of Steyr and the misty peaks of Nationalpark Kalkalpen from the terrace.

Getting There & Away

Some trains from Linz (€6.50, 50 minutes) require a change at St Valentin; there are fewer services on Sundays. Trains then continue south into Styria. The *Hauptbahnhof* has a restaurant, a travel information office and left-luggage lockers. For Wels (€10.50, 1¼ hours, hourly), most trains and buses require a change in St Valentin.

Regional buses depart from the *Hauptbahnhof* (where there's also free car parking), while city buses leave from outside the *Hauptbahnhof* to the north. Buses run to Linz (€6.50, 70 minutes) approximately hourly Monday to Friday, less on weekends. Steyr is on Hwy 115, the road branching from the A1/E60 and running south to Leoben.

BAD HALL

☎ 07258 / pop 5200

Situated 18km west of Steyr is the sleepy spa town of Bad Hall, where the big draw is **Tassilo Therme** (☎ 77 30-0; Kurhausstrasse 10; adult/child €12.10/6; ☎ 9am-9pm). The iodine-rich waters that gush from its thermal springs are famed for their therapeutic properties and leave the skin silky smooth. The outdoor pool offers massage jets and views of the Kalkalpen, while inside salt rooms, Roman baths and whirlpools vie for your attention. There's a splash pool to keep tots amused and a separate **sauna complex** (adult/child €15.20/8.40; ⏰ 11am-10pm Mon-Fri, 10am-10pm Sat & Sun) for those who dare to bare.

After drifting away in the spa, a walk in the sculpture-dotted **Kurpark** (⏰ daylight hr) opposite is invigorating. Kids and big kids love making a noise on the *Klangskulpturen*, larger-than-life musical instruments that include a glockenspiel and wind harp. To inhale the iodized salt for free, head for the central pavilion, where 1000L of the stuff filters through twig walls every hour.

A number of family-run farmhouses and guesthouses in Bad Hall offer good-value rooms; expect to pay €15 to €20 per person. Pick up a list at the **tourist office** (☎ 07258-72 00; www.badhall.at; Kurpromenade 1; ⏰ 8.30am-4pm Mon-Fri, 9am-noon Sat).

From Steyr, there are frequent buses to Bad Hall (€4, 35 minutes).

NATIONALPARK KALKALPEN

The Nationalpark Kalkalpen is a diverse and almost untouched wilderness of jagged limestone pinnacles, high moors and pristine forest. Bordering Styria, the reserve is Austria's second-largest national park after Hohe Tauern. Its valleys and gorges cut through classic alpine landscapes, dominated by **Hoher Nock** (1963m), the park's highest peak. It's particularly popular with hikers, cyclists, rock-climbers and cross-country skiers who come to glide across the glistening snow in winter.

Information on the park is available from **Nationalpark Zentrum Molln** (☎ 07584-36 51; www.kalkalpen.at, in German; Nationalpark Allee 1; ☎ 8am-5pm Mon-Fri, 9am-5pm Apr-Oct), an ultramodern, eco-friendly centre near the northern entrance to the park; staff can help with accommodation, including the 15 mountain huts within the park. A good map covering walking, cycling and cross-country skiing trails of the park is Kompass map 70 (1:50,000). Regular direct buses from Steyr to Molln (€4.90, one hour) normally only run on weekdays.

KREMSMÜNSTER

☎ 07583 / pop 6440

Looming large above the fertile Krems Valley, Kremsmünster's bombastic **Benedictine abbey**

(☎ 07583-5275-150; www.stift-kremsmuenster.at, in German; Stift 1; adult/child/family €6.50/3/14; ☼ tours 10am, 11am, 2pm, 3pm & 4pm Apr-Oct, 11am, 2pm & 3.30pm Nov-Mar) dates to 777, but was given a baroque facelift in the early 18th century. Elaborate stuccowork and frescoes shape the long, low **Bibliothek** (library), where shelves creak under the weight of 160,000 volumes, and **Kaisersaal** (Emperor's Hall). The most priceless piece in the **Schatzkammer** (treasury) is the gold Tassilo Chalice, which the Duke of Bavaria donated to the monks in around 780. You can visit all three on a one-hour guided tour.

The star attraction is the 50m-high **Sternwarte** (observatory tower; adult/child/family €7.50/3/14; ☼ tours 10am & 2pm May-Oct), dedicated to numerous schools of natural history. Spanning seven floors, the mind-boggling collection steps from fossilised starfish to the skeleton of an Ice Age cave bear. It's a giddy climb up a spiral staircase to the top floor, which displays the Keppler sextant and affords a bird's-eye perspective of Kremsmünster and the gently rolling countryside.

What can be seen without greasing the palms of the abbey with silver are the **Stiftskirche** (☼ daylight hr) and **Fischbehälter** (Fish Basin; ☼ 10am-4pm). The marvellously over-the-top baroque church is crisscrossed with white stuccowork, draped in Flemish tapestries and festooned with dark, brooding paintings. The Fischbehälter's cloisters are quite a surprise; built in 1690, they comprise five fish ponds, each centred on a mythological statue. The trickle of water is calming and you can feed the carp (for €0.20).

Getting There & Away

Kremsmünster is on the rail line between Linz and Graz (from Linz €7.60, 40 minutes); the longest you'll have to wait for a train is 1½ hours. Buses from Wels (€3.30, 30 minutes, Monday to Friday only) and Steyr (€5.70, 50 minutes) run on a regular basis.

WELS

☎ 07242 / pop 61,637

What lies on the surface is only half the story in Wels, a Roman-rooted city with hidden inner courtyards, secret gardens and a smattering of Renaissance architecture. The largest city in the Traunviertel, Wels is an excellent base to explore Linz (15 minutes away) and slip under the skin of rural Upper Austria. When the weather warms, the centre comes alive with open-air concerts, film festivals and markets.

Information, maps and audio guides (€4) of the city are available from **Tourismusverband Wels** (☎ 434 95; www.stadtmarketing-wels.at; Kaiser-Josef-Platz 22; ☼ 9am-6pm Mon-Fri), two blocks north of the main square, Stadtplatz.

Sights & Activities

Most of the action centres on the **Stadtplatz**, which is framed by slender townhouses that conceal arcaded inner courtyards. Pick of the bunch is the ivy-clad courtyard at Stadtplatz 18, nurturing palms, rhododendrons and Japanese umbrella trees. At the front, glance up to spy the 2000-year-old *Römermedallion* (Roman medallion) relief.

Nearby the **Haus der Salome Alt** (House of Salome Alt; Stadtplatz 24) takes its name from one-time occupant Salome Alt, mistress of Salzburg's Prince-Archbishop Wolf Dietrich. The illusionary red-and-cream Renaissance façade stretches back to the serene flower gardens fringing Burg Wels. Opposite is the refreshingly simplistic **Stadtpfarrkirche** (☼ daylight hr), where light illuminates the Gothic stained glass. The medieval **Ledererturm** tower, built in 1376, overshadows the western end of Stadtplatz.

Just behind the Haus der Salome Alt, **Burg Wels** is where Maximilian I drew his last breath in 1519. The castle **museum** (☎ 235 7350; Burggasse 13; adult/concession €4.15/1.60; ☼ 10am-5pm Tue-Fri, 2-5pm Sat, 10am-4pm Sun) showcases everything from canon balls to Biedermeier costumes. Must-see exhibits are the horse-drawn cider press and the cylinder-shaped room that's a shrine to traditional baking, with walls smothered in animal-shaped pastries and enormous pretzels.

Sleeping & Eating

The friendly tourist office staff can help you find somewhere to stay. In summer, the Stadtplatz and its tributaries offer alfresco dining with a lively vibe.

Jugendherberge (☎ 23 57 570; jugendherberge@ wels.at; Dragonerstrasse 22; dm with/without shower €13.35/11.45; ℗) A five-minute stroll northwest of Stadtplatz, this laid-back HI hostel features spacious dorms and a common room with cable TV.

Kremsmünstererhof (☎ 466 23; Stadtplatz 62/63; s/d €48/68; ℗) Set in a 15th-century townhouse with an inner courtyard, this three-star hotel on the main square has large, light-filled rooms with parquet floors, sunny paint-jobs and bold poppy prints.

Café Urban (☎ 460 51; Schmidtgasse 20; cake around €2; ☻ 8.30am-6.30pm Mon-Fri, 8am-1pm Sat) This convivial café's glass counter is piled high with hard-to-resist pralines and pastries – try the famous *Igel*, a hedgehog-shaped meringue.

Olivi (☎ 91 19 00; Hafergasse 3; mains €6-9; ☻ lunch & dinner Mon-Sat) This popular pizzeria serves tasty antipasti and wood-fired pizza in a buzzy setting.

Knödelwirt (☎ 472 05; Grünbachplatz 14; mains €6-10; ☻ lunch & dinner Tue-Sun) It's best not to count calories at this rustic tavern dishing up homemade *Knödel* (dumplings), including spinach, potato, strawberry and plum varieties.

Jaxx (☎ 911 956; Stadtplatz 52; ☻ 4pm-2am Sun-Thur, to 4am Fri-Sat) Perfect for late-night nibbles, Jaxx is a funky café that morphs into a party haunt by night. Munch Snaax open sandwiches (tasty little morsels at €1 a piece) on the terrace.

Getting There & Away
Trains and buses arrive at the *Hauptbahnhof*, 1.25km north of Stadtplatz. The town is on the InterCity (IC) and EuroCity (EC) express rail route between Linz and Salzburg, just 15 minutes southwest of Linz (€4, several per hour). There's also a line running to Passau (€12.20, one hour and 20 minutes, hourly) on the German border.

THE MÜHLVIERTEL

A region of misty pine forests and hills speckled with chalk-white *Steinbloass* farmhouses, you can feel you're close to Bohemia in the Mühlviertel – and not just because there's decent beer and goulash! Scratch the surface to discover a mysteriously beautiful corner of Upper Austria with abundant Gothic architecture and warm-hearted locals. Separating Linz from the Czech Republic, this offbeat region is the sort of place where you're more likely to come face-to-face with a cow than a tourist. It's pure escapism.

FREISTADT
☎ 07942 / pop 7200

A mere hop and a skip from the Czech border, Freistadt has the best-preserved fortifications of all the medieval towns in Austria and the beer isn't bad either – the nectar-loving locals are apparently so passionate about *Freistädter* brews that they avoid places where it isn't on tap. Beer aside, much pleasure can be had strolling the town's narrow streets to admire medieval gate towers and relax in the gardens that have taken root in the original moat.

Orientation & Information
The Hauptplatz is the focal point of the town centre, jammed between the old city walls. Here you'll find the **Mühlviertler Kernland tourist office** (☎ 757 00; kernland@oberoesterreich.at; Hauptplatz 14; ☻ 9am-noon & 2-4pm Mon-Fri, 2-5pm Sat & Sun), which provides information on the town and its surrounds. The main north–south route, connecting Linz with the Czech border, skirts the western section of the city walls; the local **post office** (Promenade 11) is located here.

Sights & Activities
Pick up the handy *City Walk* brochure from the tourist office, which pinpoints Freistadt's key attractions. Topping the list are the sturdy 14th-century **city walls** complete with gate towers – particularly the medieval **Linzertor** and skeletal **Böhmertor** – which reflect Freistadt's past need for strong defences as an important staging point on the salt route to Bohemia. The moat encircling the town is now given over to gardens and allotments.

The elongated **Hauptplatz** has some attention-grabbing buildings with ornate façades, such as the Gothic **Stadtpfarrkirche** (☻ daylight hr) capped with a baroque tower. Waaggasse, just west of the Hauptplatz, is lined with striking architecture, including some sgraffito designs.

Just beyond the Hauptplatz is the city's 14th-century **Schloss**, with a square tower topped by a tapering red-tiled roof. Inside is the **Schlossmuseum** (☎ 722 74; Schlosshof 2; adult/concession €2.40/1.60; ☻ 9am-noon & 2-5pm Mon-Fri, 2-5pm Sat), exhibiting 600 works of engraved painted glass. Climb the 50m Bergfried tower for far-reaching views over Freistadt.

Sleeping & Eating
Freistadt has a handful of decent places to sleep and eat; the following recommendations (apart from Camping Freistadt) are in the old town.

Camping Freistadt (☎ 725 70; Eglsee 12; campsites per adult/child/car/tent €4/2.50/3/4.50; P) This shady camping ground on the banks of the Feldaisth

---

BUYING INTO YOUR FAVOURITE BEER

Freistadt is a *Braucommune*, a town where the citizens actually own their brewery – buy a house and you automatically buy a share of your favourite tipple. Ownership is limited to the 149 households within the town walls, but if you have the spare change and *really* like your beer, properties sell for around €350,000. Realistically, the brewery cannot be taken over, as the business would have to buy the whole town in order to take control.

The arrangement started way back in 1777 when the brewery opened. In the ensuing centuries the lucky owners would receive their share of the profits in liquid form, which would be distributed in *Eimer Bier* containers holding 56L. Each owner might get up to 130 containers! Nowadays, for better or worse, owners get a cash payment of equivalent value (which, on Friday and Saturday nights, often goes straight back to the brewery).

Practically every bar in town serves the local brew, so it's not hard to see why the brewery remains a profitable business. If you'd like to learn more about Freistadt beer, there are **tours** (☎ 757 77; Promenade 7; www.freistaedter-bier.at; brewery tours €7.50; ☼ tours 2pm Wed) of the brewery; three small beers are thrown in with the price of the tour. Call ahead if you'd like to take a tour.

River is five minutes' walk northeast of the centre. The great facilities include table tennis and a sauna.

Pension Pirklbauer (☎ 724 40; pension.pirklbauer@ aon.at; Höllgasse 2-4; s/d €25/42) Nudging up against medieval Linzertor is this charming pension. Christine is a dab hand at making her guests feel at home: from the rooftop terrace to country cottage-style rooms with pinewood, floral fabrics and squeaky-clean bathrooms.

Hotel Goldener Adler (☎ 721 12; goldener.adler@ hotels-freistadt.at; Salzgasse 1; s/d €49/78; P 🖵 🕾) Polished stone slabs, wrought iron banisters and vaulted passages crammed with antique wagons and spinning wheels give the Goldener Adler its unique edge. Unwind in the sauna and whirlpool, or tuck into the famous beer-marinated Bohemian pork shoulder in the beer garden (mains €6-16).

Vis à Vis (☎ 742 93; Salzgasse 13; pizzas €6-7; ☼ 9am-2am Mon-Fri, 5pm-2am Sat) Pretzels dangle on racks at the bar at this cheery local haunt with a sunny conservatory. The kitchen whips up tasty pizzas (including vegetarian options), salads and generous portions of Austrian fare.

Getting There & Away

Freistadt is on a direct rail route from Linz (€7.70, one hour, hourly). This line then wriggles its way north to Prague; Czech rail fares are lower than those in Austria, so you can save money by waiting and buying (in Czech currency) your onward tickets once you've crossed the border.

Highway 125, the main route to and from Linz, runs adjacent to the walled cen-tre and then continues its way northwards towards Prague.

KEFERMARKT
☎ 07947 / pop 2100

It's silent enough to hear a pin drop in the tiny village of Kefermarkt, home to the **Pfarrkirche St Wolfgang** (☎ 62 03; Oberer Markt 1; ☼ approx 7am-8pm). The pilgrimage church's main claim to fame is its breathtaking Gothic *Flügelaltar* (winged altar). A masterpiece of craftsmanship, the limewood altarpiece towers 13.5m, with latticework fronds rising towards the ceiling. At the centre are three expressive figures, carved with great skill (left to right as you face them): St Peter, St Wolfgang and St Christopher. The wings of the altar bear religious scenes in low relief.

ourpick **Schlossbrauerei Weinberg** (☎ 71 11; Weinberg 2; s/d €29/50; ☎ lunch & dinner Tue-Sun; P) Perched on a hill overlooking the forest and Schloss Weinberg's red turrets is this brewery guesthouse, 10 minutes' walk from Kefermarkt. The affable owners serve home-brews and specialities like beer-drenched goulash, beer-battered schnitzel and fresh-from-the-pond trout in the vaulted restaurant (mains €6-10) or on the chestnut tree-shaded terrace. After a beer (or three), you'll sleep like a baby in one of the quiet rooms with porthole-like windows that afford snapshot views of the castle.

Four daily trains (more on weekdays) travel between Kefermarkt and Freistadt (€1.60, 10 minutes). The church is about 1km north of the train station.

THE INNVIERTEL

Ping-ponged between Bavaria and Austria over the centuries, the Innviertel is a fertile farming region sliced in two by the Inn River, whose banks are a drawcard for cyclists in summer. As well as beautiful baroque and Gothic architecture in Schärding and Braunau, the region has a few other surprises worth sticking around for: from overnighting in a treehouse (p218) to splashing around in a Caribbean lagoon.

BRAUNAU AM INN

☎ 07722 / pop 16,700

A stone's throw from Germany, Braunau am Inn is a favourite pit-stop for cyclists pedalling the Inn Trail to Innsbruck (p78). This border town has achieved unwanted attention as the birthplace of Hitler, though it would prefer to be described as *die gotische Stadt* (the Gothic city).

The long main square, **Stadtplatz**, is lined with elegant homes in pastel shades. At the northern end is the **tourist office** (☎ 626 44; www .tourismus-braunau.at; Stadtplatz 2; ⏰ 8.30am-6pm Mon-Fri, 9am-noon Sat), while its southern end narrows to the **Torturm**, a 16th-century gate tower. To the west of Stadtplatz rises the spire of late-Gothic **Stadtpfarrkirche St Stephan** (Kirchenplatz; ⏰ daylight hr). At almost 100m, it's one of the tallest in Austria.

Not far from the Torturm is **Hitler's Geburtshaus** (birth house); born in 1889, he only spent two years of his life here before moving with his family to Linz. The inscription outside his birth house simply reads *Für Frieden Freiheit und Demokratie, nie wieder Faschismus, millionen Tote Mahnen* (For peace, freedom and democracy, never again fascism, millions of dead admonish).

Sleeping & Eating

Jugendherberge (☎ 816 38; int.osternberg.braunau@ aon.at; Osternbergerstrasse 57; dm €15; ⏰ Feb-Nov; P) Directly on the Inn–Danube cycle path, this hostel 1km south of the Stadtplatz is well set up for cyclists.

Hotel Mayrbräu (☎ 633 387; Linzer Strasse 13; s/d €39/62; P) This four-star hotel's large, warm rooms are good value. A vaulted gallery full of contemporary art and a vine-clad inner courtyard add flair to the place.

Bogner (☎ 683 43; Stadtplatz 47; mains €7-10; ⏰ 9am-1am) Supposedly Austria's smallest brewery,

> ### STANDING BY YOUR NAME
>
> In the far western corner of the Innviertel stands a tiny village with a big name, Fucking (pronounced 'fooking'). Naturally the name has caused a few giggles, and a few problems along the way (signs go missing all the time), but the village is *stolz* (proud) of its unique name. Recently residents were asked to vote on a name change but decided to stick with it; village spokesman Siegfried Hoeppl stated that 'Everyone here knows what it means in English, but for us Fucking is Fucking – and it's going to stay Fucking.' The name derives from a certain Herr Fuck who settled in the area some 100 years ago.

Bogner is a rustic pub-restaurant with solid Austrian fare and several home-brewed beers to guzzle.

Getting There & Away

By train, at least one change is normally required from either Linz (€15.40, 2¼ hours) or Salzburg (€11.10, 1½ hours) by train. From Wels, there are two daily direct trains (€13.80, 1½ hours).

SCHÄRDING

☎ 07712 / pop 5200

Schärding is an easy-going town on the Inn River, with peaceful riverfront walks and a baroque centre studded with merchants' houses in myriad pastel shades.

The **tourist office** (☎ 43 00-0; www.schaerding.at; Innbruckstrasse 29; ⏰ 9am-6pm Mon-Fri & 11am-3pm Sat & Sun Jun-Sep, 9am-5pm Mon-Fri Oct-Mar), near the bridge spanning the river into Germany, is a mine of information on the town. Look no further than the **Silberziele** (silver row), a line of richly coloured houses with identically shaped gables, for accommodation and food. **Pension Lachinger** (☎ 22 68; Silberzeile 13; s/d €29/48; P) and **Haus Mayr** (☎ 30 80; Silberzeile 8; s/d €30/52) are two uncomplicated pensions with comfy rooms and friendly staff.

If you have your own transport, the approach to Schärding from Linz, via Engelhartszell along the Danube, is beautiful and certainly off the beaten track. A more leisurely alternative is a boat trip between Passau (see p208) and **Schärding** (☎ 73 50; www .innschifffahrt.at, in German; Kaiserweg 1; adult/child one-way

UPPER AUSTRIA

HIGH ABOVE THE TREETOPS

Tarzan wannabes shouldn't miss the chance to take a head-spinning walk above the treetops at **Baumkronenweg** (☎ 07763-228 92-0; www.baumkronenweg.at; Kopfing; adult/child €6/3.50 ☽ 10am-6pm Apr-Oct), a new canopy boardwalk in Kopfing, 21km east of Schärding. Stretching 2.5km, the trail is billed as one of the longest in the world and it's certainly a stunner – snaking high above misty spruce trees and comprising lookout towers, hanging bridges and platforms that afford bird's-eye perspectives over the forest. For a room with a view, check into the 10m-high **Baumhotel** (r €62-80), six pine-built tree houses perched on stilts. After some quality shut-eye, you'll awake to birds twittering in the treetops. Hotels don't get much greener than this…

€6/3, return €9/4; ☽ 11am, 2pm & 4pm Apr-Oct). Trains connect Linz with Schärding (€12.20, 80 minutes) roughly every hour.

GEINBERG
☎ 07723 / pop 1350

Sandwiched between Braunau am Inn and Schärding, Geinberg is making waves with **Therme Geinberg** (☎ 85 00-0; www.therme-geinberg .at; Thermenplatz 1; 4hr ticket adult/child €13/9.30 Mon-Fri, €15/11.30 weekends; ☽ 9am-10pm Sat-Thu, to 11pm Fri), one of Austria's top spas. In the heart of rural Upper Austria, it's a surreal experience to soak in a bath-warm Caribbean saltwater lagoon,

as underwater music plays and palms sway, but it certainly beats a chilly dip in the Inn. In the adjoining complex, saunas imitate a starry sky or smell deliciously of coconuts. After a steam, the icy sleet shower is quite a shocker. For those who want to be pampered, the Vitalzentrum offers an arm-long list of treatments, from hot stone therapy to underwater massage.

Trains operate roughly every hour between Braunau am Inn and Geinberg weekdays, less frequently at weekends (€4, 20 minutes). There are several trains daily between Schärding and Geinberg (€7.30, one hour).

Styria

Styria (Steiermark) is Austria's best-kept secret. When you ask someone in Austria for advice on the best places to visit in their country, and they answer with the mountains of Tyrol, the lakes of Salzkammergut and the cultural joys of Vienna, they're just trying to keep you out of Styria.

Austria's second-largest province is a perfect combination of culture, architecture, rolling hills, vine-covered slopes and, of course, mountains. Its capital Graz, Austria's second-largest city and among its most attractive, has one of the highest standards of living in Europe. Head south from Graz and you're in wine country, dubbed the 'Styrian Tuscany' for its uncanny resemblance to that region of glorious wine and golden sun. This is also *Kürbiskernöl* (strong, dark pumpkin-seed oil ubiquitous in Styrian cooking) country.

The eastern stretch of Styria is dotted with rejuvenating thermal spas and centuries-old castles. If you're a fan of the former, Bad Blumau is a mandatory stop, not only to take the waters but also to appreciate its unusual architecture, created from the rich imagination of Friedensreich Hundertwasser. If you prefer the latter, Schloss Riegersburg stands head and shoulders above most castles, not only in Styria, but the entire country.

The landscape of Styria's northern and western reaches is an untamed region of cold, fast-flowing alpine rivers, towering mountains and carved valleys. Complementing the area's natural wonders is a handful of man-made gems, including Admont Abbey and the Erzberg open-cast mine.

Note that the northwestern reaches of Styria stretch into Salzkammergut.

HIGHLIGHTS

- Exploring Styria's capital **Graz** (p232) and its bars and clubs
- Catching one of the fascinating changing exhibitions at **MuseumsCenter Leoben** (p241)
- Visiting Admont's spectacular **abbey** (p243) and exploring its fascinating museums
- Tripping underground, or overground, at Eisenerz's **open-cast mine** (p242)
- Cruising the mountain bike trails around **Mariazell** (p238)

★ Mariazell
Admont ★   ★ Eisenerz
★ Leoben
★ Graz

STYRIA

■ POPULATION: 1.2 MILLION   ■ AREA: 16,392 SQ KM   ■ HIGHEST ELEVATION: HOCHGOLLING 2862M

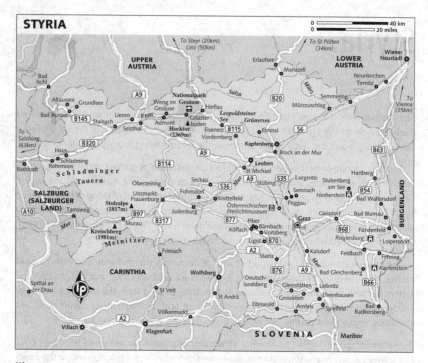

STYRIA

History

Habitation of Styria dates back to the Stone Age, and findings from the Bronze and Iron Ages are on display in Grossklein (p236). The Celts, then the Romans, followed by the Avars and Slavs, settled in the area, but it wasn't until the 11th century that Styria as a region gained its current name. At the time, Ottakar I, whose base was in the Upper Austrian town of Steyr, acquired the area through succession and stamped his seal *Marchia Styriae* (Styrian Mark) on the province. The name stuck.

When Duke Ottokar IV died without an heir in 1192, Styria passed to the Babenberg duke Leopold V. Control fell to King Ottokar II of Bohemia (see p30) and then finally, in 1276, into the hands of the Habsburgs. In the next century the population grew, but there followed two centuries of local conflicts and invasions by the Turks and Hungarians. The year 1480 was particularly dire; it was known as the year of the 'Plagues of God' – the Turks, the Black Death and locusts. Exactly 200 years later one-quarter of Graz's population was obliterated in another plague epidemic.

In the 16th and 17th centuries Reformation and Counter-Reformation wracked the province, with the Habsburg army running riot and burning anything Protestant it could find. Once religious peace returned, and the Turkish threat was removed after 1683, the region prospered. Then, in 1779, and again in 1805 and 1809, it was the turn of the French to invade. After the Nazi occupation of WWII, the first Allied troops to liberate the area were from the Soviet Union, followed by the British, who occupied Graz until 1955.

Climate

Styria is a tale of two climes; southern Styria enjoys a relatively kind climate, influenced by the Pannonian (west Hungarian) plain to the east, while much of northern Styria is subject to alpine climatic conditions.

Getting There & Away

The A2, from Vienna to Villach in Klagenfurt, runs through southern Styria, passing just below Graz, while the A9 runs an almost north–south course through the middle of Styria, making it straightforward to travel from Linz and Salzburg to Graz. The A9 also connects Graz with Slovenia, 40km to the south.

Styria's train lines are relatively sparse; the main line between Carinthia and Vienna passes well north of Graz through the region's main railhead, Bruck an der Mur. For Linz and Salzburg, a change is usually required at St Michael, 25km southwest of Bruck.

Getting Around

Regional and city transport (☎ 0316-82 06 06; www .verbundlinie.at) is based on a system of zones and time tickets. Tickets can be bought from machines for one to 22 zones, and the price rises from a single trip in one zone (€1.70, valid for one hour), to 24-hour passes for one (€3.70) or multiple zones (€55.80 for 22 zones and all of Styria). Weekly and monthly passes are also available.

In Graz, **Mobilzentral** (Map p224; ☎ 0316-82 06 06; www.mobilzentral.at, in German; Jakoministrasse 1; ☺ 8am-6pm Mon-Fri, 9am-1pm Sat) is a useful store of information on Styrian regional buses. It also sells international train tickets. The website www.busbahnbim.at has timetable and price information.

GRAZ
☎ 0316 / pop 287,700
Austria's second-largest city is possibly Austria's most relaxed, and after Vienna it is also Austria's liveliest for after-hours pursuits. It's an attractive place with bristling green parkland, red rooftops and a small, fast-flowing river gushing through its centre. Architecturally, it complements Renaissance courtyards and provincial baroque palaces with cutting-edge modern designs that fascinate, provoke or arouse curiosity.

The surrounding countryside, a mixture of vineyards, mountains, forested hills and thermal springs, is within easy striking distance, and Graz has a very beautiful bluff connected to the centre by steps, a funicular and a glass lift. Last but not least, a large student population (some 50,000 in four universities) helps propel the nightlife and vibrant arts scene, creating a pleasant, lively and liveable city.

History
Graz is a derivation of the Slav word *gradec*, meaning small fortress, and developed from a Bavarian settlement that was first documented in 1128. By 1189 Graz was a city, and in 1379

it became the seat of the Leopold line of the Habsburgs. Friedrich III, emperor of Austria and the Holy Roman Empire, resided here and left his famous motto, AEIOU (*Austria Est Imperare Orbi Universo*; Austria rules the world) inscribed all over town. In 1564, Graz became the administrative capital of Inner Austria, an area covering present-day Styria and Carinthia, plus the former possessions of Carniola, Gorizia and Istria. In 1784, with the Turks no longer a threat, Graz tore down its city walls.

Early in the 19th century Archduke Johann, benign brother of Franz I, founded the first museum in Austria, the Joanneum, in Graz. In the late 1990s the historic centre of Graz achieved the status of a Unesco World Heritage site.

Orientation
Schlossberg rises over the medieval town centre, the river Mur cuts a north–south path west of this bluff and the *Hauptbahnhof* (main train station) is 1km further west of here.

Trams 3 and 6 run from the *Hauptbahnhof* to Hauptplatz. Radiating from Hauptplatz is Sporgasse, an important shopping street, and Herrengasse, the main pedestrian thoroughfare. At the southern end of Herrengasse is Jakominiplatz, a major transport hub for local buses and trams.

MAPS
Graztourismus has an excellent free map of the central city, and also a great *city & environs* map; Freytag & Berndt's *Graz* (€3.95; scale 1:15,000) city map is also useful.

Information
BOOKSHOPS
English Bookshop (Map p224; ☎ 82 62 66; Tummelplatz 7; ☺ 9am-6pm Mon-Fri, to 2pm Sat) Lots of English books, but at a price.
Freytag & Berndt (Map p224; ☎ 81 82 30; Sporgasse 29; ☺ 10am-6.30pm Mon-Fri, 9am-5pm Sat) The best source of maps and guidebooks.

INTERNET ACCESS
High Speed Internet-Selfstore (Map p224; ☎ 0650-89 16 900; Herrengasse 3; per hr €3; ☺ 7am-10pm) A coin-operated internet space inside the passage.
Speednet Cafe (Map p222; ☎ 228 412; www.speed net-cafe.com, in German; Europaplatz 4; per hr €5.80; ☺ 7am-10.30pm Mon-Fri, 9am-10.30pm Sat & Sun) Located in the train station.

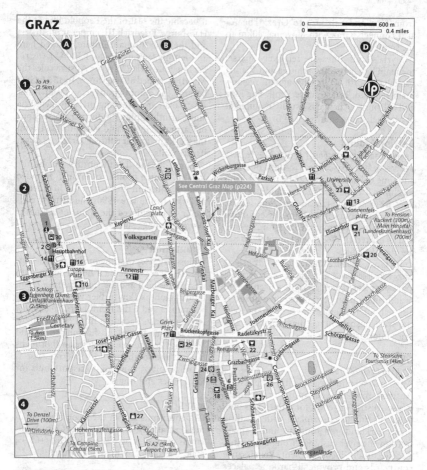

GRAZ

INTERNET RESOURCES
www.graz.at Provides a snapshot of most aspects of the city.
www.graztourismus.at The city's excellent tourist information portal.
www.info-graz.at Practical information on life in Graz; in German.

LAUNDRY
Putzerei-Rupp (Map p222; ☎ 82 11 83; Jakoministrasse 34; ☒ 8am-5pm Mon-Fri) One useful self-service laundry.

LEFT LUGGAGE
Lockers (small/large €2/3.50 for 24 hours) are inside the train station.

LIBRARIES
Steiermärkische Landesbiblothek (Map p224; ☎ 877 4600; Kalchberggasse 2; ☒ 8.30am-5pm Mon-Fri early Sep-early Jul, to 1pm early Jul-early Sep) The main library of Graz.

MEDICAL SERVICES
Landeskrankenhaus (off Map p222; ☎ 385-0; Auenbruggerplatz 1) The city's largest hospital; provides emergency treatment. It's about 3km from the town centre.
Unfallkrankenhaus (off Map p222; ☎ 505-0; Göstinger strasse 24) Emergency hospital at tram 1 terminus.

MONEY
The *Hauptbahnhof* has two ATMS.
Bankhaus Krentschker (Map p224; ☎ 80 30-0; Am Eisernen Tor 3; ☒ 8.30am-4.15pm Mon-Wed,

to 5.30pm Thu, to 3pm Fri) American Express representative in Graz.

Steiermärkische Sparkasse (Map p224; ☎ 050100 36 018; Schmiedegasse; ☯ 8.30am-12.30pm & 1.30-4pm Mon-Thu, 8.30am-3pm Fri) Full banking services.

POST

Hauptbahnhof post office (Map p222; Bahnhof; ☯ 7am-10pm Mon-Fri, 8am-8pm Sat, 1-8pm Sun) This post office is located inside the station.

Main post office (Map p224; Neutorgasse 46; ☯ 8am-8pm Mon-Fri, to 1pm Sat)

TOURIST INFORMATION

Graztourismus (Map p224; ☎ 80 75-0; www.graztour ismus.at; Herrengasse 16; ☯ 10am-5pm Mon-Fri, to 4pm Sat, Jan-Mar & Nov, to 6pm Mon-Sat, to 4pm Sun Apr-Jun,

Sep, Oct & Dec, to 7pm Mon-Fri, to 6pm Sat & Sun Jul & Aug) Graz's main tourist office, with loads of free information on the city, and helpful and knowledgeable staff. Inside the train station (Map p222) is an information stand and terminal, and a free hotline to the tourist office.

TRAVEL AGENCIES

STA (Map p224; ☎ 82 62 62-0; graz@statravel.at; Raubergasse 20; ☯ 9am-5.30pm Mon-Fri) Nationwide travel agency specialising in student travel.

Sights

Most of Graz's museums are under the tutelage of the Landesmuseum Joanneum. Entry to the Kunsthaus Graz, Neue Galerie, Schloss Eggenberg or the Landeszeughaus, including their special exhibitions, entitles you to a day

---

GRAZ IN...

One Day

Begin the morning with a coffee and cake at **Edegger-Tax** (p231) before hitting the slug-like **Kunsthaus** (p226). Grab a quick midday refreshment on the **Murinsel** (p227) and, if the kids are around, they can run riot in the small playground. Climb **Schlossberg** (p225) and take in the views from the terrace of the **Garisson Museum** (p225) before lunching at **Aiola Upstairs** (p230). Dedicate a leisurely afternoon to **Schloss Eggenberg** (p226), not missing the **Alte Galerie**, and in the early evening have a snack and quaff a wine at the bar of **Iohan** (p231) before drifting over to a table or moving to **Landhauskeller** (p231) for a full meal. After dinner, chill out in a **Bermuda Triangle** bar (p231).

Two Days

After day one, drop by the market at **Lendplatz** (p231) and later catch up on the Habsburgs by visiting the **Mausoleum of Ferdinand II** (p225). Afterwards nip into the **Domkirche** (p225) before retiring to **Promenade** (p231) in the **Stadtpark** (p225) for a light meal. Write some postcards here or stroll through the shady park, and later get a feel for medieval armoury in the **Landeszeughaus** (p224) before depriving your senses in the samadhi bath in the **Museum der Wahrnehmung** (p226). In the evening, catch a performance at the **Opernhaus** (p233) or **Schauspielhaus** (p233).

STYRIA

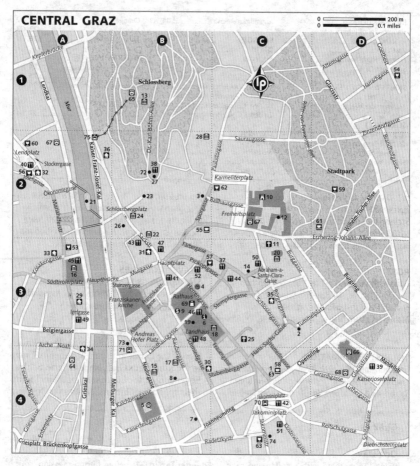

CENTRAL GRAZ

ticket for any of these. The two-day Joanneum pass (€12) covers most city museums.

HAUPTPLATZ & AROUND

The **Landesmuseum Joanneum** (Map p224; ☎ 8017 9740; www.museum-joanneum.at; Raubergasse 10; adult/child & student/family €5.50/2/11; ☑ 3-6pm Tue-Sat), founded in 1811, is Austria's oldest museum and, with 19 locations, is pretty much the gardener of Graz's rich cultural landscape. Its Raubergasse building is home to collections on geology and palaeontology, minerals and zoology, as well as one on botany (only open to groups). (Note that these restricted hours apply while it's being renovated – until about 2011).

The **Landeszeughaus** (provincial armoury; Map p224; ☎ 80 17 98 10; Herrengasse 16; adult/child & student €7/3,

tour €2.50 extra; ☑ 10am-6pm Apr-Oct, to 3pm Mon-Sat, to 4pm Sun Nov-Mar) will quite possibly rate as your favourite Austrian museum if you have a passion for armour and weapons. It houses an astounding array of gleaming pieces (more than 30,000 in fact). Most of these date from the 17th century, when the original armoury was built, and some of it is exquisitely engraved; other exhibits are rough and ready and have seen battle. This is heavy metal territory – you'll find equipment here (such as the two-handed swords) that would need a Schwarzenegger to wield it.

The stained glass window of the **Stadtpfarrkirche** (town parish church; Map p224; Herrengasse 23; admission free; ☑ dawn-dusk), southeast of the

Landeszeughaus, is an interesting anomaly: the fourth panel from the bottom on the right (left of the high altar) clearly shows Hitler and Mussolini looking on as Christ is scourged.

SCHLOSSBERG
Rising to 473m, Schlossberg is the site of the original fortress that gave Graz its name. Its wooded slopes can be reached by a number of paths, with the funicular **Schlossbergbahn** (Castle Hill Railway; Map p224; free with public transport ticket) from Kaiser-Franz-Josef-Kai, or by **Glass Lift** (Map p224; free with public transport ticket) from Schlossbergplatz. Even Napoleon was hard-pressed to raze this fortress, but raze it he did. The whole area was later landscaped and today an open-air theatre (Map p224), a great restaurant-bar and a small **Garrison Museum** (Map p224; ☎ 82 73 48; Schlossberg 5a; adult/child €1/free; ☉ 10am-4.30pm Tue-Sun) are the legacy. Perched on the southern edge of Schlossberg is the city's emblem, the **Uhrturm** (Clock Tower; Map p224). In what must have been a good deal for Europe's modernising midget, the townsfolk paid Napoleon a ransom of 2987 florins and 11 farthings to spare the clock tower during the 1809 invasion.

THE BURG & AROUND
Southeast of Schlossberg is the city's 15th-century **Burg** (Map p224; Hofgasse), now housing government offices. At the far end of the courtyard, on the left under the arch, is an ingenious **double staircase** (1499; Map p224) – the steps diverge and converge as they spiral. Farther east is the **Stadtpark** (Map p224), the city's largest green space.

Opposite the Burg is the **Domkirche** (Map p224; ☎ 82 16 83-0; Burggasse 3; admission free; ☉ dawn-dusk), a late-Gothic church dating from the 15th century that became a cathedral in 1786. The interior combines Gothic and baroque elements, with reticulated vaulting on the ceiling, but its highlight is the faded *Gottesplagenbild* fresco on the cathedral's exterior, which dates from 1485. It depicts life in the early 1480s, when Graz was besieged by its triple tragedy of Turks, the plague and locusts.

Next door is the mannerist-baroque **Mausoleum of Ferdinand II** (Map p224; ☎ 82 16 83; Burggasse 2; adult/child €4.50/2; ☉ 10.30am-12.30pm & 1.30-4pm). Construction by Italian architect Pietro de Pomis began in 1614, but the mausoleum was completed after Pomis' death by Pietro Valnegro, while Johann Bernhard Fischer von Erlach chipped in with the exuberant stuccowork and frescoes inside. Ferdinand (1578–1637), his wife and his son are interred in the crypt, although the lead roles are played by the red marble sarcophagus of Ferdinand's parents, Karl II (1540–90) and Maria of Bavaria (1551–1608). Only Maria occupies the sarcophagus – Karl II lies in the Benedictine Abbey (p244) in Seckau.

SCHLOSS EGGENBERG

Situated on the western fringes of the city (tram 1), **Schloss Eggenberg** (off Map p222; ☎ 58 32 64-0; Eggenberger Allee 90; adult/child & student €7/3; ☒ 10am-5pm Tue-Sun Palm Sunday-Oct) was created for the Eggenberg dynasty in 1625. This splendid baroque palace was constructed by de Pomis at the request of Johann Ulrich (1568–1634), who required a suitable home after becoming governor of Inner Austria in 1625.

The dominating theme of the 24 **Prunkräume** (staterooms) is astronomy and mythology. The Planet Hall, which is a riot of white stuccowork and baroque frescoes, is one highlight; the frescoes portray the seven planets (all that were then discovered), the four elements and the 12 signs of the zodiac. Most rooms are devoted to one theme, including a Chinese room and a games room. Guided tours are conducted in German every hour on the hour, though an English translation is possible (enquire in advance).

The **Alte Galerie** (☎ 58 32 64-9770; adult/child & student €7/3; ☒ 10am-6pm Tue-Sun Apr-Oct, 10am-5pm Tue-Sun Nov-Mar) is the best among the museums housed within the Schloss, with exquisite paintings and sculpture dating from the Romanesque period through to the late baroque. The palace houses three other collections, which can be visited with admission to the Alte Galerie or Schloss itself. In the **Pre- and Early-History Collection** the prize exhibition is the exceptional *Strettweg Chariot* and a bronze mask, both dating from the Hallstatt period (7th century BC). The other collections are the **Coin Collection** from Styria, and a **Collection of Roman Provincial Antiquities** covering Roman finds in the province.

The palace is set in **parkland** (adult/child €1/ free; ☒ 8am-7pm Apr-Oct, to 5pm Nov-Mar) where peacock and deer roam among Roman stone reliefs, and has a **Planetengarten** (Planet Garden; ☒ 10am-6pm May-Oct, to 4pm Nov & Apr) on the same Renaissance theme of planets.

For Graz's Kunsthaus, see the Walking Tour (right).

OTHER SIGHTS

Some other intriguing museums are: **Kulturhistorische Sammlung** (Map p224; ☎ 80 17 97 80; Neutorgasse 45; in planning) A museum with crafted applied arts from the Middle Ages to present. **Museum der Wahrnehmung** (Museum of Perception; Map p222; ☎ 81 15 99; www.muwa.at, in German; Friedrichgasse 41; adult/child/family €3.50/1.80/8, samadhi bath €45; ☒ 2-6.30pm Wed-Mon) Small but unusual collection that explores sensory illusions; the samadhi (meditative) bath is a therapeutic bath that relieves the body of all sensory input. **Volkskundemuseum** (Map p224; ☎ 80 17 98 99; Paulustorgasse 11-13a; adult/child/student €3.50/2/2.50, tours extra €1.50; ☒ 10am-5pm Tue-Sun) Museum devoted to folk art and lifestyle; highlights include 2000 years of traditional clothing.

Walking Tour

This walk covers about 2.5km of the old town and can be done in 1½ hours without stops.

Start your walk from the tourist office on Herrengasse and enormous **Landhaus (1)**, the home of the provincial parliament. The building is a design of the 16th-century Swiss architect Domenico dell'Allio, based on the style of a Lombard palace. West of this is **Landhaushof (2)**, a stunning Italian Renaissance courtyard, a three-tiered gallery connected by walkways and one of the most celebrated examples of Renaissance architecture in Austria. Back on Herrengasse, continue northwest past the **Bemaltes Haus (3**; Painted House), a splendidly decorated Renaissance ducal residence, and cross over to **Hauptplatz (4)**, the main square from 1160, which is dominated by another Renaissance gem, the **Rathaus (5**; Town Hall) from 1550. The fountain in the centre is a monument to Johann, with four women at his feet representing Styria's main rivers – the Mur, Enns, Drau and Sann. From here, follow Franziskanergasse to Franziskanerplatz, dominated by the **Franziskanerkirche (6**; Franciscan Church). The building dates from 1240 and is based on an earlier Minorite church reworked by the Franciscans, who took it over in the 16th century. Cross the bridge. Sitting splendidly on the bank of the Mur River is the **Kunsthaus (7**; Map p224; ☎ 8017 9200; www .kunsthausgraz.at; Lendkai 1; adult/child & student/family €7/3/14, tours €2.50; ☒ 10am-6pm Tue-Sun, tours 11am & 4pm). Designed by British architects Peter Cook and Colin Fournier, this world-class contemporary art space is a bold creation which looks something like a space-age sea slug. Exhibitions change every three to four months, and tours cover not only the exhibitions but also the building. Mariahilferstrasse, immediately behind the Kunsthaus, is a lively street with some good bars set among a raft of dubious nightclubs.

Continue north along the river to Mariahilferplatz, where the two towers of the Mariahilferkirche dominate a large square. A short walk ahead is the **Murinsel (8)**, an artificial island-cum-bridge of metal and plastic in the middle of the Mur. This modern floating landmark contains a café (p232), a kids' playground and a small stage. After crossing the island you reach Schlossbergplatz, where stairs and a lift take you to **Schlossberg** (**9**; p225).

From the top, follow Dr-Karl-Böhm-Allee north for the wonderful views from Schlossberg and then backtrack, taking either the lift or stairs and go left (south) along Sackstrasse, with its art and antique shops. This takes you past the **Stadtmuseum** (**10**; Map p224; ☎ 82 73 48; Sackstrasse 18; adult/child €4/2; ☾ 10am-6pm Tue-Sun), portraying the history of Graz and housing temporary exhibitions, and

> **WALK FACTS**
>
> **Start** Tourist Office
> **Finish** Landeszeughaus
> **Distance** 2.5km
> **Duration** 1½ hours

GRAZ WALKING TOUR

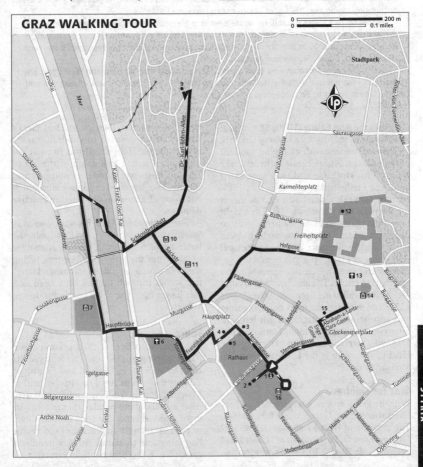

THE TERMINATOR – A ROCKY RELATIONSHIP WITH GRAZ

If you ask an ordinary Graz citizen on the street who they think is Graz's most famous citizen, the chances are they'll say 'Arnold Schwarzenegger'. Maybe it's not surprising. Arni's star-spangled biography is legendary. The son of a Graz cop. The modest childhood growing up just outside the city limits. A talented young bodybuilder who swept up multiple titles of Mr Universe and Mr Olympia. And not forgetting, of course, the fabled *Terminator* films and his meteoric rise to become Governor of California. Topping off the legend, he has recently morphed into California's 'green' crusader.

But his relationship with Graz has been turbulent. When he didn't use his gubernatorial power in 2005 to stop the execution of a condemned man, local political figures felt compelled to change the name of Graz's stadium, at that time known as the Arnold Schwarzenegger Stadion in honour of the town's most famous export.

Many local Graz citizens are quick to jump to Schwarzenegger's defence. When we asked Robert, aged 42, and born in Graz to Croatian parents, he said he admired Schwarzenegger for the way he's done his own thing. 'Schmidtbauer', aged 39, who sells produce at the Lendplatz market, echoed this view (and the sentiments of his colleague selling vegetables a few stalls further on), saying that 'He's a lot smarter than everyone thinks'.

As for the Terminator himself, he wrote a letter pre-empting the stadium name change, and demanded that his name be removed. He also returned his ring of honour to the city. 'In conclusion,' he wrote in 2005 to the city mayor, 'I want to once again expressly stress that I'll stay with all my heart a Grazer, Styrian and Austrian.'

Eva, a 25-year-old woman who grew up in Graz, said she'd seen his films and liked them. She didn't like the episode with the stadium, though. 'Renaming the stadium was idiotic', she said. 'It just wasn't right to do that.'

after that the **Neue Galerie** (11; Map p224; ☎ 82 91 55; Sackstrasse 16; adult/child & student/family €7/5.50/14; 🕓 10am-6pm Tue-Sun), with changing modern art exhibitions. At Sporgasse, turn left, take a right into Hofgasse and walk east along here past Freiheitsplatz and the city's 15th-century **Burg** (12; Castle). Just east of this is the **Dom** (13) and **Mausoleum** (14). Turn right into Bürgergasse and take the first right into Abraham-a-Santa-Clara-Gasse, which opens up to Glockenspielplatz and the **Glockenspiel** (15), where at 11am, 3pm and 6pm daily figures emerge from the clock's upper window and twirl to music. The area here and around Mehlplatz is called the Bermuda Triangle (see p232) and is one of the most popular eating and entertainment districts. Turn left into Enge Gasse and go right along Stempfergasse and you arrive back on Herrengasse. Finally, just south is the **Landeszeughaus** (16) armoury museum.

Graz for Children

With its green spaces, playgrounds and re-laxed atmosphere, Graz is made for children. The creation of **FriDa & FreD** (Map p222; ☎ 87 27 700; www.fridaundfred.at; Friedrichgasse 34; adult & child over 6/child under 6/family €4/1.50/11; 🕓 9am-5pm Mon,

Wed & Thu, 9am-7pm Fri, 10am-5pm Sat & Sun), Graz's first museum devoted to children, makes it even better. This small but fun-packed museum is aimed at kids up to the age of 12, and hosts workshops, exhibitions and theatre. Like any good children's museum, it has loads of hands-on tasks and interactive displays.

The **Schlossberg Cave Railway** (Map p224; Schlossbergplatz; admission €3; 🕓 10am-5pm), the longest grotto railway in Europe, is another highlight for the little 'uns. The trip, taking about 20 minutes, winds its way around fairy-tale scenes through tunnels once used as a safe haven from the allied bombings during WWII.

Tours

The tourist office (Graztourismus; see p223) offers a guided walking tour (adult/child €9.50/3.50) in German and English at 2.30pm daily from April to October and at 2.30pm Saturday from November to March. Also ask about its regular theme tours in town and weekend day trips outside Graz, or pick up its nifty multimedia (and multilingual) guide to sights, using a handheld computer (€7.50/8.50 two/four hours).

Festivals & Events

Graz's biggest bash is **Styriarte**, a festival featuring almost continuous classical concerts in June and July. Pick up information from **Styriarte Kartenbüro** (Map p224; ☎ 82 50 00; www .styriarte.com; Sackstrasse 17; €16-110).

Steirischer Herbst, an avant-garde festival of new art held during October, includes performances in music, theatre, film, plus exhibitions and art installations. Contact **Steirischer Herbst Informationsbüro** (Map p224; ☎ 81 60 70; www .steirischerbst.at, in German; Sackstrasse 17; €6-35) for more. **Jazz Sommer Graz** (www.jazzsommergraz.at, in German), a collection of free jazz concerts (often with an impressive international line-up), takes place in Dom im Berg from early July to late August.

Sleeping
BUDGET

The tourist office has an excellent accommodation guide and books hotels without charge.

Camping Central (off Map p222; ☎ 0676-378 51 02; freizeit@netway.at; Martinhofstrasse 3; campsites per adult/child/tent €8/5/17; ☺ Apr-Oct; P 🖵 🛒) The large swimming pool and children's playground are useful features of this camping ground 6km southwest of the city centre (bus 32 from Jakominiplatz).

Jugendgästehaus (Map p222; ☎ 70 83 50; graz@jfgh .at, Idlhofgasse 74; dm/s/d €22/33/52; P 🖵) This big, colourful and friendly HI hostel is the cheapest deal in Graz. There's a small playground for kids too.

Hotel Strasser (Map p222; ☎ 71 39 77; office@hotel -strasser.at; Eggenberger Gürtel 11; s/d €35/60; P) Beyond the uninteresting exterior of the Strasser are some fascinating pseudo-neoclassical and Mediterranean touches, with Tuscan gold and ochre blending with mirrors, along with artwork and cast iron balustrades. Rooms are comfortable but ask for one away from the busy street.

Gasthof-Pension zur Steirer-Stub'n (Map p222; ☎ 71 68 55; www.pension-graz.at; Lendplatz 8; s/d €41/74, apt €100-150) This inn combines the best of a traditional atmosphere with a bright and breezy feel, complemented by features like tiled floors in the corridors, a potted plant in each room and patios outside many of the good-sized rooms overlooking Lendplatz.

Pension Rückert (off Map p222; ☎ 32 30 31; Rückertgasse 4; s/d €52/74; P) A big plus with this pension is that it's smack-bang in the student

district. In summer the 1st floor is the best – the 2nd floor is unrenovated and the top floor gets the heat and is better for winter sojourns. Take tram 1 to Tegetthoffplatz, walk 100m in the direction of the tram route then turn right.

MIDRANGE

Hotel Mariahilf (Map p224; ☎ 71 31 63; www.hotel mariahilf.at; Mariahilferstrasse 9; s/d €51/88) Large rooms, including some with small ante-rooms, and interesting Art Deco touches give the Mariahilf a relaxed atmosphere. The interior wood creates a light ambience, and the location is excellent if you want to be near the Kunsthalle and bars on Mariahilferstrasse.

Hotel Feichtinger Graz (Map p224; ☎ 724 100; www .hotel-feichtinger.at; Lendplatz 1a; s/d/tr €50/94/129; P) This modern seminar and business hotel offers some of the best-value beds in town. Rooms are spacious, and the furnishings are modern and have a light touch, which extends to the very large breakfast room.

our pick Hotel Daniel (Map p224; ☎ 711 080; www.hoteldaniel.com; Europaplatz 1; r €59-79, breakfast €9 per person; P 🖵) Perched at the top of Annenstrasse and looking for all the world like a block of 1950s beachside holiday apartments that's lost its beach, the Daniel is an exclusive design hotel with two categories of rooms: 'Smart' and 'Loggia'. The former are smaller, though decent sized, and have queen-sized beds; they're a great deal because the price is per room, not person. The Loggia category is larger and has balconies. All rooms are tastefully furnished in minimalist designs, you can rent a Vespa (€25 per day) and there's a 24-hour espresso bar. The bathroom – but, thankfully, not toilet – wall is transparent.

Grazerhof (Map p224; ☎ 82 43 58; www.grazerhof.at; Stubenberggasse 10; s/d/tr €54/90/120) This hotel offers a central location, but few other real advantages, in a plain building; unfortunately the rooms to the yard have a wall outside the window.

Hotel zum Dom (Map p224; ☎ 82 48 00; www.dom hotel.at, in German; Bürgergasse 14; s €80-90, d €165, ste €200-322; P 🗶) Hotel Zum Dom is a charming, graceful hotel with tasteful and individually furnished rooms. These come either with steam/power showers or whirlpools, and one suite even has a terrace whirlpool. Ceramic art throughout the hotel is crafted by a local artist.

Hotel Weitzer (Map p224; ☎ 7030; www.weitzer.com; Grieskai 12; s €85-140, d €125-180, ste €300; P ☐) This four-star hotel in two buildings is just the trick if you like your pillows well fluffed each evening while you're off enjoying a sauna or romp in the fitness room. The rooftop terrace is disappointing, but everything else is up to standard here.

TOP END

Augarten Hotel (Map p222; ☎ 20 800; www.augartenhotel .at; Schönaugasse 53; s/d €115/140; P ⚡) Though not an 'art hotel', art plays an important role in the Augarten. It's decorated with the owner's private collection, which includes a great oil of the German crooning superstar Heino. All rooms are bright and modern, the end rooms have windows on two walls, and corridors run along the exterior of the building.

our pick **Hotel Erzherzog Johann** (Map p224; ☎ 81 16 16; www.erzherzog-johann.com; Sackstrasse 3-5; s €119-172, d €145-235, ste €350; mains €12-18; P ✗) Weekend deals are the thing to watch out for here, but also throw caution to the wind and splurge in one of the ostentatious theme rooms. The Wanda-Sacher-Masoch-Suite is in white and with projections of classical statues in the bathroom, whereas Orientalists will get a kick out of the sensational Moroccan room.

Schlossberg Hotel (Map p224; ☎ 80 70-0; www .schlossberg-hotel.at; Kaiser-Franz-Josef-Kai 30; s €141-181, d €187-230, ste €311-375; P ☐ ⚡) Central but away from the city tumult, four-star Schlossberg is blessed with a prime location at the foot of Schlossberg. Rooms are well sized and decorated in the style of a country inn, but the fitness room is a tacky number, with exposed air-conditioning pipes. The rooftop terrace with views is perfect for an evening glass of wine.

Grand Hotel Wiesler (Map p224; ☎ 70 66-0; www .weitzer.com; Grieskai 4; s €185-205, d €245-265, ste €300-695; P ☐) This Art Nouveau gem is the only five-star hotel in town. All but two of the elegant rooms have bathtubs, and the Art Nouveau mosaic by Leopold Forstner (1878–1936) in the breakfast room – depicting Venus stepping out of an oyster – evokes admiration even if it's while glancing up from your egg.

Eating

Whether you're after a bite on the run, coffee and cake, a cheap, filling meal, hearty Styrian fare or gourmet cuisine in splendid surroundings, Graz can give it to you.

RESTAURANTS

Stern (Map p224; ☎ 81 84 00; www.sternenclub.at; Sporgasse 3; mains €5-14; ☺ 9am-3am) During the day and early evening Stern is a fine restaurant with a focus on salads, wok and pasta dishes served at outdoor tables on Kameliterplatz; when the sun sets, its cellar-like interior morphs into a bar, featuring DJs every Friday and Saturday, and live acts on Sunday.

Krebsenkeller (Map p224; ☎ 82 93 77; Sackstrasse 12; mains €6-12; ☺ 10am-midnight) Krebsenkeller does inexpensive regional cuisine – which means lots of pumpkin oil – and appeals to locals and tourists alike, not only for its home-style cooking, but also for a lovely inner courtyard and traditional atmosphere.

Tramina (Map p224; ☎ 83 01 67; Klosterwiesgasse 2; mains €6.50-11; ☺ 6pm-2am) In the family for three generations, this is one of two restaurants in Graz – Mangolds is the other – awarded the Styrian 'Green Chef's Hat' for good ecological practice. Everything is organic in this unusual *Beisl*-gone-feral run by two sisters. It specialises in lamb, but you'll also find thin slices of beef served in vinegar and oil and half a dozen vegetarian dishes.

iku (Map p224; ☎ 8017 9292; Lendkai 1; lunch menu €5.50, mains €8-12; ☺ 9am-1am) Inside the surrealistic Kunsthaus, this sleek bar and restaurant does one vegetarian and one meat dish for lunch, and has a small evening menu offering the likes of beef medallions in red wine and basil sauce. A DJ takes the floor from 10pm Saturday.

Gamlitzer Weinstube (Map p224; ☎ 82 87 60; Mehlplatz 4; €6-17; ☺ 9am-11pm Mon-Fri) With a menu in 18 different languages, the Gamlitzer aims squarely at the tourist trade. Ingredients for its home-style classic Styrian dishes come from the local farmers; there's outside seating.

Aiola Upstairs (Map p224; ☎ 81 87 97; Schlossberg 2; mains €8-18; ☺ 9am-midnight) Ask any local where to find the best outdoor dining experience in Graz, and they'll probably say Aiola. Whether it's king prawns with pasta or corn-fed chicken, this wonderful restaurant on Schlossberg has great views, delicious international flavours, a superb wine list, spot-on cocktails and very chilled music.

Yamamoto (Map p224; ☎ 852 852; Prokopigasse 4; small/large sushi €11/19; udon €7-8.50; ☺ lunch & dinner Tue-Sat) Yamamoto is refreshingly authentic in an age when Chinese restaurants are re-inventing themselves as lucrative sushi bars; it's Japanese owned and run, and gets its sushi delivered throughout the week, so it's always fresh and, like the noodle dishes, delicious.

Iohan (Map p224; ☎ 82 13 12; www.iohan.at; Landhausgasse 1; mains €10.50-22.50, bar menu €7.50-9.50; ⏰ 6pm-1am Tue-Sat) This very stylish restaurant and bar with a Gothic vaulted ceiling is one place where you can find a seasonal salad incorporating tongue of veal and asparagus. But it's also perfect for chilling out at the bar and taking entree-like snacks.

Aiola City (Map p224; ☎ 890 335; Mehlplatz 1; mains €12-20; ⏰ 7.30am-late Mon-Sat, 9am-late Sun) In the centre, this Aiola has low vaulting, a cool lounge feel and outdoor seating on Mehlplatz.

Landhauskeller (Map p224; ☎ 83 02 76; Schmiedgasse 9; mains €12.50-21.50; ⏰ 11.30am-midnight Mon-Sat) What started as a spit-and-sawdust pub in the 16th century evolved into an atmospheric, high-quality restaurant serving specialities like its four different sorts of *Tafelspitz* (prime broiled beef). Flowers, coats of arms and medieval-style murals pack a historical punch, and in the summer outside tables look onto the stunning Landhaus courtyard.

Other recommended restaurants include:

Altsteirische Schmankerlstubn (Map p224; ☎ 83 32 11; Sackstrasse 10; mains €8-16; ⏰ 10am-midnight) Rustic restaurant serving traditional Styrian cuisine at the foot of the Schlossberg.

Stainzerbauer (Map p224; ☎ 82 11 06; Bürgergasse 4; mains €10-19; ⏰ 11am-midnight) Styrian and Austrian specialities in a lovely courtyard garden.

Magnolia (Map p222; ☎ 82 38 35; Schöngaugasse 53; 3-5 course menu €39.50-59.50, mains €15-20; ⏰ lunch & dinner Mon-Fri) Alongside Augarten Hotel, with outdoor seating, this stylish restaurant with a seasonal menu and Austro-international cuisine is highly rated.

QUICK EATS

Aside from the following listings, there are plenty of cheap eateries near **Universität Graz** (Map p222), particularly on Halbärthgasse, Zinzendorfgasse and Harrachgasse.

Mangolds (Map p224; ☎ 71 80 02; Griesgasse 11; meals €5-10; ⏰ 11am-7pm Mon-Fri, to 4pm Sat) Tasty vegetarian patties, rice dishes and over 40 different salads are served at this pay-by-weight vegetarian cafeteria.

Other good quick-eats include:

Feinspitz (Map p224; ☎ 870-0; 2nd fl Kastner & Öhler department store, Sackstrasse 7-11; meals €5-9; ⏰ 9am-6.30pm Mon-Fri, to 5pm Sat) Buffet-style restaurant with healthy salads and ready meals; also offers a kids' menu from €4 (which includes a drink and a surprise).

Mensa (Map p222; ☎ 32 33 62; Sonnenfelsplatz 1; menu €5; ⏰ 11am-2.30pm Mon-Fri) One of the university cafeterias.

Zu den 3 Goldenen Kugeln (most mains under €5; ⏰ lunch & dinner) Heinrichstrasse/University (Map p222; ☎ 36 16 36; Heinrichstrasse 18); Griesplatz (Map p222; Griesplatz 34); Bahnhofgürtel (Map p222; Bahnhofgürtel 89); Citypark (Map p222; Lazarettgürtel 55) An institution in Graz, the Goldenen Kugeln serves up possibly the cheapest schnitzel around, but still manages to make it tasty. The Heinrichstrasse branch, with its rustic air, is the nicest.

SELF-CATERING

The freshest fruit and vegetables are at the **farmers markets** (⏰ 4.30am-1pm Mon-Sat) on Kaiser-Josef-Platz (Map p224) and Lendplatz (Map p222). For **fast-food stands**, head for Hauptplatz (Map p224) and Jakominiplatz (Map p224). Supermarkets are plentiful throughout the city; there's a **Billa** (Map p222; Annenstrasse 23), a **Eurospar** (Map p224; Sackstrasse 7-11) and a **Spar** (Map p222; ⏰ daily) is located in the *Hauptbahnhof*.

Drinking

The café and bar scene in Graz is propelled by a healthy student crowd. Some of the cafés we've listed here change into bars as the night wears on, but tend not to stay open as late.

CAFÉS

Edegger-Tax (Map p224; ☎ 83 02 30; Hofgasse 8; coffee & cakes €2-5; ⏰ 6.30am-8pm Mon-Fri, 6.30am-3pm Sat, also 7am-3pm Apr-Sep) This modern café is perfectly complemented by its 1569 bakery (open 7am to 6pm Monday to Friday, to noon Saturday) next door. Apart from the yummy goodies baked on the premises, its stunning wood-carved façade is reason enough to drop by; note the small doors in the frontage, concealing ingenious hiding places.

Operncafé (Map p224; ☎ 82 04 36; Opernring 22; coffee & cake €2-5; ⏰ 7.30am-9pm Mon-Sat, 9am-9pm Sun) Operncafé is a traditional café with good coffee, homemade pastries and pleasant, suited waiters who have found a calling in life.

Auschlössl (Map p222; ☎ 81 33 68; Friedrichgasse 36; coffee about €3; ⏰ 10am-midnight Mon-Sat) Auschlössl is another small café on the edge of a park, but this time on the other side of town. It's perfect for an evening drink or a coffee break after an exhausting visit to FriDa & FreD. It often hosts art exhibitions.

Promenade (Map p224; ☎ 81 38 40; Erzherzog Johann Allee 1; snack €7.40; ⏰ 8am-midnight) Popular with all walks of life, the delightful Promenade is a Graz institution – styled on a Vienna coffee house on a tree-lined avenue in the Stadtpark.

Aiola Island (Map p224; ☎ 81 86 69; Murinsel; ☽ noon-8pm Tue-Fri, 10-midnight Sat, 10am-8pm Sun) This café on the Murinsel offers a unique experience – here you can sip a drink as the Mur River splashes below your feet.

BARS

Most bars are concentrated in three areas; around the university, on Mehlplatz and Prokopigasse (dubbed the 'Bermuda Triangle'), and near the Kunsthaus. Lines are often blurred, so don't dismiss a place for a good night out just because it serves food. Classic examples include the two Aiola restaurants, iku and Stern.

Orange (Map p222; ☎ 32 74 29; www.café-bar -orange.at; Elisabethstrasse 30; ☽ 8pm-3am) A young, fashionable student crowd gets down in this modern lounge, which has a patio perfect for warm summer evenings. DJs spin sounds regularly here.

Kulturhauskeller (Map p222; Elisabethstrasse 30; ☽ 9pm-5am Tue-Sat) Next door to Orange, the Kulturhauskeller is a relaxed cellar bar that heaves with raunchy young students on weekends.

Café Harrach (Map p224; ☎ 32 26 71; Harrachgasse 26; ☽ 9am-midnight Mon-Fri, 7pm-midnight Sat & Sun) Harrach is a long-time favourite among the art-scene students and has retained its relaxed feel.

Bierbaron (Map p222; ☎ 32 15 10, Heinrichstrasse 56; ☽ 10am-1am Mon-Sat, 6-11pm Sun) This large, busy bar just north of the university is another well-known student haunt. It has rows of gleaming silver beer pumps, and a relaxing garden.

Goldene Kugel (Map p222; ☎ 32 31 08; Leonhardstrasse 32; ☽ 10am-midnight) The Kugel has been through some tumult of late, but now its doors are wide open again to a student crowd that gathers here to nosh inexpensively and enjoy one or two of the 20 different beers.

Three Monkeys (Map p222; ☎ 31 98 10; www .three-monkeys.at; Elisabethstrasse 31; ☽ 9pm-5am Mon-Sun) Three Monkeys is possibly the most popular student bar near the university; it's loud, lots of fun, and generally known as a pick-up joint.

Parkhouse (Map p224; ☎ 80 80 80; www.parkhouse .at; Stadtpark 2; ☽ 11am-4am) On warm summer days and evenings half of Graz seems to make a beeline to this place. Parkhouse gets a very mixed crowd, but as the day fades to night

it morphs into a buzzing spot for DJs and occasional live music (usually a Tuesday).

M1 (Map p224; ☎ 81 12 330; 3rd fl, Färberplatz; ☽ 9am-2am Mon-Sat) In the heart of the Bermuda Triangle, M1 is a modern three-storey café-bar replete with rooftop terrace attracting a mixed – but often quite young – crowd. Its spiral staircase can cause a few problems after sampling a couple of the bar's 200 or so cocktails.

Stargayte (Map p222; 0664 92 47 29; www.stargayte .at, in German; Keesegasse 3; ☽ 8pm Mon-Thu & Sun, 8pm-open end Fri & Sat) This gay and lesbian cocktail bar and lounge near Jakominiplatz is popular. Thursday nights the dance floor is given over to women, and it has a permanent male-only room with a sling, plus labyrinth with glory holes.

Cafe Centraal (Map p224; ☎ 0699-172 13 415; Mariahilferstrasse 10; breakfast €3-6, snack €5-7; ☽ 8am-2am) This traditional bar and *Beisl* (small tavern or restaurant) with a dark-wood interior and outside seating has an alternative feel.

Pierre's Café-Bar (Map p224; ☎ 0699-20 21 86 82; Lendplatz 45; ☽ 5pm-2am Mon-Fri, 10am-2pm & 5pm-2am Sat) Pierre's charms appeal mostly to rolling stones who have gathered a coat of moss. Minimalism meets 40-somethings with greying pony tails who watch Led Zeppelin or Shania Twain clips on the large screen; it's perfect if you like classic rock.

Exil (Map p224; ☎ 0676-72 92 190; Josefigasse 1; ☽ 7pm-late Tue-Sat) If you like the Centraal, you'll probably like Exil even more – it's a laid-back alternative bar with outdoor seating and a couple of turntables for Friday and Saturday nights when sounds are spun; it's against the grain – empty when everywhere else is full, and buzzing when quiet elsewhere.

Stockwerk Jazz (Map p224; ☎ 81 76 74; http://stock werkjazz.mur.at, in German; Jakominiplatz 18; concerts €10-15; ☽ 4pm-1am Mon-Sat, 4pm-midnight Sun) Stockwerk is Graz's premier jazz bar for homegrown artists or international acts on tour. Relax over a beer among creaking wooden fixtures or on the summer rooftop terrace.

Entertainment

To find out what's on and where in the city, pick up a copy of the free monthly *das eventmagazin* (in German), available from tourist offices, or buy *Megaphon* (€2, in German), a monthly magazine that combines entertainment listings with political and social commentary. It's sold on most street corners.

lonelyplanet.com

STYRIA •• Graz 233

CINEMAS

Augartenkino (Map p222; ☎ 82 11 86; Friedrichgasse 24; ticket €8) Regularly shows films (mostly arthouse) in their original language.

Royal English Cinema (Map p222; ☎ 82 61 33; Conrad-von-Hötzendorf-Strasse 10; ticket €8.50) This cinema screens English-language films.

NIGHTCLUBS

Dom im Berg (Map p224; ☎ 8008 333; www.domimberg.at, in German; Schlossbergplatz; admission €5-10; ☒ see website) The tunnels under Schlossberg were once used as air-raid shelters. Today, some of them have been refashioned into a large art-clubbing venue. The sound system and light show are the best in Graz, so it's no surprise the place is often full when it hosts clubbing events.

p.p.c (Map p224; ☎ 81 41 41 11; www.popculture.at, in German; Neubaugasse 6; admission €5-10; ☒ 10pm-4am Wed-Sat) Electronic club nights with top-name DJs from Austria and abroad, as well as regular live music, are popular here.

Arcadium (Map p224; ☎ 0664-59 80 231; www.arcadium-graz.at, in German; Griesgasse 25; admission €4-7; ☒ 10pm-late) Arcadium has Latino nights Wednesdays but its real strengths are club nights and live music – everything from punk to electronic gets a showing here, mainly for a mid-20s crowd.

THEATRE & OPERA

Graz is an important cultural centre, hosting musical events throughout the year. The main venues in town are the **Schauspielhaus** (theatre; Map p224; ☎ 80 00; Hofgasse 11; tickets €3.50-46) and the **Opernhaus** (opera; Map p224; ☎ 80 08-0; Kaiser-Josef-Platz 10; tickets €1-64). Performance details and tickets (no commission) for both venues are available at **Theaterservice Graz** (Map p224; ☎ 8008 1102; www.theater-graz.com, in German; Kaiser-Josef-Platz 10; ☒ 9am-6.30pm Mon-Fri, to 1pm Sat). Both venues close in August and there are discounts for students.

Shopping

Aside from its divine pumpkin-seed oil, Styria is known for painted pottery and printed linen. A good place to pick up quality handicrafts is **Steirisches Heimatwerk** (Map p224; ☎ 82 90 45; Herrengasse 10) or **Kastner & Öhler** (Map p224; ☎ 870-0; Sackstrasse 7-11), a department store north of Hauptplatz. If you're just looking for high-street names, head for **Citypark** (Map p222; ☎ 71 15 80-0; Lazarettgürtel 55), a large shopping centre to the south of the centre.

Getting There & Away

AIR

The **airport** (off Map p222; ☎ 29 02-0; www.flughafen-graz.at) is 10km south of the town centre, just beyond the A2 and connected by train from the *Hauptbahnhof*; see p395. **Austrian Airlines** (☎ 05 17 89) has frequent flights to/from Düsseldorf (Germany), Vienna and Linz, and weekly flights to/from Salzburg, while **Welcome Air** (☎ 0800 210 211) has regular flights to/from Innsbruck, Göteborg via Stavanger and Hanover. **InterSky** (☎ 0557 448800) connects Graz with Berlin-Tempelhof and Friedrichshafen several times a week. **TUIFly** (☎ 0820 820033) has weekly connections with Hanover and Cologne-Bonn in Germany. **Lufthansa** (☎ 0810 1025 8080) has frequent flights to Frankfurt am Main, Munich and Stuttgart in Germany, and **Ryanair** (☎ 0900 210240) has frequent flights to/from London Stansted. Facilities at the airport include an **information desk** (☎ 29 02-172; departure hall; ☒ 5am-10.30pm), free internet terminals, and a bank with an ATM in arrivals, ground floor.

An infrequent airport bus also runs to the airport from the *Hauptbahnhof* but is less convenient than the train.

BUS

Postbus (Map p222; ☎ 82 06 06; www.verbundlinie.at) services depart from outside the *Hauptbahnhof* (Map p222) and from Andreas Hofer Platz (Map p224) to all parts of Styria. Indirect **GKB buses** (Map p222; ☎ 59 87-0; www.gkb.at) run to Bärnbach (€6.50, 1¼ hours) and Piber (€6.50, one hour) several times each day from Monday to Friday; more frequent services go to Deutschlandsberg (€8, two hours) Monday to Saturday. All leave from Griesplatz (Map p222), though a few begin at the *Hauptbahnhof*.

TRAIN

Trains to Vienna's Südbahnhof depart every two hours (€30, 2½ hours), and to Salzburg every two to three hours (€43, four hours). All trains running north or west go via Bruck an der Mur (€10.90, 45 minutes, every 20 minutes), a main railway junction with more frequent services. Almost all trains to Klagenfurt (€32, 2¾ hours) require a change in Bruck.

International direct trains from Graz include Zagreb (€31, 3½ hours), Ljubljana (€31, 3½ hours), Szentgotthárd (€16, 1½ hours) and Budapest (€43, 5½ hours).

CAR RENTAL

Car rental companies include **Avis** (Map p224; ☎ 81 29 20; Reinighausstrasse 66), **Hertz** (Map p224; ☎ 82 50 07; Andreas-Hofer-Platz 1), which is also at the airport, and **DenzelDrive** (Map p222; ☎ 050105 4130; www.denzeldrive.at; Wetzelsdorfer Strasse 35). See p403 for rates.

Note that much of Graz is a *Kurzparkzone* (short-term parking zone); tickets are available from parking machines on streets (€0.60 per 30 minutes).

Getting Around

Trams 1, 3, 6 and 7 connect Jakominiplatz with the *Hauptbahnhof* (Map p222) every five to 20 minutes from 4.40am to 7pm Monday to Saturday. After that trams 1 and 7 do the run alone until services end just before midnight (€1.70).

Graz has one zone (zone 101). Single tickets (€1.70) for buses and trams are valid for one hour, but you're usually better off buying a 24-hour pass (€3.70). Ten one-zone tickets cost €14.80, and weekly/monthly passes cost €9.60/32.50. Hourly and 24-hour tickets can be purchased from the driver; other passes can be purchased from *Tabak* (tobacconist) shops, pavement ticket machines or the tourist office.

Bicycle rental is available from **Bicycle** (Map p222; ☎ 68 86 45; Körösistrasse 5; per 24hr €9; ⏱ 7am-1pm & 2-6pm Mon-Fri). To call a taxi, dial ☎ 2801, ☎ 878 or ☎ 889. **Mobilzentral** (see p221) has a few city bicycles it rents for €8 per day or €40 per week.

AROUND GRAZ

All the following sights are within easy distance of Graz and make for a pleasant excursion into the countryside.

ÖSTERREICHISCHEN FREILICHTMUSEUM

Located some 15km northeast of Graz and consisting of about 100 Austrian farmstead buildings, the **Österreichischen Freilichtmuseum** (Austrian Open-Air Museum; ☎ 03124-53 700; www .freilichtmuseum.at; adult/student/child/family €7/5/4/21; ⏱ 9am-5pm Tue-Sun Apr-Oct) in Stübing is ideal for a family outing. All buildings are originals that have been painstakingly relocated to the museum site, arranged geographically as if you were walking through Austria

from east to west. Craft demonstrations are held regularly, and on the last Sunday in September the **Erlebnistag**, a special fair with crafts, music and dancing, takes place here. Pick up a copy of the English-language guidebook (€2.20) at the entrance.

The museum is about a 20-minute walk from the Stübing train station; turn left out of the train station and pass over the tracks, then under them before hitting the entrance. Hourly trains make the journey from Graz (€4.40, 15 minutes).

BUNDESGESTÜT PIBER

Piber is home to the world-famous Lipizzaner stallion stud farm **Bundesgestüt Piber** (Piber Stud Farm; ☎ 03144-33 23; www.piber.com, in German; Piber 1; tour adult/senior/student €11/9/6; ⏱ 10am-4pm hourly Apr-Oct, 11am & 3pm Nov-Mar).

Originally the farm was based in Lipica (Slovenia) but when Slovenia was annexed after WWI it moved here. About 40 to 50 foals are born at the farm every year, but of these only about five stallions have the right stuff to be sent for training to the Spanische Hofreitschule (Spanish Riding School) in Vienna. Foals are born grey, brown or black and take between five and 12 years to achieve their distinctive white colouring. Visitors are looked after by the same people who tend the horses.

In summer, you are given an information sheet with German and short English descriptions, plus a map of the complex. You make your way to several stops, where a carer waits to give explanations in German, although explanatory signs at the stations are also in English. In winter, tours are fully guided.

For information, head to the **Tourismusverband Lipizzanerheimat** (☎ 03144-72 777-0; www .lipizzanerheimat.com, in German; An der Quelle 3) in Köflach, 3km south of Piber. The perfect place to overnight is **Gasthof Bardel** (☎ 03144-34 22; gh-bardel.tripod.com, in German; Fesselweg 1; s/d €30/50; Ⓟ), right next to the stud farm. Each of the modern rooms comes with a balcony overlooking one of the parade areas. There's also a restaurant on the premises, but if you would prefer a snack and coffee, there's a café on the stud farm's grounds.

The best eating option, however, is **Restaurant Caballero** (☎ 03144-33 23-170; mains €14-20; ⏱ lunch & dinner Wed-Sat, lunch Sun), on the ground floor of Schloss Piber on the farm.

STYRIA